S0-AEZ-324

SHOEN LIBRARY - MARYLHURST

# OLDER WIDOWS AND THE LIFE COURSE

# New Perspectives on Ageing and Later Life

*Series Editors*

Tony Maltby, The University of Birmingham, UK
Debra A. Street, The Pepper Institute on Aging and Public Policy,
Florida State University, USA

This international collection of key research monographs provides a substantial outlet for the burgeoning body of research being conducted on ageing and later life issues. It brings to the wider academic and practitioner community both empirical and theoretical work in order to develop and refine policy and practice.

Encouraging both newly established and senior researchers alike, the series focuses on issues within social and behavioural gerontology with a direct practical application to the development of policy and practice in this field. Informative and wide-ranging, it will be of particular interest to academics, policy makers and practitioners working with older people.

*Other titles in the series*

Changing Worlds and the Ageing Subject:
Dimensions in the Study of Ageing and Later Life
*Edited by Britt-Marie Öberg, Anna-Liisa Närvänen,*
*Elisabet Näsman and Erik Olsson*

Ageing and the Transition to Retirement:
A Comparative Analysis of European Welfare States
*Edited by Tony Maltby, Bert de Vroom,*
*Maria Luisa Mirabile and Einar Øverbye*

# Older Widows and the Life Course

## Multiple Narratives of Hidden Lives

PAT CHAMBERS
*Keele University, UK*

**ASHGATE**

306.883
c43
2005

© Pat Chambers 2005

All rights reserved. No part of this publication may be reproduced, stored in a retrieval system, or transmitted in any form or by any means, electronic, mechanical, photocopying, recording or otherwise without the prior permission of the publisher.

Pat Chambers has asserted her right under the Copyright, Designs and Patents Act, 1988, to be identified as the author of this work.

Published by
Ashgate Publishing Limited
Gower House
Croft Road
Aldershot
Hants GU11 3HR
England

Ashgate Publishing Company
Suite 420
101 Cherry Street
Burlington, VT 05401-4405
USA

Ashgate website: http://www.ashgate.com

**British Library Cataloguing in Publication Data**
Chambers, Pat
    Older widows and the life course : multiple narratives of
    hidden lives. - (New perspectives on ageing and later life)
    1. Widows - Great Britain - Social conditions  2. Widows -
    Great Britain - Psychology  3. Older people - Great Britain -
    Social conditions  4. Older people - Great Britain -
    Psychology
    I. Title
    306.8'83

**Library of Congress Cataloging-in-Publication Data**
Chambers, Pat, 1950-
    Older widows and the life course : multiple narratives of hidden lives / by Pat Chambers.
        p. cm. -- (New perspectives on ageing and later life)
    Includes bibliographical references and index.
     ISBN 0-7546-4001-9
    1. Widows. 2. Older women. 3. Widowhood. I. Title. II. Series.

    HQ1058.C48 2005
    306.88'3'0917521--dc22

                                                                2005003229

ISBN 0 7546 4001 9

Printed and bound in Great Britain by Antony Rowe Ltd, Chippenham, Wiltshire.

# Contents

*List of Figures* vii
*Acknowledgements* ix

1   Introduction: The Experience of Later Life Widowhood             1

2   Becoming and Being an Older Widow                                9

3   The Social World of Older Widows                                33

4   Conceptualising and Re-conceptualising Widowhood                52

5   Researching Later Life Widowhood                                66

6   Out in the Field                                                91

7   Twenty Older Widows                                            107

8   Me, Myself                                                     121

9   History and Me                                                 144

10  Me and My Social World                                         164

11  Me Now                                                         190

12  Multiple Narratives of Later Life Widowhood                    226

13  Reflecting                                                     243

14  Conclusion                                                     264

*Bibliography*                                                     267
*Index*                                                           282

# List of Figures

| | | |
|---|---|---:|
| 6.1 | The fieldwork | 92 |
| 6.2 | Getting going | 102 |
| 8.1 | Multiple narratives of Me, Myself | 121 |
| 8.2 | Locating the participants within the narratives of Me, Myself | 122 |
| 8.3 | A narrative of High Self-Esteem | 123 |
| 8.4 | A narrative of Fluctuating Self-Esteem | 129 |
| 8.5 | A narrative of Low Self-Esteem | 136 |
| 8.6 | Me, Myself | 142 |
| 9.1 | Multiple narratives of History and Me | 144 |
| 9.2 | A narrative of Belonging to a Generation | 145 |
| 9.3 | A narrative of Gendered Lives | 154 |
| 9.4 | Me, Myself and History and Me | 162-163 |
| 10.1 | Multiple narratives of Me and My Social World | 165 |
| 10.2 | Locating the participants within the multiple narratives of Me and My Social World | 165 |
| 10.3 | Friends matter | 166 |
| 10.4 | No friends of my own | 172 |
| 10.5 | A joiner-in | 177 |
| 10.6 | Family first | 180 |
| 10.7 | Me, Myself; History and Me; Me and My Social World | 188-189 |
| 11.1 | Multiple narratives of Me Now | 190 |
| 11.2 | Locating the participants within narratives of Me Now | 191 |
| 11.3 | Loneliness and despair | 191 |
| 11.4 | Getting on with your life | 202 |
| 11.5 | A transition | 211 |
| 12.1 | Multiple narratives and sub-plots of later life widowhood | 228-229 |

# Acknowledgements

There are many people who have encouraged and supported me during the original study and in the current undertaking. However, I would like to say a particular 'thank you' to the following:

- The twenty older widows who participated in this study for sharing their life stories with me: I remain eternally grateful.
- Rod Chambers for his support and hard work during the final stages of finalising this manuscript.
- The editorial team at Ashgate for their patience.

And finally, a very special man to whom I can no longer give personal thanks: my father George Bone who supported and encouraged me at the outset of this study but who died before its completion. I dedicate this book to him.

Chapter 1

# Introduction:
# The Experience of Later Life
# Widowhood

## Beginnings

I first became interested in the 'lived' experience of older widows at the beginning of the 1990s as a result of a number of encounters in both my public, professional life and my private, domestic life. In my (then) role as a Lecturer in Social Care I facilitated a number of intergenerational projects, which comprised younger, mainly female, students working with and learning from older people, the majority of whom were female and widowed. The focus of these projects was to challenge younger people's pre-conceptions of old age as a time of decline and inevitable dependency and to foster instead both interdependence and reciprocity.

Increasingly, I also found some of my own pre-conceptions being challenged as I worked alongside the students and older women in a variety of care settings. In particular, I found my assumptions about the inevitable loneliness and unhappiness of widowhood confronted. I gradually began to realize that my ideas about widowhood were shaped by powerful cultural stereotypes of 'tragedy' and 'ongoing grief', and a strong patriarchal view of women alone being somehow 'less than' whole. I now know that my views were also influenced by my own personal history and my close, albeit second hand, knowledge of widowhood (my aunt and godmother, my mother-in-law, the mothers of two school friends, my father) all of whom were widowed, unexpectedly, at a young age, certainly before they might have expected to be widowed in the normal course of events, and all of whom found themselves in circumstances very different from their peers.

In the course of my work I met a diverse group of older women whose ages ranged from late 60s to late 80s, most of whom had been in one long term marriage terminated only by the death of their spouse, all of whom had different stories to tell about their present lives as widows. Their experiences covered a whole spectrum, from those who identified themselves as 'depressed' and still grieving after many years, to those for whom widowhood had been a blessed relief. I also became aware of the large number of older widows who lived in my own immediate neighbourhood. The area of the north of England in which I lived comprised mainly late nineteenth/early twentieth century terraced houses, many of which are owned or rented by single, older women. Specialist, retirement housing had also been developed in recent years. Not surprisingly then, there was a flourishing older people's 'scene' anchored in the Senior Citizen's Centre and the bowling club. It is interesting to note that as my interest in widowhood developed, these women became increasingly 'visible' to me. They had obviously always been there but were previously 'invisible'. I guessed that they were widows because they rarely had a male partner. Sometimes they were on their own, but very often they were with other women in twos or threes. And many of them seemed to be having fun! There was lots of laughter, talk and activity.

At the same time I started to read about older widows and was immediately struck by the contrast between what I was 'seeing' and what I was reading. The literature presented a much gloomier, more uniform picture than the one that was being revealed to me. I felt as though I had stumbled upon something quite extraordinary and passionately wanted to find out more. And so, in 1993, I undertook a small qualitative study which focused on the experience of five older widows (Chambers 1993).

These older women, now in their late sixties to late eighties, had been in a long term marriage, ended only by the death of their spouse, after which they had been living alone for quite a significant period of time. As such they were different from the women who preceded them and also the ones that would succeed them. The former had their marriages terminated by the early death of one partner, whereas later generations of women are much more likely to see their marriage end in divorce.


**Embarking on a journey**

This was the tentative beginning of my journey into the exploration of the lives, as I discuss in Chapter 9, of a particular 'generation' of older widows. At the end of my initial study, and as I began to review the literature in more depth, I became aware of yet more contradictions and omissions. Simultaneously, my interest in oral history and biography was being fueled by new developments in my working life. At this point I consulted Mason (1996:11-18), who recommends the researcher to ask herself five, difficult questions about the essence of her enquiry:

- *What is the nature of the phenomena or entities or social reality that I wish to investigate?* The phenomena that I wanted to investigate were the contradictions that confronted me. I wanted to explore the nature of later life widowhood as 'experienced' by older widows, in order to investigate their social reality.
- *What might represent knowledge or evidence of the entities or social reality that I wish to investigate?* Because I wanted to understand the different ways that older women made sense of their lives in widowhood, my evidence would to come from the women themselves.
- *What topic or broad substantive area is the research concerned with?* My own knowledge of the significance of the whole life course on later life, my earlier exposure to the diversity of experience in widowhood and my

strong belief in 'giving voice' to older women, convinced me that I needed to engage with the life stories of older widows, before I could even begin to understand their current experience. I would therefore have to embrace the life course of the current generation of older widows as well as exploring widowhood itself.

- *What is the intellectual puzzle? What do I wish to explain?* My intellectual puzzle was to test my conviction that widowhood was integral to a woman's whole life rather than an entity in itself.
- *What is the purpose of my research? What am I doing it for?* As an academic, I welcomed the opportunity to embark on new research, but at a personal level, as an ageing woman, I wanted to attempt to render this normally 'invisible' group of women more visible.

In summary, I wanted to find out more about the complexities underpinning both the objective and subjective experience of later life widowhood, and to ascertain the extent to which an older woman's life course impacted on her current experience. I wanted to understand how she makes sense of 'who' she is in widowhood and to do this within a framework that gives her a 'voice'.

This then was the starting point of my journey: to investigate the lived experience of later life widowhood through a review of the literature and by engaging older widows in a dialogue about their lives and the place of widowhood within those lives

## The likelihood of widowhood in later life

I now discuss, in general terms what the literature tells us about widowhood in later life. I draw attention to the fact that most older, married women will spend a significant period of their later years as a widow. I then set the scene for the following three chapters by discussing the predominant way in which widowhood is conceptualised in the research literature as a 'problem' of later life.

Gender differences in mortality and the social norm that women marry men older than themselves mean that widowhood is the norm for older women in the UK. Half of women aged 65 and over are widowed, reaching four fifths at ages 85 and over (ONS, 2001). Older widows tend not to remarry, usually through choice (Davidson 1999) and so, for many women, the likelihood is that they may spend a substantial number of years as an older widow.

In contrast, over three quarters of men aged 65 to 69 are married, 66 per cent in first marriages and 11 per cent remarried (ONS, 2001). Indeed, marriage rather than widowhood is the norm for older men. These trends seem set to continue and we are likely to see even greater numbers of older widows in subsequent cohorts. Unlike the current generation of older widows, there is a greater likelihood that future older women will have experienced divorce and remarriage. Among older men and women, the likelihood of being divorced has increased from 2 per cent to 5 per cent in the period 1980-1998 (ONS 2001). During the same period, the proportion of those who have remained 'ever single' has declined from 11 per cent to 6 per cent.

Given that widowhood is such a major feature of later life for older women, it is surprising to discover how little we know about the daily lives of older widows and the diversity of their experience. The ongoing 'lived experience' of widowhood is blurred in the literature on later life, which tends to homogenise women and is rarely alluded to in the literature on bereavement which, as we shall see, focuses on the disruption of the early days of widowhood.

## The 'problem' of widowhood

Research in Great Britain on the long-term experience of older widows is scarce. The little research there is concentrates on loss and bereavement, and focuses on the period of adjustment following the death of a spouse (Marris 1958; Torrie 1975; Bowling and Cartwright 1982). Davidson's (1999) illuminating work on gender differences in widowhood is one notable exception. North American research is more abundant (Lopata 1973, 1987; Arling 1976; O'Bryant 1982, 1987, 1991; Bankoff 1983; Ferraro 1984; Morgan 1989) but, until recently, there was a still a concentration on bereavement (Martin Mathews 1991; Jones Porter 1994; Lieberman 1996; Lopata 1996; Van Den Hoonard 1997, 1999). Indeed, a fairly uniform, problem-focused picture, which I now describe, emerges from the existing research literature.

*Loss*

Widowhood is identified as one of the major sources of loss in old age, in which the loss of a central role partner is compounded by the absence of any cultural expectations concerning a widow's proper role. Indeed, a body of literature exists which construes widowhood as a major stressful life event (see Holmes and Ray 1967) and Martin Matthews (1991) confirms that a major characteristic of Canadian widowhood research is its stress related nature. According to Bankoff (1983), the death of a spouse is a fundamental disruption which removes a key relationship in one's emotional life. Those with poor health, a lack of economic resources and poor education are likely to suffer most (Lopata 1973, 1979). According to Jerrome (1993) the loss of a partner through death involves a series of losses which include companionship, material support, a partner in a world which is couple oriented and someone to negotiate on the woman's behalf in a male dominated society. Torrie's (1975:3) description of the loss is more emotive:

> the death of a husband is in large measure the shattering of a home, as evident as any bomb blast which shears off the front of a house leaving all its intimate affairs exposed.

The literature tells us that older widows are more likely to be poor, emotionally troubled and to lack meaningful life patterns (Bankoff 1983; Gorer 1965; Gurin et al 1960; Lopata 1973, 1979, 1988; Madisson and Walker 1967; Parkes 1972). In addition, they have an elevated risk of deterioration and death (Jacobson and Ostfield 1977; Rees and Lutkins 1967). Widowhood brings with it an emotional impact and a loss of status, economic independence, mobility and social interaction (Hansson and Remondet 1988). For many older women, a combination of physical ill-health, financial insecurity, problems with housing and transport after the death of their spouse, all contribute to the loss and isolation commonly associated with widowhood (Arling 1976; Lopata 1973, 1979). Age too is a significant factor. Bowling and Cartwright (1982) remind us that it is the old who are most likely to face the crisis of widowhood at a time when they may also be adjusting to ill health and infirmity. They suggest that as a result of this, older widows are often apathetic and depressed.

For some older widows, the crisis of widowhood is complicated by an absence of DIY skills and a lack of financial knowledge, areas of married life which were managed by their husbands. In a study by O'Bryant et al (1989), 28% of widows had neither substantial experience nor preparation for handling money prior to their widowhood. Lopata (1973) found that many widows, lacking traditionally male DIY skills, felt taken advantage of by unscrupulous workmen.

*Loneliness*

Many widows experience pain, grief and loneliness as a result of the loss of a significant other (Lopata 1979). For some, the response will be resilience and adaptation (Jerome 1990) but for others, the loss of their spouse is the loss of their only intimate. Ford and Sinclair (1987:89) interviewed Mrs Hatch, whose life had revolved around her husband and family; she had no independent interests while her husband was alive, preferring to spend her leisure time in their shared love of ballroom dancing. In widowhood 'her loneliness is acute … the mechanics of life-shopping, doing things 'properly', a set of routines are the ways through the difficult days … '

It is suggested that most women who find themselves alone and without male companionship after they have lived in partnership, find widowhood very painful and disturbing (Torrie 1975). In a sample of 81 widows, Sable (1989:555), found a considerable degree of loneliness identified. One of her respondents, when asked if her bereavement had changed her, replied: 'Now, I know what fear is.'

*A mythology of widowhood*

Loss and loneliness are such key features in the literature that it is hardly surprising that widowhood is deemed to be so problematic (Pihlblad and Adams 1972; Lopata 1973, 1987; Atchley 1975; Arling 1976; Bowling and Cartwright 1982; Bankoff 1983; O'Bryant 1988; Babchuk and Anderson 1989; Sable 1989; Rosik 1989). This picture has led to the development of a popular mythology surrounding later life widowhood. Adlersberg and Thorne (1992: 9) confirm this view:

> The vast quantity of literature on older widows in our society convincingly portrays widowhood as an experience fraught with poverty, ill health, loneliness, grief and readjustment.

As Lopata (1996: 5) reminds us, the problem with myths is their 'stereotypical nature'. We begin to believe that they apply to all older widows to such an extent that 'widowhood as a problem' becomes a self-fulfilling prophecy. Hunter and Sundel (1989:21) suggest that myths are dangerous when they result in oversimplified stereotypes that influence personal perceptions, social interaction and social policy.

Our attention is also drawn to the sometimes, contradictory nature of the mythology surrounding widowhood (Lopata 1996). For example, 'older widows suffer more than younger widows' versus 'younger widows suffer more than older widows'; 'widows have close friends' versus 'older widows lose their friends'; 'sudden death is more difficult for the widow' versus 'prolonged death is more difficult for the widow' and so on. This may be something to do with the fact that in current American (and British) society there are no longer any formal rules for behaviour in widowhood; what has developed instead is a contradictory mythology. Lieberman (1994 cited in Lopata 1996:6) develops this further:

> Widows are probably one of the most misunderstood groups in America today. As pernicious as they are pervasive, the myths about widowhood are far more harmful than its realities.

He also suggests that Psychiatry and its practitioners have reinforced this problem model by viewing widowhood as a disease which requires either therapy or tranquillisers for recovery. In a later work (Lieberman1996) Lieberman acknowledges that most women, after a period of disruption in their lives during which they express their grief in their own way, experience both change and development.

*Challenging the mythology*

Adlersberg and Thorne (1992) acknowledge the influence of this pathological model when they embarked on a project that sought to find ways of helping older widows to 'recover'. From the very beginning, their preconceptions were challenged by many of the older women who were referred to them. Rather than being 'in recovery' a number of them saw widowhood as a time of opportunity and freedom. These women also reported that the myths of widowhood got in the way of them openly expressing these views to their families and friends, who expected them to feel sad and have problems. In addition, the women themselves felt they had internalized the myths and consequently felt guilty at reporting feelings of satisfaction and personal growth. Other qualitative research (Martin Matthews

1991; Pickard 1994; Davidson 1999) has started to question some of the prevailing myths of widowhood. Indeed, Lopata, a leading researcher of widowhood, who has written on the subject for 30 years, also challenges some of her earlier assumptions about the dismal and problematic nature of widowhood (Lopata 1996). Widowed herself in 1994, Lopata (1996: xiii) and with reference to the numerous myths, stereotypes and assumptions surrounding widowhood, she concedes: 'Even I found myself influenced by these at the start of the research. Many of these myths present a dismal and limiting picture of women'. Instead, she argues, we need to re-conceptualise widowhood and acknowledge that, in American society, there is no permanent role of widow (Lopata 1996 p221-2):

> ... the image of widowhood that is emerging from current research is that of a resilient widowed woman, able to work through her grief, cutting ties with the deceased, accepting life without him, modifying existing social relationships and roles and building new ones, and reconstructing the self into an independent, whole human being.

More work is needed, Lopata contends, to explore the various group and idiosyncratic identities that are uniquely combined throughout the life course. American widowhood is identified, and I would argue widowhood in later life in Britain, as an increasingly heterogeneous experience. Unique combinations of factors will contribute to this experience.

It would seem then, that a powerful mythology has developed in Western societies that widowhood, the expectation of most, older women, is problematic. Such is the power of the mythology that older widows themselves may find it difficult to subscribe to any other story, for fear of being seen as 'unfeeling' or even 'unfaithful' to the memory of their dead spouse.

**Outline of this book**

The study reported in this volume sought to go beyond this mythology by situating widowhood within the female life course and by exploring widowhood from the perspective of older widows themselves. The journey of that investigation is as follows:

- Chapters 2, 3 and 4 comprise a review the literature on later life widowhood. In Chapter 2, I explore our current understanding of 'becoming and being an older widow' and examine the inherent assumptions about this experience which are evident in much of the literature. I review in some detail the biographical assets which older women bring to later life widowhood and which have a bearing on their move from 'we' to 'I'.  My focus in Chapter 3 is on the social world of older widows and I review three 'bodies' of literature: social support in widowhood, social participation in widowhood and the social world of older women in general. In Chapter 4, I draw together a range of theories and perspectives, which have been highlighted in the previous two chapters, in order to evaluate what is more or less helpful in seeking to understand the experience of later life widowhood. I then go on to suggest a way of re-conceptualizing widowhood, which takes into account the totality of older women's lives.

•          Chapters 5 and 6 comprise the methodology and methods components of my study. In Chapter 5, I explore the theoretical concerns which underpin my fieldwork and draw on a range of research methodology and methods literature from Gerontology and Feminism. I examine in particular feminist research practice and biographical approaches to the study of later life, and argue for the importance of understanding the 'subjective' experience of those who participate in our research. In Chapter 6, I describe in detail the stages of my fieldwork from my first pre-pilot interview right through to my analysis.

•          Chapters 7 to 11 comprise five chapters of 'findings'. In Chapter 7, I present a summary of the biographies of the twenty older widows who participated in my study. In Chapters 8-11, I present a series of multiple narratives, and sub-plots, which have emerged from an analysis of my participants' life stories. Via the women's own words, I present these four chapters under the headings of: Me Myself, History and Me, Me and My Social World and Me Now.

•          Chapters 12 to 14 comprise two discussion chapters and a conclusion. In Chapter 12, I further develop my discussion and argue for the concept of 'multiple narratives' as a way of understanding the multi-faceted experience of later life widowhood. In Chapter 13, I reflect on the process of my research via an analysis of my discussions with some of the women about their participation in my study and an analysis of my field diary. I explore the impact of participating in the research on the women and myself. Finally, in Chapter 14, I conclude my journey.


## Conclusion

In this introduction I have discussed the 'beginnings' of my journey, acknowledged that widowhood is a 'women's issue' and sought to briefly introduce the 'problem' of widowhood. I have stated my intention to go beyond the current mythology of later life widowhood and provided an outline of the book. I now move on to Section 1, and in the next two chapters I review the 'problem' of later life widowhood in more detail. I then go on to draw the existing evidence together and suggest that, in order to really understand the 'lived experience' of later life widowhood, it is necessary to develop a perspective, which embraces the totality of older women's lives. I propose a way of looking at widowhood through 'a different lens' (Gibson 1996), by drawing on perspectives from feminism and gerontology. I conclude the review chapters by recommending a feminist life course perspective as a way of redefining widowhood.

# Chapter 2

# Becoming and Being an Older Widow

## Introduction

Older widows get a bad press - the word widow itself often conjures up an image of someone, who is lonely, dependent, depressed (Martin Matthews, 1999), an anomaly in a 'couple-companionate' world (Jerrome, 1993). In a study of widows in the developing world Owen (1996: 153) argued that this negative image of the older widow is both universal and longstanding: 'In fairy tales, legends and myths and nursery tales, the old widow portrayed as a hag, harridan, witch or sorceress is a familiar character'. She demonstrated that stories from all over the world depict widowed mothers harassing their daughters in law whilst possessively adoring their sons. Older widows, often the butt of 'mother-in-law jokes', are rarely described in positive terms or deemed to be worthy of respect. Such stereotypes affect both individual and collective attitudes and contribute to the experience of becoming and being an older widow.

Indeed, there has been a consensus in the literature on bereavement that the death of a spouse is one of the most stressful of role transitions (Holmes and Rahe, 1967; Parkes, 1986) and is likely to impact on the physical and mental health of the widow as well as causing disruption to her identity and self-image. It involves a major disruption to a woman's life, followed by a period of upheaval during which she gradually learns to come to terms with her loss (Vachon et al, 1976; Stroebe and Stroebe, 1983, 1987; Machin, 2000). This has generally been conceptualised through the notion of stages of grieving (Kubler-Ross, 1970; Bowlby, 1980) or overlapping clusters of reactions (Osterweiss et al, 1984; Stroebe and Stroebe, 1987; Machin, 2000). Furthermore, widowhood has been construed as one of the most serious threats to health, wellbeing and productivity during the middle and later years (Vachon et al, 1976; Stroebe and Stroebe, 1983, 1987). Pearlin (1980), for example, identified that widowhood raises depression to a higher level than pre-widowhood and other studies have confirmed significant effects on mental health following spousal bereavement (Ferraro, 1989; Bennett and Morgan, 1992). The literature has indicated that there are higher levels of depression, lowered morale and quite short term declines in health, but stability in social functioning (Balkwell, 1981; Lund et al, 1985-6; Jacobs et al, 1989).

However, within this literature, there are contradictions. For example, evidence has been presented to suggest that the health of elderly widows is not affected by the death of their spouse (Heyman and Gianturco, 1973), whereas other evidence has pointed to problematic health (Fenwick and Barresi, 1981). Such conflicting findings may of course have arisen from the variety of concepts and tools used to measure health. In a review of the literature, Ferraro (1989) concluded that widowhood results in an immediate decrease in 'perceived' good health, but has minimal long-term effect. Indeed, he argued that expectations accompanying sex and age were more important than marital status. Similarly, no consensus has been reached concerning the impact of widowhood on mortality. Although Young et al (1963) and Parkes (1972) documented high mortality rates amongst widowers six months after the death of their wives other studies have not corroborated these findings. Certainly, there appears to be no such evidence concerning older widows.

The major focus of this literature is on coping responses, coping strategies and support networks. The widow becomes socially constructed in terms of her mental health, her physical health and her loss of identity as a wife; that is in terms of major discontinuities, and her capacity to 'recover'. It is important to re-iterate however that much of this literature refers to widowhood in general rather than focusing specifically on widowhood in later life. Whilst it is true that widowhood is more likely to occur in later life  (ONS, 2001), and therefore most widows will be 'old', the assumption of homogeneity may be both erroneous and misleading.

In this chapter however, my focus is not on the immediate aftermath of the death of a spouse but rather the ongoing experience of becoming and being an older widow. My discussion centres on the biographical assets that older women bring to later life widowhood and the potential therein for growth and change in the move from 'wife' to 'widow'. It is important to reiterate both the limited amount of research that there is on 'what it feels like' to be an older widow after the initial stages of bereavement and the assumptions that are made concerning later life widowhood. Assumptions such as: widowhood is a stressful life event (Holmes and Rahe, 1967); widowhood is 'bereavement followed by adjustment to a new role' (Jones Porter, 1995); and widowhood is a homogeneous experience. I argue that these often un-stated assumptions have in many ways restricted the development of our knowledge about what shapes the experience of later life widowhood.

A small body of qualitative research (Allen, 1988; Martin Matthews, 1991; Pickard, 1994; Jones-Porter, 1995; Lieberman, 1996; Davidson, 1999; Bennett, 2000) has attempted, as part of larger studies on widowhood, or ageing and gender, to explore both the diversity and the complexity of becoming and being a widow. I draw on this work in this review, alongside the quantitative, larger scale studies of widowhood. I also draw on sources from women's history and women's studies as well as making reference to autobiographical sources in order to explore fully both the subjective and the objective experience of later life widowhood.

*Who am I?*

According to Marris (1958), a woman's life is thrown into chaos with the death of a husband. Used to defining herself in terms of 'a wife' and one part of 'a couple', she struggles to know who she is, now that she is no longer a wife. This confusion of identity, couched in terms of the question 'who am I?' has been widely reported (for example: Balkwell, 1981; Caine, 1974; Lopata, 1983; Martin Matthews, 1991; Van den Hoonaard, 1997, 1999; Davidson, 1999). Indeed, for some women, one way of answering the question, and hanging on to the identity of 'wife', appears to be the telling and retelling of the story of the death of their husbands (Bennett and Vidal-Hall, 2000).

Widowhood has been typically associated with profound psychological disorganisation. Using a symbolic interactionist perspective, Martin Matthews (1991) suggested that since interaction with significant others provides the basis for the sense of reality of the world and oneself in it, when a 'significant other' is lost, the sense of self is thrown into jeopardy. The 'me' will be changed by the loss of a primary significant other who has contributed to that definition of 'me'. This is confirmed by autobiographical accounts of widowhood (Caine, 1974; Balkwell, 1981).

Drawing on their own empirical research, Wortman and Silver (1993) provided evidence of a far greater variability in response to the loss of a spouse than this prevailing view would imply: some people show relatively little distress following their loss whereas others experience ongoing problems. They contended that differing coping responses and coping resources would impact on the experience of bereavement, citing Zisook and Schuchter (1986: 288) who have written that at the present time:

> ... there is no prescription for how to grieve properly ... and no research-validated guide posts for what is normal vs. deviant mourning ... we are just beginning to realise the full range of what may be considered 'normal' grieving.

Canadian research has provided us with examples of such variability. A study of widows in Guelph (Martin Matthews, 1982 cited in Martin Matthews, 1991) indicated that loss of spouse affected the women more than any other life event. A later study, carried out in Ontario (Martin Matthews, 1986 cited in Martin Matthews, 1991), presented a challenge to these results. Whilst 45 per cent of the sample indicated that widowhood had affected them quite a lot, and 23 per cent a lot (with loneliness and longing for the spouse reported as particularly strong feelings), 17 per cent said that the death of their spouse had affected them relatively little. A minority, 7 per cent, said compared to other life events, the death of their spouse had affected them very little. These women, who had reported not being affected by widowhood, focused instead on the continuity of their lives in widowhood and cited 'biographical factors' such as employment outside the home, ability to drive and the presence of children as having been helpful.

In a qualitative study which also employed symbolic interactionism to explore the re-alignment of the lives of older widows and widowers, Davidson made reference to Giddens' concept of 'ontological security' (Giddens, 1991) and Antonovsky's 'sense of coherence' (Antonovsky, 1979) to understand the changes experienced in widowhood:

> Both of these concepts have been defined as a sense of stability and continuity brought about over a lifetime of positioning oneself in a known, predictable and comprehensive world. Widowhood can be described as a life event which brings chaos to this established sense of self.
>
> (Davidson, 1999: 107)

She developed an 'ontological coherence - ontological chaos continuum' through which to understand how widowed persons make sense of their lives:

> ontological coherence ...............................ontological chaos
> acceptance zone....................... .................non-acceptance zone
>
> (Davidson, 1999: 107)

Most of her widowers and widows placed themselves in the acceptance zone two years after death of their spouse although, as confirmed in other research (Pollock, 1977; Bowling and Cartwright, 1982; Hyrkas et al, 1987; Stroebe et al, 1988; Lund et al, 1993; Parkes, 1996) this fluctuated depending on their own circumstances and health. Davidson (1999) argued that 'biographical assets' influence coping strategies in widows' now changing world and went on to suggest the following assets: self-identity (expressed satisfaction and self esteem); physical and mental well-being (health and functional abilities); personal autonomy (decision making and control); socio-economic status (income; former occupation; quality of environment); social interaction (social contacts, family and social roles); and gender. Others (for example Havighurst, 1972) have also contended that 'extraneous' factors will impact upon coping strategies. Generation, age, gender as well as identity and personality are all equally important and no one factor can be considered in isolation to the others; the more positive the biographical assets, the greater the chance of achieving 'ontological coherence' (Davidson, 1999). It is to these 'biographical assets' that I now turn.

## Biographical assets

*Generation and history*

It is now widely recognised that successive generations will age differently:

> ...new ... studies (have) demonstrated the powerful connections between the two forces of individual ageing and historical period by showing that the shape of the life course was different depending on one's year of birth; that is age, period and cohort intersect with each other to produce different life patterns among different age groups or generations.
>
> (Giele and Elder, 1999: 15)

Older widows are clearly no exception to this. It is of course impossible to do justice here to the complex history of the current generation of older widows, particularly in view of their individual diversity of class and ethnicity. However, in order to gain some insight into their collective history, it is appropriate to highlight a number of issues that may have shaped their life course and thus impact on their experience of becoming and being an older widow. I focus particularly on their earlier years.

Today's older widows 'came of age' in the earlier part of the twentieth century. They married in the 1930s or 1940s and according to Burgoyne et al (1987) they experienced on average longer lasting marriages than any preceding or succeeding generation. The premature death of one spouse would have ended a marriage earlier on in the century, whereas later on it was much more likely to be divorce which terminated the marriage. They learnt from childhood that they were expected to marry, be a good wife and mother and put the needs of others first. Indeed, as Verrill-Rhys and Beddoe (1992) have reminded us, in the years between the two World Wars women in Britain were left in no doubt that they belonged 'in the home':

> This notion, this domestic ideology was brought into play once again with amazing rapidity as soon as the First World War ended. It had merely been put on ice for the duration of that first conflict. Women … were persuaded and coerced back into the home to resume their 'natural' roles as wives, mothers, daughters, sisters; those who wilfully persisted in seeking employment were widely condemned as 'flappers', 'hussies' and 'women who stole men's jobs.
>
> (Verrill-Rhys and Beddoe, 1992: 6)

In such a patriarchal society, women were judged in relationship to men, whether it was their husband, their father or their brother. Many of them had little access to anything more than elementary education although some went on to train for female occupations: secretaries; nurses; or teachers (Rowbotham, 1999). In the period between the two world wars, only elementary education up to the age of fourteen was compulsory and according to Houldsworth (1988) truancy by a girl, particularly if she was 'helping mum' was both commonplace and accepted. She has provided us with an example of Dorothy Capper who, on top of attending elementary school had this exhausting domestic routine:

> My mother died when I was nine and my sister was three. My brother was seven weeks old and me granny and granddad came to live with us and she was very, very strict, a very Victorian lady. So I ceased to be a child when I was nine years old actually because I was expected to scrub all the washing on Mondays and stand at the big table and scrub my grandfather's shirts and me father's shirts and overalls and then every Friday I had to scrub the kitchen floor before I went to school and I also had to take me brother and sister everywhere I went.
>
> (Houldsworth, 1988: 51)

Those girls whose families were better off may not have experienced the same domestic routine as Dorothy but nonetheless would have been left in no doubt that education was for boys. The school curriculum was highly gendered both in terms of content and in terms of process and some of today's older widows would have been prevented from progressing in education as a result of gendered government education policies (Marshall, 2000).

For some women, the 1930s was a particularly difficult time, when their fathers and brothers were out of work; others were not touched by such poverty. For all of them though, it is highly likely that their world was centred on their own immediate neighbourhood (Young and Wilmott, 1957). The Second World War was a significant milestone in their lives, whether they experienced it as an evacuee, a teenager, a worker or a young serviceman's wife (Sokoloff, 1999). It may have been a time of great fear or even bravery for some, for others a time of great fun (Brabon and Summerfield, 1987; Verrill-Rhys and Beddoe, 1992; Rowbotham, 1999). It was certainly a time of greater mobility. However they experienced it, the war would have impacted on their life in some way. For example, some women found themselves working alongside men in a way that was unprecedented in the pre-war years. As Walker (1990) reported:

> Suddenly, it appeared women were able to do jobs previously denied to them: suddenly it was deemed that it was not necessarily harmful for small children to be left in the care of others. Such is the nature of political expediency.
>
> (Walker, 1990: 11)

By 1943, nearly 8 million women in Britain were in paid work; if part time and voluntary work are included, 90 per cent of single women and 80 per cent of married women were contributing to the war effort (Verrill-Rhys and Bedoe, 1992; Summerfield, 1998). However, Sokoloff (1999) has urged us not to read too much into this. Writing about servicemen's wives:

> Strong gendered ideologies of domestic and work structure survived intact among servicemen's wives and their communities in cities like Birmingham and Coventry, and despite the upheaval of bombing and war production, provided little basis for longer-term post-war changes in wives' statuses and roles.
>
> (Sokoloff, 1999: 27)

Some historians have suggested that the war offered women sexual liberation as never before, whereas feminist historians have tended to play down change and emphasise continuities of behaviour and mores. Summerfield and Crockett (1992) have presented an alternative perspective, which speaks of the diversity of women's experience. Women's accounts, they have argued, emphasise a wide variety of responses that include conformity to traditional norms of sexual behaviour as well as a rejection of such norms and a refusal to be subordinated.

Many women were involved in war work, such as working in the munitions factories (Summerfield, 1989) and others joined the forces (Rowbotham, 1999). Joining the forces certainly provided some of them with hitherto unknown luxuries, such as three meals a day, pyjamas, several sets of clothes and travel (Sheridan, 1990). Mothers too found themselves working for the war effort, bringing up children with absent fathers (Walker, 1990), making use of state run nurseries (Summerfield, 1989) and relying on mainly female family members and friends for daily support. Stories of family disruption (Walker, 1990) were not uncommon, nor too was experience of loss. Most of today's older women experienced the loss of a family member or friend as a result of the war, either through death, illness or as a result of moving away.

Summerfield (1989) contended that the expectation of marriage, home and dependency as the appropriate conditions for women, not only survived the challenges of war but also were major determinants of policy towards women throughout. The war, she argued, did little to alter but rather reinforced the unequal position of women in society. Women may have worked outside the home, but the bulk of wartime domestic work, whilst parcelled in the rhetoric of the war effort, was still carried out by women and their families and friends. Summerfield (1989) went on to argue that women were not expelled from the paid work force after the war, but instead they were drawn into it along lines which followed the pre-war pattern; decline in textiles and clothing and domestic service, and increased employment in food and drink, tobacco, distribution, miscellaneous manufacturing, chemicals and other expanding industries. The numbers of women employed increased in both absolute and proportionate terms in engineering, vehicles, metals, gas, water, electricity and transport. However, this did nothing to change the stratified nature of women's work, which left them less well paid than their male colleagues. According to Summerfield (1989):

> If the experience of mobilising women for war shifted the assumptions and ideologies of policy makers about women and work at all, it was in the direction of the idea that women could combine paid and domestic work without damage to industrial productivity and without undermining the concept that their first responsibility was to their homes.
>
> (Summerfield, 1989: 188)

She has challenged the view that women gained freedom during the war and then returned home without a fight after the war was over:

> In sum, the issue, which needs exploration, is what sort of change the redefinition of the double burden during and after the war did produce in women's lives. On the one hand it may have trapped women more firmly within patriarchal relations at work and at home. On the other hand it may in the long run have prompted women collectively both to attack inequalities at work and to challenge the sexual division of labour at home.
>
> (Summerfield, 1989: 190-191)

The legacies of wartime impacted on the current cohort of older widows differentially depending on their individual circumstances. What is clear though, is that they will have been subjected to both change and continuity throughout their lives, which will impact in some way on their management of the present. For example, in a text that explores journeys of widowhood, Van Den Hoonaard (2001) has noted that American and Canadian older widows who had been Second World War brides from the U.K. and Europe, seem to have managed their journey better than their counterparts, perhaps because of previous successful management of major disruption and loss.

In the post-war years, it was still possible to describe a typical family as one with both parents living at home, the father being the chief wage earner and the mother being responsible for child rearing and the home. Adult children continued to reside with family until they married and close ties were maintained with the extended family. The Beveridge Report (1942) and subsequent welfare legislation confirmed the place of women as principal carers and consolidated the notion of women's economic dependency on the male breadwinner (Williams, 1991). Beveridge made the assumption that married women would not be 'gainfully occupied' (Beveridge, 1942, para. 111) but would perform the duties of 'vital, unpaid service as housewives' (para. 309). For many women, this was not perceived as a problem. As Davidson (1999: 36) reported, the older women in her study: 'had learned from childhood that it was usual for women to look after men quite comprehensively, and that this was the basis of being a good wife'. However, they also experienced the upheaval of traditional values, to be replaced by new values more suited to: 'a brave new world of rapid change' (Davidson, 1999: 37). There was a feeling that nothing would be the same again. Notable changes also took place, partly as a result of greatly increased prosperity, new housing and improved health care.

But change did not just happen as a result of material and economic factors. According to Roberts (1998: 232): 'Other developments stemmed from evolving social and moral attitudes, which emphasised the importance of individual rights and self-fulfilment.' These changes had a significant effect on women, and the families and communities in which they lived. Whilst working class women gained in terms of better housing, more amenities and less drudgery, their lives did not seem easier and many of them may have felt more isolated in new 'homes of their own' (Giles, 1995). Some maintained contacts with neighbours but many learned in the new 'private' world, the importance of 'keeping yourself to yourself' (Giles, 1995). If they were working outside the family home (and many were), there is little evidence that gender roles changed at home. They certainly did not have equal status in the workplace; women's work was low-paid, mostly unskilled and their wages often regarded as being for 'extras' whilst the men's wages were for essentials. Working women fitted their paid jobs around the family in order to care properly for their children. Many had no choice but to do this as the nurseries, which had been available during the war years, started to close. Post war theories of child development (such as those of Bowlby, 1953), as well as political expediency, stressed the importance of women's role as principal carer in the family.

For those who stayed at home, the role of full time housewife and mother became important. Unlike their own mothers, these women had on average much smaller families. Houldsworth (1988) cited the views of a professional woman, who gave up work when she had two children in the 1950s discussing the possibility of resuming her career with another mother:

> It's our duty to stay at home' her friend replied. 'If people like us cannot stay at home with our children, then who can?' The implication being, that as they could afford not to work they should set an example to the rest. Having 'sacrificed' themselves for motherhood, these former professional women were often the loudest in their criticism of working mothers. The more they had given up, the more they needed to idealise motherhood.
>
> (Houldsworth, 1988: 125)

The role of the 'good mother' did not detract from the role of the 'good wife'. Many a childless woman still saw her role as the homemaker, who made sure her husband's tea was on the table when he came home from work.

And so, despite the interlude of the Second World War where some women, but by no means all (Rowbotham, 1999), had a taste of something different, most women returned to their role in the family home. Most of Davidson's (1999) respondents, whilst acknowledging that they 'had to work at it', reported having had a happy marriage and showed immense pride in keeping their marriage vows. For this generation, the patriarchy inherent in these marriages, whereby wives subsumed their wishes to the demands of their husbands, is a factor in the maintenance of long-term marriage (Davidson, 1999). Public policy, of course, reinforced this idealised nuclear family.

It is suggested that future historians will be tempted to look back to this period in the post war years as the golden age of the nuclear family (Roberts, 1998). Current older widows may individually agree or disagree with this but as a generation, they will all have found their lives shaped in some way by this view. Divorce, separation, cohabitation, abortion and illegitimacy were certainly around in the 1950s and 1960s, but would have affected only small numbers. As they grew older it is highly unlikely that their families would not have been affected by some of these consequences of social changes. As the children of current older widows grew up, the chances are that they will have done better educationally and financially than their parents (Houldsworth, 1988) The widows too may have found themselves better off and a greater number of them will have become home-owners. Certainly, they will have experienced better material conditions than their own mothers.

Older widows may or may not have been directly affected by the second wave of feminism in the 1960s and 1970s, but they will have been aware of the challenges being presented to many of the roles they undertook, willingly or not, throughout the life course, particularly the roles of 'good wife' and 'good mother' (Granville, 2000). They may have felt personally challenged by these new ideas or they may have even started to question previous 'certainties'. What is certain is that belonging to, and ageing in, a particular generation of women will in some way have shaped their current experience as older widows, both positively and negatively.

*Personality and 'view of the world'*

The role of personality, and a view of the world, also appears to be an important biographical asset in the transition to widowhood. Hansson and Remondet (1988) for example identified personality as one of the factors affecting the potential for growth and change. They suggested, that those with a 'hardy' personality have been shown to cope better with stress generally, and this might be expected to influence adjustment in widowhood. There is a growing consensus that personality is quite stable throughout the adult life course (see for example Sugarman, 1986; Coleman, 1994) and that personality styles could assist or undermine coping efforts in old age just as much as earlier in the life course.

In her study of 30 older women, Allen (1989) found that the meanings attached to later life transitions varied depending on the context of previous transitions and the women's perceptions and feeling about those transitions. She identified three ways of looking at life, which reflected the women's views on their present life. Firstly: I've had a dull life. Secondly: I've had a hard life. And, thirdly: I've had a full life. This view of the world had not been determined by objective circumstances in that one person's life may not have been intrinsically more exciting or more difficult than any others, but it was a subjective view of the world based on each woman's personality and individual, subjective, biography.

In a Finnish study of old age Ruth and Oberg (1996) confirmed the importance of understanding older people's view of their world, or 'ways of life', from a life history perspective as a way of understanding how they manage their current circumstances. They conducted life history interviews with older Finns who had grown up in the years before the Second World War. They found that those who felt that they had had a hard life were more likely to see their current circumstances as difficult, whereas those who felt that life had been kind were more likely to find their current circumstances favourable. The authors argued the case for a life history perspective on old age, one that takes into account issues of individual and collective biography, and subjectivity. With the exception of Davidson's (1999) comparative study of older widows and widowers, which sets widowhood within the context of 'companionate marriage', the impact of individual and collective biography on later life widowhood has been sorely neglected in widowhood research. The study reported in this book aimed to redress that imbalance.

*Age*

Just as there is now a consensus that successive generations age differently, it is also acknowledged that the experience of becoming and being an older widow follows a different course depending on the age at which it occurs (Arber and Ginn, 1991) and older widows are stereotyped as particularly disadvantaged. Is it the case that older widows are subjected to both sexism and ageism, and thus problematised (see Chapter 4) or is being an older widow really more difficult than being a younger widow? Whilst many coping resources decline with age, and stressors such as ill health, loss of peers and loss of finance are more likely to be present, accumulated knowledge and life experience increases (Wortman and Silver, 1990).

Widowhood in later life is an expectation for most older, married women and as such is an 'on time' experience. The existence of a social clock, that is a system of age norms superimposed on the biological clock, was first posited by Neugarten et al (1965; 1973). Neugarten (1977) argued that we use this social clock to assess ourselves in relation to others and to ask ourselves how we are doing in relation to our cohort. It follows that experiences are either 'on time' or 'off time' in relation our age group. Neugarten et al (1965; 1973) maintained that when the loss of a spouse occurs 'on time' the event is rehearsed and the reconciliation to that loss accomplished without shattering the continuity of the life course. It can be argued that older couples thus have the opportunity to anticipate the likelihood that one partner will die before the other and plan accordingly (O'Bryant, 1991). Neugarten et al (1965; 1973) were suggesting that where the event occurs in the life course is more important than whether it occurs at all, and that the nature of loss that is experienced is likely to vary over the life course. This may well be so, but it also has to be acknowledged that even if an event does occur 'on time', it may still be an equally overwhelming experience. For example, an older woman may have had a strong attachment to her husband of 50 years and may well have had a mutual dependence, which has enabled her to cope with some of the negative effects of ageing. With the death of her husband she may find herself unable to cope with these negative aspects of the ageing process.

The significance of age can be seen in the debate in the literature about the helpfulness or otherwise of a forewarning of the death of a spouse, in enabling the older widow to begin to adjust to her life as a widow. Some researchers have found evidence that anticipatory grief leads to better adjustment (Glick et al 1974; Vachon, Rogers et al, 1982; O'Bryant, 1991) whereas others have found little to support such a claim (Maddison and Walker, 1967; McGloshen and O'Bryant, 1988). A long protracted illness may make widowhood more difficult and adjustment poor (Clayton et al, 1973), but so too might a sudden death. Ferraro (1989) reported:

> Death stings in most cases but ... [sudden and unexpected loss of a spouse] resembles a sharp pain demanding re-organisation while [a lengthy time of caring for a spouse] is a dull chronic pain that delays life re-organisation.
>
> (Ferraro, 1989: 75)

However, it may well be that unlike younger widows, most older women may in some way anticipate the death of their spouse even if it is a sudden death and so it is likely that the impact of the death of a spouse on an older woman may well be mediated by age. Older widows, by virtue of age, are also more likely than younger widows to have previously experienced the loss of a significant other. Some might already have experienced the loss of a spouse, although whether this means they have learnt coping strategies is not clear, as there is little research in this area. O'Bryant and Straw (1991) provided some evidence of better adaptation, particularly in terms of economic and self sufficiency behaviour. However, psychological well-being does not appear to be enhanced and previous loss may well exacerbate a fatalistic attitude.

So far, the discussion has acknowledged that age is both an asset and a deficit in widowhood, so let us look further at this. Because widowhood is the norm for most married women as they age, older widows belong to a majority group (ONS, 2001) whereas earlier on in the life course they are a tiny minority. Not belonging to a minority seems to help considerably in terms of health and well-being (Fooken, 1985). Canadian research has suggested that it is easier for older women to adjust to widowhood than younger women (Haas Hawkings et al, 1985) and furthermore, women who are widowed 'on time' seem to be:

> ... psychologically prepared to accept the death of the spouse as well as their own status as widow.
>
> (Fooken, 1985: 98).

Indeed, there has been some suggestion, albeit cautious, that older women may rehearse for widowhood by spending time with widowed friends, beginning to plan and make decisions, and starting to do things on their own (Hansson and Remondet, 1988; Chambers and Pickard, 2002). Allen (1988) reported that nine of the widows she interviewed, had prepared for the transition to widowhood by building a support network over time; they had their own friends, adequate transportation and maintained good health. Once widowed, their socialisation process continued as they learned to pursue their daily activities as a widow. For younger widows, there are far fewer opportunities for this to occur.

However, there does seem to be a point where age per se becomes a disadvantage and the advantages of age may no longer apply:

> While widowhood at a young age is decidedly off time, there are also those for whom widowhood occurs so very late in life that the presence of age-related health decrements and a lack of resources may impede adaptation.
>
> (Martin Matthews, 1991: 21)

It is important to acknowledge, that older widows, by virtue of being old (and female) are also subject to the same social construction of age, and thus ageism (and sexism), experienced by all older people (Arber and Ginn, 1991; Bernard and Meade, 1993; Bytheway, 1995; Bernard et al, 2000) and may well find themselves structurally dependent both on services which restrict their capacity for growth and people who deny their independence. In societies where later life is negatively constructed, old age is potentially a stigma, that is: an attribute that is deeply discrediting (Goffman, 1969: 3). Older women (and men) have to deal with others who see them as old, even though they may reject the label old for themselves (Matthews, 1979; Andrews, 1999). Indeed, as Andrews (1999: 37) has observed, given the negative connotations of old age as a combination of incapacity, inability and ill-health, it is hardly surprising that older people in general distance themselves from it. However, by encapsulating themselves in this way and internalising negative images of ageing, older widows may, unwittingly, be preventing themselves from accessing new situations and new relationships as well as participating in their own 'erasure' (Healey 1994: 83, cited in Andrews, 1999) or 'invisibility' (Bernard and Meade, 1993; Gibson, 1996). How much they are allowed to adjust to life as an older widow may well be constrained by their own internalised ageism (and sexism), as well as that of others.

Whilst acknowledging the deficits accrued in very old age, and the negative effects of ageism, it does seem that age itself, contrary to popular opinion, has the potential to be an asset in widowhood. Certainly, the age factor is crucial in understanding the experience of later life widowhood. The ageing process itself is one of constant change and adaptation to change, which most older adults negotiate more or less successfully (Hansson and Remondet, 1988; Coleman, 1994; Kirkwood, 1999). As a person ages, there is a need to solve new problems across several domains, both emotional and practical. Many commentators (for example Langer, 1983; Rodin, 1986; Coleman, 1994) have confirmed the importance of the individual maintaining personal control over these changes. A number of transitions may occur in old age, such as ill health or loss, which can restrict an individual's range of influence over personal outcomes. If many changes occur at the same time, there may be considerable disruption and much suffering and thus adaptation may be very difficult. For example, widowhood may be a disruptive experience, involving emotional loss, loss of status, economic independence and mobility, if it occurs at the same time as age related vulnerabilities and chronic health problems. However, compared to younger widows, it may be that older widows, despite ageism and sexism, are much more able to negotiate and adapt to change because such negotiations are part of their daily lives. Furthermore, according to Andrews (1999) age gives older people, and I would argue more specifically older widows, the opportunity look back over their lives with a new ability to see and understand, a perspective which is not available earlier on in life.

*Gender*

It is generally agreed that, that just as the experience of later life in general is structured by gender (Arber and Ginn, 1991; Arber and Ginn, 1995; Bernard and Meade, 1993; Bernard et al, 2000), so too is the experience of becoming and being a widow (Davidson, 1999). Unfortunately, much of the debate concerning gender seems to have consisted of a 'who has the toughest time' approach. I do not wish to add to that discussion here, except to acknowledge that to date, there has been no consensus. Stroebe and Stroebe (1987) for example suggested that although the evidence is not really conclusive, widowers do seem to be at higher risk than widows because they gain more benefits from marriage. Atchley (1975) however, found that widowers were considerably better off than widows, particularly because they were more likely to have financial resources with which to offset social and psychological disadvantages. Yet others, (for example, Feinson, 1986) have suggested that gender has no impact on adaptation and other factors are more important. Davidson's (1999) comparative study reported a differential experience in later life, with widows managing better than their male counterparts.

However, I wish to focus here on those aspects of the debate, which contribute to our understanding of older women's experience of becoming and being a widow: the advantages and disadvantages arising from gender socialisation and women's position in society (Jerrome, 1993; Stevens, 1995). There is little doubt that the current generation of older women are likely to be severely disadvantaged in terms of the material and financial resources available to them (Victor, 1989; Arber and Ginn, 1991; Bernard and Meade, 1993; Arber and Ginn, 1995; Siddell, 1995). As a consequence they are likely to experience particular restrictions in widowhood (Arber and Ginn, 1991; Martin Matthews, 1991). They will also have to contend with the consequences of the dual discrimination of ageism and sexism (Bernard and Meade, 1993). However, as I discuss more fully in the next chapter, they are likely to be considerably advantaged in terms of relational resources (Jerrome, 1993; Stevens, 1995). Indeed, those widows who are well adapted have more varied sources of support available to them than their male counterparts.

Stevens (1995) pointed to the great diversity of ways in which women adapt to widowhood by developing a greater variation of primary relationship networks and other sources of support. As a result of both choice and scarcity of partners, they often develop alternative relationships to partner relationships. Stevens (1995) identified gender specific reasons for older women's capacity to manage these changes. Firstly, women's special virtuosity in relationships and secondly, a flexibility that is developed in the course of women's lives, in which they manage multiple careers, helps adaptation to major change in later life despite sometimes major structural disadvantage. Throughout adulthood women are subject to repeated role loss and the necessity for readjustment, and thus undergo a socialisation process that facilitates adaptation in later life.

Older widows themselves acknowledge gender differences and often recognise the strengths they bring to later life. Davidson's (1999) widows consistently spoke of their psychological strength and resilience in coping with changes in their lives. Acknowledging continuities, they reported that they felt better able than widowers to cope with being alone, especially in the private sphere of home:

> ... for this generation of women, caring, home and domesticity were comprehensible, manageable and meaningful to them. Take away the caring aspect and there was still 'safe ground' (home and domesticity): they are better able to cling on to an ontological cohesiveness learned over years.
>
> (Davidson 1999: 112)

Sheehy (1996) used the concept of status passage to understand this gendered experience. She identified becoming and being a widow as a potentially 'transformative event' for women of the Reconstruction Generation in America. (Sheehy, 1996: 354). Early socialization, she said, had taught these women that they were not complete without a man and had therefore left them unprepared for widowhood. She suggested that the women who undertake this passage successfully see themselves as survivors. While they may experience fear and loneliness at times they also gain autonomy and a gathering sense of self:

> These survivors expect to be even more self confident as they proceed through their sixties, and most look forward to being serene and ready for new challenges.
>
> (Sheehy 1996: 355)

The women stressed the importance of taking risks and challenging the expectations of others, thereby confronting the mythology and stereotypes of widowhood.

Starting 'where older widows are' and engaging with them about their gendered life world was the focus of Jones Porter's) small, qualitative study of the lived experience of widowhood (Jones Porter, 1995. She challenged the prevailing negative and problematising, 'scholarly' interpretations of the experience of later life widowhood, and pointed instead to the reality experienced by older women themselves, a unique gendered world of older women. The stories that these widows told, about their homes and their daily lives, displayed a confidence with life and increasing self-knowledge. Moreover, these women felt valued and were doing what was important for them. They had a clear recognition of changing circumstances and some of the uncertainties that accompanied those changes but these were mediated by both continuities and self-identity, particularly in and around their own home. Essentially, their home was their world. The centrality of home in these older widows stories confirms findings in the friendship literature (see Matthews, 1979; Jerrome, 1993) What is offered in Jones Porter's accounts is a richness and complexity of older women's lives and a valuing of the aspects of women's lives that they themselves consider to be important, even though they may be trivialised by others (Jones Porter, 1995).

The gendered nature of older widows' lived experience is clearly much more than whether they fare better than men. It is recognition not only of the assets that some older widows bring to later life but also of what older women themselves value in their lives. As researchers, we need to take account of this subjectivity and not allow ourselves to be seduced by objective criteria. We must also acknowledge the subjectivity of those older widows who struggle to find compensations in widowhood, who have not accrued assets (or feel that they have not) and see little to value their daily lives and recognise that for those women, life is very difficult.

*Self-identity*

One of the major challenges of widowhood then is to find out the answer to the question 'who am I if I am no longer a wife?' by garnering biographical assets of generation, personality, age and gender as they contribute to self-identity. In a major study of 600 widows, many of whom were older women, Lieberman (1996) argued:

Two conditions are pivotal in starting widows on this exploration [of discovering 'who' I am now that I am no longer a wife]: the earlier self-image embedded in the 'couple' identity and the dramatic change in the way others see you because you are a widow.

(Lieberman, 1996: 157)

This supports Martin Matthews' contention that the redefinition of attitudes and behaviours of others will contribute to the redefinition of the 'me', the sense of self, who is stepping into a new world (Martin Matthews, 1991). Lieberman (1996) went on to say that 'who' we are and 'who' we become is the product of countless interactions with people who are important to us. The self is neither fixed nor unyielding. Indeed, it does not exist in isolation but in some sense is formed by the reflections we receive from others. We gain information from lots of people, but the nature of long-term marriage means that it is often the single most important source of information about who we are. Lieberman (1996) was not suggesting that identity is in a constant state of flux but rather that the self does grow and develop over long periods of time. Identity is thus ultimately dependent on social relationships (Jenkins 1996) such as marriage that in turn have been shaped by generation, age and gender.

It is a truism to say that widowhood and marriage are inextricably linked. After all, the definition of a widow is one whose husband has died. Notwithstanding this, much research on widowhood makes little reference to the quality of the marital relationship, or at the very least makes assumptions about a commonality of experience. Yet, there is a very strong argument to suggest that it is necessary to understand both the circumstances surrounding the loss and the nature of the marital relationship in order to understand the individual experience of becoming and being a widow (Wortman and Silver, 1990).

A small body of literature has confirmed that the experience of widowhood is largely dependent on the degree to which the deceased husband was an integral part of the older woman's life and thus her self-identity, and the extent to which she had other roles (Lopata, 1973, 1979; Martin Matthews, 1991). Lopata (1973) contended that in the United States, middle class marriages were more 'companionate' than working class marriages and were thus more susceptible to disruption on the death of a spouse. She further suggested that Black American widows were more emotionally independent from their husbands and so have less to lose emotionally but were more likely to suffer financial hardship.

The tendency to 'spouse sanctification' (Lopata, 1973, 1979, 1981) which occurs in the stories of many older widows, often disguises the reality of the marital relationship. In these stories, the dead husband becomes a super-hero who possesses only good qualities (usually identified as kindness, thoughtfulness, consideration), and no faults. By implication, the marriage itself in retrospect becomes perfect: a marriage made in heaven (Davidson, 1999: 79). This memory of the good husband may be used as a justification for not remarrying (Martin Matthews, 1991), and as a way of maintaining the identity of wife (Lopata, 1979). It is interesting to note that those women who wish to maintain the identity of wife are challenging traditional orthodoxy which stresses the importance of moving from 'we' to 'I' and are thus perceived as grieving abnormally. Lopata (1979) suggested that holding on to good memories of the dead spouse may serve two further functions. Firstly to emphasise, by comparison to a glorious past, the negative aspects of the current situation. Or secondly, to assist in the working through of the current situation. Both of these are possibilities. For some women, 'spouse sanctification' may be a way of retelling the story of a less than satisfactory long-term marriage, and by implication a less than satisfactory life, without inviting either self-criticism or public disapproval. It is interesting to note that in Davidson's research interviews with older widows, where she was in the role of interested, non-judgemental listener, the tendency to 'spouse sanctification' which was apparent at the start of the interviews, disappeared altogether towards the end of the discussion, with faults and failings being reported without inhibition (Davidson 1999).

According to Lieberman (1992) the transition to 'I' is extremely daunting for a widow from a traditional marriage, that is one in which the woman's principal role has been that of 'the good wife' who has unquestioningly cared for her husband and family, always putting his needs before her own. He suggested that in widowhood, this role is a source of both distress and accomplishment. She is proud to have been 'the wife of ...' but, with the death of her spouse, the traditional wife needs to deal with her new aloneness and come to terms with a new inner life. This may be painful and may involve confronting regrets and undeveloped aspects of her life.

In a large-scale study of both younger and older widows (Lieberman, 1996) Lieberman explored further how widows see their marriages from the vantage point of loss. He suggested that high levels of guilt and anger hinder recovery and make the experience of becoming and being a widow an extremely difficult one. He highlighted a number of other factors in relation to the marital relationship, which impact on this experience. These included the following. Firstly, whether the widow regarded herself as independent or dependent. Secondly, whether she felt that marriage had stunted her development. Thirdly, whether she had regrets or sad feelings about the choices she had made in her life. Fourthly, the extent to which she idealised both the marriage and her husband, and finally, how successful or unsuccessful she judged the marriage to have been. Lieberman found that when compared to the more independent widow, women who scored high in dependency were less successful 'in recovery'). However, those who had felt stunted in marriage often experienced growth in widowhood. He acknowledged that half of the women he interviewed had major regrets about some aspects of their married lives, which led him to pose the question: 'Does regret impede recovery? In the short term having regrets clearly impacted on recovery, because many of the women who had regrets felt that they had been left with low self-esteem. In the long term, many of those who expressed regrets were able to use their feelings to make changes in their lives.

According to Davidson (1999) the women in her study recognised that in becoming and being a widow they had moved towards independence and autonomy, fostering a degree of 'separateness'. This was different from marriage, where the caring for and about their husbands, the 'attachment', was fundamental to the relationship. This separateness gave them permission to be 'selfish' which they construed as looking after themselves and putting themselves first. It is interesting to note that most of the widows were still very involved in a variety of caring relationships with others but felt differently, perhaps less pressured or obliged (by themselves as well as others) as they did in marriage.

Although not widely reported in the literature, some women have expressed relief at the death of their spouse. For such women, widowhood was a time of release from a constraining relationship. We are reminded that the death of a spouse does not necessarily signify the termination of a blissful marriage and that, for some people, the experience of widowhood may affect them substantially but not necessarily negatively. An older widow (cited in Martin Matthews 1991: 18-19) gave voice to this experience: 'Life changed. It is much quieter now. Since my husband was an alcoholic, life was not always easy before he died.'

The social construction of widowhood as a state of grieving and loneliness, in which the dead spouse is revered means that it is difficult for some older women to express satisfaction at the death of their spouse. Some of the widows who were interviewed by Adlersberg and Thorne (1992) were initially cautious about expressing positive feelings, and certainly had not shared these feelings with close family. Once trust with the interviewers had been established, these women felt able to reflect on a lifetime of always considering their spouses' needs and having little control over major decisions. Widowhood had provided them all with an opportunity to reconsider a previously accepted world view and for those women who had been in abusive or domineering relationships, widowhood had provided an escape.

As social beings, we all make choices about who we connect with and, from countless reflections with others, we select those that are important to us. When challenged by a life crisis or major change such as widowhood, the sources of feedback we have used to maintain a coherent and consistent self-image may be thrown into a state of consternation, especially if the spouse has been a major source of such feedback. We rarely think about our identity at a conscious level, except at times where either external or internal circumstances combine to heighten our awareness of 'identity consciousness' (Erikson 1980). Widowhood is perhaps, for some women, one of those times when their identity is challenged and they are painfully conscious of seeking out an identity. According to Parkes (1986) this may begin immediately or it may also come about gradually as they see their behaviour redefined by others (and thus gradually redefine themselves). For example, as I discuss in greater detail in the next chapter, widows may begin to experience feelings of 'stigma' when previously friendly people start behaving differently and a previous interaction, such as talking to a friend's husband, becomes redefined as a threat. They begin to realise that life as a single woman is different from life as a married' woman. Alternatively, they may find themselves being treated as ill or dependent by others whom they have always assumed to be equals. According to Lieberman (1996):

The struggle to maintain a coherent and consistent self-image is important for everyone but especially important for those passing through the shattering and vulnerable psychological state of widowhood. One of the greatest challenges of widowhood is to successfully forge a new identity, a struggle that can go on for years.

Lieberman (1996: 170):

A 'healthy' new self image, he argued, is the product of subtracting some aspects of personality that do not work and adding others that were always there, but found no expression when a wife. This can involve recapturing lost parts of self. Lieberman (1996) ascertained that widows who found others to mirror and maintain new views of self recovered rapidly and well; widows who maintained the old self image by using feedback from current relationships also made good recovery and adaptation. However, not all widows were able to realign identities by adding on or locating new mirrors. For example, those women who changed their self-image by letting go of important aspects of their previous selves did more poorly than those who held on to valuable characteristics. Similarly, those widows who maintained a completely unchanged self-image by basing their self-view on the distant past or on unsupported beliefs about who they really were jeopardised recovery.

In a seminal study of widowhood (albeit not specifically later life widowhood) Lopata (1973) identified three 'types' of widow whose identity had changed as a result of widowhood. Firstly, the 'modern woman' who may be temporarily passive as a result of grief but is able to re-engage:

> ... realising that the presence of her late husband resulted in a role and personality specialisation which makes widowhood difficult, she develops substitutes for his contribution by taking over certain of these functions, assigning some to others or dropping a duty or right entirely.
>
> (Lopata, 1973: 265)

Secondly, the 'lower class urbanite' who continues much of her previous life with few changes:

> Being immersed in kin relations, a very close peer group or a network of neighbours, such a woman may continue many of her previous involvement with little modification after becoming a widow.
>
> (Lopata 1973: 265)

And finally 'the social isolate'; this state of affairs occurs because of a lack of ability to re-engage or because of downward mobility as a result of widowhood. The 'social isolate' has never been highly engaged in broader society and becomes increasingly isolated as the extended kin or neighbourhood are no longer available for contact. She lacks the ability to engage in new roles, views the world negatively and is often taken advantage of.

Each of these 'types' will experience widowhood differently. So too, the perception by others of them as widows will be different. Both the subjective feelings (as defined by the woman herself) and the objective experience (as defined by others) are inextricably linked and will shape both the overall experience of widowhood and the identity, the 'me', which results from this experience.

Published autobiographical accounts of widowhood offer an insider view of some widows' struggle with self-identity. Ten such accounts were the source for Van Den Hoonaard's (1997) exploration of the meaning of becoming and being a widow. She provided a useful analysis of the crisis of identity encountered by newly widowed women and their capacity to change: 'Everywhere they went, and with everyone they interacted, they were treated differently; they even treated themselves differently' (Van Den Hoonaard 1997: 537). These women tried at first to hang on to their identity as wife, the central role in their life (as defined by them and others), but they found that they were unable to do so, no longer knowing who they were. This seemed to operate on three levels, identified by Van Den Hoonaard (1997) as: firstly, 'Don't know who they are to themselves'; secondly, 'Don't know who they are to close friends'; and thirdly, 'Don't know how they fit in to society in general'. As the gradual realisation dawned that the word 'widow' was an apt descriptor, they began to foreclose on their own identity. As I discuss in the next chapter, relationships with friends of their pre-widowhood days, who were friends of husbands, began to change and they found themselves excluded from collective gatherings of partners. Furthermore, not only were they were treated differently by their children but because they were seen as belonging to a collective of widows, they were introduced to other widows with the assumption that they would get on. They also had to physically move from 'we' to 'I' by closing bank accounts in joint names, shredding joint credit cards etc. These women all talked about the process of building a new identity, the effort involved in taking on new responsibilities and thereby learning to make decisions on their own, and the recognition that they were able to move from being a wife to becoming a widow. This was a:

> ... transformed identity... Although they would not have chosen to be widows, they like the new women they have become better than the ones they were when they were wives (and they describe themselves as) ... more at peace, more serious, braver and more confident, responsible for myself, more sociable, more tolerant, more integrated.
>
> (Van Den Hoonaard, 1997: 546)

Such autobiographical accounts quite graphically identify three levels of identity foreclosure and the tension between self-definition and social expectations, identified by others (Lund et al, 1989; Martin Matthews, 1991; Lieberman, 1996). However these widows were not typical, tending to be younger, better educated and financially sound. Whether the majority of older widows foreclose on their identity of wife is questionable and thus needs to be explored further.

**The move from 'we' to 'I'**

Not surprisingly, given the previous discussion, a number of theoretical constructs have been offered in the literature to explain the move 'from we to I', a move that has been highlighted as a 'crisis' for older women.

*A developmental task*

Adjustment to the death of spouse was identified by Havighurst (1972) as one of the major developmental tasks of adulthood. He argued that the successful resolution of this often difficult task was necessary for the mastering of other later life developmental tasks. Factors impacting on the accomplishment of this task would include the following: personal history; the society in which she lives; health; education; social world; and income. According to Parkes and Weiss (1983) resolution would only be achieved by maintaining independence, solving new problems, reconstructing life and reshaping identity.

Hansson and Remondet (1988) have highlighted the importance of establishing a new identity, independent of the deceased, because for many women, including older women, widowhood may be a significant part of their life:

> … they must somehow establish a life independent of the deceased, deal with evolving family relationships and support networks, and meet emotional, health and practical needs over the long term.
>
> (Hansson and Remondet, 1988: 140)

However, Hansson they have also acknowledged that this might require risk taking in order to explore unfamiliar ground. This is dependent on a number of factors including motivation and an awareness of the time scale involved. The older woman's current level of functioning is also significant as this will affect her ability to manage finances, maintain social networks, and live independently. They proposed a model of widowhood, configured as 'a career', as a way of conceptualising the hard work, planning and risk-taking involved in moving from 'we' to 'I'. I return to this later on in the chapter when I discuss 'growth and change'.

*Connectedness*

According to Lofland (1982: 231), there are seven threads of connectedness by which we are linked to others: the roles we play; the help we receive; the wider network of others made available to us; the selves others create or sustain; the comforting myths they allow us; the reality they validate for us; and the futures they make possible. If the spouse provided all these connections, the result would be devastating because all of the widow's connections have been severed. However, if some of these connections were provided by others (friends, family members, work colleagues, church groups etc.) and these were continued, the result would be very different. We must not assume that a spouse will provide all of these connections, particularly in later life. Individual biographies may well include connections with a variety of significant others.

It has been argued therefore that in this move from 'we' to 'I', the older widow struggles to understand who she is as her world is thrown into uncertainty. The social reconstruction of self seems to be central to the meaning of widowhood as identified in the literature. It has been suggested that for some older women, this may be defined by the absence of someone and so they will continue to identify themselves (and be identified by others) as 'The widow of ...'. However, for others there will have been role changes associated with a positive reconstruction, a new defining of self as a 'partner less' person seeing oneself as an active participant in one's world (Lopata, 1979).

This process takes time as described in the popular phrase 'time is a great healer' but, how much time is the subject of another debate. Some commentators have suggested that four years after the death of a spouse is a meaningful demarcation for older widows to come to terms with who they are (Ferraro and Barresi, 1982; Nagy, 1982), whereas others caution against setting time limits (DiGiulio, 1989). Indeed some older women themselves have reported that time makes no difference (see Allen, 1989).

There appears, therefore, to be a spectrum of widowhood experience. At one end, there is the woman who gains self-confidence and positive feelings about herself after having survived the disruption in her life. At the other end, there is the woman who becomes desolated by these events (Silverman, 1986). But what accounts for this difference? In her later work, Silverman (1987) suggested a typology of problematic accommodation to widowhood, which she described as remaining psychologically committed to the past versus satisfactory adjustment; that is, changing the way one relates to oneself or others and feeling satisfied with one's life. Many women move to positions of autonomy and gain satisfaction from newly acquired skills. Silverman went as far as to say: 'in studying the outcome [of widowhood] we cannot talk about recovery but transformation' (Silverman, 1987: 189). Evidence of such transformation has also been provided in a number of other studies (Martin Matthews, 1991; Pickard, 1994; Lieberman, 1996).

*Growth and change*

Life span development theorists (for example Baltes et al, 1980; Sugarman, 1986) have also maintained that growth and development occur throughout the lifespan, and thus opportunities for personal growth and control are possible in later stages of life. It has been suggested that older adults can continue to learn and adapt to changing life circumstances. Relating this to widowhood, Hansson and Remondet (1988: 167) claimed: 'the successful assumption of personal control rests on a widow's ability to (thus) construe her own life course.' Their starting point was that older widows are functioning participants in society and that therefore society needed to give older widows space to reconstruct their lives. Widows, they have argued, need encouragement to take personal control as they begin to compensate for change and negotiate their way as a single person. A concept of widowhood has been offered, as a beginning to a major segment of the life course rather than an end of a productive life: 'one that should be pursued vigorously in order for it to be successful and fulfilling' (Hansson and Remondet 1988: 166). A career orientation has been suggested as a useful way of understanding widowhood. This anticipates a period ahead, which can be planned for and lived rather than passively experienced. It thus implies the need to assume personal control over one's life. Fundamental to this view is the importance of looking forward:

> The stages of a typical widow's future might include the following: a time for recovery; a time for taking stock; re-establishing or restructuring support relationships and formulating personal direction for the future; a time for discovering a comfortable and satisfying independent lifestyle, and for determining an approach to maintaining economic, psychological and social functioning; perhaps a time for personal growth and change; and a time for reasoned consideration of one's last years and assertion of a degree of control over the arrangements surrounding one's own decline and death.
>
> (Hansson and Remondet, 1988: 167)

They went on to argue that after the initial psychological disruption of bereavement some widows experience growth and independence. This was confirmed by Allen (1989), who interviewed older widows as part of a larger study, which explored the life course of single and married women. For some women, the death of their spouse gave them: '… their first independent feeling of *this is my life now*' (Allen 1989: 19). For these women, independence meant a process of gaining selfhood and a feeling that they had become different. The majority spoke positively about the transition to independence and saw their current lives as a time of freedom from family and work.

For some widows then, it appears that widowhood is the first opportunity to develop a separate, independent identity without the help of their most significant other. The majority of Lopata's widows reported change as a result of widowhood and only 18 per cent saw that change as negative (Lopata, 1973). In a later study she reported that the widow: 'needs to make herself over, from a dependent person living vicariously through the husband and children, into an independent person' (Lopata, 1979: 32). Indeed over half the women in that later study felt they had personally changed as a result of widowhood. Interestingly, in Martin Matthews' Ontario study (1987, cited in Martin Matthews, 1991), although many women reported that it was the worst thing that had ever happened, they also acknowledged a general determination to make the best of it and use it as an opportunity for growth and development.

However, a minority of Allen's widows, even after many years, were heavily reliant on family, in poor health and still grieving (Allen 1989). Life had certainly changed, but for the worse. Two of them felt their lives were still dominated by previous tragedies and unresolved feelings of bitterness. It is unclear how much such feelings might be influenced by other stressors present at time of loss, such as limited financial resources, family issues and chronic health problems. Wortman and Silver (1991) suggested that this might be the case. They argued for positive change in widowhood and claimed that although some resources may be diminished by the loss of a spouse, there was every reason to expect that others might be enhanced.

## Conclusion

In this chapter I have sought to explore current knowledge concerning the factors, which contribute to the experience of becoming and being a widow in later life. Drawing on a variety of sources I have explored the complex area of identity and considered the impact of the marital relationship, age, gender and 'a view of the world' on the lived experience of widowhood. I have suggested that, contrary to popular stereotyping which structures later life widowhood as a time of vulnerability, both age and gender can be construed as assets. To what extent these assets contribute to an older widow's sense of 'who' she is, is a question I answer in subsequent chapters.

I have reflected on the lack of historical context in the study of later life widowhood and argued instead for the value of considering both ageing and widowhood from a life history perspective, one that acknowledges the impact of both collective and individual history. I therefore wish to explore further how the continuities of biography intertwine with the major discontinuity of the death of a spouse to shape the experience of becoming and being an older widow.

I have explored briefly the experience of bereavement and discussed a number of debates concerning 'the move from we to I'. However, I am interested in exploring further the subjective experience of widowhood and what it feels like to 'become and be' an older widow. It may be that just as there are many ways to grieve, so might there a number of ways to 'do' widowhood: exactly what might determine this potentially differential experience is fundamental to what follows in the course of the book.

This chapter then has focused on the widow as an individual and a number of strands have emerged. However, another significant factor which has been identified as impacting on the experience of older widows, is that of social relationships. How much does the objective experience, as defined by others shape an older widows subjective experience? The next chapter therefore situates the older widow in her social world.

# Chapter 3

# The Social World of Older Widows

## Introduction

A 'social world' consists of all those persons, and groups, with whom an individual interacts. This may be fluid and ever changing or it may show considerable consistency over time, and may consist of family, friends, neighbours, colleagues, acquaintances with whom the individual may interact for specific purposes and, of course, the individual herself. It can be argued that as individuals we gain a sense of self and who we are from our location in a social world (Matthews, 1979; Jenkins, 1996) and therefore an understanding of that world is crucial to developing an understanding the experience of becoming and being an older widow. In this chapter I explore the social world of older widows by drawing on two bodies of literature: firstly, the literature on social relationships specific to widowhood and secondly, the literature on the social networks of older women in general.

In keeping with the general framing of widowhood as a problem in the literature, and the focus on bereavement, it is no surprise to discover that much of the literature that looks specifically at the social world of widows, is framed in terms of support. Indeed, Morgan (1989: 101) argued that as a consequence, the empirical work in this area was limited:

> Instead of beginning with the fact that individuals live within networks of personal relationships and then investigating the impacts of these relationships, investigators have too often assumed that support is what is important and that relationships only matter if they are sources of support.

With reference specifically to older widows, Martin Matthews (1991: 35) noted that widows' ties with others were frequently conceptualised and measured in terms of social support and commented that this characterization may not be entirely accurate. She suggested that little consideration was given to the personal resources that a widow brings to such relationships. More importantly, she argued, these personal resources provided a context for interpreting the meaning of that support and:

> ...awareness of changes in personal resources (feelings of independence, confidence, and freedom, employment and the ability to drive) has significant implications for how the widowed view their social supports.

> (Martin Matthews, 1991: 59)

Another body of literature questions the consequences of widowhood on the social participation of older widows. It explores the impact of the characteristics of the 'survivors' on life in widowhood and tests out theoretical issues around decremental or compensation models of role loss and social participation (Ferraro, 1984). This literature highlights the different roles played by family and friends in the social networks of older widows as they move into their life without a spouse.

It is interesting to note that the literature on the social networks of older women in general which, given that the majority of older women are widows, is in fact the study of older widows, adopts a more pluralist approach. Relationships are explored in their entirety, not just in terms of support or as a consequence of widowhood. In this literature a more holistic picture emerges, which links life in widowhood to individual biography and in which older women are both key players and active participants in their own lives.

I now explore in more detail these interrelated areas of support and participation. I conclude by suggesting, in keeping with the thrust of the discussion so far, the importance of situating the social world of older widows within a life course perspective.

## Social support networks in later life widowhood

In her pioneering work on the social support networks of widows Lopata (1979) defined social support networks as that set of personal contacts through which the individual maintains social identity and style of life. A support network comprises all those people and groups who provide supports, or to whom an individual provides support and Lopata (1979) argued that in general, the degree of disorganisation in a woman's life and her support systems produced by the death of a husband depends on the degree to which the husband was an integral part of the wife's life.

Writing in 1988, Lopata further asserted that these social supports were culture bound and that this impacted on social support systems in widowhood. She cited a number of examples to support this assertion (Lopata, 1988). Firstly, the 'voluntaristic' nature of American society in which social involvement of adults is mainly dependent on their own initiative. This can be a problem for people who are not socialised into self-initiating behaviour or who do not have the confidence to enter new social relationships and social roles. Secondly, traditional American culture has discouraged older women from assertive social engagements outside the private sphere of the home with the result that they are often dependent on others, often their spouse, for links with the public sphere. This causes problems for some women in widowhood. Thirdly, friendship is viewed as a luxury in American society and is not allowed to interfere with the wife and mother role for a large part of the life course. Old age is perhaps an exception to this. Fourthly, the emphasis on 'the couple' as the appropriate social unit means that women often lose contact with personal friends when they marry, making them increasingly dependent upon family for support and friendship. Thus they can find themselves at a considerable disadvantage when widowed. Ford and Sinclair (1987: 7) confirmed a similar picture in Britain and suggested that as a result of culture bound social support systems the extent to which widows can develop a social life is restricted.

Whilst the dominant culture being described here is a rather restricted one which does not seem to either embrace or even acknowledge the possibility of diversity, it is nonetheless the case that the lives of older widows are heavily dependent therefore, not only on their own personal social support systems, but also on the definitions and resources made available to them by the rest of society. In a society that stresses the importance of the couple, an older widow often feels like a 'fifth wheel' and what used to be 'a sociable foursome becomes an unsociable three some' (Lopata, 1973: 68).

However, the culture-bound nature of social supports may also be advantageous (Petrowsky, 1976; Van Den Hoonaard, 1994). Pickard (1994) for example, illustrated how the special position occupied by female support networks (both family and friends) in the social structure of a South Wales community enables older women to cope successfully with the death of a spouse. She stressed the support and encouragement of other women and gave the example of Olwen, Menna and Ethel who, with the encouragement of other women, 'joined in ... and never turned back':

> One might almost say that for South Wales society, the social activity of widows is so widespread that it indeed provides a 'role' for widows to fall into - or at least sets a powerful 'model' for her to emulate, so that she is not so much 'in the dark' as to what to do with herself as may be supposed.
>
> (Pickard, 1994: 201)

*The importance of support networks*

The importance of specific support relationships and the networks in which they are embedded is recognised in the literature on widowhood as a stressful life event (Ferraro, 1984; Ferraro, et al 1994; Hansson and Remondet, 1988; O'Brien, 1985). According to Martin Matthews (1991), potential 'supporters' are seen to serve three functions. Firstly, to smooth the transition to the role of widowed person; secondly, to offer support and guidance as the widowed person seeks to establish a new identity that may or may not reflect the expectations of others, and thirdly, to reject or ignore the widowed person resulting in a lonely life or the incentive to develop new relationships.

There has been general acknowledgement that lack of these support relationships contributes to emotional problems and ill health in later life. Goldberg et al (1988) for example, in a longitudinal study of older women before and after widowhood, found that having few friends and not feeling close to one's family were predictive factors for women needing emotional counselling six months after the death of their spouse (see also Machin, 2000). According to Jacobson (1986), support networks are extremely complex: who gives what support to whom regarding which problems and when, is clearly significant but does not provide all the answers. Lopata (1979) too acknowledged the complexity of social supports, finding considerable variation amongst the metropolitan widows whom she studied. Those who might be involved as social supports included aged parents, siblings, children and other kin, friends and neighbours.

Research on the role of social support has attempted to ascertain who participates in the support network of older widows and the relative importance of particular sources of support. In general, the benefits from friendship networks have been consistently reported, whereas research on the family has indicated that although there might be benefits in the short term, this is not necessarily so in the long term.

*Family as support*

There is evidence of considerable agreement in the literature concerning the role of the family in widowhood. Family support is deemed to be important immediately following the death of a spouse (Ferraro, 1984; Lopata, 1973) but likely to tail off with time (Vachon and Stylianos, 1988). Pihlblad and Adams (1972) demonstrated that for up to four years after the death of a spouse there was an increase in family support and interaction, which thereafter tailed off.

Many commentators (for example: Adams, 1968; Lopata, 1979; McCallum, 1986; Gee and Kimball, 1987) have stressed the important roles that daughters play, the latter suggesting that an intimate relationship with a daughter protected against depression, both short term and long term. Horowitz (1985) however, claimed that sons provide as much emotional support, financial assistance and assistance in accessing services but were less likely than daughters to help with instrumental, hands on service. More recent research has confirmed these findings (Davidson, 1999; Van Den Hoonaard, 2001).

Adult children clearly play a role in the support systems of widows but there are conflicting research findings about the benefits of this support. For example, it is suggested that family support does not tend to be associated with daily activities, such as shopping or going to the cinema, which enhance morale (Lopata, 1973). According to Arling (1976) contrasting interests, generational differences, and a lack of reciprocity all make relationships with families difficult for older widows - even if there is love, there is not always empathy. This view was confirmed by Morgan (1989) whose findings demonstrated that if elderly widows felt they were losing their independence to their families and roles were being reversed, it was because they were fearful of losing their authority. Indeed, a close-knit family network may actually be a disadvantage (Bankoff, 1983).

Certainly in the long term the role of family support has been questioned, particularly in relation to other social supports. Nearly thirty years ago, Arling (1976) commented:

> ... contact with family members, especially children, does little to elevate morale, while friendship-neighboring is clearly related to less loneliness and worry and a feeling of usefulness and individual respect within the community ... friendship

and neighboring are more satisfying to the elderly widow because these relationships are based on common interests and lifestyles, while the elderly widows familial ties may be marked by dissimilar concerns and interests. Moreover, friendship normally develops voluntarily and is characterised by an equal ability to exchange assistance. The family bond in old age may result in a sense of formal obligation, role-reversal between elderly parent and adult child and dependency.

(Arling, 1976: 757)

Canadian research has also confirmed that although a loose family network might be a disadvantage in the early stages of bereavement, it may facilitate the re-organisation of social roles later on in widowhood (Vachon and Stylianos, 1988; Martin Matthews, 1991). It seems that high-density family networks may cause greater problems for older widows in the long run because they may hinder the take up of new roles

In a qualitative study of 55 older widowed mothers, Talbot (1990) found that power differentials contributed to older widows feeling subordinate to their adult children. She highlighted the lack of reciprocity in family relationships, which are deemed by the participants to be negative, in comparison with relationships with friends:

Some older mothers feel unappreciated by their children, some are emotionally dependent on their children, and some give goods and services to their children, at great personal cost, to maintain close relationships with their children ... older mothers may be at a power disadvantage in their relationships with their children and that this inequality may account for relationships with children being less beneficial to widows than are relationships with friends.

(Talbot, 1990: 603)

Research evidence concerning the support provided by family members other than children has indicated an equally complex and sometimes contradictory picture. Studies of siblings have found that widowhood can unite siblings and may bring emotional closeness (Anderson, 1984; 1987). This is more likely if this transition is shared. However, it is also apparent that there may be limits to the support offered as a result of this shared experience. O'Bryant (1988) noted that although older widows may actively seek out the company of a single or married sister and often describe this sibling as a 'friend', tangible help from siblings appears to be rare. For example, O'Bryant (1987) found that only 22 per cent of siblings provided some form of support to the widowed. She postulated that their mere presence as potential sources of support is their greatest contribution (see also Hansson and Remondet, 1988).

Widows are more likely than non-widowed women to identify nieces as social supports. With reference to a study in Ontario in which 70 per cent of widows reported feeling close to extended kin, especially grandchildren, nieces and nephews, Martin Matthews (1991) commented:

Other relatives' were certainly viable members of the support networks of the widowed. In terms of patterns of general contact and in terms of the frequency with which they would be called upon as sources of support, particularly on ceremonial occasions and to help resolve family problems, the role of 'other relatives' is frequently acknowledged in the support networks of the widowed.

(Martin Matthews, 1991: 47)

There would appear to be a plethora of findings, sometimes contradictory, concerning the role of family members in the support networks of older widows. This may have arisen as a result of differences in samples and research methods employed. Such findings may also reflect the complexity of family relationships. Although not really acknowledged in the literature on widowhood, research on informal care (for example Morris, 1993; Phillips, 2000; Bernard and Phillips, 2003) has reiterated that family support is given or not given (and received or not received) within the context of an individual and family history. A life course perspective enables the exploration and impact of such issues in relation to later life widowhood.

*Friends as support*

There is a general consensus that contact with friends enhances older women's morale more than contact with adult children and other family members. Unlike time spent with family, time spent with friends is often associated with positively doing something such as outings or shared interests and as such may well be perceived as supportive (Arling, 1976). Furthermore, unlike family, friends are chosen on the basis of mutual attraction (Jerrome, 1993) and as both Blau (1973) and Lopata (1973) have confirmed, peer support is an essential resource for adjustment to widowhood. Indeed, involvement with friends is linked with high morale (Arling, 1976; Hochschild, 1973; Pihlblad and McNamara, 1965; Sheehy, 1997; Van Den Hoonaard, 2001) with friendship fostering belonging.

Differences in the likelihood of friends providing support have been identified between 'young old' and 'old old' widows (Roberto and Scott, 1986). Whilst acknowledging the importance of informal support networks in confronting widowhood, Roberto and Scott (1986) suggested that maybe 'old old age' places a person at a disadvantage in terms of accessing support from friends. They have cited the scarcity of potential friends amongst aged peers and a decline in the range of social activities available. This led them to highlight the importance of defining the term 'elderly widow' in order to assess more accurately the individual's potential for peer support. More recently Morgan et al (1997), in a consideration of 'helpful' and 'unhelpful' support relationships in later life widowhood, recommended an approach that situated friendship in widowhood within the broader context of friendship in old age:

... in other words, the failure to find support from similar others might be more linked to the nature of friendship at this stage in the life course. For example, older people tend to have smaller networks that contain more longstanding friendships, and this pattern might well produce both empathy and a continuing sense of commitment in these relationships regardless of experiential similarity.

(Morgan et al, 1997: 957)

The type of help provided by friends has been a source of debate. Both Lopata (1979) and Wenger (1984) have suggested that, in the main, friends do not provide practical help either in emergencies or routinely, thus reflecting a view of friendship not rooted in, or expressed by practical help. However, Allan (1989) and Jerrome (1990) have recognized that some friends do provide help and care but that these friendships are qualitatively different from other friendships. These friends are often described in kinship terms, 'like a sister' or as 'real' or 'true' friends.

Morgan et al (1997) explored the support networks of recent widows in an attempt to find out whether some relationships are more useful than others. They looked particularly at the value of similar others in the networks of recent widows and they found a paradox: older widows spent more time with other widows but gained less support and the relationships generated more problems. This led them to suggest that the relationship with other widows is particularly important not because of the amount of support received but because of companionship:

> …widows' preference for associating with their similar others may have more to do with the nature of the companionship they share in such relationships rather than with the provision of social support.
>
> (Morgan et al, 1997: 74)

They stressed the importance of going beyond supportiveness and looking for alternative factors that lead to increased contact with other widows. They suggested that older widows spend more time together for two main reasons. Firstly, in later life they are likely to meet more widows than married women. Secondly, and perhaps more significantly, it is likely to be more convenient to make arrangements with women who do not have to take into account their husbands' needs, than those who do. So, for both numerical reasons and convenience, older widows are likely to have greater contact and experience greater companionship with friends who are widowed rather than married friends. It has been suggested that 'support' researchers often overlook the relative importance of companionship and convenience (Rook, 1987; Morgan et al, 1997).

## Type and timing of support

However, it might be unwise to make too hasty a judgement concerning the relative merits of support from either friends or family. Indeed, there is recognition in the literature that if it is to be useful, then both the type of support offered, and the timing of that support are significant (Jacobson, 1986; Vachon and Stylianos, 1988). What might be beneficial at one point might be a hindrance at another time.

In a particularly illuminating piece of research, Bankoff (1983) demonstrated that the relative importance of sources of support is a function of the phase of widowhood. Existing friendship ties, for example, may become quite tenuous in the early days of widowhood, when the need for nurture and empathy is at its greatest. According to Bankoff (1983) whether social support is harmful, helpful or inconsequential to widows' psychological well-being is dependent on a number of factors. Firstly, where the widow is in the process of adjustment to widowhood (whether at crisis stage or transitional stage), secondly, the type of support given and thirdly, the source of support (Bankoff, 1983: 837). Bankoff actually questioned the assumption of the inherent value of social support for older widows and suggested that well meaning but dependency fostering 'nurturant' support from families may be less helpful than support provided by more egalitarian based peer relationships. Help from widowed friends appears to be particularly helpful. Social exchange theory offers us an explanation for these findings by identifying loss of reciprocity as a condition under which social support may have negative consequences (Antonucci, 1985).

Morgan (1989) suggested that in the early days of widowhood, commitment is required from relationships but later on older widows seek flexibility. He too used social exchange theory to investigate a variety of different relationships that affected the adaptation to widowhood and examined how specific aspects of these relationships made the transition either harder or easier (Morgan 1989). Positive and negative aspects of relations with friends and families were coded in focus group discussions with older widows. Morgan was interested to discover which aspects of their networks widows themselves believed to be crucial in re-organising their lives. Approximately 40 per cent of all mentions of relationships were negative, with family members receiving more negatives than friends. Whereas family members showed commitment, this included problematic obligations and an inability to avoid undesirable behaviour. Friends on the other hand showed flexibility, with increases in positive relationships and decreases in negative ones. What appears to be important to these older women in their relationships with family and friends is commitment and flexibility to be judged in relation to acceptance. Those supporters whose commitments take the form of demands become a hindrance, whereas those who provide flexibility are the crucial resource. Friendship is contingent on the other person's ability to respond to the widow's needs; if the person accepts the widow's needs on her own terms, then that person is likely to remain or become a friend. There appears to be a fine line between independence and dependence and it could be argued that widows are possibly more interested in interdependence. The presence of social support may well be associated with negative outcomes and such networks may actually hinder coping.

This confirmed other research which found that higher levels of social support were consistently associated with higher levels of perceived stress (Green and Field, 1989; O'Brien, 1985) and a lack of association between involvement with social supports and perceived happiness (Roberto and Scott, 1986). For example:

> ... those widows with the most distress may thus garner more social support than those with less distress, resulting in a positive association between distress and social support ... some behaviours that are intended to be supportive, some supporters, or excessive amounts of support may provoke rather than reduce distress ... too much support may reduce one's sense of control ... Additionally, some support may be insensitive to the needs of the recipient.
>
> (Green and Field, 1989: 46-7)

Green and Field cited comments such as 'look on the bright side', 'you should be over it by now', 'get on with life', as particularly unhelpful.

*Summary*

Social support is clearly complex and there is much evidence to support the view that that one can have too much of a good thing. According to Martin Matthews (1991)

> Research findings suggest, that the potential benefits of support will be offset if there is too much support, if it comes at the wrong time in the process of adaptation, if it is too intensely focused on the widowed, or if it is offered by only those with one particular set of attributes.
>
> (Martin Matthews, 1991: 39)

Older widows can quite easily become 'invisible', and cease to be key players in their own lives if their social networks either consist entirely of support or are perceived by others to consist entirely of support networks. However, social support is only one aspect of the social world of an older widow; her participation in that world also impacts on her experience in widowhood.

## Social Participation

Another related body of literature explores the consequences of widowhood on the 'social participation' of older widows, often comparing the social networks of older widows with those of still married older women. Studies have so far proved inconclusive. Lopata (1979) for example found married women had more friends, whereas Wenger (1984) and Troll et al (1979) found that widows had higher levels of interaction. There appear to be both qualitative and quantitative differences in such relationships. It is interesting to note that older widows also feature in the literature on the social networks of older women in general. By contrast, they are portrayed here as active participants in their social world, drawing on personal resources and skills that they have accrued over the life course.

*Family*

The bulk of research on the social participation of older widows recognizes that the family is one of the most important social networks for older widows, reflecting perhaps the symbolic importance of the family in Western society generally. There has been general acknowledgement that family ties may be personally satisfying, but the assumption that the family is 'a priori' a satisfying form of involvement for older people has been challenged by some commentators (Matthews, 1986; Martin Matthews, 1991).

Considerable evidence has been provided to demonstrate that older widows do more with their friends than with their families, because family ties are generally not associated with daily activities. In several Canadian studies, Martin Matthews (1991) found that, whereas the availability and degree of contact with children was unrelated to other activities, friendship and neighbouring was positively associated with taking walks, shopping, and attendance at religious services and other organisational meetings. However, the knowledge that the family is available to 'care about' the older widow does seem to be particularly important (Jerrome, 1993; Martin Matthews, 1991; Morgan et al, 1997). Although some changes do occur within family networks during later life widowhood, such as slight increase in interaction with children in the first year of widowhood (Lopata 1973), stability of relationships from 'pre-widowhood days' has been reported (Martin Matthews, 1991; Morgan et al, 1997; Davidson, 1999).

Some researchers have stressed the importance of gender issues in family relationships, suggesting that older widows are more likely to be in contact with daughters than with sons (Adams, 1968). However this may also be the case for those older women who are not widowed and so may not be a feature of widowhood per se.

Up to four years after the death of a spouse widows are more likely to have contact with other relatives, but this declines after five years or more (Pihlblad and Adams, 1972). This may have as much to do with the ageing of relatives, than with widowhood or it may reflect the nature of pre-widowhood relationships. Class differentials have also been noted with lower class widows being singled out as having low interaction with other relatives (Lopata, 1973).

Overall there is considerable stability in family networks following widowhood. Those who have always associated with their family are likely to continue to do so, whereas those who have little family contact may see an initial increase immediately following widowhood, but then a tailing off in comparison with before the death of a spouse.

*Peer relationships*

Unlike their married counterparts, many widows acquire new friendships in later life. Lopata (1979) reported that 43 per cent of her respondents acquired new friendships, and these new friends were seen more often than other contacts. The role of friends as emotional supporters is clearly important, but less so than sociable companionship. This view has been confirmed elsewhere, for example by Jerrome (1981):

> A widespread feature of the friendships I have encountered has been the emphasis, in practice, on pleasure as opposed to help or the exchange of confidences ... the main need seems to be for companionship in an enjoyable activity, someone to do things with.
>
> (Jerrome, 1981: 192-3)

Peer relationships with other widows, what has become known as ' a society of widows' (Lopata, 1973), appear to be particularly important. It has been suggested that because widows pose a threat to couple oriented activities, they gradually become confidantes to each other (Babchuk and Anderson, 1989), often discovering a commonality of experience. Reporting on a Canadian study of widows living in age segregated housing in Hamilton, Ontario, Martin Matthews (1991) noted that the vast majority (92 per cent) recorded associations limited to older widows and indicated that their closest friend was also a widow. Pickard (1994) observed a similar pattern in the old age clubs in a South Wales community:

> With club going activities, joining Old Age clubs is a new type of social activity that does not require a partner and quickly becomes a substitute social activity, replacing things formerly done with the husband. Many widows ... throw themselves into this type of activity with great enthusiasm. In several senses then, the 'society of widows' is very helpful and acts informally in this society to guide the widow.
>
> (Pickard, 1994: 202)

However, as discussed earlier in this chapter, with reference to 'support', Morgan et al (1997) have urged caution concerning the drawing of conclusions about a 'society of widows'. Their findings led them to conclude that although older widows seek companionship with others, their relationships with other widows might be precipitated on both numerical availability and convenience, as much as on real choice.

*Friendships with men*

In contrast to these all female relationships, close friendships with men appear to be quite unusual for older widows, unless they were potentially sexual or courtship relationships (Matthews, 1986; Davidson, 1999). According to Babchuk and Anderson (1989) cross-gender friendships seem to be the exception rather than the rule amongst older women in general, regardless of marital status. It has been suggested that there are normative barriers to such friendships for elderly women; friendships with men would cause people to talk (Adams, 1985). It is possible that there is a combination of both generation expectations and individual life course issues operating in this area of relationships.

*Married friends*

In the short term, it does seem possible for older widows to maintain friendships with married friends, albeit in a mainly supportive, rather than participative role.

Morgan et al (1997) for example, found that recent widows listed husbands of friends as well as married friends amongst their supporters. However, studies have generally confirmed that in the longer term widowhood has a negative impact on friendships with married people (Lopata, 1973; Bankoff, 1983; Martin Matthews, 1991; Lieberman, 1996) leading to the establishment for some women of a completely new set of friendships. Indeed, for many older widows, friendships with married friends cease completely after the death of a spouse (Martin Matthews, 1991; Lieberman, 1996; Sheehy, 1997). Interestingly, although some widows have report reluctance about this cessation of friendships, others feel it is a strategic decision (Lieberman, 1996).

Another strategy appears to be a modification of previous relationships with married friends into sex-segregated ones (Lopata, 1979). An older widow may continue to see her female married friend but is unlikely to socialise any longer with the couple. This often places severe limitations on the friendship, with the widow feeling that she is 'fitted in' between marital responsibilities (Morgan et al, 1997).

## The impact of widowhood on close friendships

In a comparative study of older married women and older widows, Babchuk and Anderson (1989) found that although friendship ties were an important source of close emotional support for all older women, they were particularly significant for older widows. Widows certainly seem to rely on friends as confidantes more than married women. However, their overall findings have suggested that widowhood does not sharply alter very close friendship networks for older women and that regardless of marital status widows and married women over 65 have the same number of intimate friends, usually about six. Amongst both these groups, those women who have worked outside the home have the greater number of friends overall. Moreover, primary ties are with long-standing friends and few close friendships develop after the age of sixty-five. In the main, friendship networks appear to be stable and are characterised by norms of reciprocity. However, Babchuk and Anderson (1989) cautioned that their findings might be unusual as a result of a high degree of residential stability in their sample (see also Pickard, 1994; Van Den Hoonaard, 2001). Nonetheless, it is clear that there is no immediate decrease in widows' participation with close friends compared to their married counterparts.

## Confidantes

It has been generally acknowledged that intimacy support is important in building a new sense of 'I' in widowhood (Lieberman, 1996). Indeed, according to Jerrome (1993) a best friend can be both a confidante and a companion in shared activities, someone to do things for and to do things with. However, there are dissenting voices concerning the need for confidantes. For example, Allan's (1989) review of the literature suggested:

... what appears to matter is not so much having one or two friends with whom one's innermost thoughts can be readily shared, but rather being involved in different social activities that provide opportunities to socialise with others on a more or less regular basis and develop a range of less intimate friendships.

(Allan, 1989: 94)

There are certainly contradictory findings in the literature concerning the likelihood of older widows having intimate friends. One body of research (for example, Pihlblad and Adams, 1972; Lopata, 1973; Petrowsky, 1976; Adlersberg and Thorne, 1992) suggested that widows are less likely than others to have intimate friends particularly when compared to women who have been married for a long time. In her later work however, Lopata (1979) found that most of her widows had close friends both before and following the death of their husband and that some had close friends for the first time since widowhood. Similarly, Strain and Chappell's (1982) review of the literature on friendship concluded that most studies indicate that elderly persons have at least one confidante, although in their study in Winnipeg, four fifths identified having a confidante but only one third identified this as a friend.

Ferraro (1984) reported that widowhood results in an immediate increase in the probability of having an intimate friendship and Adams (1985), in a study of older women's friendships, found that most of the respondents had at least one 'emotionally close friend'. Wright's (1989) study also confirmed that the friends of older widows are often close confidantes, suggesting that a close friend is often a worthy substitute for a co-resident companion. Widowed women are more likely to depend on friends when worried or depressed compared with their peers who are still married. It has been suggested elsewhere by Anderson (1987: 133) that: 'being widowed ... is related to friends entering older women's emotional support systems.'

Matthews' (1983) work on the close friendships of older women is particularly illuminating here. She differentiated between friendships where the other person was valued as both unique and irreplaceable and a friendship that was valued for its relational provision (and therefore replaceable). This differentiation enabled older women to better clarify 'close' and 'not close' friendships and resulted in the reporting of smaller numbers. The results confirmed that close friends were not necessarily those who were seen regularly and proximity did not appear to be an issue with emotionally close friends. They may live at a distance but the knowledge that they 'care about' is sufficient. Other studies have confirmed this. For example, in Adams' (1985) study of older women's friendships, almost four fifths of respondents had an emotionally close non-local friend.

Given such conflicting conclusions it is difficult to get an overall picture of the likelihood of older widows having a confidante. The differences in findings seem to result from variations in methodology, differing definition, or variables such as class, age, health, regional differences, individual biography and life course issues amongst those studied. It may also be, as O'Connor (1992) suggested, that generational differences concerning the nature of close friendship have been ignored in much of the literature to date. Older widows may well have close friendships in their own terms, but the use of an expression such as 'intimate confiding' as a definition of close friendship is one used to describe such friendships in the 1970s and 1980s and ignores:

> ... the reluctance of many elderly people, who had grown up in the 1920s and 1930s to discuss intimate topics, such as money or sex, with anyone, especially those who are not relatives- regardless of their closeness.
>
> (O'Connor, 1992: 123)

*Neighbours*

Neighbours are not always distinguished from friends in the literature and it may well be that for some older women with high residence stability, neighbours have become friends over the years. Lopata (1973) found low levels of involvement in connection with service exchanges, but suggested that neighbours were likely to be helpful in the short term. Widows are more likely than married persons to visit neighbours frequently (Kohen, 1983). As with friendship networks, participation with neighbours is generally stable but may increase rather than decrease, particularly if the experience of widowhood is shared (Martin Matthews, 1991). Both friends and neighbours are essential in helping older widows to maintain daily activities and to adjust to their new circumstances. As Arling (1976: 84) indicated: 'neighbours and friends are a better resource (than family) for avoiding isolation in old age'.

*The particular role of friendship in the social networks of older women*

Older widows are the principal actresses in the social world of older women and this is reflected in the literature on the social networks of older women. However, by focusing primarily on age and gender, rather than marital status per se, these studies have reflected a more holistic, even optimistic, view of the social networks of older widows.

Although the family still remains important for many older women, the potential importance of friendship with other women in later life is recognised. According to O'Connor (1992: 118), friendship may well be: 'one of the few available sources of social integration, status and companionship' in later life. Friends can be a source of identity and worth in old age. This is particularly important in Western society where being old and female tends to be negatively constructed (Matthews, 1981; Matthews, 1986; Arber and Ginn, 1991; Jerrome, 1991; Bernard and Meade, 1993; Gibson, 1996; Bernard et al, 2000). Indeed, longstanding friendship has the potential to offer self-validation in a way that relationships with family or sometimes a spouse appear unable to do. As Jerrome (1981: 191) confirmed: 'old friends are valued for their role in preserving one's self image and confirming one's sense of worth'.

Older women's friendships are extremely complex and diverse but there is often a lack of clarity in the literature, not least because of a lack of consensus concerning what constitutes a friend in later life (O'Connor, 1992). It has been suggested that 'friend' encompasses the following: the purely sociable companion; the longstanding but no longer face-to-face relationship; the very close and/or identity enhancing relationship; and the friend who is like a sister (Jerrome, 1993; O'Connor, 1992). Often the type of friendship has not been differentiated, thus rendering comparisons and overall conclusions difficult and sometimes rather simplistic.

There has been some suggestion that age itself has a negative impact on the development of friends in later life (Cumming and Henry, 1961; Ferraro et al, 1984). However this has been challenged by those who point to older women's capacity to make and keep friends throughout the life course (Jerrome, 1981; Matthews, 1986; Adams, 1987). It has been argued that this capacity is one of women's strengths and in later life places them at considerable advantage compared to their male counterparts (Gibson, 1996). O'Connor, (1992: 122) for example, demonstrated that for all older women age is a contributory factor in the development of new relationships, particularly those which are based on companionship. In a longitudinal study of a small community sample Adams (1987) noted that the women averaged more friends in 1984 than in 1981. Interestingly, the women saw their friends less frequently and felt emotionally distant from a higher percentage of them, although they lived closer to a higher percentage of them. Adams's study raised the possibility, that old age may be a period of greater freedom from social constraints and hence provide the opportunity to try out new patterns of sociability, albeit within the sometimes, formidable limits imposed by health and economic resources.

In Jerrome's (1981) study of older women, the majority had made new friends in old age. Indeed a substantial minority had met their 'closest' friend after retirement. Further evidence has been provided by Antonucci (1985) who suggested that, compared to younger groups, older people are more likely to report satisfaction from friendships, less likely to wish they had more friends, and report fewer negative feelings about them.

*Reciprocity*

Reciprocity is a key element of friendship, in the same way that it is a significant aspect of support (see earlier discussion). Rook (1987) found that reciprocity was greater with friends than with adult children and was more strongly related to satisfaction. Ties with others made an important contribution to well being only when they involved positive affect and sociability and not when they simply provided support (Rook 1984). This was confirmed by Blieszner and Adams (1998) who identified that relationships with friends are not always positive and can be problematic, for example, if the other participant in the relationship becomes difficult, too close or makes too many demands thereby testing the boundaries of reciprocity.

We must beware however of exaggerating the importance of reciprocity. According to Jerrome (1990) some close friendships will tolerate temporary inequalities in reciprocity in the knowledge that they will be, or have been, redressed. It is certainly important, but some friendships have a protective quality that brings them closer to kinship in response to ill health or disability.

*Barriers to participation*

There would appear to be barriers to older widows' participation in a social world that result from factors other than widowhood. For example, as early as 1976, Arling identified health and financial resources as significant predictors of social involvement. He found that the healthiest of the elderly widows had greater contact with family, neighbours and friends, and participated in more daily activities. The most economically deprived had fewer neighbours that they knew well enough to visit and had less contact with relatives other than children. Lack of money limited both interpersonal relationships and participation in activities that require financial resources. These results were later confirmed by Ferraro (1984) and Allan and Adams (1989), with the latter citing the availability of private transport as a key factor in participation.

Some commentators have noted the differential impact of earlier educational history on the social world of older widows (Lopata, 1973, 1979; Atchley, 1975; Ferraro and Barresi, 1982). Although education makes little difference to involvement with friends and family or interpersonal relationships generally, poor educational attainment is cited as a barrier to participation. Those older widows who are more educated participate in more activities such as meetings, reading books and newspapers, attending clubs and so on.

Finally, it is worth noting that some women have internalised ageist and sexist views and feel that the company of women will always be inferior to the company of men. The negative feelings that these women have towards other older women can mean that become very isolated in later life, where older widows predominate (Ford and Sinclair, 1987; Jerrome, 1993).

However, all of these findings on the social networks of older widows need to be treated with some caution and certainly cannot be viewed in isolation from other aspects of older widows lives. Two issues in particular need to be considered. Firstly, where the change from wife to widow places an older woman in relation to her peers is crucial to her engagement in a social world. Both similarity and difference from others are salient in the potential development or hindrance of friendship in later life. And secondly, the extent to which individual and collective biography helps or hinders the development of social networks in widowhood. I now discuss each of these in turn.

*Widowhood as normative*

More than forty years ago in a major study of widowhood, Blau (1961) argued that differences in findings concerning the friendship networks of older widows were dependent on the prevalence of widowhood in a locality or community. She suggested that widows look for friends among others with similar characteristics to themselves and that a large pool of older widows may ameliorate the potential adverse effects of widowhood on friendships. Using the theoretical framework of 'social clock' (see Chapter 4 for further discussion of this), Blau (1973) later confirmed that widowhood only affects a woman's friendships if she is placed in a deviant position relative to age and class peers. So the situation for a younger widow would be very different from that of an older widow. This suggests that it is not widowhood per se which impacts on relationships, but its effects on the person's interests and experiences relative to others in a similar situation (see also Petrowsky, 1976; Pickard, 1994; Van den Hoonaard, 1994; Lieberman, 1996).

It does seem then that older widows experience a shifting or realignment of relationships dependent on the commonality of their situation; some networks become more active, whereas others become less so. In addition, some new networks are activated. Furthermore, the length of widowhood for some women means that new friendships made at this time become longstanding over a period of time. Although some roles may be lost, it does seem that there is huge potential for replacement.

*Older women's social networks and the life course*

Matthews (1986) is one of the few commentators to have confirmed the importance of situating social networks in later life within individual biography. She contended that the exploration of the social world of older women was limited by a lack of definition of what constituted friendship and a lack of attention to life course issues. To redress this imbalance, Matthews (1986) engaged older women in developing guided oral biographies around the topic of friendship. This process enabled her firstly, to gain an understanding of those older women's subjective experience of friendship and secondly, to locate that concept of friendship within the life course. She argued that a biographical research process, underpinned by a life course perspective, enabled women to identify 'turnings' in their lives (such as stages in the family life cycles or work history) and to explore the impact of these on the present.

In addition, Matthews (1986) highlighted the importance of friendship styles over the life course and identified three ways of doing friendship: 'Independent'; 'Discerning'; and 'Acquisitive'. Each one, she suggested, will provide different resources in later life, which for the vast majority of older women will be a time without their spouse. As this clearly has important implications for the potential experience of later life widowhood, I propose to look at these friendship styles in greater detail.

According to Matthews (1986), women, who practised the 'Independent' style had only known their current friends for a short period of time. They had usually encountered these friends by chance or circumstance rather than seeking out friendship. They had little support from, or participation with, friends earlier on in the life course and had generally relied heavily on spouses and kin for social networks. New friends were likely to be from their own age cohort, with friendships based on the meeting of immediate needs and the pursuit of particular activities. Essentially, although these friendships were with age peers, they were not based on any common biographical experience so did not provide any sense of continuity of self for the individuals involved.

By contrast, the 'Discerning' had maintained relationships with others whom they had known for a long time; as such, there was a sense of biographical continuity that enabled parts of the self to be preserved. There were no new friendships in their networks, only long term ones, which supported the historical self, the individual as she had been in the past.

The 'Acquisitive' included both lifelong biographical friends and those of immediate significance in their social networks. Both long and short term relationships featured in their social world. Matthews (1986) cited as an example of the acquisitive style of doing friendship, a woman who had distinct periods in her life: childhood; early marriage; childrearing; widowhood; job and retirement. She had drawn friends from each of these periods of her life and, as a consequence, some friendships were still maintained but others had ceased.

Jerrome (1981: 193) demonstrated that in later life generally, and in widowhood specifically, older women compensate for the loss of close ties and the decrease in leisure in a number of ways: some extend or deepen existing relationships; some grow closer to siblings, cousins or sisters in law; some become good neighbours or assume responsibility for others; and some acquire new friendships through voluntary work or moving house. Matthews (1986) developed this further by suggesting that choices will be dependent on 'friendship styles' arising out of individual biography:

> Those who use the 'independent style' for example cannot decide to 'extend and deepen relationships' and 'the discerning' are unlikely to 'acquire altogether new friends.
>
> (Matthews, 1986: 144)

Matthews' thesis then is that in order to understand older women's experience of relationships and the impact of those relationships on self, it is as essential to consider the impact of the individual (and generation) life course as it is to consider the impact of other changes in later life. How an older woman manages and responds to her social networks in widowhood will be influenced by her style of relationship over the life course.

*Summary*

The literature on the social participation of older widows generally seems to have highlighted considerable stability in all relationships, whilst acknowledging that some changes do occur. However with the exception of the work of Matthews (1986), there does appear to have been an overall focus in the literature on the 'status quo ante', a return to normal, with the older widow portrayed as a one dimensional character who has no history or no future. This indicates a sizeable gap in the literature that I would argue greatly limits our understanding of the experience of later life widowhood.

**Conclusion**

In this chapter, I have presented a picture of the social world of older widows as portrayed in the literature on later life widowhood and have demonstrated that it is often framed in terms of support. I have shown that the literature on social participation has emphasised continuities with life before widowhood, whilst acknowledging that some changes in relationships do occur. I have also drawn on literature from the social world of older women, with particular reference to Matthews' work, which both employed a biographical approach to friendship and located relationships within the whole life course. Her analysis of friendship styles is a helpful contribution to our understanding of how older widows 'do' friendship. It is important to locate the social world of older widows within a framework, which acknowledges 'old' and 'female', and recognises that both of these have been structured throughout the life course.

Major later life events such as widowhood, can re-organize an individual's life (Morgan et al, 1997); it is therefore entirely fitting that we pay attention to how a woman's network of personal relationships may change in widowhood. However, there is a danger that we may only reference those relationships to the event of widowhood, rather than the widow's life course. If we start with exploring an individual's life course relationships, there is a real possibility that we may gain a greater understanding of the older widow's social world.

Two key questions have arisen from this part of the literature review that are fundamental to any inquiry into later life widowhood. Firstly, in what way does the 'objective' experience, as defined by others in her 'social world' shape an older woman's subjective experience of becoming and being a widow? And secondly, how do the continuities and discontinuities of those relationships with others impact on that experience? A biographical approach to the study of older women's lives situating widowhood within the life course, such as that adopted by Matthews (1986) in her study of friendships, would seem to offer one way of answering these questions. In Chapter 4, therefore, I argue for a re-conceptualisation of widowhood within the life course.

# Chapter 4

# Conceptualising and
# Re-conceptualising Widowhood

## Introduction

This chapter concludes the review of the literature by drawing together a range of theories and perspectives highlighted in the previous two chapters, in order to evaluate what might be helpful in seeking to better understand the experience of later life widowhood. I argue the limitations of some of these perspectives, suggesting that their restrictive nature has served to reinforce a problem model and thus perpetuate the negative mythology of widowhood. I also acknowledge the insights and helpfulness of other perspectives. Arising from this, and in keeping with the thrust of the discussion in the previous two chapters, I then go on to suggest a **re**-conceptualization of later life widowhood which, by drawing on a life course perspective situated within gerontology and feminism, takes into account the totality of older women's lives.

## Widowhood as pathology

I noted previously that a large body of widowhood research is still located within the grief and stress literature. Widowhood is often construed as pathology, from which a woman needs to recover. One consequence of such conceptualization, according to Jones Porter (1994), is that when it is assumed that the death of a spouse is such a stressful event, researchers are more likely to frame data collection in terms of grieving and coping and thus perpetuate the pathological model. Such a perspective focuses on a particular point in time in which the event of widowhood occurs, rather than on the older woman herself and the continuities and discontinuities she brings to that event. Because the event itself is medicalized and incorporates the language of illness and recovery, by implication the older widow herself becomes pathologised. Although this approach may be helpful in conceptualising the early stages of widowhood and the changes a widow undergoes, it is not particularly helpful in developing our understanding of how older widows experience the rest of their lives, nor does it offer us insight into how they make sense of that life.

## Widowhood as a loss of role

As indicated in Chapter 2, a number of major studies on widowhood have used role theory as their framework (Cumming and Henry, 1961; Blau, 1973; Lopata, 1973, 1987). This presents widowhood as a major crisis of role identity that often precipitates an older woman's disengagement from society. Indeed, it can be argued that this model is particularly strong in the popular construction of later life widowhood where phrases such as 'she is lost without him' and 'she doesn't know what to do with herself now that she is a widow' are quite common in both family and professional discourse. This theoretical perspective is not however without its critics.

Some changes in roles within the family in the early stages of widowhood were identified by Ferraro (1984). He noted, particularly, the changes between mothers and daughters where the daughter might take on the 'mothering' role for a period of time. However considerable stability of role was generally observed. The effects of role loss in widowhood are not consistent and as discussed in Chapter 2, are more likely to occur as a result of other factors surrounding widowhood, such as poverty, ill health and/or very old age rather than widowhood per se. Indeed, Ferraro (1984) actually questioned the utility of a decremented model of role loss and pointed instead to a compensation model in which a shifting or realignment of relationships takes place. Older women lose the role of wife but they compensate for this loss by adopting or adapting to other roles. Interestingly, although Ferraro developed a less restrictive and more helpful model of widowhood than that of 'role loss' he did not draw on experience across the life course in this discussion. Instead, his focus has been on 'current' rather than 'past' roles.

It would seem that the overall focus within role theory is on the individual action (or inaction) of the older woman, a woman who is seen as a solitary actress in her world, and on discontinuity.

## Symbolic interactionism

The usefulness of role theory in developing our understanding of widowhood was questioned by Martin Matthews (1991: 9) who argued, instead, for a symbolic interactionist approach in order to be:

> ... better able to ascertain the basis of responses to bereavement and widowhood and to account for factors that role theory cannot adequately consider.

Examples were provided in the previous two chapters, which highlighted Martin Matthews' (1991) acknowledgement of the way in which the roles and attitudes of others as well as the older woman herself bring about change in later life widowhood. Role theory, she argued, placed too much emphasis on the older woman as a solitary agent, rather than recognizing that she is only one player amongst many. Instead, Martin Matthews (1991) theorised widowhood via the interactions that older women have with the society in which they live, and the meanings that are attached to those interactions. Widows are construed as active players in their own world with all sorts of uncertainties and with both continuities and changes in their relationships with others.

Davidson (1999) also employed a symbolic interactionist approach in her study of older widows and widowers because it acknowledges the richness and complexities of their lives. The use of symbolic interactionism is an important development in theorising widowhood and has the advantage of acknowledging both the potential diversity of the experience of later life widowhood, and also the way in which older widows' lives may be shaped by themselves and others in their social networks. However, there are also limitations to this theoretical approach. In particular, a lack of exploration of the significance of interactions with society and the meanings attached to those interactions over the life course, on present understanding. Indeed, Martin-Matthews (1991) acknowledged that a life course dimension may be useful in developing our overall understanding of older women's experience and recommended that this be considered in further studies of widowhood.

**Social clock theory**

As I discussed in the Introduction, and again in Chapter 2 in relation to 'Age' as a biographical asset, widowhood in later life is an expectation for most, older women. As such it has been theorized as a 'on time' experience by Neugarten and her colleagues (Neugarten et al, 1965; Neugarten and Datan, 1973; Neugarten, 1977). They have posited the existence of a 'social clock': a system of age norms, which is superimposed on the biological clock. Neugarten (1977) argued that we use this 'social clock' to assess ourselves in relation to others. To re-iterate, this may not make the actual 'event' of widowhood any easier for older women, particularly during the period of bereavement, but it may ultimately impact on their understanding of the experience and the possibilities offered. More specifically, and contrary to popular mythology, the expectation of such an 'on time' event may also mean that many older couples will have discussed the probability of one of them dying and may even have made arrangements. Gerontological literature reminds us that in general older people are much more likely to talk about the prospect of dying than their younger counterparts (see for example Lieberman and Tobin, 1983). Social clock theory certainly offers an explanation as to why later life widowhood may well be, or be perceived to be, very different from widowhood earlier on in the life course, both from the perspective of the older widow and also those of others in her social world and beyond. It also reminds us very strongly of the necessity to acknowledge age as a factor in widowhood research.

**Widowhood as a status passage**

This perspective was developed by Sheehy (1997), as highlighted in Chapter 2, and in many ways can be construed as a logical development of the work of the social clock theorists. Sheehy (1997: 354) identified widowhood as a 'transformative event' for women of the Reconstruction Generation in America. Her work has been particularly helpful in developing our understanding of widowhood as part of the life course and our knowledge of how women 'manage' their widowhood at different points in that life course. Sheehy acknowledged the role of widows as active players in their own lives and also took account of individual and collective history. Later life widowhood is acknowledged as a major milestone in the life course of women, and one which, according to Sheehy (1997) most women manage effectively. Within this perspective, widowhood is theorized as part of the life course and therefore not abnormal. As such it becomes an accepted (if not always acceptable) part of the female life course, rather than being viewed as an illness or a condition.

## Social exchange theory

Social exchange theory, as highlighted in Chapter 3, with reference to the empirical work of Morgan (1989) and Morgan et al (1997), identified loss of reciprocity as a condition under which social support may have negative connotations (see also, Antonucci, 1985) The support given to older widows, particularly by family, often leaves them in the role of passive recipients or patients and can leave them feeling powerless and dependent (Watanabe Greene and Field, 1989). Silverman's (1986) work with self-help groups identified the importance of mutual exchange and understanding in the becoming and being a widow. In these self-help groups older widows and widowers provided mutual support and practical help on the basis of reciprocity (see also Jerrome, 1981, 1990, 1991, 1993; Babchuk and Anderson, 1989).

Exchange theory seeks to explain the consequences for the older woman of potential power imbalances that may occur in later life widowhood. For example, if an older widow feels that others are making decisions for her, when previously she has made her own decisions, it is theorized that she is more likely to experience low self-esteem and possibly depression. In this case, the consequences are as a result of the lack of reciprocity rather than widowhood and yet they are likely to be attributed to the state of widowhood. This is particularly helpful in developing an understanding of why some relationships are more helpful than others, especially if a life course perspective is employed.

## Revisiting theoretical perspectives on widowhood

Widowhood therefore has been theorized as an event, a transition or an ongoing experience that happens to a particular individual, usually in later life, when her spouse dies. For some women, these theoretical perspectives suggest that this may involve a significant loss of role whereas for others it may involve a readjustment to different roles. It may or may not involve a change in relationships with others. What is certain is that in some way, those relationships themselves will impact on the older woman's experience. I would suggest that, in addition, we ought not to ignore the fact that all of this takes place within a societal and political context, which will structure both the objective and subjective experience of widowhood. 'Widowhood' in later life is therefore not a neutral concept; how it is defined and conceptualised will depend on current societal norms and behaviour concerning marital status, age and gender.

However, it is equally important to acknowledge that later life widowhood does not occur in isolation to the rest of older women's lives but as an integral part of their life course and as a consequence it is highly likely that past experience will impact on the present. Clearly widowhood is an extremely complex and diverse experience and one that will vary over time. I would certainly endorse the observations of Jones Porter (1994: 33) that we need a fresh perspective on the life world of older widows, one that is sensitive to the totality of older women's lives and is: 'grounded in conversation with older widows'.

### Embracing the totality of older women's lives

The vast majority of the literature on later life widowhood offers us little explanation concerning the actual experience of becoming and being a widow at the beginning of the 21st Century. The symbolic interactionist approach of Martin Matthews (1991) in Canada and Davidson (1999) in the U.K. are notable exceptions. In addition, the work of Neugarten et al (1965; 1973; 1977) and Morgan et al (1997) also provide valuable analyses of differential experiences. However, the bulk of literature does not really address the issue of widowhood as an integral part of the female life course although Sheehy's (1997) work on status passage and Davidson's (1999) situation of later life widowhood within companionate marriage, do at least acknowledge that widowhood has a gendered past.

I have argued so far that, to date, the theoretical perspectives that have been developed and the blurring of the lived experience of widowhood with the acute state of bereavement have limited our understanding. I have also argued that the study of later life widowhood has been located within a body of literature whose focus has been grief and adaptation rather than subjective experience and identity. To summarise, existing perspectives lack: a community context, a life course and biographical understanding and a sense of widows as agents of their own lives. Indeed, they stop short of considering widowhood as an ongoing lived experience. In order to explore the experience of later life widowhood as an integral part of older women's life course, we need to look beyond the widowhood literature and draw on a range of theoretical perspectives, which enable us to look at this experience through a different lens (Gibson 1996).

Experience has many layers. It exists in the present but it also has a past. Our current experience always has a relationship with our past. Experience is something we gain, even if it is not always valued, as a result of age (Bytheway, 1995). Over twenty-five years ago Johnson (1978) highlighted the importance of the past for understanding the ageing of an individual when he argued that our present is sculpted from our past. In order to understand the totality of the experience of older widows we must surely pay attention to their life course and each woman's unique biography. Not to do so means that we run the risk of interpreting her widowhood in isolation from the rest of her life. Collective, or generational, as well as individual biography, will contribute to our understanding of her present experience (Giele and Elder, 1999). Experience also has subjective and objective dimensions. How older widows construct their identity as women, both in the present and in the past, and their relationships with others, will affect their experience as older widows. Furthermore, that experience will also in some way be mediated by the perceptions of others.

Individual experience is structured by the society in which that individual lives. Feminist scholarship, for example, has argued that women's lives are gendered. This occurs throughout the life course, for example in domestic relations (Oakley, 1974), caring responsibilities (Finch and Groves, 1983) and lack of access to financial resources in old age (Arber and Ginn, 1991). Widowhood and widowerhood in later life are very different experiences (Davidson, 1999): older men who are widowed, tend to remarry fairly quickly after the death of their spouse or they die (Gibson, 1996; Sheehy, 1997), whereas older widows are much more likely to live alone for many years. Davidson (1999) has also highlighted the gendered nature of adaptation to the loss of a spouse.

In order to explore these complexities of experience and to seek a perspective which both embraces the totality of older women's lives and acknowledges that older widows are 'ageing' women, I now turn to the literature relating to the life course within social gerontology and feminism which seems to offer a contribution towards a **re**-conceptualisation of later life widowhood

## Social gerontology and the life course

The study of social gerontology has moved away from a focus on old age per se and the discontinuities associated with functionalist theories of ageing such as disengagement theory (Cumming and Henry, 1961) and role theory, to an acknowledgement of old age as part of the life course. Old age does not occur in isolation but is the accumulation of a lifetime's experience and happens on a number of fronts, which I now briefly describe.

Firstly, the political economy perspective highlights the impact of an individual's location within the social and economic structure during the earlier part of their life course, on their old financial status, their social location and the life choices available in old age (Townsend, 1981; Phillipson, 1982, 1998; Walker, 1993). Although not predictive, this perspective acknowledges in particular the way in which advantages and disadvantages accrued earlier in the life course impact on an individual in old age. An example of this would be the way in which many older women find themselves with reduced access to financial resources in later life as a result of a history of part-time, low paid, low status employment or a lifetime's financial dependence on a spouse (Arber and Ginn, 1991).

Secondly, the role of historical location. Riley et al (1972) stressed the importance of 'cohort' for understanding how different groups of older people manage the experience of old age. More recently, Giele and Elder (1998: 11) have argued the case for a life course paradigm that incorporates four elements: development of the individual; history and culture; social relations; intersection of age, period and cohort. These elements collectively impact on the ageing of an individual and contribute to different trajectories of the life course. Without an understanding of both individual and collective biography, we cannot really understand an individual's experience of ageing (see also, Birren et al, 1996).

Thirdly, social gerontologists are increasingly acknowledging the importance of the subjective experience of ageing, as encapsulated in biographical studies. Birren, for example, (1996) suggests that the interest in the life course of ageing individuals has come about due to a belief:

> ... that something important has been left out of our scientific knowledge generating system in its studies of adult change and ageing. It is becoming increasingly clear that what has been omitted are the experiences of growing old and being old.
>
> (Birren, 1996: ix)

This cannot be understood in isolation from historical location or political economy. Ruth and Oberg for example, explore the ways of life of Finns from the generation of the Wars and the Depression and argue that gerontological knowledge, based solely on current circumstances, is inadequate: 'Ageing must be seen as a continuation of an integrated process, starting with an earlier life, where the life lived gives meaning to old age' (Ruth and Oberg, 1996: 31).

Central to the work of Ruth and Oberg, and to biographical approaches generally, is the way in which the life that has been lived is reflected on, and given meaning to, in old age. Phillipson (1998: 24) identified this as: 'the 'reflexivity' of the self'. This idea is paralleled in the sociology of the self (Giddens, 1991) and examples can also be found in the literature on 'disability and identity' (see Thomas, 1999 for example). According to Giddens:

> Self-identity is not a distinctive trait, or even a collection of traits, possessed by the individual. It is the self as reflexively understood in terms of her or his biography.
>
> (Giddens, 1991: 53)

Narratives, or stories, he argues (see also Ruth and Kenyon, 1996) play a key role in the construction of lives:

> The existential question of self-identity is bound up with the fragile nature of the biography, which the individual 'supplies' about herself. A person's identity is not to be found in behaviour nor, important though they are, in the reactions of others, but in the capacity to keep a particular narrative going. The individual's biography, if she is to maintain regular interaction with others in the day-to-day world, cannot be wholly fictive. It must continually integrate events, which occur in the external world, and sort them into the ongoing 'story' about the self.
>
> (Giddens, 1991: 54)

I explore the issue of subjectivity further in Chapter 5 but suffice it to say here that a life course perspective enables us to theorise that an older widow's identity is constructed and reworked in the light of her own individual biography. This is influenced, and shaped, by the historical and social context in which she has lived. As I argued in Chapters 2 and 3, we cannot begin to understand her current experience without paying due attention to these factors. Furthermore, such a perspective acknowledges change over the life course and thus incorporates the potential for future development.

The life course perspective therefore acknowledges that an individual's ageing will be influenced by personal, social and historical factors. Thus, in order to understand the trajectory of an individual woman's life course, we must pay attention to **all** of these influences.

## Theorising women's development over the life course

Social gerontologists have looked to theories from life-span psychology to support the notion that the potential for development exists throughout the life course, and that development occurs on a number of fronts (Sugarman, 1990; Bernard and Meade, 1993). The traditional approach has been to view life as a series of stages, often identified through chronological age (Buhler, 1935; Havighurst, 1953, 1972; Levinson, 1978; Gould, 1980). This developmental notion of a stage focuses on those things a person needs to know at a particular point in the life course in order to be judged by his/herself to be reasonably happy and successful. However, Bernard and Meade (1993) found this approach to be very deterministic, failing to acknowledge the individual process of development, which incorporates the social, political and economic environment (see also Llewelyn and Osborne, 1990).

Erikson's model (1959, 1963, 1980, 1982) is one of a changing individual in a changing world. He identified eight stages in which a series of psycho-social tasks or crises are to be negotiated, the successful negotiation of which leads the individual through to the next stage. The successful negotiation of Erikson's final stage, that of ego-integrity versus despair, is characterised by an acceptance of one's life as it has been lived. Lack or loss of ego-integrity will lead to despair and a fear of death. For some older people this crisis may be faced as a result of the death of a spouse. Coleman (1994), whilst questioning whether Erikson's state of integrity is too idealistic, conceded that nonetheless his work does highlight some of the key elements of later life and the special adjustments necessary. A lack of a sense of fulfilment, for example, can be crucial in later life and may account for some of the despair reported at the time of widowhood. As discussed in Chapter 2, there is some evidence to suggest that those widows whose marriages have been less than satisfactory are likely to find adjustment to widowhood more difficult than those widows who report a satisfactory marriage (Lieberman, 1996). Erikson also drew attention (Erikson, 1982; Erikson et al, 1986) to the place of 'generativity' in the ageing process; that is the important role of establishing and guiding the next generation, seeing beyond oneself to the wider society. Some of Lieberman's (1996) older widows clearly identified that widowhood had 'freed up' time and space for them to develop such a role, but they were certainly in the minority.

Feminist theories of development, in particular the work of Gilligan (1983, 1993) have challenged Erikson's theory, suggesting that it focused on the male as the model of normal development. The emphasis in his model of adult development is one of the emergence of the individual and the task of achieving autonomy and independence. Gilligan's (1993) study of younger women led her to conclude that women's psychological development over the life course is different to that experienced by men. Women's development, she asserted, is concerned with relationship building and connectedness and should be seen as a continuum along which women move from a point where they do not recognise their own needs, to a point where they recognise the legitimacy of their own needs alongside the needs of others. Gilligan (1993) argued that rather than achieving autonomy and independence women instead embrace mutuality and inter-dependence.

Silverman (1987) employed Gilligan's feminist model of development in her research with widows who participated in self-help 'widow to widow' groups. She recommended us to consider widowhood as a stage in the life course that is a change in the life circumstances in which the individual relates to herself differently than in the past. 'Widowhood' is thus construed as an opportunity for women to reach 'mutuality and interdependence'. Silverman proposed that such a conceptualisation enables widowhood to be understood both as an ending and a beginning. She found differences amongst widows based on appropriate or inappropriate accommodation to the new stage of life: those women who were committed to the past found the transition to widowhood difficult, whilst those who saw a change in themselves often felt satisfied with their life (Silverman, 1986). Both Gilligan and Silverman are asserting that in order to really understand women (of all ages), we need to acknowledge the gendered nature of their development over the life course.

## Feminist gerontology

The links between social gerontology and feminism therefore add another dimension to this discussion. The acknowledgement of the gendered nature of later life is fairly recent in Gerontology; what might be tentatively termed a 'feminist gerontology' has begun to emerge. We are beginning to explore and understand the impact of gender in later life both at an individual and a societal level. Initially, this was a response to the androcentrism underlying most gerontological work. The experience of women was either ignored (for example in studies on retirement) or highlighted when it differed from the dominant male pattern (mortality and morbidity). More recently, older women's lives have been studied in their own right, with the recognition that later life is a predominantly female world (Matthews, 1979, 1984; Gee and Kimball, 1987; Allen, 1989; Arber and Ginn, 1991; Bernard and Meade, 1993; Gibson, 1996; Browne, 1998; Bernard, et al 2000).

At the same time that gerontology was uncovering gender, feminism was discovering old age. Reinharz (1986) has suggested that from the start of second wave feminism in the 1970s, feminists working within the three major perspectives of that time, radical, liberal and socialist (Jaggar, 1983, Tong, 1989) were developing analyses of ageing (De Beauvoir, 1970; Olsen, 1982; Sontag, 1978). However, until the 1980s, feminist concerns with women's issues earlier on in the life course such as reproduction, childcare, domestic and caring responsibilities and employment opportunities were paramount (Bernard and Meade, 1993). In fact, in highlighting the unequal burden of care imposed on women at mid-life, there is an unfortunate tendency in some feminist literature to portray older women as the burden (Lewis and Meredith, 1988). Furthermore, Macdonald (1989) argued that older feminists have often been seen as a source of embarrassment to their younger colleagues:

> From the beginning of this wave of the women's movement, the message has gone out to those of us over sixty that your sisterhood does not include us ... You do not see us in your present lives, you do not identify with our issues, you exploit us, you patronize us, you stereotype us. Mainly, you ignore us.
>
> (Macdonald, 1989: 6)

According to Reinharz (1986) there are several reasons for this. Firstly, feminists like everyone else have been socialised in an ageing-phobic culture so are just as likely to fear ageing as anyone else. And secondly, the very development of an early feminist consciousness among women stems from a rejection of the world of their mothers:

> ... to some young feminists, the world of their mothers seems unattractive, 'politically incorrect', a product of false consciousness. These women have yet to learn about sisterhood across the life cycle.
>
> (Reinharz, 1986: 507)

As mainstream feminists have aged, some have belatedly begun to be interested in older women's issues (Greer, 1991; Friedan, 1993; Sheehy, 1997) but the field is not yet vast. One notable exception is the work of Browne (1998).

Feminist gerontologists however, in raising awareness of older women's structural disadvantage, have highlighted a number of areas of concern. For example, although old age brings with it the likelihood of discrimination on the basis of age, older women are likely to suffer the double jeopardy of ageism and sexism (Sontag, 1978; Bernard and Meade, 1993; Bernard et al, 2000). Older women live longer than men, but they are more likely to experience disability, make greater use of hospital services and be institutionalised during their later years (Gee and Kimball, 1987; Arber and Ginn, 1991; Victor 1991). Writing from a political economy perspective, a number of authors have highlighted the disadvantaged position of older women with regard to income and housing (Peace, 1986, 1993; Arber and Ginn, 1991; Minkler and Estes, 1991); older women are more likely to live alone, with less access to financial resources than older men.

However, Gibson (1996) recommended caution; the study of older women (and by implication older widows), by both feminists and those gerontologists interested in older women, has been defined an ongoing tendency to see older women in terms of problems. Whilst not denying the problems some women experience Gibson has argued:

> It is my contention that the particular lens through which older women have come to be viewed is one that selectively includes only certain aspects of being old and female ... by focusing on issues of disadvantage, feminist analyses of old age have tended to obscure not only the heterogeneity of old women but also the aspects of being old and female that are a source of both celebration and strength. While there is no doubt that women face a number of adverse physical, emotional and mental, social and economic eventualities in their old age, such eventualities do not represent the totality of their experiences.
>
> (Gibson, 1996: 434-5)

Furthermore:

> Much is made of the greater propensity of old women to widowhood, which is readily associated with a range of financial, social, psychological and sexual difficulties. Comparatively little is made, however, of the closer instrumental and affective ties that the women experience with family and friends.
>
> (Gibson, 1996: 438)

In highlighting the gendered nature of ageing, we have begun to see the life circumstances of older women, and older widows in particular, as unfortunate. By looking at the lives of older widows in their entirety, through a different lens, it is possible to identify the strengths that women bring to later life. These include: their greater experience of and their commitment to the private sphere; their involvement in the informal economy; their connectedness to others over the life course; their experience over the life course in moving between the formal and informal sectors and the private and public spheres. Moreover, women's experience of maintaining family links, establishing friendship networks (Jerrome, 1993), working with others, juggling roles and dealing with uncertainties over the life course, may also be a source of strength and serve them well in old age:

> Death of spouses, family and friends is undisputedly a more frequent experience as one ages, the erosion of established networks an unavoidable corollary. The very interruptedness of the traditional woman's life course tends to provide a context in which the reestablishment or replacement of network members is not a new experience.
>
> (Gibson, 1996: 439)

Indeed, as Rossi (1986: 160) so succinctly observed:  it is perhaps fortunate that it is elderly women rather than men who tend to outlive their spouses.

Feminism, combined with a life course perspective from gerontology, offers the possibility of focusing on the uniqueness of women's lives in order to better understand their experience of later life widowhood. A feminist perspective on later life widowhood offers the possibility of understanding the social reality of later life widowhood via the actresses involved. Despite feminism's early lack of interest (and, some would argue, a continuing lack of interest) it is possible, whilst not subscribing to any one theoretical strand in particular, to identify elements of feminist theory which are useful to the development of a different perspective on widowhood.

## Feminist theory

Stacey (1993) for example suggested that feminist theory comprises a body of knowledge, which: offers a critical explanation of women's subordination; focuses on the centrality of experience and provides an explanation and analysis of how and why women have less power than men. I argued earlier that similar elements have been lacking in widowhood research. It is perhaps useful to re-iterate these here in the context of feminist theory. Firstly, widowhood has been researched and usually conceptualised as a problem. Secondly, there has been little focus on the experience of later life widowhood and thirdly, explanations and analyses are lacking of why, despite their numbers, widows are largely invisible.

Before I explore the usefulness of feminist theory in furthering our understanding of the experience of widowhood, it should be acknowledged here that the elements highlighted by Stacey (1993) have been, and still are, the source of much debate within feminism itself. Questions such as whether women have or do not have a shared identity and the 'category woman' versus the 'politics of difference' debate, have been ongoing (Stanley and Wise, 1990; Harding, 1991; Browne, 1998; Beasley, 1999; Granville, 2000). From its origins as a white, middle class, heterosexual theory of women's subordination (arising out of second-generation feminism) there has increasingly been recognition, according to Reinharz (1986), that women represent a highly diversified group. Whilst recognising women's subordination and critically analysing their role in society, it is important not to see all women as equally powerless: we need to acknowledge women's differential strengths and differences.

Nonetheless three threads in particular can be discerned within these debates that are pertinent to the current discussion. Firstly, the commonality of 'femaleness'. Although different strands of feminisms embrace different political and philosophical perspectives on what constitutes the concept of womanhood, what does seem to be a common feature is: 'the consideration of women as the subject' (Beasley, 1999: 18). As Delmar (1986) confirmed, the concept of womanhood is placed centre stage in feminist theory. Stacey (1993) suggested that the 'category woman' debate is constantly changing as feminist theories grapple with both multiple meanings and shared identity. She argued that 'woman' had different meanings at different times and cited Riley (1988), who recommends the strategic use of the term 'woman', but always foregrounding it in terms of both subjectivity and current discourses. In exploring the experience of later life widowhood therefore, attention must be paid to difference as well as similarities, and to both objective and subjective experience. We need to acknowledge the voice of older widows alongside other discourses and to recognise the interaction of these discourses on the experience of older women.

The second thread relates to this concept of 'experience'. In the 1970s and 1980s 'malestream', so-called neutral social science, was challenged because of its inclination to universalise experiences associated with men and to describe men's experiences as if they were common to all human beings (see discussions by: Stanley and Wise, 1990, 1993; Harding, 1991; Maynard and Purvis, 1994; Granville, 2000). Feminist writers began to invoke 'experience', both their own and that of other women, as a way of getting women's voices heard. The purpose of giving authority to individual and collective experience was to expose mainstream approaches as highly gendered (women in relation to men). The view was put forward that knowledge is always situated:

> There is no view from nowhere, indeed the view from nowhere may well itself be a male construction of the possibilities for knowledge.
>
> (Bordo, 1990: 137)

This 'malestream' view of the world presented women's lives as 'other', with men as subjects and women as objects (de Beauvoir, 1974). The realm of the personal was coded as female and therefore 'other'. Instead, feminist writers, from all strands of feminism, have started to emphasise the importance of the 'private' as well as the 'public' arena as areas of significance for the generation of knowledge and theory (Oakley, 1986; Stanley and Wise, 1990; Harding, 1991; Granville, 2000, 2001). This has led to a redefinition, by feminist writers, of politics and social life, as captured in the phrase 'the personal is political'. By insisting on the study of women's experiences as both valuable and essential, the study of women's lives is brought to the forefront. Feminists such as Stanley and Wise (1990; 1993) have continued to argue the epistomological importance of experience for understanding the world we live in. By exploring the experience of older widows from the perspective of older women themselves, and by valuing that experience, it becomes possible to gain knowledge and understanding of their world, which may not otherwise be accessible. Smith (1975, cited in Anderson, et al, 1987: 107) argued that feminist theory: 'must begin 'where we are' with real concrete people and their actual lives, if it is to do more than reaffirm dominant ideologies about women'.

The debate concerning patriarchy is the final thread. Patriarchy relates to the nature of male dominance in society. Different theorists have argued in favour of the historical, material and political nature of women's subordination (for example Mies, 1986), pointing to women's roles in society being mainly confined to the private sphere, women having less access to resources and power and so on. Others have stressed the operation of patriarchy at a psychic level, arguing that the valuing of the male over the female operates at an unconscious level and has its origins in the formation of our earliest sexual identities (see Mitchell, 1974; Mitchell and Rose, 1982). There does however seem to be an overall consensus that women's lives are structured in one way or another by patriarchy and any discussion of women's experience has to be analysed in recognition of this. The current generation of older widows are no exception and so any discussion of their experience must take account of this.

Feminist theories therefore enable us to locate the discussion of later life widowhood within the context of **all** women's lives in a number of ways. Firstly by recognising both similarities and differences of the female experience, secondly by valuing women's experiences as contributing to new forms of knowledge, and finally by confirming the impact of patriarchy on a number of levels on women's lives. I explore these ideas further, in relationship to feminist research practice, in the next chapter.

## Conclusion: re-conceptualising widowhood

In this chapter, I have re-visited theoretical perspectives highlighted in Chapters 2 and 3, and ascertained what is helpful in furthering our understanding of later life widowhood. I have then gone on to explore theoretical perspectives from gerontology and feminism and argued their potential usefulness in developing our understanding of later life widowhood. The common factors that emerge from this discussion, in relation to later life widowhood, are gender, age, development and the life course. These components can be construed as 'a feminist, life course perspective', that builds in the possibility of growth and development over the life course, embraces the totality of older widow's experience and provides a different interpretative lens through which to understand that experience. Such a perspective acknowledges the impact of both age and gender in constructing women's lives over the life course. It also acknowledges that within the category 'woman' there will be considerable diversity as a result of differential experience during that life course. It places women's personal experience at the centre of that discussion but also acknowledges that past and previous experiences will have been constructed within prevailing societal norms of age and gender. It further acknowledges that current experience in widowhood is an integral part of that life course. This re-conceptualisation thus enables a redefinition of widowhood as an 'expected' and understandable part of the female life course to which older women bring both the advantages and disadvantages which they have accrued throughout their lives.

A logical conclusion then from the preceding discussions is that no single perspective will suffice if we are to really understand the experience of later life widowhood. I have acknowledged that there are both benefits and limitations to traditional ways of conceptualising and researching later life widowhood. I have gone on to argue that it is possible to re-conceptualise later life widowhood by situating it within a feminist life course perspective, which draws on both gerontology and feminism. This potentially moves us away from a problem model and allows the focus of attention to be on the totality of older widow's experience. If we are to truly understand this experience, we need to transform prevailing knowledge paradigms to incorporate these older women's lives.

# Chapter 5

# Researching Later Life Widowhood

## Introduction

I begin this chapter by highlighting a number of concerns about existing research on widowhood in later life. I then go on to discuss the potential of a qualitative approach which draws on feminist and biographical practice, both for uncovering the subjective and differential experience of later life widowhood and for engaging older women in the research process. This combined approach acknowledges that as women we have a story to share, which is fundamental to really making sense of and understanding 'who' we are.

I suggest that adopting a life story approach allows the possibility of understanding later life widowhood as another integrated chapter in a woman's life, rather than an event that is separate and distinct. I review the literature supporting a biographical approach to interviewing, taking heed of the issues raised and identifying elements of good practice. I then explore the validity and the reliability of life story research and the ethical issues that must underpin the whole process. Finally, I discuss an appropriate theoretical framework for analysis.

## Existing research

A review of the research on later life widowhood raises several methodological issues which need to be resolved before embarking on further research: timing of the research; the nature of data collection; the underlying assumption of homogeneity; and the emphasis on discontinuity. I now summarise each of these in turn.

### Timing of the research

Many of the studies reviewed in earlier chapters have taken place within three years, or less, of the death of the spouse (Pihlblad, and Adams 1972; Lopata, 1973, 1979; Atchley, 1975; Arling, 1976; Bowling and Cartwright, 1982; Bankoff, 1983; O'Bryant, 1988; Babchuk, 1989; Rosik, 1989; Sable, 1989). This is generally recognised as a time of grieving (Parkes, 1986; Bowling and Cartwright, 1982; Nieboer, 1995) confirmed by autobiographical accounts of widows themselves (see Van den Hoonaard, 1997) and as such, hints at the limitations of much existing research in relation to the ongoing experience of later life widowhood (Chambers, 1994; Davidson, 1999). The implications for further widowhood research are clear

- a period of at least three years after the death of a spouse would seem to be a more appropriate timing if the focus of the research is to be the ongoing experience of widowhood.

## The nature of data collection

Data collection has been largely quantitative and carried out through the use of large scale surveys and structured interviews (Pihlblad and Adams, 1972; Lopata, 1973, 1987; Atchley, 1975; Arling, 1976; Bowling and Cartwright, 1982; Bankoff, 1983; Babchuk and Anderson, 1989; Rosik, 1989) or case histories within the grief literature (Stroebe and Stroebe, 1988; Sable, 1989). We are presented with a vast array of facts and figures, which explore the 'objective' experience of widowhood but tell us little about the subjective experience. Not surprisingly, older widows' voices are sadly lacking in these studies. Until fairly recently few studies had attempted to engage with older widows and explore widowhood, as it were, 'from the inside'. The work of Davidson (1999) in the UK and Martin Matthews (1991) and Van den Hoonaard (2001) in Canada are notable exceptions. Indeed, Martin Matthews (1991) has confirmed that research that more fully addresses the social meaning of widowhood is certainly needed. A qualitative approach that engages with older widows may have the potential to elicit this subjectivity.

## Assumption of homogeneity

There would appear to be either a lack of recognition of the diversity of the experience of widowhood or a failure to make explicit the potentially differential experience of widowhood. Martin Matthews (1991) has suggested that there is an inappropriate assumption of homogeneity within the literature; the widowed, and particularly the older, female widowed, are frequently treated as a homogenous group. The complex biographical assets of age and gender have not always been made explicit. Older widows have often, for example, been submerged in studies within the general widowhood literature, despite the fact that widowhood is more likely to occur at the end of life than at any other time in the life course. In a critique of the literature Martin Matthews (1991) cited the following: Lopata (1973) included women over 65 but 81% of her study group were widowed before 65; Morgan (1976) studied women in the age range 45-74; Bankhoff's studies (1983) had a mean age of 51; Vachon et al (1977) used an age range of 22-69; Haas-Hawkings et al (1985) surveyed an age range of 49-83 with a mean age of 66. However, as Lopata (1973) suggested over thirty years ago now, age differences in the timing of widowhood are crucial in understanding the differential experience of widowhood because of the way a woman's life is immersed in other roles and the way others see her. In an earlier chapter I highlighted the significance of age as both a biographical asset and a biographical deficit. Furthermore, I also demonstrated that the generation to which a woman belongs and whether widowhood is 'on time' or 'off time' both have the potential to affect the experience. I would concur with Lopata (1973) concerning the importance of diverse socio-economic factors, particularly education but would suggest that these may also be age-related.

However, the significance of age is acknowledged in some widowhood research. For example, Arling's (1976) study only included widows who were over 65; Scott and Kivett (1980) sample covered an age range 65-99. Indeed, Lopata's later study concentrated on older widows (Lopata, 1979). However, as I argued in Chapter 2, so often in these studies age is construed as a deficit. More recently, Davidson (1999) explicitly focused her attention on the experience of later life and argued convincingly for the recognition of both age and gender, in furthering our understanding of the differential experience of older widows and widowers.

I would argue therefore that research on later life widowhood should start with an assumption of diversity rather than homogeneity, acknowledging the complexities of age and gender and that research methods should be employed that enable this diversity to be further explored.

*Discontinuity*

Finally, as Martin Matthews (1991) confirmed there is a tendency in the research literature to treat widowhood as a separate, distinct period of a woman's life to be studied in isolation from the rest of the life course. And yet, as I demonstrated in Chapter 4, theoretical perspectives from gerontology confirm the significance of a life course perspective in understanding later life. Quantitative approaches, particularly those employing secondary analyses of large surveys, focusing as they do on data collected 'on', rather than 'with', widows' have tended to reinforce this view.

This is further compounded by feminist researchers who, as discussed in Chapter 4, have only recently 'discovered' older women. Whilst placing great emphasis on the continuities in women's lives they have, with some exceptions (Browne, 1998; Bernard et al, 2000), tended to ignore the lives of older women in general. In contrast to the exploration of younger women's lives, there is a real lack of research from a gendered, life course perspective, which explores the lived experience of ageing women who become widows. We know so little about the continuities that these older women bring to later life widowhood and even less about how these continuities enable them to make sense of the glaringly obvious discontinuity: the death of a spouse.

In the next part of this chapter, I argue the case for a different approach to the study of later widowhood that addresses these concerns. This approach comprises a number of threads encompassing qualitative, feminist and biographical perspectives. I explore each in turn, whilst acknowledging that the threads are nonetheless inextricably linked.

## The potential of qualitative research

I have argued in previous chapters and earlier on in this chapter that with some exceptions, we have very little understanding of the subjective experience of widowhood. Gubrium and Sankar (1994) have informed us that qualitative research starts from the assumption that it is possible to obtain a profound understanding about persons and their worlds, from ordinary conversations and observations. This approach acknowledges the considerable ability people have to know things about their own lives, one another and their respective worlds. Within qualitative research, the researcher's role in obtaining the facts of experience is made very explicit as she seeks to understand the multi-faceted and complex nature of human experience from the perspective of those being researched. It is suggested that qualitative research: 'makes the often invisible, un-reflected, aspects of life, explicit' (Gubrium and Sankar, 1994: ix).

Jaffe and Miller (1994: 53) confirm that the goal of qualitative researchers is to understand social life by seeking to explore the meaning or understanding of the participants in the research project. They caution against an oversimplification of 'meaning' and suggest that: 'in any particular instance, the meaning we create is circumscribed by other meanings that we and other members of society have created'. Bringing reciprocity into the research relationship, and encouraging older women to be co-participants in the creation of new knowledge, provides an opportunity to tease out meaning both in terms of positionality and embeddedness; the world we see is both the same (what we share) and different (differently positioned or situated in reference to it). This is particularly important when researching with participants who are of a different age, race or gender than the researcher. According to Jaffe and Miller (1994: 54): 'Meaning construction and identity formation give the researcher and the researched shared and yet crucially different realities and are mediated by broader forces or social structures.'

Qualitative research is particularly useful in situations where variables are unknown and where difference is important; it permits flexibility and sensitivity. Since it is grounded in a philosophical position that is broadly interpretivist (Mason, 1996), qualitative research is primarily interested in how the social world is interpreted, understood or experienced by the actresses involved. In my research, these principal actresses were older widows. Mason has stated:

> Qualitative research aims to produce rounded understandings on the basis of rich, contextual and detailed data. There is more emphasis on 'holistic' forms of analysis and explanation in this sense than on charting surface patterns, trends and correlations.
>
> (Mason, 1996: 74)

In order to achieve this, it is suggested that qualitative research needs to be systematically and rigorously conducted, yet flexible and contextual. It should involve critical self-scrutiny by the researcher and should produce social explanations to intellectual puzzles. Attention must be paid to ethics and this must be made explicit throughout the whole endeavour.

*Subjectivity*

Both Martin Matthews (1991) and Jones Porter (1994) have recommended an approach to the study of later life widowhood that is grounded in conversation with older widows, and makes use of widows' own words to tell their stories. A qualitative approach that engages with older women and encourages them to tell their 'life stories' is one way of gaining this 'insider' perspective. Such an approach enables an exploration of the subjective experience of later life widowhood through a 'subjective' research process. Gubrium and Sankar (1994) and Andrews (1991) have confirmed the value of the subjective in qualitative research. In fact, Andrews goes even further and challenges the notion of objectivity at all stages of the research process from the conceptualisation of the project through to the final end product

There are parallels here with both the disability and the feminist literature. Increasingly, disabled women have been encouraged to 'speak out' and tell their stories in order to both claim and validate their experience (Morris, 1989; Morris, 1996; Thomas, 1999). The bringing in of the personal, that is the writing of the self, is one hallmark of feminist approaches. It allows voices to be heard but also gives rise to new ways of knowing, understanding what knowledge is and how it is produced. According to Thomas (1999: 69) it: 'reminds us that all knowledge is situated, that knowledge is a social product bearing the marks of time, place and social positioning.'

Feminist inquiry thus offers a frame for this new qualitative approach to the study of later life widowhood. Accordingly, I now turn to the literature on feminist research practice to explore in some detail its potential for exploring older widows' lives.

## The potential of feminist research practice to explore the reality of older widows' lives

According to Holloway (1999) feminist research focuses on:

> ... the experience and perceptions of women. Feminist approaches do not prescribe methods of analysing research but suggest ways of thinking about it. The intention is to make women visible, raise their consciousness and empower...
>
> (Holloway, 1999: 88)

Such an approach therefore fully acknowledges the gendered nature of all women's lives. Furthermore, as Reinharz (1992) has reminded us, underlying all feminist research is the tenet that women's lives are important and for feminist researchers:

> ... females are worth examining as individuals and people whose experience is interwoven with other women. In other words, feminists are interested in women as individuals and as a social category.
>
> (Reinharz, 1992: 24)

This echoes my own quest, which was to understand both the subjective (individual) and the objective (socially structured) experiences of later life widowhood.

*Developing feminist inquiry*

Feminist scholars are thus interested in research practices that enable us to understand the social reality experienced by women of different ages, class, race, culture, sexuality and disability. If we add marital status to that list it is possible to imagine the possibilities for widowhood research. Feminist research came about initially as a reaction against 'positivist' research, which was identified as both 'male' and 'androcentric' (see Chapter 4) and the notion of value-neutral research, in particular, was challenged (Stanley and Wise 1993).

It has been recommended (Stanley and Wise, 1990) that feminism be present within the research process in the following ways. Firstly in the researcher/researched relationship, which challenges the traditional 'malestream' research relationship of separateness and objectivity. In feminist research researchers are encouraged, or even expected, to engage with the person who is participating in the research. Secondly, in the recognition of the validity of emotion; a feminist researcher is actively encouraged to research the subjective and feelings are acknowledged as valid data. Thirdly, in the intellectual biography of the researcher; feminist research acknowledges and makes visible the role of the researcher and her own intellectual biography as part of the research process. Fourthly, in managing the different realities and understanding of the researcher and the researched; feminist research encourages a dialogue between researcher and researched to tease out the different meanings and realities they both bring to the research relationship. And finally, in the complexities of power in both research and its written products; feminist research pays great attention to the power relationships inherent in research and actively seeks to redress, wherever possible, that power imbalance. Where it is not possible to redress that balance, feminist researchers are encouraged to reflect on the impact of that imbalance on the research process. Furthermore, in writing up the research feminist researchers pay considerable attention to language, which should not demean or discriminate against those researched and, wherever possible, there should be an agreement, between the researcher and the researched about the language that is used. Feminist researchers are encouraged to reflect and comment on all of these issues, even if it is to acknowledge that they are not always achievable.

Feminist research therefore has been interested in exploring women's perceptions, experiences and feelings and has attempted to make women visible. The emphasis has been on equality and mutuality in the research relationship; interaction and collaboration have been seen as essential. Central to feminist research has been feminist theory (Stanley and Wise, 1993), the recognition of an alternative social reality and the need to contribute to the improvement of women's lives (see Chapter 4).

*What is feminist research practice?*

According to Maynard (1994) there has been a general acceptance by feminists of a distinctly 'feminist' mode of enquiry but no agreement on what this is. Indeed, she has questioned the idea that feminism is a method for conducting research. Harding (1987) too has argued against a distinctive feminist method of research. She suggests that there are only so many methods, but how the method is used may be different. For example this might include: listening carefully to what is being said, seeking to understand or observing behaviours and settings that traditionally have not been thought worthy of exploration. She has acknowledged a feminist epistemology and has confirmed that feminist research has challenged who can be a 'knower' and what is 'knowledge'. Subjectivity, it is argued, is knowledge:

> ... feminists have argued that traditional epistemologies, whether intentionally or unintentionally, systematically exclude the possibility that women could be knowers or agents of knowledge; they claim that the voice of science is a masculine one; that history is only written from the point of view of men; ... that the subject of a traditional sociological sentence is always assumed to be a man. They have proposed alternative theories of knowledge that legitimate women as knowers.
>
> (Harding, 1987: 3)

Harding (1987) has also identified distinctive features of feminist research. Firstly, women experience phenomena they think need explanation and feminist research generates its 'problematics' from the perspective of women's experience. Secondly, there is recognition of the importance of using women's experiences, revealed by women, as the source of social analyses. And finally, questions that need answering are rarely in forms such as pure truths but rather enable us to understand and change. Feminist research should therefore be for women and offer explanations for women (see also Reinharz 1992). Harding (1987) claimed that:

> ... while studying women is not new, studying them from the perspective of their own experience so that women can understand themselves and the world, can claim virtually no history at all.
>
> (Harding, 1987: 8)

Kelly (1988) preferred the phrase 'feminist research practice', arguing that what distinguishes feminist research is the questions that have been asked. Feminist researchers are part of a process of discovery and understanding with the goal of creating useful knowledge to be used by ourselves and others in order to make a difference. Indeed, Kelly et al (1994) went on to question some of the orthodoxies of feminist research. For example, whilst agreeing that feminist research is on and with women, they contended that we must pay attention to the ways in which women's lives are structured. Further, in the challenge to 'androcentric' research, feminist researchers have tended to use qualitative approaches in a rather uncritical manner, often assuming an automatic value for participants of participating in research projects. They have suggested (Kelly et al

1994: 36) that we need to look more critically at the experience of 'participation' and consider the potential for harm on participants of 'intrusions' into their lives: 'Several feminists have noted recently that the fact that in-depth ethnographic methods reduces distance, means that the potential for harm increases.' It was their contention that the notion of reflexivity, which is so integral to feminist research, ought to extend to our participants such that they concluded: 'we are now committed to self-consciously studying the impact of participation in research, which includes inviting feedback from participants on our research design' (Kelly et al, 1994: 36).

Feminist research often makes claims for the empowerment of participants. However, Kelly et al (1994) have challenged this claim, arguing strongly that participation in a research project is unlikely to transform the condition of a woman's life. We certainly need to ask about the benefits for women of participating in our research but we must not overstate 'empowerment issues'; it is the researchers who really have the power and who have a vested interest in the end product.

> It is we who have the time, the resources and skills to conduct methodical work, to make sense of the experience, and locate individuals in historic and social contexts.
>
> (Kelly et al, 1994: 36).

It is suggested that we can and should involve our participants in discussion about the data and even to some extent in the analysis, but it is illusory to think that full involvement and empowerment is possible in anything other than a participatory research project.

By contrast, Opie (1992: 64) has presented an alternative view of empowerment and research, arguing that there are several ways that women may be empowered through participation in a research project. Firstly, through their contribution in making a social issue visible and secondly, through the therapeutic effect of being able to reflect on and re-evaluate their experience as part of the process of being interviewed. Both of these, she has contended, are valid.

*The role of the feminist researcher*

Feminist researchers have challenged objectivist/positivist claims of researcher invisibility by situating the researcher explicitly within the research process. The role of the researcher is made explicit in feminist research. In fact, critical reflection of the researcher's role in the production of data is part of the analysis. Feminist researchers claim that this strengthens the quality of the research. Paradoxically, introducing this subjective element into the analysis makes the work more objective because it makes subjectivity visible (Oakley, 1981). And, according to Miller (1991, cited in Stacey, 1997: 64):

> For many feminists, the introduction of personal criticism (writing the self) is a strategic disruption of the smooth surface of the abstract universalising theories that have constituted women in 'lack, invisibility and silence'...
>
> (Miller, 1991: 7)

It is acknowledged that the researcher has considerable power in research relationships. In order for others to assess the influence of this power and thus evaluate the validity of the findings, the researcher needs to consciously address her, own role. The idea of controlling researcher bias is illusory (Oakley, 1981) and instead the researcher becomes an active player in a reciprocal research relationship. As a consequence, she also becomes involved in the construction of findings. A feminist researcher will therefore spend time explaining the purpose of her research to participants, the assumptions underlying it and sharing her own experiences. Oakley (1981) argued strongly for exchange and participation both on ideological grounds (offering support to other women) and as a pre-requisite for establishing trust and furthermore contended that involvement enhances rather than jeopardises data:

> ... the mythology of 'hygienic ' research with its mystification of the researcher and the researched as objective instruments of data production must be replaced by a recognition that personal involvement is more than dangerous bias - it is the condition under which people come to know each other , and to admit others into their lives.
>
> (Oakley, 1981: 58)

Making the research process explicit (placing the researcher and participants in the same critical plane) is an attempt to make the researcher's influence more visible. It is also an attempt to redress the power imbalance inherent in the research relationship, particularly when the participants are from marginalized groups. The task is to develop commonalities in order to share knowledge. Neysmith (1995) has acknowledged that even though commonalities in research relationships may sometimes be few, it is still important to develop links of recognition. However, there is also recognition that without an appreciation of why it is important to do this, the process can be seen as: 'ritualistic at best and condescending at worst ...' (Neysmith, 1995: 107). I now explore this issue further.

*Acknowledging the limits of feminist research practice*

Andrews (1991), who has been critical of an approach that overemphasises commonalities, particularly gender, at the expense of acknowledging other differences such as age, class, race, culture, and education, recommended caution regarding over-identification. Such a view was echoed by Sangster (1994) who confirmed that in stressing commonalities we could be masking our own privilege. Our analysis for example may be different from that of those we are researching; they may reject both the image we portray and our feminist perspective. Our view of the world may be different from their view and we must recognise that it is our privilege and access to knowledge that enables us to interpret. We must therefore acknowledge differences and not overemphasise the collaboration; after all whose is the end product?

A number of researchers (Stacey, 1991; Bornat, 1993; Standing, 1998) have reminded us that however equal methods of access and interviewing are, the researcher holds the real power when we take women's words and thoughts into the academy. Researchers decide which words to use, how to interpret the words and how to represent the women's voices. Indeed, Bornat (1993) and Standing (1998) both noted that some of their participants requested that they 'tidy up' their words for publication. As feminist researchers we must be prepared to acknowledge our power and our responsibility in this unequal relationship but certainly not exploit it (Stacey, 1991).

*Women's voices as 'gendered scripts'*

Anderson et al (1987) have stressed the role of feminist research in listening to women's voices. Indeed, in order to find out about women's lives, we need to let women talk about their feelings and to explore with them what their language means. Daley (1998) writing about women's memories of the Second World War, suggested that women's memories of the past are couched in terms of how they felt about particular situations rather than necessarily factual. Furthermore: 'memories have been shaped by prevailing ideas of gender appropriate behaviour and values' (Daley, 1998: 243). What women remember and retell and how they tell it, conveys much about their individual and collective experience. Alongside this, feminist research also allows us to consider the silences and the omissions in women's stories (Bornat, 1993).

According to Sangster (1994) women's narratives are liable to be characterised by understatements and avoidance of the first person, with often little mention of personal accomplishments. Being embedded in family life may shape their view of the world and their role in it and even impact on their consciousness of historical time, such as their use of benchmarks that often accord with the family life cycle. Ray (2000) drew on feminist autobiographical criticism to argue for the notion of 'gendered scripts' as a way of understanding and interpreting women's stories. These are socially and/or culturally constructed scripts that women use, either consciously or unconsciously to tell their stories. Ray (2000: 75-76) has argued that cultural scripts, which define: 'the "appropriate" ways to live and tell about a life' are constraints, alongside the more predictable ones of lived experience and memory, in the telling of a life story. Furthermore:

> ... a life story is interesting primarily for the way it reveals - to use feminist critic Sidonie Smith's words – 'the way the autobiographer situates herself and her story in relation to cultural ideologies and figures of selfhood ....' In particular Smith shows how the ideology of gender 'has always constituted **a** if not **the** fundamental ideological system for interpreting and understanding individual identity and social dynamics'...
>
> (Ray, 2000: 77)

According to Ray (2000) the female self in autobiography is:

> ... typically self-effacing rather than self-promoting; oriented toward private rather than public life; responsive to others needs and desires before her own; more likely to foreground relationships and subjective states to over accomplishments; and anecdotal in her means of expression

(Ray, 2000: 77)

Therefore, when we listen to women's voices, we need to be aware of prevailing ideologies relating to the lives of women at different times and we also need to be prepared to explore their emotional and subjective experience. We must both tune into and value these gendered scripts. This leads feminist researchers to seek an approach that allows women to reflect on their experience and choose for themselves which experiences and feelings are central to their own past.

*Theorising experience*

The legitimacy of women's understanding of their experiences is one of the hallmarks of both feminist theory and feminist research practice. Feminists attach epistemological importance to experience, suggesting that experiential accounts can act as windows on the 'social'. However, there is no such thing as raw experience; people's accounts of their lives are culturally embedded and I, the researcher, am also both culturally embedded and involved in interpretation because my work is theoretically grounded. According to Maynard (1994: 23): 'No feminist study can be politically neutral, completely inductive, or solely based on grounded theory, this is a contradiction in terms'. When researching women's lives we need to take their experience seriously but we also need to 'take our own theory seriously and use the theory to make sense of ... the experience' (Cain, 1986: 265). An interpretative and synthesising process that connects experience to understanding, must then take place.

Furthermore, Skeggs (1995) has cautioned that experience is always 'mediated'; those being researched give researchers an account, an interpretation or a representation of their lives. What we researchers then write up is also mediated by our experience and our personal, situated view of the world (Riessman, 1993). There is not a straightforward link between experience, and truth and knowledge. Accessing experience as researchers does not mean we access and reproduce something unmediated. Our task becomes one of understanding the interpretations in operation on the part of the researcher and the researched as part and parcel of the substance of the experience related.

*Summary*

Qualitative, feminist inquiry is therefore a way of both enabling the voices of older widows to be heard and exploring the experience of later life widowhood. Moreover, it has the potential to enable both the participants and the researcher to be active participants in the research process. It offers the possibility of collaboration in the process of data generation and a more equal research relationship. However, it also has its limits as I have outlined. This is particularly important to acknowledge when researching with a marginalized group such as older widows.

Reinharz (1992) has noted that although there is no particular feminist research method, the unstructured or semi structured interview is often favoured by feminist researchers. Indeed, Anderson et al (1987: 104) have contended that the feminist biographical interview is a particularly useful tool to use to find out about: 'previously overlooked lives, activities and feelings of women. When women speak for themselves, they reveal hidden realities: new experiences and new perspectives emerge.'

I now move the discussion to consider the potential of such a method for researching later life widowhood.

## Biographical methods of research

The life story or biographical method was central to the Chicago School of Sociology that in the 1930s developed the gathering of life stories as a method of data collection (Plummer, 2001). Fundamental to this approach to research was the choice of subjects from whom the life stories were to be drawn; they were 'ordinary' people, whose lives were either not 'visible' or were considered not respectable. Sympathy with the subjects' position was implicit. According to Chamberlayne et al (2000) present day interest in biographies has its origins both in the 'more general qualitative backlash', that questioned positivist assumptions of quantitative analysis as the more specific developments in feminist research, gerontology and disability discussed in an earlier chapter.

The biographical method has the potential to help both the researcher and the researched to understand the pattern of a life in relation to the present. Atkinson (1998: 3) has argued that: 'as a method of looking at life-as-a-whole and as a way of carrying out an in-depth study of individual lives, the life story interview stands alone.' The biographical method thus acknowledges both subjectivity (Atkinson, 1998) and the totality of a person's life (Miller, 2000).

### *Narratives*

In my study, I have subscribed to what Miller (2000) calls the 'narrative' approach to life story collection:

> The narrative approach bases itself fundamentally upon the ongoing development of the respondent's viewpoint during the telling of a life…'story'. Understanding the individual's unique and changing perspective as it is mediated by context takes precedence over questions of fact.

> (Miller, 2000: 15)

In keeping with Ruth et al (1996) who suggested that life as a story is something other than a true verbatim copy of the life lived, I was interested in the way in which each older widow perceived her life history and her perception of its impact on the present, rather than factual information about her life. I recognise that this implies acceptance of the nature of the narrative interview as one in which the interplay between the participants and myself was the core source of information. Indeed, I would argue that it was the manner in which the life story developed and was related during the course of the interview(s) that provided the essential avenue to understanding. This requires an acceptance that there is not one single objective reality that is factual and which exists at a level of abstraction beyond the interview. The story that each woman told me is the story she chose to tell me at a particular point in time. For Miller (2000: 17) this situational view of reality as fluid is an essential part of the narrative approach. Arguing from a more specifically feminist perspective, the Personal Narratives Group (1989) have confirmed the importance of this view:

> When talking to someone about their lives, people lie sometimes, forget a lot, exaggerate, become confused, and get things wrong. Yet, they are revealing truths. These 'truths' don't actually reveal the past "as it actually was" aspiring to a standard of objectivity. They give us instead the truths of our experiences.
>
> (Personal Narratives Group, 1989: 261)

Narrative life stories therefore have to be accepted for what they are: an individual's own account of her life, seen through her own memories at a point in her life. This does not detract from their value as a method of data collection instead it adds a unique dimension, the subjective, to our understanding of later life widowhood.

*History*

The historical context is another important issue in the life story interview. In keeping with the 'Life Course Paradigm' of Giele and Elder (1998) time and time related issues are central to the holistic viewpoint that lies at the core of the biographical perspective. Plummer (1983, 2001) for example, referred to the centrality of the historical experience. This historical approach does not necessarily rely on factual information but rather allows individuals to reflect on external events as they have impacted on their lives.

*What is a biographical interview?*

There are many answers to this deceptively simple question. Yow (1994: 168) for example defined the biographical interview as: 'the account by an individual of his or her life that is recorded in some way, by taping or writing, for another person who edits and presents that account'. However, for Atkinson (1998: 8) the life story interview comprised: 'the story a person chooses to tell about the life he or she has lived, told as completely and honestly as possible, what is remembered of it, and what the teller...wants others to know of it, usually as a result of a guided interview by another.' This is not simply the recording of a testimony but rather an interaction between the interviewer and the interviewee. As a researcher, the life story interview offered me an opportunity to gain greater insight and understanding of the subjective experience of women who have become widows in later life and enabled me to better explore the 'meaning' of that experience from their own perspective (Di Gregorio, 1986; Dant and Gearing, 1990).

*Why should women participate?*

Oakley (1981) highlighted the positive effects of taking part in an interview for those being interviewed, an important consideration for feminist researchers who wish participants to 'gain' from the research process. Yow (1994: 118) however stated that this 'gain' is dependent on the interviewer communicating to the woman being interviewed: 'you have something to say that I think is important; I listen and I accept that your version of the story is true for you; I seek to understand rather than to judge'. Furthermore:

> ...the process of reflecting during an oral history interview can be a way to understand anew some things that happened and a means of coming to accept the things that have hurt. Each person is creative in the way that she or he weaves from various life experiences - both the pleasant and the devastating - a whole cloth ...
>
> (Yow, 1994: 119)

There are a number ways in which an individual might gain from taking part in a life story interview (Atkinson, 1998). Through the telling of her story, she might gain a clearer perspective on her own personal experience and feelings; this can bring greater meaning to her current life. This is akin to participating in a life review (Butler, 1980) in which an individual both reflects and takes stock of her life, whilst sharing it with an interested listener. She can gain joy and satisfaction from this sharing and it has the potential to be a purging and/or a validating process. In some cases, it can help an individual see their life more clearly and perhaps enable her to make changes. Allport (1942) for example, suggested that some people tell their life stories to others because they sense an opportunity to justify the way they have lived and they like to give their own perspective on life. They might want the life story for someone else such as a child or grandchild or they might just value an opportunity to talk to an interested listener. For others, there is the desire to create order from disparate events and yet others may participate for altruistic reasons, such as passing on knowledge to future generations (Erikson et al, 1986).

However we need to be cautious not to overstate the gains because not everyone either enjoys or benefits from telling their story. Indeed, the work of Coleman (1986, 1996) has challenged the view that reminiscence is a natural process of ageing in which everyone willingly engages and concludes instead, that there are a number of different responses to reminiscence. Some people want to reminisce and find it a positive process. Some people do not want to reminisce and do not feel the need to do so. However, another group of people do not want to reminisce because they find the process of reviewing their life to be both painful and negative. This last group looks back on life with regret and is unable to make changes. As a researcher therefore, it is essential to acknowledge that not all women will automatically wish to participate in life story research.

## Feminist practice and life story research

I have situated my life story research with older widows within the framework of feminist inquiry, which, as I discussed earlier, sees reflexivity and collaboration as part of the research process (Oakley, 1981; Burman, 1989). The interviewer and the interviewee are working in partnership, with the interaction being seen as fundamental to the research. The Personal Narratives group (1989: 201) have suggested that life stories collected through such feminist research reflect the collaboration between the 'original narrator' who tells her life and 'the interpreter' who records or analyses various dimensions of the relationship between narrator and interpreter. And according to Yow (1994: 187) researchers must:

> Be open to the possibility of different ways of framing the life experiences. Seeking to understand the narrator's view of the life, contrasting it with your view of the life, and presenting different ways to interpret the meanings of the evidence result in a rich biography, not a one dimensional account.

However, feminist life story research is not solely about reflexivity and collaboration, it is also grounded in feminist theory (see Chapter 4 and earlier this chapter). The Personal Narratives Group (1989: 4) have confirmed that women's personal narratives are essential primary documents for feminist research: 'since feminist theory is grounded in women's lives and aims to analyse the role and meaning of gender in those lives and in society'. In this book I do not subscribe to any specific feminist theory but rather, as discussed in Chapter 4, draw on some of the common threads of feminist theories: woman as subject; the centrality of experience; the foregrounding of the 'personal is political'; diversity; and patriarchy.

Widowhood in later life is an individual experience but one, which because it takes place in a social context and has a history, is nonetheless socially structured. Therefore, the use of feminist life story research to research later life widowhood has the potential, firstly, to enable an exploration of historical and social differences and similarities which women bring to later life widowhood, and the structures in which these have taken place and thus allow the emergence of the whole person in her social and highly gendered world. Secondly, such an approach has the potential to challenge some of the stereotypes of later life, particularly those that have problematized later life widowhood (see Chapter 4). Older women suffer from a process of negative stereotyping that portrays their lives as emotionally narrow or deprived (Bernard and Meade, 1993; Gibson, 1996). A life history approach allows the possibility to see beyond that stereotype and see the individual throughout her life. Indeed, feminist disability literature (for example: Morris, 1989, 1992; Thomas, 1999) has taken this further suggesting that the very process of allowing disabled women's voices to be heard has the potential to both engage and empower. I argue in the course of subsequent chapters that this is also the case for older widows. And finally, life history accounts reveal the differences older women bring to later life (Bornat, 1993). A biographical approach thus acknowledges that widowhood is only one part of a woman's life and therefore such an approach enables women to tell their story and situate widowhood within their whole biography.

*The interactive nature of feminist life story research*

A life history interview therefore is not simply the recording of one woman's story by another. It is an interaction of two people who come together for the purpose of the research, both with their own agendas whether conscious or unconscious. These agendas need to be teased out in the discourse in order to evaluate the content of the discussion. A feminist biographical interviewer must pay heed to differences as well as commonalities.

Typically, it is the researcher who exercises most power in the interview; it is she who initiates the project (Andrews, 1991) and sets the parameters even in a semi-structured or unstructured interview. Borland (1990) has also reminded us that it is likely that as interviewer we will have had our consciousness formed in a different social and historical reality and therefore it is crucial to open up an exchange of ideas with our interviewees in order not to just gather information to fit our own paradigm. In employing a feminist model of biographical research we must adopt a non-hierarchical approach and make reflexivity part of the process.

Along with other feminist researchers, I acknowledge the challenge to so-called hygienic research (Oakley, 1981) and argue for exchange and participation on both ideological grounds (offering support to other women) and as a way of gaining trust in order to better understand interviewees' experiences. This involvement enhances rather than jeopardises the quality of my data and allows for considerable flexibility. As Anderson (1991) has suggested, the spontaneous exchange that can take place within such interviews offers the possibility of freedom for researchers and interviewees alike.

The interactive nature of the interview allows for clarification in the way that quantitative methods do not (Jack, 1991). An unstructured or semi-structured interview provides the opportunity for women to talk about what is important to them rather than being guided along pre-conceived paths. For example, a negative view of widowhood would emphasise problems, whereas providing women with the opportunity to talk about their past and present allows an exploration of the issues which are important to them. Within a feminist model, the interviewee is always encouraged to say what she thinks rather than what she thinks the researcher wants her to say. However, as Bornat (1993) has noted, there is never absolute flexibility and freedom:

> However friendly and informal, an interview cannot be the same as a conversation. It has a product, an account which one person takes away either on tape or as notes. It has a formal beginning and an end which means it may leave things unsaid, ideas unspoken. It is usually a one way process of questioning with one person dictating the direction and pace.
>
> (Bornat, 1993: 25)

Barriers, both of context and difference, exist and the researcher must be respectful of them. There is a delicate balance to be struck in feminist biographical research, where the researcher is concerned with issues of power, between enabling the voice of older women to be heard and achieving an end product. Given that the actual process of carrying out biographical research is so crucial it is worthy of further discussion.

## Conducting a life story interview

Dant and Gearing (1991) have written that although there is no single or correct way to conduct an interview, openness and involvement from the beginning are important. This is of course essential for those engaged in feminist research practice. The researcher needs to be honest with her interviewees in order to build and maintain trust. The first communication, whether by telephone or by letter, must be seen as the opportunity to start this process. This is particularly important when initial contact is made by a third person. The interview can then be an opportunity to explore and share within an ongoing, trusting relationship. In the current study, for most of the older widows it was the first opportunity they had had to share their life story. Others had encouraged them in the early days of bereavement to express their grief and, latterly, to 'move on' or 'get on with your life', but few had had the opportunity to reflect on their past experiences and relate these to their current situation.

   The process of sharing a life story can be empowering for older women and humbling for the researcher. As Bornat (1993: 23) revealed: 'as an interviewer I always find myself in awe as I listen to older people's life experiences'. She noted an overwhelming sense of inequality, in which the researcher must be sensitive to the memories and feelings that are being shared. Respect, understanding and empathy must be integral to the interviewing process. Following the advice of Anderson and Jack (1991: 25) I learned when interviewing older widows to listen 'in stereo' to what was or was not being said and to go beyond stereotypes to find out what was really being shared. When practising feminist research and listening to women's words we must be careful to receive: 'both the dominant and the muted channels clearly...tuning into them carefully to understand the relationship between them' (Anderson and Jack, 1991: 25). This includes listening to the silences as well as the words.

A biographical interview is thus a very effective method that allows the interviewer to ask questions not only about events but also about motivation, reflection, interpretation and feelings. It is of its very nature structured by 'biography' but the form of the interview may be quite unstructured, thus allowing a woman to tell her story and express her thoughts in her own way, in the order she chooses. Thompson (1990) however has questioned the existence of a completely free flowing interview - there has to be a beginning, a scene setting and the purpose of the interview must be explained. This in itself can cause problems of unspoken assumptions and expectations that shape what follows.

It is clearly essential to think very carefully about the skills that are necessary to conduct this type of research. Although not specifically referring to feminist biographical interviews, Mason's caution to qualitative interviewers is highly relevant:

> ... in the absence of a pre-designed set and sequence of questions, the qualitative interviewer has to prepare themselves to be able to 'think on their feet' in the interview itself. They have to do this quickly, effectively, coherently and in ways which are consistent with their research questions. They need to be able to ensure that the interview interaction actually does generate relevant data, which means simultaneously orchestrating the intellectual and social dynamics of the situation. ... A qualitative interviewer has to be ready to make on the spot decisions about the content and the sequence of the interview as it progresses.
>
> (Mason, 1996: 43)

The formidable task of conducting such an interview is highlighted:

> At any one time, you may be: listening to what the interviewee is...currently saying and trying to interpret what they mean; trying to work out whether what they are saying has any bearing on 'what you really want to know'; trying to think in new and creative ways about 'what you really want to know'; trying to pick up on your interviewee's demeanour and interpret these; ...reflecting on something they said twenty minutes ago; formulating an appropriate response to what they are currently saying; formulating the next question which might involve shifting the interview onto new terrain; keeping an eye on your watch and making decisions about depth and breadth given your time limits.
>
> (Mason, 1996: 45)

Add to this the complexities of feminist research practice outlined earlier and it becomes very apparent that qualitative, feminist life story interviewing is not to be undertaken by the fainthearted!

## Validity and reliability

The very nature of the reflexive, collaborative feminist life story method means that no two researchers will carry out, or analyse the data from, an interview in the same way (Atkinson, 1998). Runyan (1982: 3-4) has suggested that: 'critics of life history method argue that such studies are based on retrospective and introspective data of uncertain validity'. However, it has been argued by others (Plummer, 1983; 2001; Andrews, 1991; Atkinson, 1998) that validity is dependent upon the intent or the purpose of the investigation and the very essence of life history research is to understand the way in which the person who has lived it recalls a life. Perhaps of greater importance is the issue of internal consistency: what is said in one part of the narrative should not contradict what is said in another. There are inconsistencies in life, but stories of what happened and what did not happen, should be consistent within themselves.

The application of the following criteria is recommended:

- Corroboration: does the transcription still sound like the original narration? It is important to check with the narrator and enable her to claim ownership of her script (Plummer, 1983; Atkinson, 1998).
- Persuasion: does the story strike a resonant cord, does it persuade, compel, delight, stimulate or invite us? (Andrews, 1991; Atkinson, 1998).

One test of success is whether those being studied accept the researcher's account and whether it rings true, what has been described as a 'member test of validity' (Atkinson, 1998). Although acknowledging that this 'test' has been subject to debate (Bloor, 1983), Atkinson (1998) has nonetheless claimed:

> The underlying standard here is that the story teller has the final say in telling the story, even after it has been transcribed, because he or she is the one telling the story in the first place and is the one to determine how it all fits together, what sense it makes, and whether or not it is a valid story.
>
> (Atkinson, 1998: 61)

Plummer (2001: 155) too has long argued that in life story research validity should come first, reliability second: there is no point being very precise about nothing! If the subjective story is what the researcher is after, the life history approach becomes the most valid method. Indeed, both Plummer (2001) and Atkinson (1998) have refuted the need to apply standard, quantitative tests of reliability and validity to life story research.

The question of validity as raised in discussions of practitioner research is also pertinent. McLeod (1999), for example, has argued that although practitioner research makes use of the validity criteria associated with a wide range of qualitative (and quantitative) research methods, there are also additional criteria, which need to apply. Firstly, there is 'descriptive validity', that is 'the accurate and sensitive description of the phenomenon being studied' (McLeod 1999: 18). Secondly, 'personal validity', that reflects 'the personal trustworthiness or credibility of the researcher' (McLeod 1999: 18). In order to meet these criteria of validity, the study must include sufficient detail of the research participants and the overall context in which the research is carried out. In addition it must provide sufficient information on the researcher's role, and engagement, in the study 'for the reader to be able to make a judgement concerning authenticity, ownership and personal integrity' (McLeod 1999: 18). In effect, it is suggested that the study must be explicitly honest and open. As well as being 'valid' therefore, the study also needs to be ethical.

## Ethical Issues

Feminist researchers are as concerned to produce an ethical research design as to produce an intellectually coherent and compelling one. Ethical considerations thus need to be addressed within the whole research design. For example, access to participants and their participation must be on the basis of informed consent. We need to be particularly vigilant when accessing participants via so-called 'gatekeepers' to ensure that no coercion has taken place (Sapsford and Abbott, 1992).

Biographical research with older women is potentially extremely ethically sound in that the older woman has the choice of selection, what to say and what not to say. Further, the older woman is the expert on her own life and so the power relationship is potentially more balanced than in other types of research. It is vital that the researcher does not abuse this. For example, as the relationship between interviewer and interviewee develops the interviewee is likely to feel safe and offer more information than maybe she would have done in a more formal research interview. Stacey (1991) has reminded us that we must not abuse this very intimacy that the relationship generates; otherwise we are in danger of oppressing the very people we sought to empower through the research process.

The essence of in-depth biographical interviewing is that there are subtle ethical issues in the interpersonal relationship, which are not easy to define. Power is not equal but tipped in favour of the interviewer. Indeed, Patai (1987) has concluded that the possibility of exploitation is built into every research project that uses human beings as sources of information:

> We ask of the people we interview the kind of revelation of their inner life that normally only occurs in situations of great intimacy and within the private realm. Yet these revelations are made within the context of the public sphere- which is where in an obvious sense, we situate ourselves when we appear with our tape recorders and our notepads ... while shyly curious, interviewees never, to my knowledge, make a reciprocal exchange a condition of the interview. And researchers are always much less frank than they hope their subjects will be.
>
> (Patai, 1987: 18)

Accordingly, Miller (2000) has cautioned the researcher to set ground rules and agree a contract. It is important not to build up expectations of the research relationship developing into a social one, nor to make promises, which cannot possibly be fulfilled. He warned of:

...the possible vulnerability of participants in a biographical study means that the usual strictures about giving potential participants in a study a clear enough explanation so that they can exercise a truly informed consent deserve even more emphasis than usual. As well as taking care during the collection of information, researchers should ensure that the closing of an interview relationship is done with care and should make it possible for respondents to contact the research team at a later date.

(Miller, 2000: 105)

There is both intensity and an intimacy in feminist life story research, which does not exist even in other qualitative research methods. As such, it is vitally important that researchers pay heed to ethical issues at every stage of the research process: ethical access; framing ethical research questions; ethical data collection; and ethical analysis (Mason, 1996). The interviewer must constantly question her own feminist research practice to ascertain that it is ethical and to be prepared to justify it (Reinharz, 1992). It is important for the researcher to think about what she asks and also how she asks it.

Informed consent, an essential pre-requisite in most research in gerontology (Kenyon, 1996), is a fundamental requirement in feminist biographical research if there is to be mutual trust between the researcher and the narrator. Although not specifically discussing feminist research practice Mason's (1996) recommendations that we ask ourselves the following questions concerning informed consent, are particularly helpful for feminist researchers. Is it consent to:

- Participate in the interview? Is that the same as agreeing to answer every question I ask? What about opportunities to withdraw at any stage? Do I renegotiate at several points during the interaction?
- Give me the right to use the data collected in whatever way I see fit? Does the woman understand that 'data' might include, for example, non-verbal communication or 'off the record' information?
- Give me the right to interpret and analyse the data, make comparisons with others (even though she might not be familiar with the techniques of data analysis)?
- Give me the right to publish or reproduce the data and the analysis?

(Mason, 1996: 58)

It may never be possible to get consent that is truly informed, but the researcher needs to reflect these questions in the research process and think through the implications. In summary, Mason (1996) has recommended that the researcher should take the issues of informed consent more rather than less seriously.

The researcher needs to think carefully about how she guarantees confidentiality, particularly when, in the interests of validity, she wants to make explicit the phenomenon and the context under study (Mason, 1996; McLeod, 1999). The very nature of qualitative, biographical research generates rich, detailed data. How this is to be presented, and how much the participant wishes to be visible, needs to be openly discussed. Anonymity is not always desired and there may be occasions when some participants wish to be identified (Yow, 1994).

Confidentiality and anonymity therefore must be negotiated as part of informed consent.

There is an added responsibility on feminist researchers to make sure that consent remains informed and that participants are neither exploited nor come to any harm. Renegotiating informed consent at each meeting, making explicit the research process, and involvement at all stages of that process, are all ways of ensuring that this happens.

*A cautionary word on feminist research ethics*

Feminist research ethics however are sometimes hard to manage in practice as Skeggs (1995) has acknowledged:

> I began the research with some knowledge of feminist research ethics: I wanted to reciprocate, not exploit, not abuse power, to care, to empower, and to be honest. Putting these principles into practice was often difficult
>
> (Skeggs, 1995: 197)

Her aim was to make visible 'young working class women' but most of her participants rejected the label 'working class' that she was using in her analysis; indeed they were expending vast amounts of money and energy into **not** being working class. Despite the rejection of this label by her participants, Skeggs (1995) needed to use her academic frameworks to make sense of their situation. Drawing on Harding (1991) Skeggs (1995) contended:

> … it may be … useful to think about knowledge being produced through different discursive sites in which the researcher and the researched have different access to discursive resources. I had access through higher education to feminist and sociological explanations, which led to my understandings.
>
> (Skeggs, 1995: 200)

This may well be extremely helpful advice when as feminist researchers we find ourselves at odds with our participants and our own feminist ethics. We have to take responsibility for our own academic frameworks and in the course of doing so surely we are only acknowledging our differences.

## Data Analysis

Having discussed these complexities in some detail, I now move on to the analysis of feminist life story interviews. As Thomas (1999) has reminded us:

> Narratives are representations involving interpretation and selection in their construction (the 'telling'), in their consumption (my 'reading') in their reproduction (my 're-presentation'), and in their further interpretations (your 'reading').
>
> (Thomas, 1999: 7)

There are indeed many ways of 'telling', 'reading', 're-presentation' and 'interpretation', all of which may be valid (Riessman, 1993). My analysis in the current study consists of a thematic analysis (Luborsky, 1994) of older widows' life stories, which is informed by a feminist, life course perspective which, as I argued earlier, has the potential to enable us to see later life widowhood through a different lens and will be guided by feminist research practice. My analysis therefore, although grounded in the words of the women who participated, is modified by the perspective that informs it. According to Kelly et al (1994):

> The most basic yet fundamental feminist question has always been 'why?' Exploring with individuals why they think and act as they do enriches our understanding, and is a far stronger base from which to explore potential change than knowing only what they think and do.
>
> (Kelly, 1994: 39)

This is not an easy task and Jack (1991: 18) has recommended the following stages in our analysis. Firstly, when carrying out the interview:

- Immersion in the interview
- Not intruding
- Not interrupting or diverting
- Following the narrator's lead
- Noting our own personal discomfort

And, secondly, when the data has been collected:

- Immersion in the data (written/ tape recorded)
- Listening to ourselves
- Listening to the woman's moral language
- Listening to the meta statements (where the woman stops and comments on her own language/ thoughts)
- Listening to the logic of the narrative and recurring themes
- Trusting our own hunches
- Noticing our own areas of confusion/ uncertainty
- Honouring integrity and privacy

In this way, Jack (1991) suggested that through 'listening' and 'noticing' we analyse the complexities of women's lives, and start to answer the 'why?' question. But how do we manage the vast amount of data that this process generates within a life story interview? .

According to Atkinson (1998), there are three stages in the analysis of life stories: reading the story as a whole; understanding the parts; drawing out patterns and themes or sub-plots. This is corroborated by Miller (2000: 132-35) who contended that these three stages are inextricably linked. Firstly, the biographical life history is constructed, with factual details being clarified and ordered. This is similar to Miles and Huberman's (1994) recommendation to render the data manageable. Secondly, a thematic field analysis, or what Luborsky (1994: 193) identified as the discovery of 'life themes', is conducted via a process of coding. Life story researchers acknowledge that the story that is told is, of necessity, selective, and so the narrated story will represent: 'a sequence of mutually interrelated themes which between them form a dense network of interconnected cross references' (Miller 2000: 133). The purpose of the analysis is to elucidate those themes, which then enables the researcher to move on to the third stage and 'dig deeper' (Miller 2000: 135) to understand the past and present experience of those participating in the research, via the sub-plots in their narratives.

For life story researchers, this analysis is thus the active construction of the respondent's view of her life. Feminist practice takes the analysis one stage further by firstly incorporating reflexivity and collaboration and secondly by engaging with feminist theory.

**Conclusion**

In this chapter I have drawn on the literature to explore both the methodology and the method, which has underpinned the current study. I have discussed both the 'why' of qualitative research and feminist research practice and the 'how' of carrying out feminist, biographical, life story research. Indeed, I have justified my intention to use such a feminist, qualitative approach by highlighting the limitations of previous research. Further, I have justified my intention to engage in feminist research with older women for ideological, personal and practical reasons. I have noted the importance of paying attention to the interaction of the research relationship and the role of the researcher within that process. I have also highlighted the importance of understanding the diverse, subjective experience of research participants, whilst acknowledging the problematic nature of experience, which itself is structured by prevailing conditions. I have discussed the need to address power relationships in life story interviewing, and stressed the importance of feminist researchers working hard to redress that imbalance wherever possible (whilst acknowledging that it may not always be possible and that there will be limitations to the process). I have also highlighted the complexities of carrying out semi-structured life story interviews and the challenges presented 'in the field'. I have explored the problematic area of validity and drawn attention to the importance of ethical research, at all stages in the research process. Drawing on Mason (1996) I have indicated that although it may not always be possible to get true informed consent, feminist researchers must pay more rather than less attention to this part of the research process. Finally I have acknowledged that feminist research practice is often difficult and that as a researcher I have to take account of my own academic frameworks to make sense of the world, which is inhabited by my participants.

In the next chapter I discuss my experience of carrying out feminist, biographical research. I discuss my data collection and the procedures used to analyse that data. Throughout, I reflect on the experience of putting research theory into practice and discuss the many dilemmas I encountered.

# Chapter 6

# Out in the Field

## Introduction

This chapter is about research design and practice and the application of the theoretical perspectives and ideas discussed in the previous chapters to the study of later life widowhood. Novice researchers will find this helpful in learning about the reality of applying theory to practice and undertaking work 'out in the field' whereas more experienced researchers will be able to compare and contrast their own techniques and experiences with those of the author. I make no apologies for the inclusion of such a technical chapter: my message throughout the book and in this chapter in particular is that the way in which we carry out our fieldwork has implications for quality and type of data that we collect. Therefore, I explain how I set about gathering the data (the stories which tell of the subjective experience) and I also explore the dilemmas and complexities that I faced out in the field. I detail the interactions that took place within the interviews and demonstrate how I tried to address the inherent power imbalance. I pay particular attention to the ethical issues that arose during the course of the fieldwork. Where appropriate, I have reflected on my own role in this whole process. I return to this later in Chapter 14, where I look back in more detail on both my role and my feelings about being an active participant in the research; at that point, I also discuss the reflections of the other participants.

It is important to remember that although the study was situated within feminist research practice, it did not actively set out to bring about change in the lives of the older widows participating in the study. I was however interested to explore the potential of feminist, biographical research to engage older widows through the telling of their stories, and to consider the possibility that this might incorporate personal change for some individuals. As a co-participant in the study, I was seeking to better understand each participant's experience of widowhood, to value that experience and to learn from it. Furthermore, the act of 'writing up' makes visible to others the differential experience of the participants and thus has the potential to challenge prevailing mythology.

In order to set the scene for what is to follow, I summarize below the stages in my fieldwork. Underpinning this is a research design that incorporates a feminist, life course perspective to explore the lives of older widows. The study relies on the qualitative method of data collection and analysis of data from loosely structured biographical interviews. This is reflected in the various stages of the research:

| Stages in the Fieldwork |
|---|
| 1. Test out the potential viability of life story research by engaging in a 'conversation with a purpose' with a friend and neighbour, who is an older widow. |
| 2. Begin a personal field diary in which to record my own feelings and reflections on the research process and my role within it. This will also be a useful tool through which I can critically evaluate my skills, comment on non-verbal interactions and raise ethical issues should they arise. |
| 3. Formulate procedures for contacting potential participants and develop a broad framework for interviewing, which incorporates content (biography) and process (feminist research practice). |
| 4. Make contact with a small sample of older widows in order to pilot the structure and process of the interviews. |
| 5. Conduct a series of tape-recorded, loosely-structured life story interviews with a small sample of older widows. |
| 6. Transcribe each interview and return the transcription of the interview to each woman. |
| 7. Conduct a second interview:<br>     - To clarify/amend/confirm/discuss the content of the transcription<br>     - To discuss the 'process' of the life story interview |
| 8.  Return amended transcriptions. |
| 9. Commence analysis of the pilot interviews. |
| 10. Deliver by hand/Send 'potted biography/summary of key events' by post. |
| 11. Revisit the structure and process of the interviews in the light of the pilot, make changes if necessary and then extend the sample until 'saturation' point. |
| 12. Repeat stages 5-10 for main fieldwork phases. |
| 13. At a later stage in the study (post analysis) return to discuss the overall findings (both content and process) with those women, who agree to still participate (acknowledging that this is likely to be a small proportion of the original participants). |

**Figure 6.1      The fieldwork**

**Testing the water**

An early decision was taken to hold a 'conversation with a purpose' with a neighbour who is an older widow, as part of my preparation for beginning the study. I was able to explore with her the possibility of using a biographical approach, the feasibility of engaging older women in the telling of their life stories, and ways of encouraging them to situate widowhood within that life story. I was able to explain in layperson's terms, my quest for qualitative, rather than quantitative, data in order to better understand the current 'lived experience' of later life widowhood. The story she had to tell, and the meanings she attached to that story, were more important than purely factual data. Our 'conversation' enabled me to explore the possible nature of the interaction, identify ways of beginning and ending the interview, explore potential content and generally discover the mechanics of carrying out a tape recorded interview as well as the reality of engaging in 'feminist research practice'.

In order to more rigorously test out the process, I subsequently undertook five pilot interviews The sample, an opportunistic sample gathered via neighbours, an ex-colleague who worked for the local Age Concern office and previous contacts, comprised five, older, white widows. They shared the following significant characteristics: all had been widowed at the age of 55 years or older ('on-time'); all had been widowed for more than five years (not in the acute state of bereavement); and none of them had remarried (all described themselves as 'widow'). From these pilot interviews a number of issues arose concerning: initial introductions; interview format (structure, the return of the transcriptions and second interview, field diary); ethical issues; level of involvement; and time.

Given that these issues were fundamental in undertaking subsequent fieldwork, I now briefly discuss each of them in turn.

*Initial introductions*

The importance of initial introductions was confirmed. Even with the women who were known to me beforehand it was important to outline the scope of the study, to set the parameters and establish initial informed consent. Having a prior discussion with each participant was essential in order to ensure that the consent given to share a life story was truly informed. Initial contact was by telephone, and each interview took place in the woman's home at a time convenient to her, thus bringing greater equality into the research: she was on her own territory whereas I was the visitor. A timetable was confirmed and privacy ensured. The use of the tape recorder was always discussed beforehand and fortunately it was not seen to be a problem. At the initial interview, more detailed introductions occurred and the purpose of the research was explained again. The tape recorder was switched on immediately as soon as initial politeness permitted.

*The interview format*

I had no original formal interview schedule but, as a result of my initial learning, the following format was used in the five pilot interviews.

I summarised the purpose of the interview and the way in which I hoped it would proceed, both in my initial contact (usually by telephone) and then again at the initial meeting. I re-iterated the overall commitment and timetable which was:

- There would be an initial interview, which would last about an hour and a half (two sides of a 90 minute cassette). This was based on an acknowledgement in the pre-pilot discussion that beyond this time it is difficult to concentrate. If the woman felt that she had not been able to fully tell her story within this time a further interview would be arranged within the very near future.

- The interview(s) would then be transcribed and returned within (at the most) 6 weeks. This time span allowed for time-consuming transcription to take place but also kept it within a reasonable time limit to maintain interest and continuity.
- There would then be a follow up interview to discuss the content of the transcription and the process of the research. I took very seriously the impact of participating in the research process for the older women who chose to be involved. A crucial stage in my research design therefore was this opportunity for each woman to discuss 'what it feels like to tell my story' and to reflect on her participation and role in the ongoing research.
- There would be contact by post to endorse a summary of key events/ biography.
- For those women who were still interested, there would be an opportunity at the very end of the study to discuss the overall research findings.

In line with my commitment to ethical research, I then discussed informed consent, confidentiality and anonymity. Within this discussion I highlighted the possible ways in which the data might be used: the research study itself, journal and conference papers, book chapters and so on. I confirmed her right to stop the interview at any point; to ask for the tape recorder to be switched off; to withdraw from the study at any point (during or after the interview). I acknowledged that I would try my utmost to maintain confidentiality and anonymity and that she would have access to the transcript in order to eliminate possible identifying factors. I reassured her that anything which was said when the tape recorder had been switched off (at her request) would not form part of the data, unless she specifically requested it to be so. I then asked each woman to choose a name by which she wished to be known in the research. I gave each woman my home telephone number and my work address so that she could contact me anytime during her involvement in the research.

*Structure*

I took note of Thompson's (1990: 199) comments concerning the impossibility of having a totally unstructured interview in my initial contact with each of my participants (see Chapter 5). I did not have a series of prepared questions that I wished to follow but I did have a very broad outline. I tried to stress to each woman, that I was interested in 'her' story, that I was exploring 'widowhood' as part of that life story and that it was up to her to decide how that story was to unfold. Despite these attempts, I am sure that I nonetheless inadvertently set expectations in my initial introductions. My body language and symbols, my age and background would have all set parameters to the discussion. I would argue however that although this does not affect the overall quality of the data that I collected, it does need to be part of my analysis and discussion of my findings.

I started off therefore by reaffirming my interest in her life before and after widowhood, but stressing that I was interested in her story. My review of the life story literature suggests that it is useful to break the ice by asking for some biographical information, so I asked for specific details relating to later life widowhood - age, how long married, when widowed. I then confirmed my interest in her life story and requested her to start wherever she wanted. If asked, I would prompt with the following 'life stages', gleaned from the literature: childhood; young adulthood; mid-life; getting older; life now. I re-assured her that there was no 'right' or 'wrong' way of telling this story.

She was then requested to begin her story at whatever point she wished. Major transitions and life events concerning school, family, work, friends, courting and married life, health and social life were discussed if they arose, as were any other significant events. The discussion explored events, experiences and feelings both now and in the past. The discussion was certainly not one-way. In line with feminist research practice, I disclosed appropriately, openly answered questions when asked, made observations and asked further questions in order to seek clarification. This was a collaborative process that we were engaged in and we explored together the changes in her life over the life course, talked about her life before and immediately after widowhood, her life 'now' and speculated about the future.

Although the discussion sometimes appeared to be rambling and disjointed, each woman told her story in her own way. At times it felt rather perilous and it was tempting to opt for a more structured, biographical interview with a more rigid framework. However, I felt that this would limit the discussion to my issues and concerns rather than each individual woman's issues and concerns. As Yow (1994: 173) reminds us, life story interviews are a quest in which the unexpected often turns up: 'part of the pleasure is in its serendipity'.

I was very aware of difference even in these initial pilot interviews. We were different in age, education, and generation and consequently our roles as women had been structured at different times. I was keenly aware of these differences and so too at times were the women. For example, generational perspectives on marriage, societal attitudes and expectations of women were alluded to with comments such as: 'your generation wouldn't have put up with that would they?' or 'its so different now. At times, despite my positive reinforcement of their expert role in the telling of their story, they would defer to me as the academic researcher and in response to a follow-up question would respond with 'you'll know better than me about that'. Nonetheless, there was also recognition of a commonality of gender that cut across age, generation and education and on several occasions this was referred to with phrases such as 'you'll understand that being a woman', or, 'well after all as you know that's what happens when you are a mother'. The inclusive 'we' was used often. These assumed differences and commonalities were a rich source of discussion, as we challenged each other's assumptions, and added considerably to our interaction.

These pilot interviews confirmed the flexibility of this more unstructured approach, although there were moments of uncertainty and silence in these early stages when I longed for the safety of a more structured schedule. However, the gains, particularly in the development of a more interactive and reciprocal relationship, and the data that was generated, were far greater than the tension. Consequently, this approach was used in subsequent interviews.

### A cautionary note

I actively sought involvement with the women who participated in the pilots and neither disguised my quest for information nor my sheer delight and interest in listening to their stories. I attempted on each occasion to make the research encounter as enjoyable and meaningful as possible. However, I was careful not to build up expectations that could not be fulfilled. From the very beginning I was completely open and honest about the boundaries and limitations of the research relationship.

### The return of the transcriptions and second interview

Each interview was transcribed verbatim and returned to its owner for a further discussion of the content, the overall flavour, and to explore any afterthoughts that had arisen as a result of the interview or when reading the transcriptions.

I also discussed with each woman, her feelings about the process of the research and my role in that process. Because these were pilot interviews I also asked for any other comments concerning the future conduct of the research. All five of the women confirmed their enjoyment and interest in the interviews, acknowledged that they felt satisfied with the structure of the interview and were comfortable with my interviewing skills. I did consider that their uncritical stance at this time might have been more a reflection of the inherent power imbalance than my skills (I discuss this further in Chapter 14). However, the loosely structured process had worked well enough for me to feel able to continue with this for subsequent interviews. Each woman was given a typed transcription of her interview to do with as she wished.

### Field diary

I kept a field diary during the pilot stage in which I recorded, at different times, the following: physical environment; my feelings; notes on non-verbal communication; conflict of values; power relationships; difficulties / problem areas encountered by me; my own skills; general observations on the process These observations were ongoing and recorded as soon as possible after each interview. As such, they clearly influenced subsequent interviews. Encouraging reflection through the use of a field diary, by checking and clarifying the transcripts with interviewees and through follow up interviews, were all ways in which I tried to achieve a balance of power in the research. The diary proved to be extremely useful during the pilot stage for highlighting my own feelings about the interviews, and so I continued to use it in the subsequent interviews. My own self-reflection at the end of each interview, as well as the comments of each woman, fed into the next interview. As such, each interview was part of the whole.

*Ethical issues*

During the pilot interviews, I discussed ethical issues as part of the interview format. On reflection this did not feel satisfactory and certainly did not conform to the ethical standards recommended in Chapter 5. Consequently, in the subsequent interviews, a 'Statement of Ethics' (see Appendix 1) was constructed and handed out and discussed at the beginning of the first interview. This served to signal the first stage in the collaborative process in which the women were co-participants in the research. It both formalised the process of conversations with a purpose and gave each woman written information about the study, which, if she wished, she could share with others. It also enabled me to make explicit my attempts at ethical research with my participants. As before, I assured confidentiality and also assured each woman of her right to withdraw at any point and to make changes in the transcriptions. I reiterated this at the second interview, where again I referred to the statement of ethics. In the event, none of the women did withdraw from the research but some changes were made to the transcriptions: removal of some comments concerning third parties; factual information corrected; more details given. I concur with Andrews (1991) here in the view that no story is fixed and that any changes made to the original story are as valid as the original story. What matters is that each woman is comfortable with her story. At each meeting I renegotiated informed consent; I felt this was important to maintain trust. As I discuss in more detail in Chapter 14, this trust enabled me to gain sometimes very intimate material, but also created a moral obligation not to cause harm.

*Level of involvement*

I looked to feminist research ethics when considering how much involvement degree of control respondents would have at different stages in the study; for example sight and comment on transcript accuracy, sight and comment on interpretation, sight of final product. I also considered at the pilot stage, that the women might be involved in analysis. The five women agreed to check over the transcripts and to reflect on the content at a second interview but were reluctant to enter into further discussion, suggesting that I 'knew best' what was needed for analysis. This seemed to me to represent a real power issue, but in retrospect it might also have been an acknowledgment by the five women of my academic background, knowledge and skills, which they did not share. In my quest for sound feminist research practice, perhaps I was in danger of not acknowledging our difference and instead trying to mask power differentials.

After careful consideration of the debates in the feminist research literature, and after discussion with other feminist researchers, I took the following decision. After the pilot stage, I decided to involve the women in the discussion of the transcriptions, in identifying key themes in their lives and to provide the opportunity for feedback on their involvement in the research process. However, I chose not to involve the women in the analysis of the data or in the presentation of the final product. I discuss this further in Chapter 13.

*Time*

Time was another factor identified as crucial in the research process - all the pilot interviews and the transcriptions took a long time (an issue confirmed by Ruth, 1996). Each interview lasted somewhere between two and four hours and each collection of tapes could take between sixteen and thirty hours to transcribe. The transcriptions took a long time because I found I was replaying the tape several times in order to recreate the interview and immerse myself in the content. The whole process of the initial interview (and sometimes a second interview), transcribing the tape, returning the transcriptions, a follow up interview, and further transcription, was thus extremely time consuming but absolutely necessary in order to collect the data I needed, within the framework I had set myself.

**Sink or swim**

I now discuss the main body of the fieldwork.

*Sample*

The five women who participated in the pilot stage of the research constituted an opportunity sample; as discussed earlier, there are clearly limitations to opportunity sampling. For example, it is not possible to generalise from such findings and in addition, there may be similarities in the sample that may not mirror the whole population. However, it is important to acknowledge two points. Firstly, the current study was not seeking to generalise from the experience of the participants but rather to learn from their experience. And secondly, each woman spoke as an individual rather than a representative of any particular group. Indeed Jerrome (1990) argues for the importance of studying the individual and the idiosyncratic, and suggests that social situations do not have to be typical to be illuminating. Therefore, using a variety of recruitment sources the final sample included differences of age, length of widowhood, education level, number of children, housing tenure, ethnicity and disability, in what was still nonetheless an opportunity sample. The three selection criteria of age at widowhood, length of time widowed and current marital status remained constant. Given the lack of research, which gives voice to 'ordinary' older widows, such a sample, despite acknowledged limitations, provided a unique view of an otherwise silent world.

The final size of the sample was initially kept open, as suggested by theoretical sampling (Arber, 1993; Mason, 1996). As the data collection and analysis progressed however, it became apparent that a very large amount of data (on both the content of life stories and feedback on the research process) was being collected from each person. For a variety of reasons I took the decision that a final sample size of twenty women was adequate for the purpose of the study. These included: the diversity of the sample as it developed (see Chapter 7: Biographies); my quest for an in-depth, 'insider' perspective of the experience of later life widowhood; the variety of stories which were being told to me and the need to do justice to these stories; and finally, that nothing new was emerging from my data. The very detailed nature of (feminist) life-story work outlined in the previous chapter, suggests that we can learn a lot from 'smaller' populations (Bornat, 1993).

*Conducting the interviews*

The interview format remained the same as it did during the pilot phase. Each taped life-story interview lasted about ninety minutes (some were shorter and three requested a second interview). Sometimes this included a break for refreshments but on other occasions, a social part took place after the tape recorder had been switched off. This presented me with a dilemma - was this conversation 'off-tape' part of my data or not? I solved it by asking each woman if she minded if retrospectively I took notes of such conversations. These notes were then added to the final transcript and were checked/approved/modified by each woman. There were also times, during the interview, when an individual woman asked for the tape recorder to be switched off. This was usually to share a secret that she wanted me to know but would not form part of the research data. Again, this presented a difficulty- I could not after all 'un-hear' such a secret. Therefore we agreed that in my presentation of the data it would be permissible to write that there were areas of the woman's life that she shared with me, but were not to be made available to others. However, I made a promise that the secret itself would not be included in the data to be presented, analyzed and discussed.

Nineteen women agreed to be interviewed on their own, but one woman for whom English was a second language requested that the contact source, an interpreter who was known to both of us, be present so that she could conduct the interview in her first language. I was sensitive to her needs, aware of potential power imbalances of race, age and language, and felt that this was entirely appropriate. Instead of an initial telephone call, I paid a pre-arranged visit to her house with the interpreter prior to the interview. We talked about the research and what I hoped to do with it, the possible structure of the interview (including the use of the tape recorder), and raised issues of confidentiality and informed consent. I reflect further on this interview in Chapter 13.

This was not the only interview in which power issues were apparent, although it was the only one in which issues of race and language were addressed. I have noted elsewhere that I could not eradicate the inherent power of the younger, educated, white researcher and to do so would be to ignore difference. However, in all the interviews, I tried to address any power issues that were raised in one form or another. Situating the interview in a place and at a time to suit each woman was one way of addressing the power imbalance- I was always aware that I was the visitor and was courteous at all times. I made sure that each woman was given plenty of time in which to tell her story and I took pains to demonstrate my genuine interest and enthusiasm. I paid attention to both my verbal and body language and actively listened at all times. I took note of disabilities and always took advice on where I should sit, and what would be best for the individual woman. I did not make assumptions about literacy and always offered to read both the Statement of Ethics and the transcription. I made sure that I kept each woman informed about the progress of the research but also acknowledged the right of each individual woman to participate as much or as little as she wished. Each of the interviews was an interaction between the woman and myself, so that on each occasion I shared information about myself and always answered direct questions as honestly as possible.

I constantly acknowledged and demonstrated the 'expert' role of the participants and interestingly, there were many times when I actually felt the less powerful person in the interaction. On one occasion for example, I found myself particularly overawed by the rather grand surroundings of her home and the expectations placed on me by the woman I was interviewing. More often, I felt humbled by the openness with which women told me their stories. However, I do nonetheless acknowledge that my perception of the situation may well have been different to that of the women I was interviewing.

After each encounter I continued to write in my field diary, using the format tested during the pilot stage. At a personal level, this was a useful process. I found that each interview was both exhilarating and exhausting - writing my thoughts down was one way of resolving these emotions. At a professional, research level, the diary provided me with a useful tool for reflection and analysis. In addition to my observational notes, it was a record of my ongoing skills as an interviewer and the process of life story interviewing. Although I told each of the women that I made notes after the interview, I did not openly share the contents of the diary and nor did any woman ask to see the diary. I did usually make reference to my observations in the follow-up interview, in particular those relating to my interview practice and skills or concerns/ questions that I had after the interview, or after listening to the tape recording. At the time, I took the view that the diary was both an academic tool and a safety valve for me the researcher. I explore this further in Chapter 13.

*The follow-up interview*

Sixteen of the women, from the overall sample of twenty, agreed to participate in follow-up interviews, having previously received a copy of their transcription. These interviews lasted between thirty minutes and two hours. The four women who declined, expressed satisfaction with the content of their transcription but did not want to participate in a further interview. Reasons that were given over the telephone or in writing included: 'too busy'; 'I shall be going away and I have a lot to do'; 'I enjoyed the interview and I will keep the copy of it but I don't want to do another interview'; 'I don't think I can tell you any more'; 'I'll get in touch with you when I've got time'. None of the four openly expressed dissatisfaction, although non-participation could be interpreted as such (see Chapter 13).

The 16 follow up interviews, which were tape-recorded, were in two parts. The first part consisted of checking the transcription for inaccuracies/ additional information/ parts to be omitted. As with the previous interviews, informed consent and confidentiality were always re-negotiated. This follow-up interview also enabled a test of internal consistency to be applied to the transcriptions. Most of the women had thought of other things they wanted to say, either after the interview or on reading the transcription. Some of them had written down their thoughts and/or discussed the story with others. Thus, a lively discussion ensued which confirmed the ownership of the story. Several women expressed concerns about their grammar or their use of English. This is yet another difficult area. The transcriptions were written verbatim and, although I spent considerable time reassuring these women of the differences between written and spoken language (phrases rather than full sentences, hopping from one point to another etc.), for the few there was some dissatisfaction with the written product and a need to 'tidy' it up before claiming ownership. One woman in particular took great pains to correct her script and was clearly unhappy about the way it looked initially. Another woman said she enjoyed telling and reading her story so much that she now felt inspired to have a go at writing a longer version of her story, for her own satisfaction. Unlike the transcription, it would be written 'like a composition'. There are clearly both advantages and disadvantages to returning a written transcription as opposed to a taped recording. All the women enjoyed having a final typed copy of their story, for personal consumption, to show to family, or to put somewhere 'safe' and bring out when they wished, and most of them were clearly very proud of their story. I took the view that the advantages outweighed the disadvantages.

The second part of the follow-up interview involved a reflection on the process of participating in a life story interview. As with the first interview this was an exchange rather than a question and answer session. We both participated in the discussion, identifying areas of importance, improvement, concern and pleasure from participation in the first interview. I certainly saw it as an opportunity to critically appraise my skills and some of the women felt able to enter into the spirit of this part of the discussion. Others used it purely as an opportunity to reflect on their own feelings and felt unwilling/ unable to comment on my skills. All of the women, who participated in the follow up interview expressed satisfaction at being offered the opportunity to reflect.

A detailed analysis and discussion of these reflections, along with my own feelings (drawn from my field diary) about the process of carrying out the research and the complexities therein are raised in Chapter 13.

**Making sense**

Having outlined how I undertook my fieldwork, I now briefly describe the way in which I carried out my analysis. I include this process in the chapter in order to demonstrate to the reader the way in which I made use of academic frameworks and techniques but nonetheless ensured that both the experience and voices of older widows were fairly represented.

*Familiarising myself with the transcriptions*

The tapes of the interviews were listened to several times before transcription was undertaken. I found the processes of listening and transcribing to be extremely useful as they helped me to gain even greater familiarity with the stories of individual women's lives. The ultimate aim of my narrative investigation was the interpretation of the experience of later life widowhood, using a life course perspective and so immersion in the whole of the life stories was essential. Following Atkinson (1998) and Miller (2000) I read and reread each story as a whole, with the objectives of understanding the parts and thus drawing out patterns and themes.

*Getting started*

Initially, I used the data to extract enough 'quasi-factual' (Miller, 2000) information to write a summary of each woman's life story that captured key events in her life (I present these summaries in Chapter 7: The Biographies.) This biography was then confirmed with each woman. These summaries were useful in enabling me to focus my attention on both the flavour and individuality of each life and the component parts, and provided a useful reference point. I had these readily at hand when going through the transcriptions.

I wanted to make sense of the life story which was being told so with each transcription, I highlighted with a pen the biographical issues that were raised, and noted down key points on a separate sheet of paper. This went beyond the recording of factual data and instead I started to engage with each woman's subjective experience. I show an example here of how I began this process.

| Example: Evelyn |
| --- |
| Ability to cope with responsibility; independence; strong sense of self; the role of family; women's lives; making relationships; enjoyment of life/seizing the moment; choice; activity; hard work; war years; risk taking; adaptability; busyness; shock of husband's death; friendship; other widows; ill health; best friend/ kindred spirit; contentment; making relationships; choice; telling her story/ life review; making sense. |

**Figure 6.2    Getting going**

I compared and contrasted my findings across the first, five transcriptions, and began to develop a tentative list of ideas or themes with which to explore subsequent transcriptions. This process was then repeated chronologically with each of the next six interviews, as the transcriptions were completed and verified, and the summaries confirmed. At this stage before I began my coding, I was particularly interested to highlight issues relating to 'then' and 'now' in order to conceptualise continuities and discontinuities. I then repeated this process with each of the final nine interviews, as I processed them, adding to the list where necessary. A final, more confident list of themes was compiled.

Drawing on the work of Ruth and Oberg (1995) I went through all of the transcriptions again, noting generalised statements or seemingly throw away remarks denoting attitudes about self, life in general, or life now, which would also inform my analysis. The statements were extremely helpful in terms of expressing attitudes and ways in which lives are lived and understood and hinted at a variety of narratives, which might be found within the individual stories

*Conceptualising the parts*

At this point in my ongoing analysis, I was able to conceptualise a number of 'parts' (Atkinson, 1998) that were emerging from the comparisons and emerging themes and which I identified as:

- Me, Myself (the continuities of 'myself' over the life course)
- History and Me (generation and gender issues)
- Me and My Social World (relationships with family and friends over the life course)
- Me, Now (the 'me' as a widow within the context of my life history)

The list of themes and ideas was thus re-organised and re-coded into these five parts[1] that formed the basis of the final coding system. At the same time as I was beginning to develop my coding system, I was also noting down issues relating to the life course, feminist theory and feminist research practice. These subsequently informed some of my code headings.

This coding system and my notes, were finally applied manually to all the interview data. This was an exciting, albeit extremely time-consuming, process. Because I was interested in reflexivity and the process of the research, I also coded a final part that I have chosen to call: Me, Telling My Story, that is the discussion I had with my participants concerning our respective roles and feelings in the process of biographical research. This final coding was applied to the transcriptions and my field diary. As process is integral to all of the stories and the emerging narratives, I incorporate some of the discussion arising from 'Me, Telling My Story' within subsequent chapters as well as in Chapter 13, where I reflect in more detail on the process of the research

*Emerging narratives and sub-plots*

As the coding proceeded, a number of narratives started to emerge within each of the parts. At this point I returned to the statements about life in general and took note of Polkinghorne's (1995) recommendation to identify the 'type' or 'narrative'

---

[1] My choice of the words 'me', 'my' and 'myself' to describe these parts was deliberate, and symbolises the 'voice' of each participant.

of life, that each life story depicts. I used the content of these statements, and the results of my coding, to construct what I have chosen to call 'multiple narratives' for each of the 'parts'. For example within Me Myself, there were three narratives of 'self' over the life course. I have described this thus:

- Multiple narratives: Me, Myself
    o   High self-esteem
    o   Fluctuating self-esteem
    o   Low self-esteem

In History and Me, two narratives were evident:

- Multiple narratives: History and Me
    o   Belonging to a generation
    o   Gendered lives

In Me and My Social World, the following narratives were evident:

- Multiple narratives: Me and My Social World
    o   Friends matter
    o   No friends of my own
    o   A 'joiner-in'
    o   Family first

And in Me, Now:

- Multiple narratives: Me Now
    o   Widowhood is loneliness and despair
    o   Widowhood is a time of getting on with life
    o   Widowhood is a transition

I was constantly seeking consistencies across life stories; the key is always to see the story first. I found that, as I gained confidence with the process, I was starting to uncover what I have chosen to call 'sub-plots' within the narratives. For example in the narrative of 'High self-esteem' within 'Me Myself' the following sub-plots were evident:

- Me Myself:
    o   High Self Esteem:
        - Feeling secure
        - Values
        - Self-confidence
        - Learning from experience
        - Independence
        - Regrets for others

I was constantly making meaning from these narratives. As Atkinson (1998: 65) has commented: 'there is no stronger, clearer statement of how the person sees and understands his or her own life than his or her own narrative of it.' I tried not to impose my own ideas on the data but instead to interact with what was emerging in my analysis (Lofland and Lofland, 1995). As the narratives and sub-plots started to emerge, I returned to three of the women to seek their views on the authenticity of those narratives and sub-plots, either from their own experience or that of friends who were widows. I was asking if these narratives 'rang true'. Borland (in Patai, 1991), in a powerful discussion entitled 'that's not what I said', demonstrated the importance of involving women in such stories resulting from data. Her work was a reminder that my consciousness has been formed at a different time and social reality than the women I was researching. It was important therefore to talk to some of the women about my ideas before committing to writing. This was not the same as giving either control of the analysis or textual authority and interpretation but was instead an exchange of ideas to make sure I was not collecting information to fit my paradigms. The three women, with whom I met separately, were comfortable with the narratives and felt that my emerging analysis enabled them to make sense of their own experience and that of others. In summary, I wanted to make connections, to analyse and interpret but not to make judgements.

## Situating myself

A feminist researcher often uses the strategy of starting from her own experience both to define research questions and to have access to useful sources of data (Reinharz, 1991). She often starts with an issue that is important to her. My starting point, as I outlined in my introduction, was older women in my own neighbourhood whose company and friendship I value, and whose lives seemed to contradict much of what I read in the literature on later life widowhood. My initial groundwork (the 'conversation with a purpose' and the pilot interviews) and the subsequent time I spent interviewing and chatting socially with all of the women, was essential if I was ever going to begin to understand their lives. I am a woman with an academic background, a professional job and three adult daughters. I am now fifty-three years of age, with a husband to whom I have been married for thirty-three years. Potentially I have very little in common with some of the women whose life experience I was seeking to understand. However I demonstrated throughout my fieldwork genuine empathy and interest in each woman's life experience and an acceptance that each individual had access to knowledge that I could only gain through her story. Indeed, I was the 'learner' and she the 'expert'. Only she could help me to explore the apparent paradox that I had observed. As for commonalities, we shared the following experiences: gender in a patriarchal society; marriage to a man older than myself; the varying roles that women experience during their life course. Indeed, long conversations with my mother in law (herself an older widow) about our roles as women had identified both our shared and differing experiences. I too have experienced loss, albeit not the loss of a partner. My mother died when I was 21 years old and in the final year of an undergraduate degree and my father, who did not remarry and with whom I had a very close relationship, died during my fieldwork. I am acutely aware of the mixture of emotions I have experienced as well as the changing experience of this loss over time.

I was aware throughout the period of my fieldwork that I was both an avid listener and an active participant in the research process. The data that has been collected is a product therefore of both of these roles. I consider that this added to rather than detracted from its quality. The very fact that I was an active participant, engaged in active listening and relationship building enabled me to gain the trust of twenty women who openly shared with me their life stories.

## Conclusion

In this chapter I have outlined in detail the fieldwork component of the present study. I have demonstrated how I applied my chosen research methodology and method, discussed in the previous chapter, in my quest to understand the experience of later life widowhood. In doing so I hope to have given the reader a taste of what it felt like to be out in the field. I have also, by explaining the way in which I made sense of my data, anticipated what is to follow. In the next chapter, I introduce the reader to the twenty widows who participated in the study and I then go on in subsequent chapters to make sense of their stories.

# Chapter 7

# Twenty Older Widows

## Introduction

In this chapter I set the scene for the multiple narratives that follow in the next four chapters by introducing the twenty women who took part in the study. This is a deliberate attempt on my part to raise their profile; so often, this type of information is to be found only in the appendices of books. I take the view that the rightful place for this information is within the main body of the text; after all, the twenty women, although not representative of all older widows, are pivotal to the current study.

## Pen-portraits

Each pen portrait is a summary of a life story shared with me and confirmed by each individual woman. Biographical details such as age, length of widowhood etc. are those given at the time of the interview. Each woman is introduced by the name she selected.

**Jean** is 72 years of age and has been widowed for seven years. She has three children and eight grandchildren. Jean left school at the age of fourteen and has had numerous manual jobs, both part time and full time. When she was eighteen she met and married Albert who was in the Merchant Navy. She was pregnant when she got married. Her father was vehemently opposed to the marriage (her mother died when she was still at school) and offered her little support as a young mother. Primarily for financial reasons, Jean has juggled work and home commitments throughout her married life. She also acknowledges that she has always enjoyed meeting other people and work outside the home offered her such opportunities. She worked in a munitions' factory during the war, with the children in nursery, and subsequently undertook shop or bar work to fit in with family commitments. Money was always 'tight' and she and Albert lived in rented accommodation, initially provided by the council and latterly by a housing association. For most of their married life, Jean and Albert coped with his ill health and increasing disability. Despite that, and within the confines of family life, they were both very sociable.

In retirement, they had made new friends who, along with the family, helped Jean when Albert died. Jean is now an active member of the local senior citizens' centre where she serves on several committees; she joined the centre six months after Albert's death. With her friend, Phyllis, she has been instrumental in starting up 'dancing afternoons' at the club; dancing was her passion before she was married but she gave it up during her married life. She has numerous friends, of whom Phyllis is a special friend. Jean now lives in a one bedroom flat in the next housing association block to where she lived with Albert. She regularly attends a Methodist church and feels her religion is an important part of her life. She is in regular contact with her children and grandchildren but fiercely maintains her independence (with the knowledge that any one of them is on the end of the phone should she need help). She is very content with her life.

**Phyllis** is 75 years of age and has been widowed for ten years. Her husband was older by thirteen years. Two years after the death of her husband she moved house and area to look after her only son, who was divorced, and her grandson. For most of their married life, Phyllis and her husband ran a village pub. Although this provided them with a readymade social life, it imposed many restrictions on their family life. They had been retired for a number of years when he died. She has a lifelong interest in sport, initially as a participant and latterly, as a spectator. Phyllis regretted the loss of her freedom when she went to live with her son and grandson and after a further two years she moved to her current accommodation: a flat she rents from a housing association, in the same area as her son.

She has always been and still is a very sociable person, enjoying the company and friendship of others, especially her special friend, Jean. Phyllis is now very active at her local senior citizens' centre and with Jean was instrumental in setting up the dancing afternoons. She has a man friend who lives in the same accommodation, but says she would not consider remarriage. Despite some ill-health and the loss of sight in one eye, she leads a very full and active social life in which female friends play a large part. She describes herself as a regular churchgoer, Church of England, and attends services locally. She continues to have contact with her son, her new daughter-in-law and her ex-daughter-in-law, but feels they all get on separately with their own lives. She is confident that she can call on any of them if she needs help. She worries about her health, but on the whole is happy with her life. She acknowledges that her life would not have been so full had she remained in the village where she spent all of her married life.

**Vera** is 67 years of age and has been widowed for twelve years. She has three sons, all of whom are married and live away from the area. She moved to her present flat six months after the death of her husband, having not lived in the area for nearly thirty years. In retrospect, she regrets this move and wishes she had not allowed herself be influenced by others; she made too many big decisions while she was still in a state of shock. Her husband was a meteorologist, working with the RAF. Because of his job, Vera and the boys moved regularly, both in this country and abroad. Before marriage, Vera worked full time in an office (after leaving school at the age of fourteen) but her husband never wanted her to work once they had children. She had a very active social life within the RAF, but with the exception of two married ex-school friends living in Stockport, no friends outside of forces life. She has one older sister, who also lives in Stockport, but they are not close.

Although Vera now feels it was a mistake to move so soon after her husband's death, she felt she had no ties where she was living. She still feels a sense of loss and has found it difficult to build up a network of close friends with whom she can spend time at weekends. For most of her life she has enjoyed living in what she describes as a 'male world' and has found it difficult to value the predominantly female world she now inhabits. Nonetheless, her weeks are full as a result of becoming a volunteer at a local volunteer job shop, and she has been instrumental in setting up a Widows and Widowers Club. Ill health has prevented her from participating in sporting activities, which she used to enjoy. When she was younger and living in Stockport, she had strong religious beliefs and was an active participant in her local Church of England. However, personal experiences and events in Cyprus and Northern Ireland have led her to question her faith and she no longer feels commitment to any church. She is saddened by this and is envious of people who do have faith.

She is in telephone contact with her sons but does not see any of them regularly. Occasionally she goes to stay with them, but only when they ask her; she feels she wouldn't initiate a visit herself. She is not happy with her life but feels powerless to make changes; she struggles to see herself as an individual and was much more comfortable as one part of a couple.

**Edith** is 64 years of age and has been widowed for nine years. She has a large but close family of sisters, brothers-in-law, nieces and nephews but she has no children of her own. She always worked during her married life, predominantly in the mail order business, but her husband Donald managed all the household finances and business. She looked after the daily running of the home but he did all the organising. They had an active social life with family, married friends and neighbours. They regularly went on holiday and were able to buy their own bungalow in Stockport. Edith continues to have a very close relationship with her family and her in-laws.

In a short period of time, Edith experienced a series of losses of people close to her. Not long before her husband died, she had nursed her own mother and subsequently her brother, who both died of cancer. Six months after Donald died, her mother in law also died. After this time, she suffered from clinical depression, which resulted in what she describes as 'a breakdown' and admission to hospital for a period of time. Although her family were very embarrassed by her illness, Edith feels it was an important turning point.

Since that time, she has been rebuilding her life. She sold the bungalow and bought a flat in a complex for retired people; she has decorated and furnished it completely on her own. She has developed a new social network through volunteering at the local volunteers job shop and joining a craft class. On Fridays, she works at the local market on a hardware stall. Edith has strengthened her friendship with her younger, ever single, sister. Although they live separately, they now spend weekends and holidays together. She now manages all her own household business and organises holidays for herself, her sister and friends. She now has a strong belief in herself and her capacity to manage her life; she feels she has become a different person.

**Evelyn** is 89 years of age and has been widowed for twenty years. She was unable to have children but has a very close relationship with her niece and her family. She left school at sixteen, knowing that she wanted to become a nurse. She tried a variety of other jobs until she was old enough, at eighteen, to gain employment as a fever nurse before going on to Doncaster Infirmary to complete her training. Evelyn had already qualified as a nurse when she met and married Sidney. She became a nursing sister and then, after further training, a midwife. She worked in hospitals in South Manchester for many years and was in charge of a first aid post during the Second World War. In her forties, Evelyn gave up nursing to run a boarding house in Blackpool. She had no qualms about leaving nursing and was a successful Blackpool landlady for twenty-five years. She and her husband then retired to Lytham-St.-Annes because of Evelyn's ill health. They had been there three years when he died; although he had been ill, his death was still a surprise.

Evelyn remained in Lytham for a number of years after Sidney's death, making friends and building a small but active social life. As a result of increasing frailty and her wish to be nearer to her only family, she was enabled to move to her present accommodation in Stockport: a bed-sit within a sheltered housing complex run by the local council. She receives help with personal care but remains independent. Evelyn has made friends with both the care staff and her neighbours. She has one close friend and neighbour whom she regards as both kindred spirit and confidante. She enjoys her own company and is content with her life.

**Elizabeth** is 84 years of age and has been widowed for thirteen years. She now lives in a semi-detached bungalow in Stockport. She was born in Shropshire and had been married to Ivor for forty-five years. She has three children and many grandchildren and great grandchildren. Elizabeth met her husband when they were both 'in service' at a large country house in Cheshire. After an extended courtship, during which time she ran away to work for several years in London, they married. As a young mother, Elizabeth spent most of the Second World War apart from Ivor, who was in the Eighth Army. For a large part of her married life she ran a bakery business with Ivor, living and working on the premises. Her husband died not long after they retired from the business and she wishes they had had more time together in retirement.

She felt very sad when he died but feels she coped with the bereavement with help from her family. She is very close to her two daughters, one of whom lives nearby, and her son and their families. She maintains close links with her husband's family and spends time with her two sisters in law, one of whom is also a widow. She has a close woman friend whom she first met as part of a couple when she and Ivor were on holiday in Yugoslavia; as widows they have become great friends. She has good neighbours who call in for coffee. Elizabeth's daily life revolves around her own home where she has many visitors and keeps busy. In addition, she still visits other people, making use of public transport and travels to a newly built 'out of town' shopping centre making use of a free bus. Her health is no longer as good as it was and she has days when she does not feel so well. Elizabeth has worked outside the home all her married life and although she still keeps very busy, she enjoys not working to a timetable. She feels in control of her life and enjoys her independence.

**Jennie** is 73 years of age and lives in a terraced house in Stockport. She was born in Wigan and was an only child. She spent a very happy childhood in Leeds and moved to Manchester just before the Second World War. She married John during the war and moved to Stockport in 1948. They were married for forty-six years. John died seven years ago when they were on holiday in Germany and Jennie has remained in the house they shared. John had previously had a stroke and Jennie had been his principal carer for a number of years prior to his death.

Jennie strongly believes in the importance of family duty and loyalty. She has two daughters who both have children. At different times, Jennie has provided a home for one granddaughter and one grandson. She maintains close links with her daughters, even though they live some distance away, and willingly gives practical help whenever she is able. She knows that they will always reciprocate. Jennie has always juggled family life and paid work in a variety of cotton mills; she still works part time as a quality controller in a local mill. The 'work ethic' has always been very important to Jennie, something she attributes to her upbringing in a family who owned small businesses and always worked hard.

She and John were always very sociable and she continues to have a network of friends. She has a circle of single female friends, some widows and others ever-single, with whom she goes on day trips and holidays. Jennie is a devout Christian and is very active in her local evangelical church. Her faith enabled her to cope with John's death and she feels it gives her an optimism to live her life to the full.

**Patricia** is 67 years of age. She has been widowed for just over five years. She married Bob when she was twenty-one years of age; he was sixteen years older than her. She was born in Manchester and has been buying her semi-detached house, an ex-council property, on the outskirts of Stockport for fourteen years. She has actually lived in the house for thirty-five years. Patricia has one daughter, Wendy, who has not married and lives in a small village about ten miles away. They are in daily contact by telephone and meet up at least once a week.

Patricia had an unhappy childhood; her parents were divorced, there was very little money and she was often left to look after her younger sister while her mother went out to work. When she was ten years old, she was evacuated to Staffordshire; she has bitter memories of this time. These experiences made her determined to be a 'good' mother and she is sad that she only had one daughter. She would love to be a grandmother but thinks it unlikely now. Patricia left school at fourteen and worked at a music shop in Manchester until she got married. She met her husband when she was ballroom dancing; he was an instructor. For many years their lives revolved around the national ballroom dancing circuit and they took part in many competitions. Bob worked nights as a printer from the time their daughter was born, which meant that Patricia and Wendy spent a lot of time on their own. Patricia also found that it was difficult to get out and meet other people; she has never had any close female friends. She has a younger sister whom she sees fairly regularly.

Patricia's health is no longer very good and she describes herself as 'very lonely'; her sole companion is her dog, Daisy. She rarely goes out socially apart from with either her daughter or her sister and worries about being a burden on her daughter. Inside the house she is very self sufficient; she does all her own decorating, enjoys craftwork and spends a lot of time sewing. She sells her work via a craft shop.

**Pat**[1] is 66 years of age and is a close friend of Jennie; she is part of a circle of older women, who are all either widowed or ever single. Pat lived at home after leaving school at the age of fourteen and went to work in the family firm. She was enjoying learning all about the garment making business, with a view to eventually taking charge, when her mother became ill; she had to give up work to care for her mother, her father, her grandmother and her brother. Her mother subsequently died and Pat's father remarried fairly soon afterwards. Pat did not get on with her father's new wife so she returned to work in the family business. She then had a sexual relationship with a married man who worked for her father and became pregnant; she was twenty-seven at the time. She had a son, but did not marry the boy's father. Her own father would not allow her to return to the family home so she lived on her own with her son until she got married. She combined paid work with bringing up her son; she continued to get an income from the family business but had little time for a social life. When her son was seven, she met a divorced man with two daughters and married him. They had another son together. During their seven-year marriage, she and her husband developed friendships with other married couples but these friendships stopped once she became a widow. She found herself quite isolated again with little opportunity to meet others in the same situation.

---

[1] Pat does not meet the criteria of the sample because she was widowed in her early forties, after a seven-year marriage. However, she identifies herself as an older widow, and as such she was included in the study.

Now in later life, Pat has moved to a terraced house and found herself surrounded, both socially and geographically by women like herself, women with whom she has developed strong friendships. She regularly attends church, although she feels she does so for social rather than religious reasons. She has also rekindled a friendship with her brother. She continues to receive an income from the family business and has few financial worries. Pat has had to be independent for most of her adult life and has always felt 'different' from other women. Now as an older woman with other older widows, she no longer feels this difference.

**Katherine** is 86 years of age and lives in a flat in a retirement complex in Stockport. She moved here after she was widowed. She has been widowed for five years. Katherine lives on a state pension and housing benefit. She was born in Manchester and was the third child of four. She was married twice but her first marriage lasted less than twelve months. (She did not talk about this marriage beyond giving this information). She married Stan soon afterwards. She has one daughter from this marriage, two granddaughters, two great granddaughters and a great, great grandson. Money was always scarce so she combined paid work with bringing up her daughter and then, subsequently, her granddaughter who lived with her. She worked for many years as a school meals assistant for Manchester City Council although she says she would rather have been a lady of leisure. Katherine has a group of female friends whom she has known since her early twenties. She and Stan, her husband, were always tolerant of each other's interests and so Katherine regularly went dancing and on holiday with her friends whilst Stan was always able to pursue his interest in boxing.

Katherine has continued to spend time with these friends since Stan died. She loves to travel and feels her friends are the most important aspect of her life. She spends time with her granddaughter and her family, but feels strongly that different generations have different needs and expectations. Although she has always been very independent and a strong supporter of women's rights, she felt quite vulnerable when Stan died, particularly at night. This surprised her because she and Stan had both talked about the fact that one of then would die first. She was happy when her family suggested she move to the retirement complex. She has always been fit and healthy but recently had been to the doctors because she was feeling unwell.

**Ellen** is 73 and lives in Stockport. Her husband died in 1990 after a period of illness. She has recently, with the help of one son and his wife, bought her council house. They have just moved in with her and are converting part of the house to a 'granny flat'. She is looking forward to this arrangement which she feels will benefit them all. Ellen was born in Birmingham where, after leaving school at fourteen, she worked in a factory. She joined the ATS in 1941 and met Joe, her future husband, when they were both stationed in Gloucester. This was an important time in her life during which she feels she gained confidence and independence. She was married in 1945 and has three sons. They all moved to Manchester, to live with Joe's mother, when the war ended, and then moved to Stockport when the boys were older. In order to supplement the family finances, Ellen combined paid work with looking after her family. She had a stroke in 1973 from which she has completely recovered.

She has always been close to her three sons and their families and maintains strong links with Joe's family. Like Jennie, she feels that family duty and loyalty are very important. She and Joe had always been regular churchgoers with strong religious beliefs and Ellen continues to be very involved with her local church. Many of her social activities are with friends from the church. She finds that her faith is a great comfort to her. Both Ellen and Joe had maintained links with their forces days via the British Legion, and Ellen is still very active in her local branch of the ATS. She has one best friend, a single woman of a similar age to herself, who is also a neighbour. They spend a lot of time talking to each other, usually in each other's houses and they often go out together on coach trips.

**Farzana** is 63 years of age. She has been widowed for eight years. Two of her sons and their wives and children live with her at her house in Stockport. Farzana was born in Pakistan. She left school at the age of twelve when her mother died and went to live with her sister in law who took over the care of the family. She was married at seventeen, having met her husband formally at her in-laws' house. She has six children, three born in Pakistan and three in Stockport.

She came to Stockport in 1969 to join her husband who, with other men from Pakistan, had been recruited the previous year to work in the local iron and steel works. She still lives in the same house she moved to in 1969. Her other sons and daughters and their families all live nearby and regularly visit. Farzana particularly enjoys the visits from her grandchildren and the support she gets from her children. She has some close friends from Pakistan whom she meets at the mosque; they have all been friends since they came to England with young children. In the 1980s the iron and steel works closed so Farzana's husband went to work firstly in a bakery, but latterly ran his own business on Stockport market.

Although he was not in good health, he was not really ill so it was a surprise when he died of a heart attack. At that time, four of Farzana's children were still unmarried so she had a lot of responsibility. As a Muslim, she always puts her trust in Allah and she believes her faith has helped her to cope. She feels she manages well now she has got used to having all the responsibility, which she would have shared with her husband. She spends most of her time at home with her daughters in law, who sometimes take her shopping, or she goes to the Mosque. Her religion is very important to her; she says prayers five times a day and recites the Koran.

She feels her life is very different now, not because she is a widow but because she is getting older and her children are grown up. Her life has centred on her children; she has never worked outside of the family home. Now her family look after her; for example, her daughters in law do all the cooking. She has a pain in her leg when she walks and her diabetes sometimes gives her problems. She lives her life from day to day, trusting in Allah to get her through any difficulties. Her world is her family.


**Betty** was born in Rochdale and is 73 years of age. She moved to South Manchester in 1933. She was married for thirty-three years and has been widowed for sixteen years. Her husband was ten years older than her and died of cancer after a short illness. She lives in a rented house, the family home, in Stockport with her youngest son. Her family experienced extreme poverty in the 1930s but her father's sister paid for Betty to attend a boarding school in Blackburn. She loved her school years but her hopes for higher education were thwarted by a lack of family money and the intervention of the war. Betty was prevented from joining the forces by her family and instead went to work for an insurance company. She met her husband after the war. They had three children and lived on a very low income, struggling to make ends meet from week to week. Betty started childminding and then did a series of part-time jobs while the children were growing up, moving on to work full-time as they got older. She was the one who took responsibility for ensuring that all the bills were paid and so took 'any job that was going' in order to supplement the family income.

Her husband died when she was fifty-seven; he had no private pension and she only had access to the state pension. Betty continued to work for a printer and now works as a cleaner for several private clients. Her health is not as good as it was and she worries about the future. She has always worked hard to maintain a good standard of living and cannot imagine what life would be like if she was not in employment. She remembers her husband's death as a difficult time, especially coming home after a day at work. She has always had her own interests outside the family home, particularly amateur dramatics, and her own friends, and that helped at the time. Betty has recently become a school governor at her local Catholic primary school. She has always been a practising Catholic and her faith is important to her. She has three close friends, who are all widows, one of whom is her best friend and confidante. She is not close to her children or grandchildren; they all get on with their own lives.


**Doris** is 81 years of age and was born in Blackpool. She moved to Stockport when she married at nineteen years of age. She was widowed five years ago. When her husband Walter died, she sold their bungalow and has used the profits, and other money he left, to pay for her care in a residential home. She says it was the first time in her life that she was able to please herself and describes the move as 'liberating'.

She had a happy, if rather pampered, childhood and a rebellious youth; she left school as soon as she was able and worked in a gown shop. She met her husband at a staff dance and they married soon afterwards. He was a very possessive man who didn't want her to work for anyone else. Consequently, she worked for him as a secretary all his working life, initially in his office and then latterly at home. Doris describes her husband as 'controlling' and feels that marriage was a disappointment; she put up with the relationship because she was financially dependent on her husband. They both had affairs during their marriage.

She has three sons, with whom she is still good friends, who all have families. Her sons all live away from Stockport but they visit her regularly and keep her supplied with books. During their married life Doris and Walter had many couple friends, mostly older than themselves, but Doris has never had a close female friend. All of her couple friends have died. She has always liked her own company and has never been a 'clubby' person; her passions, gardening and reading, were solitary activities. She has no real friends in the residential home but gets on well with the staff. Doris's health is now poor but nonetheless she feels in control of her life. She makes choices about how to spend her money and how she will spend her time. She still reads a lot and, whenever the weather permits, sits in the gardens or in the conservatory overlooking the gardens.


**Bee** is 68 years of age and has been widowed for five years. She has no children, although her husband had a son from his first marriage. She married Harold when she was twenty-seven and he was fifty-four. She has lived in the same bungalow in Stockport for forty years. She describes herself as wealthy and is able to enjoy travel and a full social life. Before she was married, Bee was financially independent, enjoyed her office job and had a very busy social life. However, her husband was a successful businessman who did not wish his wife to work; she agreed to this and consequently, she has never worked since her marriage. She learnt to play golf and bridge and discovered she was good at both. These two activities became (and continue to be) major passions, taking up most of her daytime. She has little contact with her mother and sister; her husband and friends were the focal point of her life. William and Bee had a very full social life throughout their married life and regularly gave parties, travelled, spent time with mutual friends. In addition, Bee has always had a circle of her golfing and bridge friends.

Bee cared for her husband at home prior to his death, with the help of nurses, but eventually he moved into the local hospice where he died. They had previously talked about the probability of him dying first and she was well informed about both practical and financial issues; William had already appointed a financial adviser for Bee, who has continued to help her. Bee still has many close friends who are very important to her, and she is able to afford to make choices in her life. She had recently met an American man while she was on a cruise and has embarked on a new relationship. At the moment she is enjoying the relationship but has no idea what the future holds.


**Joan** is 74 years of age and was born in London. She has been a widow for twenty-two years. She had recently moved to live with her daughter and son-in-law in a purpose built flat in their house, having lived in the family home for fifty years. She married David during the war years when she was eighteen years of age. Joan saw little of her husband, who was sent abroad for a number of years until the end of the war. Joan's early years at home and school were very happy, but her education came to an abrupt halt as a result of the Second World War. She has regrets about the impact of the war years on her loss of education and opportunities, but incorporates these feelings into a stoical attitude to life. Joan moved to Stockport after the war and had two children. She missed her parents and at school holidays returned to London to visit them. Joan never did paid work (her husband did not approve of working mothers) but she did work for a time as a volunteer for an adoption agency. She also had an active social life, which revolved around the tennis club and the amateur dramatics society. She has always found it easy to make friends and enjoys the company of others.

Her husband died unexpectedly in the bath at home, following a massive stroke. She was supported during this time by a number of people, in particular her son, her daughter and son-in-law and many close friends. Joan has a group of female friends whom she sees regularly and until two years ago also had a male partner. They did not live together but they shared an active social life. He died after a period of illness, during which time she cared for him. She has three grandchildren and values her relationship with them. Joan's health is variable, and she worries about what will happen when she is no longer able to drive; she does not want to be dependent on her daughter.

**Mags** is 79 years of age and was born in 1919 in Salford. She has been widowed for 15 years. She was the eighth child of nine. In early infancy, she contracted infantile paralysis. She was unable to walk until she was 7 years old and then needed the support of callipers. She spent half of her childhood in a children's home in the country, and the rest of the time with her large but very close family in Salford. She has remained close to her family and feels strongly that families should stick together. It was always assumed, by her family and others, that Mags would never be able to work outside the family home. In fact, she went out to work from the age of fourteen and continued until she was fifty-seven, becoming an extremely skilled sewing machinist. She describes herself as very determined, but realistic about her limitations.

After her mother died, Mags moved to live with her sister and brother in law, whom she regarded as second parents. It was through them that she met Jim, who was already married. They met secretly for a while and then, despite family opposition and disapproval, decided to live together. Eventually, they married and were re-united with Mags' family. When Jim became ill, Mags was his principal carer.

After his death Mags was depressed for a while; it was the first time in her life she had lived alone. She gained a full driving licence and started spending time with her family again. She supported her sister when she too became a widow, and then when her sister became ill, Mags again took on the role of carer. With the subsequent death of her sister, Mags moved to Stockport to live with her niece; they lived together for ten years and jointly bought and furnished a mobile home. With other members of the family, they had regular holidays abroad. After a very bad fall, Mags was advised to move into residential care. She still sees her family regularly and is involved in the planning for the next holiday abroad.

**Eunice** is 69 years of age and was born in Lancashire. She has been widowed for eight years. She belonged to a close family who were all Christians, and the church has always been integral to her life. She married Laurie, who was also a Christian, when she was twenty-four years of age, just after he had qualified as a civil engineer. Eunice was a clerical worker and successfully studied part-time for her local government examinations. She had been very disappointed to fail her eleven plus and since that time she has taken every opportunity to improve her education. When her daughter was born, Eunice gave up paid work and became a full time mother. She had two more children. They all moved to Stockport in 1965, primarily for the children's education.

Although Eunice and her husband did a lot together, particularly family and church activities, they each had their own interests and friends. Laurie was very involved in his work and Eunice became involved with the Red Cross (and has continued this involvement ever since), initially by enrolling on a course and running a cadet group and later progressing to a high position within the organisation.

Eunice's first daughter died unexpectedly at twenty-four years of age. Eunice describes this as the worst time in her life. As a result of this experience, Eunice initiated a bereavement support group at her local church and successfully completed a Certificate in Counselling.

Eunice's husband also died unexpectedly following a heart attack. Her daughter and son have supported her and so have her friends. Eunice moved to a smaller house in the same locality two years after Laurie died. She now lives near to her brother, who is also widowed, and several friends. She is still very active with the Red Cross and with her local church, attends a keep fit class, does voluntary work and attends adult education classes. She has a group of close female friends with whom she goes to the theatre and on holidays. She has a very good relationship with her daughter and son, and they regularly spend time together. She still misses the companionship of married life but would not consider remarrying. Her faith is very strong and central to how she sees herself and the world around her.

**Sylvia** is 73 years of age and was born in Stoke on Trent. She moved to Stockport when she was four years old. She was widowed when she was fifty-nine, after thirty-nine years of marriage. She now lives with another partner but has decided that they will not remarry. Her childhood years were difficult. Her father had his own kennels and was frequently away from home meeting up with other dog breeders and owners. Sylvia was expected to work in the kennels when she came home from school and she had little opportunity to make friends. She passed her scholarship examinations but was unable to continue with her education because of the cost.

Sylvia started work as an office junior and became pregnant when she was seventeen. She refused to have her daughter adopted and three years later met John, whom she married. They subsequently had another child and Sylvia gave up paid work. When Sylvia's father died, her mother moved in to live with her and John. She lived with them for the next thirty years. Sylvia returned to work when the children were older and her mother helped in the house. John was ill for a number of years before he died and so too was Sylvia's mother; she was their principal carer. Eventually, Sylvia's mother was admitted to residential care and four weeks later John died. Sylvia has never had any close female friends; she and John used to go out dancing when he was well, but latterly they had spent most of their time at home.

She felt very alone when her husband died and started drinking heavily. She joined a bereavement club and then decided to go back to the dancing club she and John used to attend. It was here that she met James, her new partner. Sylvia's daughter does not approve of the relationship and they are now estranged; this saddens Sylvia greatly. She has always felt that family members should support each other, just as she and her mother did, and cannot understand her daughter's hostility. Her relationship with her son and his family is close and they have welcomed James. Sylvia still has few friends of her own, although she and James have a very active social life, and does occasionally worry about what she would do if anything happened to him. Most of the time she lives life to the full and continues to enjoy her new relationship.

**Dorothy** is 71 years of age and was born in Stockport. She has been widowed for five years. Her childhood was not particularly happy and she spent some time living with her grandma. She did not enjoy school and left when she was fourteen years of age. She had a number of jobs but could not settle to anything in particular. She met her husband, Roy, when she was sixteen, but fairly soon afterwards they both enlisted in the forces. She enjoyed forces life and feels that she would have made it her career had she not had to leave on medical grounds.

She was married in 1948 and, after initially living with family, moved into a new council house. She has three sons. She juggled work and home life in order to supplement the family income, but always put the children first. Like Patricia, she was determined to be a 'good' mother, but also acknowledges that she was, and still is, a very possessive mother. It saddens her that her sons, now, have little time for her nor do they understand how she feels. Her interests were centred on the house, sewing and baking. There was little time for socialising, because either she or Roy worked in the evening. In later years, she felt they did very little together and regrets this. She became a school dinner lady, a job she did for twenty-five years and was very upset when she had to retire.

After an accident at work, Roy had to retire and was ill for a long time before he died. These were difficult times and Dorothy still feels guilty about the times when she lost patience with him. She always refused to discuss the possibility of one of them dying, even when Roy made out his will, and was surprised when he died. Dorothy has found widowhood very difficult, especially birthdays and anniversaries, but she has tried to keep busy. She has some close friends, who are either ever single or widows, and she works part time. She is also a volunteer at the primary school where she was a dinner lady. She tries to look forward and has devised strategies such as planning holidays and organising her week in order to ward off her sadness. She feels she has always been insecure and this is exaggerated now she is on her own.

## Conclusion

This chapter has thus set the scene by introducing the twenty widows whose life stories are at the heart of this book. The following four chapters, grounded in the words of those women, comprise the multiple narratives that derive from an analysis of those stories: Me, Myself; History and Me; Me and My Social World; and Me, Now.

# Chapter 8

# Me, Myself

## Introduction

In this chapter I present and discuss the multiple narratives that have been derived from an analysis of the part of the women's life stories that relates to Me, Myself. This is essentially a discussion of identity - a self that is reflected on when looking back over the life course and circumstance. I suggested in Chapter 2, that we rarely think about our identity at a conscious level, except at times where either external, or internal circumstances combine to heighten our awareness of identity consciousness. The giving of a life story to an interested listener provides such an opportunity. I also argued in Chapter 4, that narrative and biography/autobiography are at the core of identity in modern life: there is a close connection between personal meaning, identity and life story.

In giving her personal biography, each woman, to a greater or lesser extent told the story of the way in which she has perceived herself over the life course. She talked, from her own perspective, about the perceptions of others, ways in which she has managed her life and how this has either helped or hindered her in widowhood. These perceptions were reflected in the story which was told, the way in which it was told and through phrases which sum up a personal view of 'self'. She hinted at an identity which has been both self ascribed and sometimes confirmed or contradicted by others.  She provided examples of the way in which she had drawn on aspects of her 'self' to manage events in her life via recurring life themes. Although there were idiosyncrasies in the way the women explained these life themes in their individual stories, there are a number of narratives or overriding accounts that embraced the themes. As I discussed in the Chapter 6, it is useful to view these themes as comprising a spectrum of multiple narratives:

| High Self-Esteem | Fluctuating Self-Esteem | Low Self-Esteem |
|---|---|---|

**Figure 8.1    Multiple narratives of Me, Myself**

At one end, are life themes of self-determination, self-confidence and autonomy, which are embraced by what I have chosen to call a narrative of 'High Self-Esteem'. Women who voiced this narrative expressed self-belief and an awareness of their own sense of autonomy. They told a story which looked back positively over the life course and in which they felt comfortable with their 'self'. In many ways this is contrary to a popular stereotype of the current generation of older women who are often portrayed as having lacked autonomy and a strong sense of self throughout their life course. At the other end of the spectrum is the narrative of 'Low Self-Esteem'. The stories that embraced this narrative contained life themes of emotional dependence on others, a lack of self-belief, and low confidence. The women who told these stories reflected unhappiness with their life and uncertainty about themselves. Some of the women told stories that are between these extremes. Their life themes embraced a narrative of fluctuation/ variation between managing and not managing, sometimes feeling confident sometimes not, feeling good about themselves but at times feeling very unsure of who they were. Self-esteem was variable and the life story is often encapsulated in the phrase 'if only'.

As figure 8.2 demonstrates, each woman's life story encompassed one dominant narrative:

| |
|---|
| *High Self-Esteem*<br>Eunice; Jean; Jennie; Evelyn; Elizabeth;  Farzana; Katherine |
| *Fluctuating Self-Esteem*<br>Bee; Betty; Doris; Ellen; Joan; Mags; Pat; Phyllis |
| *Low Self-Esteem*<br>Dorothy; Edith; Patricia; Sylvia; Vera |

**Figure 8.2    Locating the participants within the narratives of Me, Myself**

I now explore in detail the multiple narratives arising from the women's stories of Me, Myself:

**A narrative of High Self-Esteem: 'I've always known who I am, what I wanted to do, I've had a good life'**

The overriding narrative here is of a strong woman who feels she has been able to influence her own life. Life events have been managed with considerable self-awareness and self-confidence; strength, resilience, and autonomy have been confirmed by the words and actions of others. This is not to say that challenges or crises have not arisen; this is not after all the narrative of a charmed life, but a life in which it has been possible to exercise some influence over those challenges and crises or at the very least to manage them successfully. The narrative reflects a subjective experience of well being, a contentment with self and life as the following sub-plots confirm:

```
┌─────────────────────────────────────────────────────────┐
│  A narrative of High Self-Esteem                          │
│    • feeling secure                                       │
│    • a strong value base                                  │
│    • self-confidence                                      │
│    • learning from experience                             │
│    • independence                                         │
│    • regrets for others                                   │
└─────────────────────────────────────────────────────────┘
```

**Figure 8.3    A narrative of High Self-Esteem**

*Feeling secure*

Feeling valued by those around them, and the sense of security which comes from that validation, is significant and was expressed by all of the women in this narrative. Eunice, for example, talked vividly about a childhood in which she felt loved and able to be the person she wanted to be:

> (My father) found a new estate being built in Denton, near St. Anne's church. And I was thrilled to bits with this house and what I particularly remember is that the gates were all painted pink...they hadn't been properly painted. We were all so excited. So I started at the local school and made friends ... and we grew up in that area, during the war, and that's where I lived until I got married. Well I always knew I was loved at home and my parents encouraged me ... that makes such a difference you know.

Jennie echoes the importance of growing up in an extended family who cared:

> My parents, they did a lot for me, they helped me in every way. I had a wonderful childhood, I was the only child and my childhood, well I knew I was precious ... I had a family closeness, right from the beginning.

Despite failing her scholarship examination, Eunice was able to enjoy her secondary modern school, which enabled her to 'grow':

> I failed the scholarship, I was terribly disappointed, I was on the borderline ...but I got through, my parents helped me ... (at the secondary school) I made friends with all kinds of people, I was secretary of one of the houses, and vice captain and games captain. And school vice captain. Oh, I loved my time at school I was very happy there. I left when I was 14, I think now I was a late developer. When I left school I had a choice of jobs and I got a job at a cotton firm in Manchester. I had such a strict interview for the job and I was only the post girl (laughs)! I had to have an exam in English, Maths and Geography. My first job was travelling all round Manchester delivering the letters. We had to find out where all the streets were and I so loved going up and down in the lifts! ... I've always tried to make the most of opportunities, I always wanted to learn and find out more.

For Eunice, this feeling of security continued throughout her marriage, a marriage in which she was both an individual pursuing her own interests and career in the Red Cross and a partner, sharing other aspects of her life with Laurie:

> ... right from the beginning we led separate lives but together ... there were so many things I wanted to do and of course Laurie was such a private person ... but we had such a lot in common as well. We had a caravan and that was great for me, I could move and get around and we both loved the open air and travel ... although we had separate interests, we had a lot in common. We were very good companions. There was so much we did together and thought alike about things. It was a good balance.

Unlike some of the women in other narratives whose sense of security was fragile, these women felt that they were loved and valued by those around them. This certainly did not make them complacent, but instead provided them with an inner strength on which they could draw in times of stress without feeling undermined by others. Evelyn for example suggested that this sense of security was one of the main reasons why she never felt lonely: 'I've never felt lonely, I'm not a lonely person ... I suppose you could say I've been happy with myself, secure.'

*Values*

A strong value base that provides both a reference point and a sense of continuity is also integral to this narrative. This is expressed mainly in terms of faith or spirituality. Jennie and Farzana for example, had strong spiritual beliefs, which have always guided their lives and given them an inner confidence and a confidence about their place in the world. Farzana has always been guided by her Muslim beliefs and her lifelong trust in Allah. When her husband died, she had absolute belief that, once her grief had subsided, she would manage her life: 'I managed, I knew I would manage. I am a Muslim and I believe in Allah, he helped me. It was difficult but I managed.'

Speaking about her faith, Jennie says: 'I feel that God helps me in my life, he always has done.' When Jennie's husband took ill and subsequently died, they were in Germany on holiday together. She gained considerable comfort from her faith at that time, and welcomed the support of the nuns who cared for him before his death. Jennie has managed many changes in her life, including a number of major family difficulties, with a confidence that all will be well.

Like many of the women in this narrative, Eunice has a strong sense of her own values, which are underpinned by her faith. This faith has helped her to manage some very difficult times:

> My faith has always been so important to me. I really do have deep faith and throughout my life that has been so important to me. My mother and father were Christians, and I was brought up as a Christian. I was a Sunday school teacher for many years. Laurie and I used to sing in the church choir and we were both active in the church. My faith has helped me through very difficult times ...

Values are expressed in other ways than through faith. Each of these women had a strong belief in 'family values', with the family being an anchor (albeit not exclusively for all of them). The women attributed this, in the words of Jennie, to: 'it's the way I was brought up'. For Farzana, Jennie and Eunice family values were integral to their faith. I discuss the family further in Chapter 10 but suffice to say here that Jean, Jennie and Katherine for example often made reference to friends or work colleagues being: 'like a family.'

There was also a strong 'work ethic' expressed by these women that again was often attributed to their upbringing. Each one spoke with pride of her work efforts but also had a tendency to minimise those efforts with the assumption that this was what they expected of themselves and others. Indeed it is interesting to note that during my conversation with Elizabeth, I enquired how she managed to juggle a busy family life with working in the bakery, she looked at me in amazement and said: 'I just did, its what we did, we believed in hard work!'

*Self-confidence*

The development of confidence over the life course is significant. In telling her story, for example, Jennie exemplified the self-confidence of a woman who had always made the most of life's circumstances and had few regrets. This self-confidence had been validated by those around her, both family and friends, and had given her considerable self-worth which she had taken into widowhood. She had few regrets about her life and felt that this helped her when John died:

> We'd had a good life together and I'd had my life too, my working life. I mean, I did what I wanted to, John would never stop me, he knew what I was like! (When he died)… We were having a lovely time on holiday, John really enjoyed it, and we were both together, I've no regrets. And that's how I've looked upon it you know. I had a good life …
>
> (Jennie)

Farzana was able to manage the major life change of moving from one way of life in Pakistan to a completely new life in Stockport with the confidence, as a devout Muslim, that Allah would help her get through any difficulties:

> At first it was different, so different, so difficult. But then you get used to it … and then I came here to this house. I have lived here all the time. And then all my children went to school in Stockport.
>
> (Farzana)

Like Jennie and the others, she had few regrets about her life, summed up in the phrase (which she used on several occasions): 'My life has been good. Allah has been good to me'. This is despite the difficulties arising from her husband's redundancy and subsequent ill health and the disruption this caused for family life:

He used to work for a steel firm but they closed and then he became ill. Then he worked for a short time in the bread factory but that wasn't so good. And then he had his own business in the market but he only did that for a short time. He was not in good health, it was difficult ... But I was strong.

(Farzana)

Farzana has gained considerable self-esteem from her roles of wife and mother, roles which were validated by her husband, children and friends. She has never worked outside the family home, but instead has had a career as a wife and mother. Her story therefore is not the story of a woman who is independent of her family, but rather the story of a woman who gains considerable self-confidence from her role within the family. She continues to build on these earlier experiences.

This self-confidence enabled each woman in this narrative to feel 'at ease' with herself as an individual, and to express satisfaction with life. Evelyn echoed the views of others. Reflecting on her life in the past, she said: 'I like being with people and I like my own company ... wherever, I am at ease.' She had successfully embarked on a major life change when she left nursing, a career that she had enjoyed, to pursue a new career with her husband as a Blackpool landlady. This had been quite a risky business:

When I first started the guest house, it was all strange to me ... I'd only ever cooked for the three of us. Sidney, myself and his father. I'd never done any big cooking so I went to lectures run by a big wholesalers to help me with quantities ... and the first summer I didn't have many guests, I never advertised but our first visitors were the people I'd worked with (when nursing) in Doncaster and it built up from there ... we didn't know how we'd manage but we did. We never made a lot of money from it, we fed them too well, but we had twenty-five years of happy times there.

(Evelyn)

These women were comfortable with themselves and had a strong sense of 'I'. They were satisfied with the life they had led and had few regrets; to the contrary, they have learned from experience.

*Learning from experience*

This capacity to draw positively on previous experiences in order to manage new situations has contributed to growing self-confidence among this group of women. When Eunice's daughter died, she was able to accept the support of others and also felt able, at a later date, to make use of this experience to make changes in her own life and support others. She has a strong awareness of how difficult this was at the time: the death of a daughter, who was only in her twenties, was a completely 'off time' experience. After her husband's death, she gained strength from this earlier experience as well as drawing on her faith in order to manage her life as a single person:

(after oldest daughter died) my faith kept me going and then when Laurie died …
I really do believe that I shall meet them again. When my husband died I was
prepared for some things that maybe some people who are bereaved for the first
time aren't. You see cards, well when they came through for my husband they
didn't hurt me as much and I knew I would manage.

(Eunice)

She remembered the feelings of shock when her husband died and the
numbness. But throughout her bereavement she had a strong sense of her own
strength and knowledge that she had the inner resources to make sense of and
manage her aloneness. Like many of the other women whose stories encompassed
this narrative, she had a strong sense of self and her own autonomy; she was self-
contained but able to ask for, as well as give, help without feeling compromised in
any way.

Jean told a story of resilience throughout the life course, learning from
experience and coping with major life changes such as Albert's increasing
disability, his unemployment, and the move to a new neighbourhood. She
described what objectively has been a 'hard' life:

I've always done what I needed to do. You just have to do it. My husband didn't
earn very much; when he first came out of the navy, he couldn't get a job, then he
went working nights but that wasn't suitable. Then he got a job at Oldham
Batteries but he was ill … he was in the naval reserves but he was discharged
because he had a patch on his lung. He was off work for two years and I worked
as a stewardess at the cricket club … in 1954 we had National Assistance but then
in June 1955 Albert got back to work. When he came home at night, I used to go
to work making gas cookers, near where we lived …I suppose I've always been
busy, but then I've always been healthy. And you just have to get on with it don't
you?

(Jean)

## Independence

'Independence' is a word that featured often within this narrative. It describes a
feeling of personal autonomy, the need for personal space and also the objective
experience of having managed alone.

Jean was proud of what she described as her independence over the life
course. It is both a subjective feeling and the objective reality of having personally
successfully managed some difficult life events. She was very aware that others,
including her family, have recognised and valued her need for independence. She
took pride in this, feeling that it had contributed generally to her overall well being
and specifically to how she felt about herself. Jean talked about gaining
independence throughout the life course and responding positively to the
challenges before her:

I had to be independent. My father wasn't very pleased with me marrying Albert
… I worked all the time the children were growing up … you just learn to cope …I

would have liked to have been a 'lady of leisure' but I do enjoy a challenge (laughs).

In a similar way, Elizabeth, described herself thus: 'I've always been independent I think'. She offered the following examples as explanation. As a young girl, she had left her Shropshire home to work in service in Cheshire and then London. She talked about this as a deliberate decision on her part, given the limited choices for girls of her age in rural Shropshire, and not one into which she was pressurised in any way. On the contrary, her mother had tried to dissuade her. During the war years (which I describe in more detail in the next chapter) she had felt strong as a woman on her own with a young child. Indeed her story was that of a self-confident young woman, who took this self-confidence and independence into adulthood and later life. Her description of the time when her husband died is telling: 'I knew I would cope. I can cope on my own, I think I have always been able to do things on my own.'

Katherine spoke little of her early years but portrayed herself as an independent woman in her adult years. It had been important to her to have a life that was separate from her husband as well as sharing their family life together:

> I've always had a lot of independence, its been important to me ... yes I think it has (P. Did you know many women who saw themselves as independent in marriage?) No, no, a lot of them have been subdued, perhaps I was a bit unusual... I've always been a fighter for women's rights, well I've always spoken up ...
>
> (Katherine)

Katherine's story, like those of Jean and Farzana, told of a woman whose life has objectively been difficult. She and her husband lived on a small income that required them both to work outside the home. However, like many of the women, she looked back with few regrets. She feels she had the space within her marriage to be the person she wanted to be, she had her own friends and her own interests (see Chapter 10) but balanced this with a relationship in which she felt valued.

*Regrets for others*

Although there are few personal regrets within this narrative, there are regrets for her partner. Reflecting on her retirement from the guesthouse, Evelyn said:

> We just walked out of the guesthouse in Lytham Road and into a retirement flat in Lytham. It's a shame we didn't do it sooner, he only had three years there.

It is interesting to note that Evelyn's regrets were for Sidney, reflecting a sadness that he was not able to find the satisfaction with life that she clearly had. For her part, once she had retired, she had 'seventeen happy years living in the flat', and for the first time had a best friend, whom she valued greatly. This friendship is discussed in more detail in a Chapter 10.

In her story, Elizabeth also regretted that her husband had died before he was able to 'enjoy his life'. This is in keeping with what the literature tells us about gendered scripts (see Chapter 4). When giving positive personal accounts, women often feel the need to insert such reservations or regrets, perhaps because they are so unused to talking warmly about themselves.

*Summary: narrative of High Self-Esteem*

This narrative then articulates a strong sense of 'me as an individual', and includes an awareness of the multiplicity of roles undertaken over the life course. The self-confidence that has developed has enabled adaptation to, and in some instances active embracing of, new roles and new circumstances. The need for autonomy has been recognised by others and there is an explicit value base that underpins both life choices and the management of major life events. Bereavement, for example, was certainly not an easy time, but was managed with the help of lifelong self-esteem.

**A narrative of Fluctuating Self-Esteem: 'I never really pushed myself forward but I got by in the main, only sometimes I think, if only…'**

This narrative reflects a 'self' that fluctuates between managing and not managing, sometimes feeling confident, sometimes not, occasionally feeling self-assured but at times feeling very unsure. There is no absolute certainty of validation by others and self-esteem is not entirely intact. It is a narrative of women whose inner self and outer self are often contradictory. There is not absolute confidence of managing although in fact the narrative describes good managers who have self-pride. In reflecting back over married life in particular, there are a number of regrets, usually encapsulated in sentences beginning: 'if only'. Thus the hand of cards that life has dealt is perceived as a mixture of good and bad. Although there is a feeling that too often the roles that have been played out were those demanded by others, there is a strong recognition that structural issues have contributed to this in some way.

So unlike the consistent narratives of 'self', which are located at either end of the taxonomy, this narrative is one of inconsistencies and contradictions. I now discuss the sub-plots of this narrative.

| *A narrative of Fluctuating Self-Esteem* |
| --- |
| • ambition versus 'I might have' |
| • becoming 'someone else' |
| • a bit of a rebel |
| • pride |

**Figure 8.4    A narrative of Fluctuating Self-Esteem**

*Ambition versus 'I might have ...'*

This tension was integral to the narrative. So many of the women reflected a frustration with themselves and their lives when they look back over their life course.

Phyllis, for example, described herself as a clever schoolgirl, who was particularly good at sport. At school, she had ambitions to be a PE teacher but: 'I was not encouraged from home'. Instead, she did a variety of 'unfulfilling office jobs' and when the war started married a man who was thirteen years her senior. Apart from the war years when they were apart for some of the time, they spent all their working lives together. They managed public houses, what Phyllis describes as 'public life':

> Of course, when my husband was in the war, that was a very different life, then when he came out we went into public life. It's not an ordinary life. (Tell me what you mean by ordinary) Well, its not that you lead separate lives but you become independent. Its not like living in a house ... I was married forty- three years and my husband's been dead ten years. Apart from the last ten years, most of that was spent in public life. You put on an act a lot of the time ...

Phyllis described herself as a confident woman who has always been surrounded by people who value her. (I discuss her social world in more detail in Chapter 10.) However, as a consequence of the life she led, she lacked a private world and a world in which she could be herself. Instead, she put on a public face, and latterly, regretted her unfulfilled ambitions and the lack of opportunity for personal development: 'You miss a lot in life.'

Joan and Betty echoed these sentiments. For Joan, the war years had intervened crucially in her life. Her schooling ended abruptly and very soon afterwards she met her husband, a young officer, and married at seventeen years of age:

> While I was younger I thought I wanted to be a teacher, when I was fourteen or fifteen. Before the war started I had visions of being a teacher, particularly sport and dancing ... I would have loved to have played at Wimbledon ... I should have been able to do things but I missed out ... there were so many periods in my life where I might have made a success ... everything in my story was 'I might have...
> (Joan)

Joan's story was one in which 'might have' predominated. Like many of the women whose stories encompass this narrative, she feels both frustrated by circumstance and yet angry with herself:

> There again, I would have gone in for ice skating but my husband was coming home from Africa, and I'd been for some auditions in Blackpool for a summer show, but I pulled out because my husband was coming home and I hadn't seen him for three years and he was going to be posted near to London. So I left St. Anne and went down. So that was another period when I might have made a

success, everything was I might (original emphasis) ... (when the children were young) I used to go off and do my little bit of visiting for the Adoption Society. Sometimes, I would have to go quite a long way and it would take a whole day. I used to go to Alsager, I went there quite a lot and I ended up going back to Alsager for a tennis course. I wanted to be a tennis coach, but I didn't make it; I was ill during that time and had to have an operation, so I didn't make it. I'm a failure really, I never finished doing what I wanted to do.

After she had read her transcript, she reflected ruefully: 'I should have been able to do these things, but I missed out.'

This feeling of 'missing out' is a recurring theme, which is articulated individually but also collectively in that there is a sense of 'we' in this narrative, a reference to a generation of women. (I discuss the important issues of generation and gendered lives in the lives of these older widows in more detail in the next chapter, History and Me.) It is worth noting here that, in this narrative, there was a strong sense of lives structured by 'others'. As a consequence, there was self-blame and anger at inaction and missed opportunities, but also an awareness of a bigger, gendered picture which, to some extent, tempered those feelings. This awareness set this narrative apart from the final narrative which, as I discuss later, encapsulates internalised regrets and self-blame.

*Becoming someone else*

Alongside the frustration of missed opportunities, the narrative of fluctuating self-esteem also revealed a 'self' which was, in some ways, 'coerced'. Betty, for example reflected on becoming the manager of finances and the organiser in the household even though she did not really want that role:

> We lived in a small flat for fifteen years, I suppose because my husband was not a good provider ... he was a very good husband and a good father but he was an artist and he lived up there somewhere, you know in the clouds. He was very clever and he should have made a fortune but he was not a businessman and you couldn't guide him, he was an architectural sculptor, extremely good at what he did but it was always hard going, very hard going financially ... and so I took over the finances, I became the one who, well I always had to take responsibility and I had to take responsibility and I had to keep things on an even keel because my husband didn't. (So would you describe yourself as fairly independent and autonomous when you were married?) Well, I had to be ... I think he made me into something I really wasn't ...I perhaps wouldn't have been like that with a different partner but then one would never know, he wasn't the type, well I've always wanted somebody to lean on and I've never had anybody to lean on, I've always had somebody that leant on me ... Because of that I had to push, take on more and had he been well, had time not been so tight, I could have done a lot more, updating my qualifications and got on a lot better. Who knows, it's supposition isn't it?

Bee's story was somewhat different, but also reflected a change in 'self' as a result of the actions, or in her case insistence, of a husband. Unlike Betty she had no regrets about this but was very aware of the change within herself. She married when she was twenty-seven, to a man who was twice her age. Until her marriage, she had lived independently since leaving school:

> From being eighteen until I was twenty-seven, I worked for the railway. I had my own flat and I loved my job. I was in the accounts department, working with engineers. My hobbies were tennis and dancing and I loved them both. Also I did an awful lot of social work for the railway with the staff association, organising drama festivals, arts festivals, things like that. I had no intention of getting married because I was very happy, and I couldn't have children so I saw no need to …

When she married, Bee's husband insisted that she give up her job and not undertake paid work:

> My husband said when I got married, 'You are not going to work, I want you here'. What do you think of that? (Well, I suppose I am wondering how this very independent woman you have just described, who loved her job and the freedom it gave her, managed this demand?) Well, I was determined my marriage was going to be a success. My husband was a very wealthy man, and I'm a monogamist, one only, and I'd seen what my mother and father had had to struggle through in the 1930s and I was determined my life would not be the same. So he said, I want you here and when I come home from work, I want my dinner ready and if I say go, we go …so whatever he said, we did …

Bee had created a different life for herself around her new role (described in more detail in Chapter 10, Me and My Social World) but was very aware that she had changed from the 'self' she was before she married, at her husband's insistence. It was a trade-off she was prepared to make:

> I loved my job, I always wanted to go to work and I knew I wanted to get on. I've always been a very positive person, not over ambitious, I've been very positive and practical. People have always said I have a lot of common sense … if I hadn't met Harold, if I hadn't had money, I would have got on with my life, because I am a positive sort of person … but meeting him, I had to become a different person and I had a very good life, we had a very happy marriage for thirty six years, we travelled the world, but yes, I became a different person.
>
> (Bee)

### 'A bit of a rebel'

There was also a hint within this narrative, which did not appear elsewhere, of rebelliousness, which took a number of forms. For example, some women told the story of a rebellious young woman who, in marriage, outwardly lost her rebelliousness but really, secretly kept it hidden inside herself. Doris, for example talked of her parents' relief when she married at nineteen years of age:

> I was nineteen when I married ... I liked my own way and my parents were relieved (laughs) they never knew where I was, what time I was going to be back, I was a rebel ...everyone said so.

She described herself as 'very green' when she married, with very high expectations of marriage, totally undomesticated and expecting her husband to be as indulgent as her father had been:

> I thought he was like my father, he was a wonderful man, everything my mother did was right ... I thought, I'll be like that. But it wasn't, my husband was a very possessive man, very selfish ... he had to have his own way or he sulked and I couldn't stand that, so I never used to cross him ... I suppose it was a good marriage really, it wasn't ecstatic but, you know, it was alright, we didn't fight. If he got his own way, we didn't quarrel ...

Doris maintained that she never really lost her rebelliousness but kept it hidden and conformed for a quiet life. She managed the house and the family and her life seemed very ordered: 'I had to become domesticated ... but then I'm very adaptable really.' Her escape was her garden, which was her own private space:

> We didn't have very much of a social life, but it didn't worry me. I had my garden. I was very keen on gardening, I loved gardening it was such an escape. We had three quarters of an acre. He wasn't interested in it. So I could do whatever I wanted, it was mine. I loved gardening and hated housework so what I did was I employed a woman to clean three times a week and I could spend my time in the garden - it felt so naughty (laughs).

(Doris)

Like so many of the women, she revealed an awareness of the structured nature of her life: 'I just put up with it, you did in those days.'

So many of these women spoke of keeping a significant part of themselves hidden in order for their marriages to survive; in doing so, some of them put what they saw as their 'true self' on hold.

Mag's story was particularly telling. She had been disabled since childhood and was very aware from her early years of the limitations placed on her by others, because she was female and disabled:

> I've always been a devil you know. (Tell me what you mean by that?) Well when I was at the home, the Crippled Children's home, I used to go there periodically, I can remember I tried to run away twice and they brought me back ...And then, my mum said I would never be able go out to work, and I'd never be able to go out with boys. There was enough at home to keep me busy, so I could help her in the house. Well I stuck it for three weeks and then the devil in me, well I went out without telling her and got a job because all my mates got jobs. And I worked from fourteen till I was fifty-seven. I never had a break, you know how you have a break to have children, well I never had children and I worked until I was fifty-seven.

Even her courting was rebellious. Jim was a friend of her brother-in-law and was already married when he and Mags met:

> He was teaching me to drive and one thing led to another and I did a bit of dodging. (What do you mean by 'dodging'?) Well you know, not straightforward, I suppose. I used to go out in my car and meet him and get in his car because my sister and her husband were a bit straight laced. She was worried for me, but we dodged a lot, Saturday afternoons ... and then we decided I would go and live with him, well in them days it was bad you know, we weren't married.

She was happy to settle down and eventually marry Jim and no longer felt the need to openly rebel. She had proved her mother wrong - she had a job and a husband; nonetheless her rebellious streak was always just below the surface.

*Pride*

As highlighted in the introduction to this chapter, this narrative was not just about regret, or subjugation of self, or inconsistencies, although these are important strands of the narrative. These women knew that they had a lot to be proud of in their lives, have clearly gained a lot of satisfaction from what they have achieved and, in many ways, feel good about themselves.

Mags described herself as always having been a fighter and is clearly very proud of having confounded the low expectations arising from both her gender and disability. She worked for many years as a seamstress and takes great pride, both in the skills she acquired and also in the praise and respect she received from others, especially members of her family:

> I used to do so much sewing. I've made wedding dresses, all my nieces and girls I worked with, Jim used to do all the housework while I sewed (laughs). They all said nobody could sew as well as me ... I've even made leather jackets ... and I liked doing it properly, I won't put up with less than perfect.
>
> (Mags)

Betty, Ellen and Phyllis also gained pride and satisfaction from being good workers. Despite the frustrations of her job Phyllis, for example, knew that she was an excellent publican - her customers told her so. Ellen knew from the references she received each time she changed jobs, as her sons grew older, that she was a valued worker. Even though they had to juggle these roles alongside others throughout their lives, they gained both satisfaction and confidence from knowing that they had skills that were recognised by others:

> I got a job at a printer's and I stayed there five years, well by then I was running the office. There was only the boss and myself and I was in charge of all the accounts, he said I could do it better than him. That was very, very interesting because I liked printing. And I was valued by the Company. I really did like it and I was stepping up a little bit each time, getting a little bit more money.
>
> (Betty)

Both Doris and Ellen were proud and satisfied at having raised a family whom they knew cared for them. Ellen's own family of origin was not particularly caring or supportive, but that was not the relationship she had with her sons. She recalled what happened when her husband was first ill:

> He was fine really, there were no problems; there were no worries about anything. We carried on 'day to day' … We were very, very fortunate because we'd got a family that cared. Anything that he wanted, he could have, and me of course. I am so proud of my boys, I must have brought them up right (laughs).
>
> (Ellen)

Bee and Joan both remarked on aspects of their life which have given them satisfaction, pride and self-confidence. Having made the decision that she would be a full time wife, Bee set about this with enthusiasm and was rewarded for her efforts by the approval of her husband and mutual friends, and by her own self-approval:

> He was well taken care of … everyone said so. I was a good wife to him. He liked his food and I made sure that he was well fed (laughs). With not having a family, you see he was my husband, my baby, everything you see. I hadn't got any money; I had no money. I had to depend on Harold giving me it … but he was always the first person in my life, the first consideration if you like.

Despite her reiteration of 'might haves' and the declaration that she was a failure, Joan reflected proudly on many areas of her life. She had worked as a volunteer with an adoption society:

> I did … voluntary visiting. I had an aunt who was in London with an adoption society, which was very much to the fore in those days. They wanted visitors, particularly when I moved up north. So I'd got a little Austin Seven in those days and I used to do all this visiting. They used to bring the babies home from the adoption society and I'd go to their house before they brought the baby home and I'd vet the house, and then I'd go back three or four times after, up to six months I think, before the adoption went through. And during that time, I used to write all the letters … I was learning from scratch …
>
> (Joan)

This pride was sorely tested around the time of her husband's death. She managed to cope with a number of family problems that followed her bereavement, with a confidence which took her by surprise:

> … when my husband died, there was all that fuss over my son's wedding, and then they didn't get married and I had to support him … that was so difficult but yes, I managed it all.
>
> (Joan)

*Summary: narrative of Fluctuating Self-Esteem*

Yet again, it is the subjective experience, which locates this narrative and which renders the overall experience of 'Me, Now' different from the other narratives. The immediate impact of widowhood for each of the eight women was both distressing and unsettling. On looking back, she may have had regrets about some aspects of her life, and how others had seen her, and wished she had had the confidence to manage some situations differently. She may also have had an awareness of the structural issues that impacted on her life and limited any real choice. There was, however, the knowledge that she had managed other situations well. Each one, in her own way, brought these contradictions to widowhood.

## A narrative of Low Self-Esteem: 'I've never felt sure about myself, I've always done what others wanted'

At the other end of the spectrum is a narrative that tells of emotional dependence on others, a lack of confidence. Many of the life experiences and challenges within this narrative are objectively very similar to those within the previous two narratives. However, more importantly, the subjective experience is one of not having coped well with life events. Furthermore others, often husbands or members of family of origin, have seemed to confirm, or sometimes even reinforce these feelings. There is often self-blame for this lack of confidence and lack of self-esteem, and certainly no censure to either individuals or society. Interestingly, it is this very narrative that is sometimes portrayed as the stereotype of women of the pre-war generation, that is one who is downtrodden, dependent on a partner for identity, lacking in coping skills. I now discuss the sub-plots of this final narrative of Me, Myself.

| *A narrative of Low Self-esteem* |
| --- |
| • powerlessness |
| • a lack of self-confidence |
| • lonely |
| • failing to live up to expectations |
| • always being grateful |
| • no individuality |

**Figure 8.5    A narrative of Low Self-Esteem**

*Powerlessness and a lack of self-confidence*

Powerlessness, and the lack of self-confidence which arises from it, is the key feature of this narrative. All of the women in this narrative expressed many regrets about their lives, but with a resignation that they felt powerless to do anything about it. I discuss the process of telling these stories in Chapter 13, but it is worth noting here that for both Vera and Patricia, some parts of the research process were particularly painful. They enjoyed the company of and talking to an interested listener and were very keen to participate in the research but, nonetheless, initially found it difficult to read their own life stories because they contained so much unhappiness.

Vera's mother died when she was young and she lived with her sister up to getting married. Once married, she went wherever her husband's job demanded. Throughout her life, she never had to take the initiative but relied on others, especially her husband, to make decisions for her. She has never been independent and, whilst acknowledging that she had had many skills, she observed that she had always lacked confidence and, on reflection, had always had low self-esteem. This lack of confidence had been further compounded by widowhood:

> Until you are widowed you can't imagine what it is like, it is completely different than I thought it would be. It sapped my confidence, and I had very little of that ... I'd always followed my husband ... Suddenly you are on your own.
>
> (Vera)

Patricia confirmed that she too had always lacked confidence and had doubted her capacity to cope with life events. She had felt both neglect and abandonment as a child, in particular as an evacuee at the beginning of the Second World War. From a young age, she was required to undertake caring responsibilities for a younger sister, which left little time for herself. There had been a brief period as a school leaver when life had been both exciting and in her control: 'the happiest time of my life apart from when I had Wendy ... I met so many people and felt so free'. Otherwise, life had been:

> ... difficult. I've always taken the world on my shoulders, if you like, tried to look after everybody, and that's probably why when I got married, I just carried on. But I got the type of man who would let me.
>
> (Patricia)

On reflection, her marriage had been a disappointment, which eroded her confidence even further. She described her husband as:

> ... a silly man ... he was like the eternal teenager, he never grew up. I used to say to my daughter, all he wants is just his television and chair at the fire ... I was the worrier, not the breadwinner, but the worrier.
>
> (Patricia)

She expressed the view that being married decreased her already low self-esteem.

*Lonely*

Loneliness was identified as a feature of this narrative. Not just loneliness in widowhood, but a loneliness that spanned the entire life course and is both emotional and physical. Patricia's story reflected those of the other women in this narrative. She had often been lonely, particularly when her husband worked on the night shift as a printer. Her compensation had been to devote herself to her daughter:

> ... he started to work nights just before she was born ... well, all through her childhood. It made for loneliness really, a lot of it. I didn't go out much at all in those early days. She came to me a lot ... there was only me there, especially at night ... I never left her alone with him, he was frightened to death of her waking up and me not being there.
>
> (Patricia)

The desire to be a 'good mother' had been so important, firstly because of her own lack of parenting and secondly, because it provided her with a clearly defined and satisfying role:

> I wanted to be here for her and have a meal ready for her. I'd be here to look after her, be a proper mum. And I was, I was always here.
>
> (Patricia)

However, life at home became an isolating experience that eroded her confidence even further. Unlike Farzana, for example, she had not felt validated by her experiences within the home. When Wendy, her daughter, was in her teens, Patricia had been given the opportunity to take a job in the box office of a famous theatre, a job similar to the one she had loved as school-leaver; but overcome by self-doubt she had turned it down: 'I felt relieved at the time ... but I was sorry afterwards'. I asked what she meant by 'sorry' and she replied that she regretted it because it might have been an opportunity for her to do something she was good at, to meet new people, and to re-enter a world where she had been happy. When her husband died, her isolation continued and her self-esteem decreased even further. She lacked confidence in her own ability to handle the new situation, a sentiment echoed by Vera and Dorothy, and, in the short term, by Edith and Sylvia.

*Failing to live up to expectations*

Implicit in the narrative was a disappointment with life and a feeling of not having lived up to the expectations of others, or of letting oneself down. Dorothy echoed the experience of the other women in this narrative, describing an unhappy childhood during which she had tried very hard, but without success, to please her parents:

> I was the eldest and my brother and sister, there's two years between each of us and the other two were very sickly, and mum got diptheria and she had to go into hospital and dad couldn't cope with the three of us so I came to my granny's here in Romiley. I stayed here for quite a while ... and then I went back home, but I was always in trouble, my sister was the baby and I got into all sorts of things, I think it just continued from there. I seemed to get into trouble with my mum and dad ... I tried hard to be good but I suppose I was a naughty girl.
>
> (Dorothy)

Joining the army, a life event she managed successfully on her own, had been one way of trying to please her parents. Reflecting on her father's response at the time, she said: 'anyway, he was quite proud then, the fact that 'my daughter's in uniform' and I was so pleased...' Even in the army, despite enjoying the life and being pleased with her contribution to the war effort, she was nonetheless unable to fulfil her ambition to be a nurse, finding herself instead on kitchen duties.

Dorothy, like Patricia and Vera, perhaps as a result of her own unhappy experience and a desire for a clear role, desperately wanted to be a good mother to her sons. She did this as well as she could, but on reflection worried that she had been an over anxious and possessive mother. Although she had worked outside the family home, she invested a lot of herself in motherhood and did not welcome her boys growing up and moving away. She described her life as 'hard', was often tired, had many regrets about her life and a very low opinion of herself: 'I didn't have the confidence to do so many things, there were lots of things I couldn't do. I suppose I still lack a lot of confidence.' The one time in her life when she did lived up to expectations was when she was a school dinner lady. She was recognized by the staff and children as someone who actively contributed to school life and as a consequence, felt valued and gained self-esteem. When she had to retire on grounds of age, the school marked the event:

> I was a dinner lady across at the school, I did that until I was sixty-five, I did twenty-five years over there, twenty-five years. I was broken-hearted to leave ... I did love the children, and the teachers were so kind and when I retired I used to sit upstairs and watch them playing out at lunchtime and get all upset ...I just couldn't help it and Roy used to say, that school, that's more your home than here. The headmaster phoned the council to see if he could keep me, they wanted to keep me you see, but they said 'no'. They had a surprise party for me you know when I retired, the teachers and the children, and bought me presents, I have two lovely roses for the garden ...
>
> (Dorothy)

Dorothy conceded that her family did not really appreciate the significance of the job for her self-worth. In fact her husband, as the above comment demonstrates, openly expressed hostility concerning the amount of time and energy she devoted to what he saw as 'just a part-time job'. It is interesting to note that Vera too reflected that her voluntary work in the RAF had not been valued by her husband; it was just something she did to fill her time and could be dispensed with each time they were posted to a new base.

Dorothy grieved for a long time when she had to retire and acknowledged that it was a very difficult life event, which within a year was followed by the death of her husband. She tried very hard to manage the funeral, but following the funeral a family row concerning the site on which to scatter her husband's ashes, had left her feeling even more devalued: 'I felt that I couldn't even get that right. I thought I was doing what Roy would have wanted but now I'm not so sure.'

*Always being grateful*

Within this overarching narrative of Low self-esteem, there was also a strong feeling of gratitude to others for tolerating inadequacies or failure to live up to expectations. Sylvia most strongly expressed this feeling. For a significant part of her life, she had felt an overwhelming gratitude which led her to take on responsibilities for others and 'be busy' without a lot of thought for her own happiness or well being. Looking back, she reflected on her growing lack of self-confidence and self-worth:

> I got myself pregnant. I wasn't married, I was an unmarried mother as they call them now ... I went into an unmarried mothers' home in Heywood to have the baby. It was such an awful place, to punish you I suppose ... she was three months old when I came home and I had to go to work because in those days, you got nothing once your maternity allowance was up. I know I didn't feel very good about it all ...
>
> (Sylvia)

Her mother supported her in caring for her daughter, and Sylvia was extremely grateful. She was able to return to the firm where she had previously worked 'in the offices'. However:

> I had to go into the works because I'd never finished my, well I was going to night school for shorthand and typing, but of course that all stopped when I had Susan so I just worked in the factory. I'd been to the grammar school, but it counted for nothing afterwards...
>
> (Sylvia)

Sylvia had not expected to get married and recalled that she was very grateful when John asked her to marry him:

> I suppose my marriage was happy. Well, he was a good dad, and a good husband, nothing out of the ordinary. We never had any real major upsets and I think I was very grateful. When I had Susan, I suppose I thought that was it.

In later life, when her children had left home, Sylvia became a full time carer for both her mother and her husband. Her gratitude to both of them, as well as a certain amount of resignation, was apparent when she remembered this time in her life:

> I very often had them both ill together. She (her mother) was repeating herself and so on and I was acting as a buffer between them ... when John died, she said 'thank goodness we've never had a cross word' and I thought, yes but only because I was in the middle ... But I don't regret it because they'd had a good relationship for years.
>
> (Sylvia)

*No individuality*

A Narrative of Low Self-Esteem spoke of individuals who lacked autonomy, only ever achieving identity in relation to others. A number of the women reflected that, ironically, this did not seem to matter when they were wives but it presented a crisis when they became widows.

Sylvia had been a good daughter and a good wife, who judged herself in relation to how well she looked after her mother and husband. The impact of losing both these people, for whom she had felt so much gratitude and to whom she had devoted all of her time and energy, was not surprisingly devastating. She suddenly realised that she had very little else in her life and no confidence in her own ability to manage on her own. She did not know 'who' Sylvia was without these other people:

> I went from looking after two of them to nothing ... it was a bit traumatic really, especially with my mum going into a home four weeks beforehand. I started drinking, I started buying bottles of whisky and I'd have three or four before I went to bed and many time I'd be half way upstairs and you'd just crumble and have a good cry ... many times during the day, I just used to get on the bus and go into Stockport because I couldn't stay in the house ... I was so lonely.
>
> (Sylvia)

Edith too did not recognise herself as an individual. She told the story of a married life during which she relied totally on her husband. He made all the important decisions and she concurred; it never occurred to her that it should be any different. Her family were aware that he was the decision maker and were grateful that he was looking after Edith. She summed it up with the statement: 'Everyone knew us as Donald and Edith.' This was not problematic when her husband was alive but when her husband died she began to see it differently:

> I'm still me, I'm still the Edith that was with Donald but other people didn't see me like that ...it was like I wasn't a person, I was part of Edith and Donald.
>
> (Edith)

It was as though nobody, not even Edith herself, really saw her as an individual. This was exacerbated by a lack of self-belief and no self-confidence. In reflecting back over her life, she recognised that it had always been thus but that it was disguised when she was part of 'Donald and Edith'. It took Donald's death, and the time she spent in hospital, for her to begin to really value Edith.

*Summary: narrative of Low Self-Esteem*

Within this narrative therefore there is considerable self-doubt. A lack of self-confidence, reinforced by the behaviour of others over the life course, has resulted in feelings of being undervalued and unsure. It is a narrative in which 'Me, Myself' exists only in relation to other people. Life events have been difficult to manage and it has been difficult to accept support from others, without being further undermined. The death of a husband, and the consequent bereavement, only served to confirm this narrative.

## Conclusion

In this chapter I have demonstrated that there are a number of narratives of Me, Myself, which have impacted differentially on the experience of later life widowhood. There is a spectrum which ranges from at one end, a narrative of high self-esteem which tells of women who have felt good about themselves as individuals throughout their life course and who have managed life events with confidence, to a narrative which tells of women who have low self-esteem, who have always felt devalued and perceived themselves to have lacked the confidence to successfully manage life events. I summarise it thus:

| Me Myself |
| --- |
| *High Self-Esteem* |
| • feeling secure |
| • a strong value base |
| • self-confidence |
| • learning from experience |
| • independence |
| • regrets for others |
| *Fluctuating Self-Esteem* |
| • ambition versus 'I might have' |
| • becoming 'someone else' |
| • a bit of a rebel |
| • pride |
| *Low Self-Esteem* |
| • powerlessness |
| • a lack of self-confidence |
| • lonely |
| • failing to live up to expectations |
| • always being grateful |
| • no individuality |

**Figure 8.6    Me, Myself**

This chapter has focused on the individual within life stories and the place of the self which is reflected on when looking back over the life course. These multiple narratives of 'self' are a stark reminder that the experience of widowhood does not exist in a vacuum but is located within personal biography and identity which are constructed over the life course. However, these multiple narratives of 'self' are only one part of the experience of my twenty participants, as the following three chapters will demonstrate. The next chapter therefore explores the place of a common history in the lives of the twenty older widows and analyses the impact of this common history on the management and experience of later life widowhood.

# Chapter 9

# History and Me

## Introduction

I highlighted in both Chapter 4 and Chapter 8 the increasing recognition by gerontologists of the importance of historical location for understanding the experience of later life. In this chapter therefore, I discuss the multiple narratives derived from an analysis of the wider, historical, issues that are both explicit and implicit in the women's stories. These are yet another part of the jigsaw which makes up both the individual and the collective experience of later life widowhood. The narratives tell of events and structures as well as attitudes towards and opportunities for women at different times in their histories.

In the telling of a life story each participant identified herself, to a greater or lesser extent, in terms of generation and gender and talked of the impact on her life of belonging to a collective 'we'. This is demonstrated in figure 9.1

| Belonging to a Generation...............Gendered Lives |
| --- |

**Figure 9.1    Multiple narratives of History and Me**

Firstly I explore the narrative: Belonging to a Generation. This is of necessity focused on the period about which the women talked most, their childhood and early adult years; the historical time which identifies them as a generation. Secondly I explore the narrative: Gendered Lives. I then conclude the chapter by discussing the place of history in the lives of older widows and suggest that we can have no real understanding of the experience of older widows without paying attention to the historical context in which they came of age.

## A narrative of Belonging to a Generation

Each participant in the study had her own individual biography, but like all of us she shared a common history with others. Clearly, the impact of this common history on each individual will vary but there are nonetheless powerful shared memories and experiences that contribute to a narrative of generation.

The pen portraits demonstrate that women who participated in the study encompass an age range from 64 years to 89 years. Nevertheless, whether they were a child or an adult during the years 1939-45, they all situated themselves historically as belonging to the pre-Second World War generation. Indeed talk of

'The Thirties' and 'The War Years' predominated in most of the women's stories. Therefore, although there are both commonalities and differences in the historical issues that were raised, the overriding narrative was one of belonging to a particular generation. This was a generation who experienced massive upheaval and change, but also a generation who had greater hopes and expectations than those who had preceded them. The sub-plots to this narrative are summarized in figure 9.2.

| • Difficult times for some |
| --- |
| • The War Years |
| • Changing times |

**Figure 9.2    A narrative of Belonging to a Generation**

*Difficult times for some*

Within this sub-plot there was an understanding of the difficult times some families experienced in the 1930s and the impact thereof. These were years that for some were fraught with problems, often precipitated by unemployment and poverty. Memories of those times have remained to the present day and, in some instances, still influence the management of finances in particular.

Betty's father, for example, had a series of jobs during these years. He was an intelligent man, a brewer, who lost his job during the Depression. She told of his search for work and the way in which he took any job so the family would have food on the table. She remembered some very hard times:

> I was born in Rochdale. Because my father was a brewer, he worked at the local brewery in Rochdale and then we moved to Bolton …he moved to another brewery there because the one he was at, it was going down. We hadn't been there very long and of course the brewery went into liquidation overnight, it was the bad old thirties you see and things like that were happening all the time. And so we left Bolton and came to Manchester because my mother had relatives in Manchester … my father had a terrible time and he literally took anything he could get in the way of work. I mean, he was a staunch Tory and he sold the Daily Herald as though he had supported it all his life. You know, all sorts of things. I mean he travelled for a glassware company that was tied up with the brewing trade. It was a very hard struggle for my mother.
>
> (Betty)

This had been a very difficult time and often entailed him working away from home, including a job in South America at the very beginning of the war. Betty had been close to her father and reflected that these absences had been painful. Her mother, used to a much higher standard of living before marriage, struggled to live on a low income and there were often rows in the family. A sister of her father offered a solution:

It was hard going. Then one of my father's sisters who was well to do, she was married to a man who was a director of a company called G&W Collins who were wholesale provision merchants, so they were very comfortable and she said if they wanted help, unload one member of the family, she would be agreeable to pay for me to go to boarding school. So when I was nine I went to boarding school until I was sixteen. I learnt to be very self-sufficient.

(Betty)

Betty continued to identify with her father, both in her attitude to work but also her instinct for self-preservation. Throughout her married life and latterly during widowhood she has had a fierce determination to manage financially. Indeed, as I highlighted in Chapter 8, she had indicated her resentment that her husband not been 'a good provider'. At the age of 77 and suffering from severe arthritic pain, she still worked as a cleaner in order to preserve her standard of living.

Bee too, has been determined never to experience the poverty she knew her parents experienced during the 1930s: 'I'd seen what my mother and father had had to struggle through in the 1930s and I was determined my life would not be the same'. She identified this as an important factor later on in her life and suggested that it had made her determined that her marriage would succeed, even if it meant having limitations imposed on her life.

For Elizabeth, life during the twenties and thirties had been quite different. As a young woman, she left the potential poverty of rural Shropshire to work 'in service'. Along with many of her contemporaries, she joined a domestic agency through which she was able to find a job in a large country house in Cheshire. Her story about her life in service provides an interesting insight into the hierarchical, controlling relationships between the owners of the large houses and their staff. For example, she and Ivor (her future husband who was then a butler) were unable to meet openly as friendships between staff were disapproved of. Elizabeth talked about 'courting':

It wasn't allowed really; we weren't supposed to do this. We couldn't go out at the same time but we did manage to get in at the same time. But they did find out and they did offer for us to be married and stay as cook and butler. But we didn't want to …

She had not been ready for marriage and certainly did not want to be pressurised into marriage by her employers. To the contrary, she wanted to find out more about what life had to offer: an early example of the 'free spirit' she has exhibited throughout her life:

I hadn't finished roaming then. I wanted to go to London, which I did. We both left, he went to Darlington and I went to London … I was there just over three years. I went to work for Lord Camrose, brother of the newspaper people; I went as head kitchen maid. There were five in the kitchen there. That was easy really because they went to the country every weekend so we only had the staff to cook for … although sometimes there were thirty of them.

(Elizabeth)

As a widow of eighty-five years, despite considerable health problems, Elizabeth was certainly in control of her own life. She was still extremely well organised and enjoyed showing off the domestic skills acquired so many years ago to children and grandchildren. She still seized opportunities for adventure with great enthusiasm and she regularly visited friends and family using public transport. At the time of interview, she had recently been on a train journey with her youngest daughter back to Shropshire and spent time in the village where she was born.

*The War Years*

Stories about the Second World War, 'The War Years', loomed large in this narrative: Belonging to a Generation. With the exception of Farzana, who had lived in Pakistan at this time, all the women confirmed this time as a significant period in their history, one that has impacted on their lives both in the past and the present. Age, geographical location, marital status and new opportunities all played a role in this.

For some, it was a time of sadness and lost opportunities. Patricia was one of the younger women to take part in the study. Born in Manchester in 1929, she was ten years old when the war broke out. Along with many children from large cities she had been evacuated to the country and separated from her family:

> It was a bit of a tough childhood really. The war started on my 10th birthday, and on September 3rd we were evacuated to Great Harwood. My mother came along, and Maureen (her sister) would only be, well if I was only ten she would be four, I suppose. My mother came and she stayed at another house with Maureen and I was a bit further, the other side of the village with a very, very nice family with one other girl from my school.
>
> (Patricia)

The time that followed this was one of great unhappiness for Patricia. Indeed, she reflected that she had carried this sadness with her throughout her life, right into widowhood; not surprisingly she became tearful when describing this time. She vividly describes the disruption caused to an already chaotic life; her parents had separated and her mother was very unsettled away from Manchester:

> We'd been there about a month I think and my mother said she was coming home, going back home. She was doing some sort of job helping with other children; I don't really know properly what she was doing. And I wanted to go with her but she said no. Well I've never, ever forgotten it. Because I sobbed and sobbed...I desperately wanted to go home.... and she wouldn't, she was a harder woman than me... in fact a couple of years before she died she said, you never really understood, did you, why I left you in Great Harwood. Because she knew, after all those years and I don't think I ever forgave her for it. I was so unhappy when they went home. She took my little sister with her. The lady, Mrs. Martin was very kind to me but I was so unhappy until sometime in the November, one Sunday,

> Mrs. Martin came to me and said, 'there's a visitor for you Patricia' and it was my father. I was delighted to see him and he asked if I was happy and I said no. So he said 'right we're going home'. So he went to Mrs. Martin and said 'pack Patricia's clothes, she's going home, I'm taking her'. She said 'you can't do that' and he said, 'I'm taking her'.
>
> (Patricia)

Patricia graphically described her mother's reaction on seeing her.

> And I'll never forget the greeting I got when my mother opened the door and saw who it was. She said, 'what have you brought her home for?' She wasn't too pleased to see me but I'm afraid I didn't care much. I was home and that was it. I never went back of course. I just didn't understand at the time and I'm afraid I still can't see how she could do it.

Her mother had subsequently worked in a munitions' factory, leaving Patricia to look after her younger sister. She had grim memories of those times, conceding that she had to grow up very quickly. She remained convinced that her lack of self-confidence and lack of trust of others had its origins in her very disrupted childhood.

In Joan's life story, the war years predominated. Indeed, even in the follow up interview she returned to her feelings about the war years. She reflected that they were crucial in shaping her future life, both because of meeting her husband and the direction her life subsequently took, and also in terms of missed opportunities. Joan was fifteen and living in Kent when the war broke out and she had to leave school suddenly:

> My school suddenly closed because of the air raids and an insurance company came to the school, they had evacuated from London. And that was the end of my education! While I was younger I thought I wanted to be a teacher and before the war started I had visions of doing this. There was a college in London, Dad put my name down for me to go and I would have gone there when I was 16. So what would have happened then, I don't know. I think I would have made it.

Instead, Joan worked for the insurance company who took over her school and continued to work for them when the company moved back to London. This brought her face-to-face with the after effects of the bombing in London. The family moved, temporarily to East Grinstead and it was here that Joan met her future husband. Like many women of this generation, the war provided a number of women in the study with the opportunity to meet men from other parts of the country and from different backgrounds; Joan's husband had lived in the North West of England. She provided an illuminating insight into the role of women in wartime marriages as well as reflecting on the necessity to 'live for the moment':

> My husband came down there (to East Grinstead), he was with some ambulance corps, he came down and we loved dancing and that's how we got together. At that time, that was our social life, the dancing ... I was married at 18, its very

young isn't it? It was the war, my husband was an officer in the army and he was going abroad and he so wanted to get married, so there was no question about it. It was difficult for my parents but life was so different in the war.

(Joan)

Her husband then left for service abroad, initially for twelve months and then for a further two years. Joan was a married woman, but still very young:

When I got married, of course I was ready for 'calling up' then. But they didn't seem to know what to do with me. I was married and only 19 when my husband left. So I got myself a job at the NAFFI at Reigate … and I didn't leave there until the war was over. It was odd really, I mean there were these sort of socials and parties and you longed to go out and have a little flirt really or meet somebody new, but you couldn't because you were married. But there were many stages when I thought, that was a silly thing to do. You really do if you're honest with yourself. I mean I couldn't because my parents would have been in a really bad way about it … in those days, you didn't think about separating or divorce, even with the war.

When her husband finally came home from Africa a lot of adjustment was needed to resume married life:

… when he came back it was very odd, very odd. I'd been a married woman in name. It was even odder than when you're first married and the first night because you've been together leading up to it, but this was suddenly somebody else was going to get into bed and you've been on your own for three years, it was quite a shock really.

(Joan)

There was no question of the marriage not working and so Joan adjusted to what was expected of her by her husband and society at large. Joan's philosophy of 'you just have to get on with it' was one that clearly has its origins in her early years.

Elizabeth spent the war years in rural Cheshire with her daughter. Her husband had been away in Africa for four years. She too acknowledged the readjustment when he came home: 'you had been in control all those years … it took some adjusting. You get to rely on yourself and cope'. Like Joan, she took the decision that despite the difficulties, her marriage was going to work.

Both Elizabeth and Joan, despite their very different wartime experiences, acknowledged that the independence they had during the war years was evidence that they were able to look after themselves and make their own decisions. This knowledge had proved to be extremely useful for them as older widows.

For some of the women, the War years offered life chances previously unavailable. The war years offered Ellen, for example, an escape from inner city Birmingham. On leaving school she had a factory job, but was able to leave it to join the Auxiliary Territorial Service (ATS) in 1941 at the age of seventeen and a half. Ellen still regarded this as a turning point in her life:

A lot of us had never had things we got in the army. We all got lovely pyjamas and things like that. We needed them because the anti-aircraft girls roughed it a lot, but a lot of the men never realised. And you'd always get big boots, you got plenty of everything you'd never had at home. For me, and a lot of others in the army it was luxury; three good meals a day we were fed, it was a different kettle of fish to home. I think we sort of grew up in, well I often say, we grew up in a few weeks. It was a great experience. I've said to my grandson, my eldest grandson, I'd never seen the sea till I joined the army. I started off at High Legh, that's where we trained in the beginning and then we went to Shropshire to a camp and then we were sent down to Painswick, in Gloucestershire, I was on anti-aircraft duties…that's where I met my husband. Then we stayed there for about twelve months and then we went to Falmouth. We were there for D Day. It was a wonderful experience. I mean all those ships and boats and everything else. They were all there one day and the next morning we were going up on the Aircraft Recognition, you had to do that first thing in the morning, and the sergeant said, you're going to get such a shock when you get up on the gun park. And there wasn't a ship in sight … nothing was there, because you see nobody could write home, we couldn't write home for three months. So everybody knew there was something going on … it was such a wonderful experience, I think we all got a good deal out of being in the forces. … I would have spent all my life in Birmingham.

(Ellen)

'The Forces' continued to live on in Ellen's life; she belonged to her local ATS Association and regularly attended meetings once a month. She had some close friends with whom she shares these early memories and a tremendous sense of communal pride.

*Changing times*

The war years were a time of change for many women, but so too were the years immediately following the war. Two examples are provided to highlight the sub-plot of changing times that is inherent in this overriding narrative of generation.

Living arrangements were particularly complex in the post war years and many of the women, who might have expected their lives to follow the pattern of housing experienced by their mothers, found themselves instead in very different circumstances. Some had moved from one part of the United Kingdom to another, leaving their childhood home. For some, this had been a tremendous wrench but, as I explore later, this was not something a woman questioned.

Joan, Doris and Bee had all been married to men who had the financial means to purchase a house. Joan and Doris were able to purchase newly built houses on small housing estates in Stockport. This had been an exciting time and certainly something they had never done before. For Joan, it was a huge adventure:

Well, we came up here, I can remember it now. We came on the train and, of course, I had to have my hat on because I always wore a hat in those days and I lost my hat in the taxi. We were picked up in a small car, I think the driver worked for the firm and he took us, he said he knew of two houses for sale, and we had to look at them quickly. It was quite exciting. We decided to have the one in Cheadle because we had hardly any money ... we were very fortunate because you couldn't buy houses in those days (immediately after the war) and this one, it was built before the war, but not finished because of the war, so it had stood like a bombed shell, but we managed to get round the builder, who had lots of friends who wanted it ...

Thinking that they would only stay there for five years, she had then lived in the same house for fifty years, only recently moving to live with her daughter.

Ellen's experience had been somewhat different. She and her husband had moved initially to Manchester to live with her mother in law. Her husband's sister and her family also lived there:

> We lived in his mother's house. She was a lovely woman; my own mother couldn't have been nicer. She was really good. We lived in a big house, we had a bedroom upstairs and a room downstairs of our own. And so did his sister and her husband. And then his mum and his other brother shared the kitchen and a bedroom, they had a curtain across. The biggest room was for them and then his sister ... and of course we had David, who was born in Birmingham, and then we had Stephen who was born two and a half years later and Kenneth was two years after that; they were born at his mother's, Stephen and Kenneth. We stayed there until 1963 when we moved here.
>
> (Ellen)

When the opportunity arose, Ellen with her husband and boys and like many of her contemporaries, moved to a newly built social housing estate in Stockport. Although she remembered this time with excitement, she had also clearly enjoyed living in an extended family household, particularly valuing the relationship with her mother-in-law. At the time of the study, she was re-creating this arrangement with her oldest son and his partner. She had clearly thought long and hard about this and had learned lessons from the past, especially about personal space and the company of another woman. She shared these thoughts:

> Somebody said to me, 'do you think you'll be tied with having David and Tina living with you?' but I said, no, not really. I can't see there being many disadvantages. They're out all day for a start, they go out at twenty five to eight in the morning; he takes her up to the station on his motor bike then goes off to work. He finishes work at four o' clock and then he's home and getting her a cup of tea ready when she comes in. I usually do the veg and before they go to work in the morning I usually say I'm going off to make my bed in case they want to talk about anything ... even when they're at home at night I say, well I'm just going up to watch a programme so they've got an hour. I can't see it being a disadvantage because I've got my own space. That was the idea, because there's an empty room. They said they didn't want me to live upstairs but I said, I do, I want my space because you do want your own space. Whatever, you need a little bit of time to yourself ...and Tina and I, well we're like friends, so no I don't see it being a problem.
>
> (Ellen)

Having somewhere nice to live, often with a garden, and somewhere to call 'home' is a recurring theme. All of the women realised this dream in some way in the post war years. The provision of relatively cheap but good, rented social housing enabled a number of the women to bring up their families in conditions that were so much better than those they had experienced themselves as children. They certainly fared better than their own mothers. The rapid growth of house building enabled those women whose husbands (or parents) could afford it, to take advantage of the private housing market. Many of the women had remained in the same family house throughout their married lives and some have only relocated in widowhood.

Some women identified the period immediately following the war as a time of opportunity. Elizabeth's husband had come home from the war determined to set up his own business. Although she had been initially reluctant, she went along with this idea and, with a loan from the bank, they bought a bakery and grocery business. Together they built this into a very successful enterprise but Elizabeth recognised that this was because of the times as much as their own hard work:

> We made it successful, but I think in a way the times helped, because there was a lot of building and a lot more houses were being built, and the town was growing; there were a lot of families here, young families. And of course your own reputation helps ...
>
> (Elizabeth)

Evelyn too had taken advantage of the changing times by giving up nursing and buying a guesthouse in Blackpool. She and her husband had been to Blackpool for a short break and realised that a lot more people were taking holidays than in the years before the war. They decided to take advantage of this and make some changes in their life:

> Well I was nursing and my hubbie was fed up with his work, he wasn't very happy. We went to Blackpool on holiday, lots of people did, and we saw this house advertised. We got details of the house, looked at it and I fell in love with it, we never looked at anything else. We went home, both gave our notices in, and sold our house quickly. We only took the soft furnishings with us. It had only been a guesthouse for a year so we walked into it as it was. I didn't know how we'd manage but we did. We never made a lot of money from it, we fed them too well. We had 25 years of quite happy times there...
>
> (Evelyn)

The gendered nature of many of these 'opportunities' is explored in more detail in the narrative of gendered lives later in this chapter.

For Farzana, one of the younger women who took part in the research, the post war years had involved even bigger changes. She was born in 1934 in Pakistan and married in 1952. In the early 1960s her husband, along with a group of other Pakistani men, came to Stockport to find work. They were some of the first Pakistani immigrants to come to the area in any sizeable number. These men had been recruited to work in the local iron and steel industry that existed at that time. (It closed down completely in the early 1980s). Although not a large group, (a much larger Pakistani community lived in nearby Manchester) the men, who worked together, settled in one part of Stockport. Some of the men had been well educated in Pakistan, but found themselves doing heavy manual work. They provided support for each other and when Farzana and her three children came to join her husband in 1968 there was an already established support network. Although this was a major change for Farzana and her three children, (she had three more children whom she referred to as 'my English children') she presented it in her story as of little consequence. This may have been as a result of telling her story, via an interpreter, to me a white woman living in Stockport and a desire to therefore minimise the problems, but it also seemed to reflect her attitude to life (as discussed in Chapter 8). Her strong religious belief and her role within the family provided her with a point of reference and continuity:

> ... my husband was here and I was with him. I came here to this house. I have lived here all the time. My husband bought this house ... this is my home, there is no-one left in Pakistan now, no in-laws, everybody is here. I go there for a month but not to move back. Stockport is my home now.
>
> (Farzana)

*Summary*

A narrative of belonging to a generation clearly situates the lives of this group of older widows within a certain historical location and identifies them as a group who have lived through a particular historical period. In doing so, it separates them from those who were born earlier or later. Integral to this narrative, perhaps with the benefit of hindsight, is a mixture of stoicism and optimism: putting up with the 'now' but anticipating better times ahead.

**Gendered lives**

The second overarching narrative in relation to History and Me is that of gendered lives. The recognition by some of the storytellers that women's lives are gendered was raised both in Chapter 8 and in the narrative of belonging to a generation in this chapter. In so many ways the women recalled how their lives had been structured by gender. They made it clear in the telling of their stories, the role that both the government (or society) and powerful individuals (usually husbands, fathers or brothers) had played in structuring their lives. Some women were very aware of the impact of patriarchy on their lives, but for others, the telling of their story provided them with an opportunity to reflect on these structural issues with the benefit of hindsight and the knowledge of the sometimes different experience of their daughters and granddaughters. I discuss the following sub-plots to this narrative:

| • Education |
|---|
| • Becoming a wife |
| • A woman's place is in the home |
| • Working lives |
| • Breaking the rules |

**Figure 9.3    A narrative of Gendered Lives**

*Education*

For many of the women, formal education had been a passing phase in their lives, whereas for others it comprised missed opportunities or lost chances. Thirteen of the twenty women left school at the age of fourteen when compulsory schooling ended. Hating school so much, Doris had actually left before that time but was made to return by the school board. Farzana's mother had died when she was twelve years old necessitating a move to live with her sister in law and thus leaving school: 'There was no choice. I was a girl. When I was in the sixth year of schooling my mother died, so I finished my education.'

Only six women went on to study beyond compulsory school leaving age. All of them chose, or were encouraged by others to choose gendered educational routes. Indeed, none of them considered that any other options were available to them. Vera and Bee for example, both took part-time night school classes in shorthand, typing and bookkeeping whilst working full-time. With the exception of Evelyn who undertook nurse training, none of the women pursued full-time higher education. Indeed, only Eunice had committed herself to lifelong learning. Having left her local secondary modern school at fourteen years of age, she then went on to study, with the support and encouragement initially of her family and latterly her husband, both at night school for her Matriculation and in her local Diocese as a Sunday school teacher. She later entered adult education as a mature student and studied part-time for a Certificate in Counselling. She also enrolled for numerous courses as part of her work for the Red Cross.

For many of the women then, school was a prelude to marriage, with work perhaps intervening for a while and both the gendered curriculum and the attitude of family reflected this. There was an emphasis on domestic or clerical skills they would need in their future lives. They were not encouraged to read widely or think for themselves. After all, as Betty commented: 'we didn't need to think to be housewives.'

Both Dorothy and Katherine were obliged to leave school at the earliest opportunity in order to supplement the family income. Dorothy did not really enjoy school apart from cookery lessons and felt that school offered little to girls from her economic background. Certainly, her family saw little need for her to be educated:

> I didn't like school, only when it came to baking and knitting, my hobbies. No I wasn't very happy at school at all, I didn't get much from it. In fact, I started work at eleven, after school because mum used to work in a corner shop that was a

bakery and mum used to do the baking there. I used to go to the shop after school and she showed me how to do baking, she said it was more use than school. I started off with muffins and then teacakes and then bread.

(Dorothy)

Even for those women who found school a rewarding experience, there were difficulties. Eunice, for example, loved school and had been sorely disappointed not to pass her eleven plus examination. Having been told she was borderline, she had later found out that the eleven plus results were skewed in favour of boys. She was cross about this:

I failed the scholarship and I was so terribly disappointed. I was on the borderline … I've always had a chip on my shoulder about education and any chance I've had to do studying, I did.

(Eunice)

Class, as well as gender, impacted on the education of many of the women. Reluctance or an inability to spend meagre family finances on education for girls appeared in several stories. Sylvia passed her school scholarship and went to the local grammar school but after a period of illness fell behind with her schoolwork. Her mother had then decided that the family could no longer afford the money needed for the uniform and books. Sylvia reflected ruefully on this time:

I went to Romiley School and I really liked it, I was happy at school. Then I passed my scholarship and went to Stockport High. But my mother couldn't really afford to keep me there because of the uniform and it was before free books, I think that came in not long after I'd been there, but she couldn't afford to keep me there. She managed to buy my first uniform but as I grew out of it, she found it very hard to renew it and by this time my dad had started drinking so we were short of money. And then, when I was fourteen I had diphtheria very badly and was in hospital. I was off a full term and I found it very, very hard when I went back to catch up with the work, so she wrote to the authorities and they allowed me to leave. So my dad made me go into the kennels full time.

Betty had loved her boarding school education and acknowledged that, courtesy of her aunt, she had a privileged education. However, unlike some of her school contemporaries, she was not able to take further advantage of her education by going on to college or university. There were no grants available and her own family could not afford to support her. Her aunt had provided her with a sound education thus far, but was not prepared to support her further and so she had to leave:

I was sixteen when I left school because in those days, unless you were going on and taking your higher school certificate, which of course I didn't think I'd ever be able to do … There were two things I really wanted to do, one was I would have liked to have been a P.E. teacher, that was one thing or I would have liked to have been, well they didn't call it physiotherapists then, they were massage students. But both were very expensive courses and of course there just weren't any grants and this was, well when I was leaving, it was wartime so there was nothing.

(Betty)

Joan had hoped to go on to college but as discussed earlier in this chapter, the war intervened. She had hoped to train as a Physical Education teacher and, unlike Betty, would have been financed by her parents. After the war she was a young married woman and fairly quickly became a young mother. Unlike the many young men (married and unmarried) who took the opportunities offered to them to train as teachers, via shortened courses, her life had taken a different direction. Her responsibility, reinforced by government policy, was to care for her husband and family and there was no question of going back into education. Joan deeply regretted her lost educational opportunities, which she attributed to the war but also society's attitude towards women:

> One of the problems was that after the war I was a married woman and that was different to being a married man. And then I had these children and there wasn't the support... I feel I was never well educated sufficiently, well it was the fault of the war and being married, you just didn't go back ...

For these women who found their own education thwarted, education became an important issue when they became mothers. They did not want their daughters and sons to suffer the same restrictions they had experienced and so offered encouragement and support. For others there is still a feeling of lost opportunities.

*Becoming a wife*

For those women who were married just before or during the war, life as a wife began when their husbands returned home from the forces. A number remember that there had been little negotiation about how their lives were to develop; they obeyed their husbands.

Joan moved to the North of England with her husband, who was expected to join the family firm. This entailed leaving her closely knit family and friends:

> It was dreadful moving away, it was dreadful. I hated it...and later, when I had the children, every school holiday, I'd be in that car with the children, down south we'd go ...

(Joan)

Ellen moved from Birmingham to Manchester. Her husband's family came from Manchester and that was where he hoped to find work. It was out of the question to disagree with this. Indeed, her father made sure that she knew what was expected of her:

We stayed in Birmingham until...well I was there with the baby, Joe was still in the forces, I can't remember exactly when he came home. David was about eleven months when he eventually came home and he wanted to go back to Manchester, well he was born in Manchester and his mother was there. So I decided, well I don't think I decided, my father said to me, 'You're married, you go where your man's work is now'. He said, 'its an understood fact that where your man goes, you go too'. Well that was the days, that was the thing then. So of course we upped and left and came to live round here.

(Ellen)

When Elizabeth's husband came back from the forces, he decided he no longer wanted to work in service as they had both done in the pre-war years. He had tasted a different world and he now wanted his own business. Elizabeth didn't really want to take on such a large commitment but felt she had little choice but to agree:

Well it was my husband that wanted it; I didn't want a business, not a shop and certainly not a bakery business, but I went along with it and we were there twenty-three years. We did it because he wanted to do it really; it mattered to him.

It is interesting to note that none of the women, even Elizabeth who has always regarded herself as an independent woman, considered doing anything other than follow their husbands' wishes. It was what was expected of women and they went along with this view. As discussed in Chapter 2, this was reinforced by post-war social policy. Husbands were the breadwinners (even if Elizabeth and Ivor were co-workers) and so the women did what was expected of them.

*A woman's place is in the home*

The message that was given to women after the Second World War by public policy and voiced by many husbands, was that not only was a woman to be defined by her 'wifely' status but that her place was in the home. For some of the women, this proved to be the reality.

For example, once her husband had returned home from his wartime duties, it was made quite clear to Joan that her place was to be in the home:

Well, there was no question of going to work, no question at all. Oh my goodness, there was a home to be run and children and everything like that. Sometimes, if I grumbled about money, he would say, 'Well you can always get yourself a job', but he didn't mean it, oh no. My place was in the home. And there were many women like me.

Eunice, who did not question her role in the home at the time, reflected that with hindsight it was strange to think that women put up with this situation. She noted that there had been practical reasons, particularly concerning child-care after the war. If you had no family nearby it was very difficult to find child-care and of course child-care was the domain of mothers, not fathers. However, she also acknowledged that it was not just about child-care but rather the powerful, gendered philosophy and policies of the time:

> I automatically gave up my job and I do think a woman very often loses out. Well you did then; now I suppose you would go back to work and use your skills.
>
> (Eunice)

For others, family finances meant that they had to combine paid work and domestic duties. However, it is very clear from their stories that no matter how many hours they worked outside the family home, they were still the providers of care for their family and they had sole responsibility for running the home. Even if a husband was in and out of work (as in Jean's story), the domestic sphere was still the responsibility of the woman.

*Working lives*

If they did work, the jobs available for women were both limited and gendered. Katherine, Evelyn, Elizabeth and Jenny, who all began their working lives before the Second World War, worked in traditional female occupations. Evelyn completed her nurse training and became a state registered nurse; Elizabeth was in domestic service and Katherine and Jenny worked in the cotton mills, where there were strict gender divisions.

With the outbreak of war, opportunities for some women were to change dramatically. With vast numbers of the male population otherwise occupied, there was a great shortage of labour. The war years, according to those women who were old enough to be of working age, provided opportunities that would not have been available during peacetime. Some of the women, for example Jean in the munitions' factory, were allowed to take on new working roles. However, overall this does not seem to have made a big impact on their working lives. Many continued in traditional female roles: Dorothy, for example, continued to work in the kitchens once she had joined up; Joan and Betty both had clerical jobs in the burgeoning insurance industry. Betty was adamant that bright girls who were unable to go to university had a small number of career choices: 'There was nothing for bright girls who didn't go on to university, there was only teaching, civil service and insurance, and I went into insurance!'

The way in which women's lives were structured was clearly reinforced for Betty by the reaction of both her mother and brother to her request to volunteer for one of the women's services. Unlike Ellen and some of the other women, Betty was neither encouraged nor supported by her family to join up. She describes how this decision was made for her:

> I was a bit ambitious then. But my brother, who was in the forces of course, said to my mother (because my father was dead, he died at the beginning of the war): 'You mustn't let Betty go into the forces, they're all morally bad, all the girls, they're immoral.' So of course, this frightened my mum to death and she said, 'No

you can't go into the forces, you're not to and you wouldn't like it.' Oh I hated him, I really hated him!

(Betty)

She was resentful that, as a girl, her brother made this decision for her. Nonetheless, there is a resignation about this, after all women's lives were structured and women were powerless to do anything about it: 'I was desperately disappointed that I didn't join the forces but that's how it was.' Betty also noted, with irony, that although she certainly gained promotion more quickly during the war years, she found that her promotion didn't continue after the war when the men returned:

> I went as assistant cashier but the cashier was called up to the forces and so I took over his job then, well I had my own department by the time I was nineteen, I had my own typist, it was marvellous. It only happened because it was wartime…when he came back of course, he became chief clerk and I had to work for him.

After the war the women's working lives continued to be gendered, with some women becoming full time housewives and others tending towards some of the new and booming female occupations. These included the textile industry; the school meals service; domestic work outside the home; food and drink industries; shop work; clerical work and mail order companies. Many of the women combined part time, low paid work with looking after their families, continually juggling roles as Ellen illustrated:

> I used to go cleaning when the boys were younger, to buy little extras and what have you. And then as they got older, you know a bit older to take care of themselves, ten or eleven, I got a job at the BBC in the canteen and I worked there for about eight years. And then of course the travelling was getting harder and harder, backwards and forwards and doing all I had to do here, so I left there. Then I went to work across here, it used to be John Williams' and I worked in the warehouse. Then I moved from there and went to work for Fine Fare on the same estate … and I still had everything to do here. It was a busy life.

However, these women later paid the penalty of low paid, part time work when, as pensioners, they found themselves dependent on their husband's income for a state pension. None of the twenty women had access to her own occupational pension:

> I never built up a pension, there just wasn't the money, and of course women didn't. I would have had a better pension if he'd earned more, the same with Helen (friend) she only has a state pension. And yet, the years we worked …

(Betty)

A small number of the more financially secure women undertook voluntary work, again a predominantly female arena. Joan, Vera and Eunice all spent a lot of their time doing mainly welfare work, which took them outside the family home. This was clearly considered to be acceptable to their husbands because they were not earning money and therefore not undermining the male role of breadwinner. Joan worked for an adoption agency, Eunice continued with a life long commitment to the Red Cross and Vera worked for an RAF welfare group. However, while her husband was away overseas for twelve months, Vera learnt to drive and then worked for the WRVS as a bookkeeper. As long as this did not interfere with her primary roles of wife and mother, he was prepared to tolerate this aberration. Doris's husband accepted her working but only if she worked for him:

> My husband was very possessive and didn't like me working for anyone else but him, so we opened a little office of our own in Blackpool ... and then after that, I worked as his secretary at home for years, all the time really.

All of these women who stayed at home were financially better off than some of the other women who had to continually juggle motherhood and work in order, as Ellen recalled, 'to make ends meet'.

Evelyn, Edith and Mags, who like Bee, had no children, all continued to work full time as married women. They worked in female jobs (nursing, mail order and sewing respectively), but each had domestic responsibilities in addition to paid work. There were clear divisions of labour within their households as Edith described:

> I didn't have to pay a bill or do anything like that. I looked after the house, and I suppose I looked after Donald but he did all the sorting out of bills except the phone bill, I used to pay that. And he did the big jobs around the house and looked after the car ...

There was a powerful message in the women's stories about their working lives: a woman's place was in the home, except if she had to work to support the family finances. If she had to work outside the family home, then there was a limited choice of jobs. These tended to be predominantly female and were often short term or low paid. Their working lives, both inside and outside the home, were strictly gendered.

*Breaking the rules*

So powerfully were women's lives gendered that when they broke the rules they were severely censured. The stories of those women who were unmarried mothers exemplified this censure. To be a 'good' wife and mother was to be applauded and of course expected, but to be an unmarried mother was shameful and defied the rules by which women were expected to behave.

Sylvia, for example, was sixteen years old and starting her career as an office junior, when she became pregnant:

Then I got myself pregnant, well I wasn't married...I was an unmarried mother as they call them now ... I made a stupid mistake, well he was a good looking boy and one thing led to another but I should have known better. My dad was furious, wouldn't talk to me...I went into an unmarried mothers home in Heywood to have the baby. It was such an awful place, to punish you I suppose. You knew you'd done wrong, it wasn't a very pleasant experience ... it was a very bad winter, deep snow drifts when I went in on New Years Day, we had to get the train from Romiley to Manchester and then from Manchester to Heywood ... I don't know what I would have done without my mum, she used to come and see me on the train. When Susan was born, I was going to have her adopted, but when she was born I couldn't, she was my baby, it was my mistake not hers ... and my dad said I wasn't to bring her home, he didn't come to visit me ...but my mum said I could and she would help me, I suppose I had an extremely good mother, I couldn't have brought Susan home without her ... she was three months when she came home.

Sylvia remained ashamed of breaking the rules. Indeed, the very words she used to tell her story reflected that self-blame. For example: 'When I had Susan, I suppose I thought that was it ... when I brought Susan home, I expected to be on my own for the rest of my life'.

When Pat became pregnant at the age of twenty-two, she was living in the family home. Her mother had died and her father had remarried. She knew that she had to get away from home and hoped to keep her pregnancy secret:

When I found out I was pregnant I went to Crossley Hospital in the middle of Delamere Forest...a TB hospital, to work there and I didn't tell anyone in the family. I went into Crewe, in those days you went into a home if you had an illegitimate child and I was the only one ... by this time, my father had found out about the child because one of my aunts came to see me and realized what had happened and my father said that I could keep the child but that I wouldn't be able to go home again because, of course, his new wife wouldn't have me at home.

(Pat)

Disapproval of women who did not conform to the rules was explicit and reinforced by both men and women. Pat, who had a private income from her father's business as long as she did not return home, was more able to manage this disapproval than Sylvia, who found herself totally dependent on her mother for support.

*Summary*

The overarching narrative of gender confirms the structured lives of this particular generation of older women. Integral to this narrative of gender, again with the benefit of hindsight, is an interesting and complex blend of acceptance, resignation and anger.

## Conclusion: The place of historical location in the lives of older widows

As a generation of women the twenty participants clearly placed themselves within a historical location that they identified as a time of change. As women they were expected to both adjust and adapt to the challenges and restrictions of that change. More importantly, they had collective memories, both good and bad that have helped to shape their lives as older widows. This interplay between the past and the present in terms of women's lives is an important part of the overall story of later life widowhood.

In Chapter 4, I discussed the significance of the past in understanding the present lives of older people and suggested that our present is sculpted from our past. By making reference to historical location, I am arguing that not only is there an individual past, as discussed in Chapter 8, but also a collective past which because it has both sculpted and structured the lives of all women, contributes to the present, to 'Me, Now'. The lives of the current generation of older widows have been sculpted within a particular historical location and this is yet another part of the complexity of later life widowhood.

In this chapter therefore, I have explored the role of historical location in the lives of older widows, thus adding yet another piece to the jigsaw that is later life widowhood. Through the discussion of multiple narratives of generation and gender, I have sought to understand something of the women's collective history and thus situate the experience of later life widowhood within this common history of a particular generation of women. As the figure below demonstrates, 'History and Me' is now placed alongside 'Me, Myself' as yet another part of older women's lives, which contributes to the multiple narratives of later life widowhood.

| Me, Myself | History and Me |
|---|---|
| *High Self-Esteem* | *Belonging to a Generation* |
| • feeling secure | • difficult times for some |
| • a strong value base | • the War years |
| • self-confidence | • changing times |
| • learning from experience | |
| • independence | |
| • regrets for others | |
| *Fluctuating Self-Esteem* | *Gendered Lives* |
| • ambition versus 'I might have' | • education |
| • becoming 'someone else' | • becoming a wife |
| • a bit of a rebel | • a woman's place is in the home |
| • pride | • working lives |
| | • breaking the rules |
| *Low Self-Esteem* | |
| • powerlessness | |
| • a lack of self-confidence | |

| • lonely<br>• failing to live up to<br>  expectations<br>• always being grateful<br>• no individuality | |

**Figure 9.4    Me, Myself and History and Me**

In the next chapter, Chapter 10, I add a further part by examining the multiple narratives relating to the social world of older widows over the life course.

# Chapter 10

# Me and My Social World

## Introduction

In the literature reviewed in Chapter 3, I demonstrated that the study of the social world of older widows has been restricted by a focus on support. The literature on widowhood largely ignores the impact of older widows' capacity or incapacity to engage and connect with others in a variety of social networks over the life course on their current relationships. And yet, using the evidence from the literature on friendship in later life as a starting point, it is suggested that we cannot really make sense of social networks in later life without an understanding of individual and collective biography, the narratives of self, explored in Chapter 8 and the narratives of generation and gender, explored in Chapter 9. In this chapter therefore, that complex life course experience is acknowledged in an exploration of the social world of older widows.

In telling their stories so many of the women in the current study made reference to turnings in their lives, that is, the way in which they both developed and maintained their connectedness to others during periods of change. These included: getting married; becoming a mother; children attending school; illnesses of family members; and so on. That these turnings have been managed within clearly gendered lives is nowhere more apparent than in the multiple narratives of their social worlds. The demands on their time, from husbands, children, other family members and work, and their acceptance or not of these demands, have shaped their social world. For some of the women, juggling work outside the home with housework and family commitments dominated their lives and left little time to develop social networks beyond the family. For others, the friendship of other women has always been important and opportunities have been sought to develop and maintain these friendships. There were many different ways of managing competing demands and relationships and a variety of social skills and level of confidence were discernable. Indeed, some women have been more connected than others throughout the life course and, as discussed in Chapter 8, these relationships have either reinforced or detracted from older widows' feelings of self-esteem. There is also evidence of different friendship styles.

This chapter takes as its starting point the view that what older widows tell us about their social world over the life course, their priorities and their capacity to connect with others, enables us to better understand their current social networks, a significant part of the experience of later life widowhood. Analysis of the interview data yielded four multiple narratives, encompassing both formal and informal networks. These are summarized in Figure 10.1.

| Friends matter |
| --- |
| No friends of my own |
| A 'joiner-in' |
| Family first |

**Figure 10.1   Multiple narratives of Me and My Social World**

As Figure 10.2 demonstrates, one or two narratives predominated in each woman's story, with a narrative of family often being juxtaposed with one of the other narratives.

> - *Friends matter*
> Bee; Betty; Ellen; Eunice; Jennie; Joan; Katherine; Mags; Phyllis
>
> - *No friends of my own*
> Doris; Dorothy; Edith; Elizabeth; Evelyn; Farzana; Jean; Pat; Patricia; Sylvia; Vera
>
> - *A 'joiner-in'*
> Bee; Betty; Jean; Joan; Phyllis
>
> - *Family first*
> Dorothy; Edith; Elizabeth; Ellen; Evelyn; Eunice; Farzana; Jean; Jennie; Joan; Mags; Patricia

**Figure 10.2   Locating the participants within the multiple narratives of Me and My Social World**

I now explore in detail the multiple narratives arising from Me and My Social World.

**Friends matter**

In this narrative friends feature as significant others at different points in the life course. Furthermore, even though different friendship styles are discernable, identity has been confirmed through friendship. The term friends usually refers to female friends, or sometimes couple friends, who range from acquaintances through to close 'like a sister' friendships. Rarely are male friends mentioned earlier on in the life course, and more specifically during married life (except as part of couples) although as I discuss in the next chapter, Me, Now, male friends or new male partners sometimes feature in widowhood. I now explore the sub-plots, summarized below in Figure 10.3.

| |
|---|
| • My friends are part of my life, the social me |
| • The constituents of friendship |
| • Friend-makers |
| • It must be awful not to have friends |
| • Significant female friendships over the life course |
| • Restrictions |

**Figure 10.3   Friends matter**

*My friends are part of my life, the social me*

Being a friend and having friends throughout the life course confers a desirable identity, one which confirms a social me. Based on choice and reciprocity, even if sometimes deferred reciprocity, the friendship of other women, offers companionship in shared interests and the possibility of a listening ear, a confidante. According to this sub-plot, a woman who has friends knows that she too is a companion, a confidante to others and thus valued.

Katherine has always had a group of female friends, who have been a significant part of her social world. She and her husband had separate interests, which they were both eager to pursue. Reflecting on the role of friendship over her life course and its significance in her social world, Katherine highlighted particularly the importance of friendship in marriage, and the implications for widowhood:

> It's been part of my life. I think you're lost without them (friends), I do really. Even though you've got a husband. I mean some husbands and wives never go out without one another and when anything happens, the other's lost.
>
> (Katherine)

Friendship then is durable and provides emotional support as well as companionship in shared activities.

Throughout her married life, Eunice's social world had always extended beyond her immediate family and her neighbourhood. This was a deliberate choice on her part, initially to follow up her own interests to ease the potential isolation caused by her husband's devotion to his work, but also because she recognised that she needed friendship: 'I realised early on that I would have to have some interests because Laurie was deeply involved with his work.' She became an active member of the Red Cross, an almost exclusively female group, and developed an extensive network of friends and colleagues. The friendships extended beyond the time spent together at the organisation; recreational activities were shared and holidays or weekends away were organised. As a consequence, colleagues became real friends. Eunice was proud to count herself as both a receiver and giver of friendship. When her oldest daughter died, these friends provided her with tremendous emotional support:

Friends from the Red Cross, they were my friends, they were very much part of my life and they helped me so much...they were here, they cooked meals, but it was more than that, they were here ...and that was so important to me, they were my friends.

(Eunice)

Betty did not share the same interests as her husband and was aware that their social needs were very different. She wanted to meet friends with similar interests, whereas he did not. When her children were young, her social world consisted of her immediate family and people from church but as the children got older she felt the need to move outside the family and pursue her own interests:

My husband was never interested in the things I did. He would always give me support but he didn't need to go out and meet people like I did. I was the sociable one (laughs).

(Betty)

Betty was proud of her identity as a sociable person. During her married life, it differentiated her from her family and confirmed her value outside of the family home.

Friends have always featured in Bee's social world. Indeed, she identified herself as 'a social animal' who has always needed friends more than family. Her husband had a son from a previous marriage, but there was little contact between them. Nor were there any strong bonds with her own family of origin. Meeting new people and spending time with friends was a significant part of married life. Friends provided both a social life, comprising sailing, golf, bridge, parties and holidays and a social network of support. They offered companionship but also affection and support in times of crises. Bee in her turn has always offered the same:

Friends were very important, we always had lots of friends ... I suppose being a Lancashire person, your door is always open ...My friends have been wonderful and I always think, 'As you sow, so you will reap' and its always been that way, and since ...

(Bee)

*The constituents of friendship*

Friendship was differentiated from family relationships by choice and talk was an essential component of this relationship. Many of the women identified talking and listening with similar others as the defining element of friendship. For example, for Betty, friendship was: 'what you put into it ... you tell each other things, and you ring them up and tell them things'. This perception was endorsed by Ellen: 'You can talk to a friend...and they can talk to you.'

True friendship is based on reciprocity, even though at any one time it might not always be equal and require effort. Ellen acknowledged that you have to work at friendship and be prepared to be a receiver as well as a giver: 'I always think that if you let people do, well you've got to want to do things with people but you can't be too independent to not let people come and do for you'. This reciprocity is confirmed by Phyllis: 'I always like to be doing something for somebody; but you have to let them help you as well … friends really matter to me.'

*Friend makers*

Some women possessed the skills and the confidence associated with making friends and practise what was identified in the literature review as the 'acquisitive' style of friendship.

Katherine, for example, had always been a friend maker and this was clearly understood and accepted by her husband:

> He was a kind of reserved man and I used to have friends that I used to go dancing with. He always knew where I was, they were local friends who I'd had for donkey's years. I've always had friends. Oh I used to go dancing and on days out. He would never go abroad for a holiday but he never objected to me going with my friends…I've been friends with them for as long as I can remember … Two of them have never been married. Ann, she lost her husband. The Brown sisters they have never been married. Another two, well one was a widow and a couple of them were married. I met them at the local Community Centre dancing and this is where we kind of mixed together… now they are all widowed or never married.
>
> (Katherine)

Phyllis too identified herself as a friend maker. She had maintained many of her earlier friendships and continued to make new friends:

> People just seem to adopt me…it's always been the same, I always collect people. I've always had a lot of friends. I am still in touch with people I went to school with. I write to three friends from school at Christmas; it's a long time to keep in touch. Once I make a friend I never lose them.

She and her husband had been publicans for many years and the pub itself was a significant part of her social world. Many of her earlier friendships developed from this environment. She described her life as a publican:

> … its not like living in a house… all of my married life, forty three years, was spent in public life. The pub was the focus of the village; we had outings and ran sports and social clubs. I've always met a lot of people. You had to be like that in the pub trade; you had to be able to change and adapt. I've always been able to make friends … it's most probably the life I've led. I'm very choosy about my friends but once I've made a friend, that's it. I have some very good friends now and I've quite a few friends I can visit.
>
> (Phyllis)

Jennie had little time for friends earlier on in her life course but nonetheless she too described herself as a friend maker. Both she and her husband worked outside the family home and life was very busy. As the children got older they started to develop a network of friends, some of whom were his friends but many of whom were Jennie's friends: 'I mixed with his friends but they weren't my kind of friends. But no, I think we went out more with my friends'. Friends mattered more to Jennie than to her husband and she knows that she has always been skilful at making and keeping friends, who have provided her with companionship, emotional support and importantly, fun:

> Where I worked, the girls, we all keep in touch with one another and there are three of us, all birthdays together. And there's another girl but she's left because of there being no work, made redundant. We've gone out together for our birthdays; we all collect and save up. And now, we've started line dancing, we all go…on a Monday night. You're just like a family.
>
> (Jennie)

### *It must be awful not to have friends*

Within this overarching narrative of the importance of friends, friendship had always been important for defining the social self and in many ways was as important, if not more important in some instances, than family. Life without friends was judged to be intolerable and those older people who appear to have no friends are considered to be lonely and to be pitied. Not having friends was certainly not to be recommended.

Katherine acknowledged that she spent more time with her friends than her family, and that this has been ongoing throughout her life: 'Oh friendship is so important, its part of life. It must be terrible not to have friends, a terrible thing to be entirely alone, oh it must be'. Indeed, she gave a dire warning of what might happen if you do not have your own friends:

> Some husbands and wives never go out without one another and when anything happens to one the other is totally lost. I had a sister that died on a holiday in Spain and her and her husband never went anywhere without one another, they were absolutely wrapped up with one another and he was totally lost when she died …that's what I mean about friends.
>
> (Katherine)

Bee too, confirmed that her closest networks were with her friends: '… it must be awful not to have friends, good friends. I've always had friends, I don't know what I'd do without my friends, especially now …'

### *Significant female friendships over the life course*

Significant friendships over the life course, although usually managed within the restrictions of marriage, were also evidence of sociability and thus valued. Not everyone is able to be a friend maker but a style of friendship akin to what was identified in the literature review as 'discerning' style, was evident in the study.

Ellen had not had many friends but she did have significant, longstanding friendships. For example, having served in the ATS during the Second World War, she had maintained a long association with ex-members of the ATS. Her husband had belonged to the British Legion and separately they maintained their forces friendships. Indeed, Ellen still regularly attended meetings and conventions:

> Well when Christmas comes I think I must get about 250 Christmas cards…we all send one another cards and there's always a little bit of something on about where we're going and they'll try and meet. We have our meeting once a month and Kath always picks me up and when we've had our meeting we usually nip in to have a cup of coffee or a cup of tea somewhere … there's usually about twenty so they all love to see all the grannies walking in for a cup of tea … oh, there's a great friendship between the association.

Making the most of opportunities for friendship at particular times in the life course is evident. For example, although Mags had a disrupted childhood, moving between home and the Crippled Children's Home where friendships were difficult to sustain, her early working life provided her with opportunities to develop friendships and extend her social world outside her family. She vividly recalled these friendships:

> I used to get up trips for the girls, we used to pay a shilling a week … we'd go to Manchester, Blackpool, anywhere … I've been really lucky as regards my friends and workmates.
>
> (Mags)

She still had a friend from this time: '…we phone and write now but I don't see her as much. She came once or twice when I was married to Jim; she phoned me when I was at Norah's and here'.

By contrast, Doris had made friends with her neighbours when she and her husband first bought their house:

> There were eight of us who all bought houses together … and we all made friends together and we all kept the friendship going. And one used to call on a Saturday morning for coffee …

She had been particularly friendly with the women although they did tend to be daytime and weekday friends. These friends were all older than her but, at the time, their lives were similar: husbands at work, children at home and then school and so on. However, in later life the age difference became telling: '…all of our friends were older than us and so in their seventies they all died, even in their sixties; our greatest friend died at sixty and I do miss them; we were all very close.'

Joan's interests in drama and sport had enabled her to build up a network of companions throughout her life course. She had close friends at school and met new people when she moved north. From a wider circle of companions, she had gathered a small circle of close friends:

My friends were those who played tennis or swam, all the sporty things I liked to do … I have some wonderful female friends; there were six of us went out to dinner last night; they're great my female friends, very supportive; we six always celebrate birthdays and Christmas; they are friends from the amateur dramatic world, we support each other, we share a lot.

(Joan)

## Restrictions

For some women, the change from being a single woman to becoming a wife and mother had transformed their social world from one consisting of friends and family to one centred on family. This was particularly so in the case of some of the women who lived in families where money was scarce. They did not question this. As women, their social world was their family and friendship was sometimes peripheral. Even paid work, usually part time, outside the home did not always allow for the extension of friendship networks. However, whenever opportunities arose, even if they were sometimes short lived, they were seized upon with enthusiasm.

During the early part of their married life for example, Dorothy and her husband had lived on a newly built social housing estate. When her children were younger, Dorothy's social world consisted primarily of her family and a well-developed support network of other women on the estate, in a similar situation to herself. There were regular parties for the children at Christmas and New Year and the women would often meet at each other's houses. However, Dorothy's husband decided that the area 'was going downhill' and decided they should move house and she reluctantly went along with his decision: 'I didn't have any choice in the matter'. She found that this decision impacted on her social world. It was difficult to keep up these friendships when she moved house and now she concedes that she was saddened by this change:

I stayed friends with them over there for quite a few years. I used to go and see a couple on alternate weeks; they'd come here and I'd go there. And gradually it petered out, it got harder and then one left and the other had grandchildren, so it just petered out.

(Dorothy)

Like many other women she found that there were difficulties developing a social world outside the family and her manual job. Once Dorothy had moved away from the supportive network of friends, lack of money and family life determined her social world:

I didn't have any time outside the house because when I wasn't usheretting, Roy was working overtime…after his tea he went to work for a friend of ours in his garage so we didn't really get out; well we used to go out once a month, his mum used to come and babysit… that was the only time we used to go out. We didn't have couples as friends, we didn't go out with couples. By the time we got home at night, we were too tired and we had a lot to save up for.

Although Ellen maintained her forces' friendships, there was little time to develop many others. She has three sons and during the years they were growing up money was very scarce. She too needed to juggle manual work, caring for her sons and her husband, and looking after the house:

> I used to go cleaning when the boys were younger, to buy extras and what have you; there was no time for anyone else. I knew girls at work but we all had our own lives.
>
> (Ellen)

However, despite the restrictions, there was still the knowledge that friendship was possible. These women knew they could make friends and be friends, even if they had to acknowledge that at times in their lives, friendship was 'on hold'.

*Summary*

This narrative of 'Friends matter', confirms the role of friendship in women's lives. Friendship provides both a means of being and of doing and as such offers the possibility of an identity which is separate from the family, as well as the opportunity to participate in a wider world.

**No friends of my own**

In direct contrast there is recognition in this narrative that friends have played a minimal role in identity formation, support networks and participation. Either other social supports and opportunities for participation had been available, for example, via the family, or individuals had experienced a lack of such opportunities. Thus, the impact of never really having friends of my own is varied, and the sub-plots reflect this difference:

| |
|---|
| • no need for friendship |
| • no time for friends |
| • I don't know how to make friends |
| • a social life but no real friends |
| • full time employment |

**Figure 10.4   No friends of my own**

*No need for friendship*

Where other social support systems, such as the family, are both reliable and culturally reinforced, there is no place for friendship. Farzana was the only woman in this study for whom there had been no need for friendship; her family have always provided her with support, validation and companionship, thereby meeting her social as well as her emotional needs. Indeed, she has not experienced loneliness throughout her life: her role of wife and mother and latterly, older widow, have always shaped her identity and given her status and purpose. Her family have always been her social world and this is both underpinned and reinforced by her faith. She remembered having had female friends when her children were little, but these friends were always the wives of her husband's friends. She had certainly never confided in them even though they shared similar experiences, because her husband was always her confidant:

> I don't know any widows, but I think it is mainly the family… if there was someone, we would meet for social reasons perhaps, but we would not seek support from each other.
>
> (Farzana)

## I don't know how to make friends

A lack of skills in friendship making is offered by some of the women as a reason for never having had a friend. In direct contrast to the friendship makers, these women don't know how to make friends. Patricia, for example, who disclosed loneliness throughout her life, had never had a close friend, certainly not one from whom she both sought and gave support:

> I've never shared my feelings; well you didn't when I was a little girl, not in my family … I didn't have friends at school …all in all, it wasn't a very good childhood. Mother was out at work for long hours … I was in charge of Maureen … so from ten years old I grew up very quickly.

Her relationships with other women have always been cautious and she has often felt inferior in the company of women, a feeling that was confirmed for her on many occasions. For example, she said: 'I didn't like being in an office with all these girls; I always felt they were more city-slick than me'. And during her early married life friends were dancing friends, acquaintances of her husband, certainly not people who offered either support or companionship. In fact she had viewed them as competitors, both as dance partners and for his attention: 'He was a good dancer; unfortunately all the ladies knew it. And it caused a lot of problems'.

Opportunities for Patricia to learn to make friends were few and far between and were curtailed even further by domestic responsibilities. Her husband had started to work the night shift before their daughter was born and this continued all their married life. He worked until he was 70, when he died:

> Once he started working nights, if you were ever asked to go anywhere … you couldn't, so that, well they don't ask you again. I don't know where half the people I used to know are and as I say, when my husband started to work nights, that put an end to it all…it does kill family life; I mean when other people are sat down all together of an evening, you are on your own.
>
> (Patricia)

On the nights when her husband was not working he used to go and play pool with other men at the local pub; his social world extended beyond the family. Patricia continued to feel resentful of this and had realised the limitations it put on her life, both when she was married and now. She recognised that her lack of friendship skills derived partly from her own personal life course and a lack of self-confidence, but also acknowledged that the structured nature of her life and perhaps all women's lives had rendered friendships difficult:

> when you get married, you lose friends, you lose contact with other people...which is wrong I suppose, I made a lot of mistakes ... I was the lonely one and I am now.
>
> (Patricia)

## No time for friends

For others, family responsibilities and women's gendered roles therein, often restricted the amount of time available for friends. Sylvia's story illustrated this well. She had few female friends throughout her life course. Instead her life was dominated by family matters: working in her father's kennels, motherhood at an early age, her marriage, another child, juggling work and home and latterly, caring for her mother and her husband. This left little space for friendship:

> I've never had a group of female friends. I've nobody that I kept in touch with from school. Maybe it's the fact that I had to settle down so early and I never went out with friends and my family were there, well my mum was. You see when I was a child I didn't have much of a childhood with respect to playing out, I had to work.
>
> (Sylvia)

Sylvia became a mother at 17 but did not marry the father of her child. She married John a few years later and subsequently had another child. She acknowledged that initially her life had to revolve around her daughter. Although she had help from her own mother, it was made quite clear that her daughter was her responsibility. She had no friends her own age because her life was so different from the lives of her contemporaries and on reflection she noted the difference between my life and hers: 'I never had a group of female friends, not like your girls, not like you do...I've never done that.'

Once married she wanted to spend as much time as she could with her family and only when both her children were at school did she return to work, to a manual job, in order to augment the family income. Her social world at this time was located within her family. There was a daytime friend whom Sylvia saw occasionally, but there were clear boundaries to this friendship: 'We never went out socially with them as a foursome. When she and I met up, we never really talked, only chatted'. Only when the children were older and Sylvia and her husband started to go dancing did friends begin to enter their social world. Even then it was only peripheral: 'We had no real close friends.' Indeed, as her husband became progressively more disabled even the couple friends started to drop off. As her caring role increased, her social world became even smaller:

> There were two who we used to go dancing with, they used to call in occasionally but they gradually drop off because … you're not going out anymore. The friend who came yesterday, I only went to see her once every three weeks instead of seeing her every week. No we didn't have many friends …it was very hard when I look back.
>
> (Sylvia)

She never questioned this; indeed to the contrary, Sylvia just accepted that as a woman her social world consisted of her immediate family. Her husband had friends from work with whom he socialised, but she did not.

### A social life but few real friends

Some women drew a very real distinction between a social life and real friends. Ostensibly, Vera's social world consisted of her husband, her three sons, and the many couples she and her husband met on the RAF (Royal Air Force) bases where they were stationed. Her husband, although a civilian, had officer status and they were part of a wide social circle of officers and their families. However, it was a social circle that was dependent on his officer status and the family's location on the RAF base:

> Although you have a good social life in the RAF, you don't really make friends as such. I once reckoned it up, we had twenty houses in our married life…to move house wasn't anything to me, I've done it all my married life. You meet someone, start to get to know them and then you have to move on… you don't keep in touch. You don't make real friends…
>
> (Vera)

Reflecting back over her life, she acknowledged that although she was part of this wide social circle, she did not have many friends. She always enjoyed the company of men, having lived in a predominantly male world, but found it problematic to develop close friendships with other women. She reflected that she only ever had two close friendships, both friends from her schooldays, one of whom died a few months prior to the interview: 'That's just left one friend now. We go out once a week for lunch and we talk. I miss my other friend'.

Edith only became aware in retrospect that she had no real friends of her own. Although I discuss this in more detail in the next chapter, Me Now, it is worth noting here that like other women of her generation, many of the people she had counted as friends had been couple friends, whom she shared with her husband. They were companions in shared activities, contributors to a social life, but that was as far as the relationship went. During her married life this had been unproblematic. After all, her identity at that time was founded on her role as the wife of Donald, and 'Edith and Donald' had friends. Only when Donald died and she became a widow was this revealed as a problem when she found herself friendless. As Edith tellingly recalled: 'When my husband was alive, it was all 'Donald and Edith' this and that but its amazing when he died, they didn't want to know, they were still couples you see Pat.'

*Full time employment*

Only two of the women who participated in the study were employed full-time outside the home for most of their married lives. Unsurprisingly for women of this cohort they also had total responsibility for the family home, leaving little opportunity to develop a social world outside of work and home.

Evelyn nursed full time until she was fifty. As a ward sister, her working hours were long and unsociable and *s*he devoted a lot of her time and energy to her job. She had friends at the various hospitals but these friendships did not extend beyond work. Looking back:

> I never really had time before (for friends). Even when I was nursing, I had a good colleague but we never went out together, shared time together because we were too busy...
>
> (Evelyn)

When she was fifty, she embarked on a new career as a seaside landlady. Although the intention was for a joint enterprise, her husband continued to work full time in engineering whilst Evelyn ran the business. The nature of the work meant that she had little free time and her social world comprised her husband, her niece and family and one couple with whom there were occasional outings.

Elizabeth also worked full time during most of her married life. She and her husband had their own bakery and shop: as described in the previous chapter, this was not a venture that Elizabeth had embarked upon with great enthusiasm. She also managed the roles of caring for her three children and looking after her home:

> I used to help in the bakehouse in the morning and then I'd take over the shop. I would often start at half five to six in the morning. We hadn't been there long when I had Liz, I'd already got Pat, and then three years later I had Philip. (P. So how did you juggle all of those roles) Well it wasn't juggling (laughs) you just did, you managed your time and what you didn't have time for you didn't do.
>
> (Elizabeth)

Needless to say, there was little time for a social world beyond the family and the shop.

*Summary*

This narrative of 'No friends of my own', confirms the diverse experience and identity of those women who have not had access to friendship throughout their life course. Choice, lack of opportunity, or lack of confidence and skills, all characterise this diversity.

### I've always been a joiner-in

A joiner-in is identified as a woman who joins formal organisations or clubs associated with a particular interest or purpose. She positively thrives on the expectations and predictability associated with joining in, enjoying the companionship of similar others. For some of the women in the study, this had been a lifelong activity and they drew a very clear distinction between those who identify themselves as joiners-in and those who do not. The former have acquired and practised the skills of putting themselves into new situations with similar others and knew the benefits of group activities. This sometimes made them impatient with other women who do not join clubs, particularly those who were so clearly lonely; perhaps because the obvious advantages of participation had been clear throughout their own life course. The following sub-plots are discussed:

| |
|---|
| • proud to be a joiner-in |
| • managing change |
| • not joining in. |

**Figure 10.5  A joiner-in**

*Proud to be a joiner-in*

The identity of a person who joins in was claimed with pride. It set a woman apart from those who did not actively participate and suggested both energy and organisation.

Jean, despite the limitations imposed on her social world during her married life, identified herself as someone who, given the opportunity liked to join in. She had always liked being with people, enjoying the company of others in more formal activities:

> In my teens, I went to a dancing club, and then I didn't do a lot of sport but I did do a lot of walking. I was in a youth club, a sort of social club with some older members from the choir, where we went on hikes. I used to go walking with them and then we started a keep fit class. I was sixteen or seventeen... I've always wanted to join anything that was good fun. When the children were born, well I was too busy... but now I join in everything I can.
>
> (Jean)

Phyllis and Betty too confirmed their identity as joiners-in. Firstly Phyllis:

> I've always joined things. My family was very sporty. My father was a big sportsman, my son is and my grandson... before I was married I used to dance and

> I used to play hockey, all the usual things, guides, sporting clubs. My husband was keen on joining clubs too; he was a keen sportsman.

And secondly, Betty:

> I'd always joined things. I was in a drama group and I used to go tap dancing and that sort of thing so I'd always something that I did.

Bee went even further, identifying herself as a serial joiner-in, both before her marriage and throughout her married life. Before marriage, she had belonged to a tennis club and was the social secretary in the engineering department where she worked. Once married, she was encouraged by her husband to participate in clubs, particularly those clubs that he considered to be suitable and which would not impinge on her full-time wifely duties. She greatly enjoyed the identity associated with participation and had invested considerable energy in joining-in:

> There was the Yachting Club, then there were my friends from bridge and then there was the golf club. He (her husband) said I was a natural and he encouraged me. I got to be an eleven handicap, you see and I used to go to other golf clubs, such as Northenden. My day was taken up and that was fine, as long as I had his tea on the table.
>
> (Bee)

*Managing change*

Joining-in provided continuity and was a way of managing change, or 'turnings', at different times during the life course.

For Joan, this had been a very deliberate process which she knew from previous experience would help her to manage a major life change and settle into a new environment. For example, Joan said that when she and her husband originally moved to the north of England after the Second World War: 'I knew when I came up north that I must **join**' (original emphasis). She set about forming a women's tennis group, with a crèche for the children and joined an amateur dramatics society: 'I'm a member to this day, and recently they've made me an honorary member'. The fact that, as a girl, she had been a joiner in and a skilled sportswoman, provided her with continuity and enabled her to move easily into new groups and meet new people and thus manage, more easily, what might have been difficult times.

Bee, too, has used joining-in as a way of managing change. She played golf and bridge before she was married, but had never really had time to pursue these activities when she was working full-time. Once married, joining in provided her with an opportunity to both fill her daytime, and to move into a new social circle to which she was eager to belong: '...where I would meet other members of a particular social circle, where people tended to know of each other' (Bee).

Those women who identified themselves as joiners in clearly saw considerable advantage in being this way. They were able to bring the skills and continuities acquired over the life course to new situations and recognised that what had been useful at earlier 'turnings' in the life course, might well be useful at later periods of change.

*Not joining in*

It is worth noting that, just as some women claim the identity of perpetual joiners-in, there are others who are quite vociferous in identifying themselves as never having been inclined to participate in clubs or organisations.

Doris for example recognised herself in this way: 'I'm not a clubby person at all; I don't think I ever have been.' Elizabeth has been asked on many occasions to join local organisations but has declined to do so:

> I've been asked many times to join but I haven't, and I haven't since (widowhood). I think you miss out when you don't really. The Evergreens and that sort of thing, they have quite a lot of outings. I've just never felt that I wanted to join things.
>
> (Elizabeth)

However, both Doris and Elizabeth had other social networks that enabled them to engage and connect, so that even though Elizabeth recognised that there might be benefits to participating in clubs, not joining in has not been problematic. For others, this was not the case. Patricia described herself as 'not that type of person', who joins clubs:

> Oh I could never walk in anywhere on my own but then as Wendy says, 'If I felt like that I'd never go anywhere'. But she's very different from me, very different and she gets annoyed with me for being as I am. And my mother was like me. I used to try to get my mother to join in things to go to clubs and she'd say, No I don't want to, and now I'm saying it.

Although she had come to recognise the limitations of this stance, including real loneliness and the frustration caused to her daughter, Patricia considered herself unable to change: 'Its just how I am, I'll never change now'.

*Summary*

This narrative confirms the identity of those women who are lifelong participators or joiners-in in formal organisations and demonstrates the advantages of this identity. Equally, there are others for whom joining-in is abhorrent. As I discuss in the next chapter, for those women who have few other connections, this abhorrence proves to be a liability in widowhood.

**Family first**

This narrative is one in which a woman's social identity is confirmed first and foremost within the family: it is the place in which her social needs are met, through her role as wife, mother, sister or daughter. Moreover, in putting the family first, she is fulfilling the expectations of both her generation and gender. The centrality of the family in women's lives is integral to this narrative, even for those women who described their relationship with family as 'not close', and often sits alongside other narratives. The following sub-plots are discussed:

| |
|---|
| • an ideology of the family |
| • interdependence |
| • family as friends |
| • a small but very close family |
| • dependence |
| • a lack of closeness |

**Figure 10.6   Family first**

*An ideology of the family*

A powerful ideology of the family underpinned the Family first narrative. This ideology encompassed both the institution of the family as good and also women's roles within the institution. This often manifested itself as idealised concepts such as a 'real family' (as opposed to those families who are unfortunate enough not to be) which conjured up images of warmth, togetherness and exclusivity. The good wife and mother (as described in Chapter 9) who always put her own needs second, had her social needs met within this family. Indeed, many of the women who participated in the study often spoke about themselves only in terms of family roles and relationships.

Jennie for example, made many references to being 'a real family' when describing her relationship with her own parents, aunts, uncles and cousins, and also with her children and grandchildren. She explained what she means as follows:

> Well, we care for each other. We can rely on each other. It's what being a family means…I know I can always rely on my family. They (my family) did a lot for me, helped me in every way…and there are my grandad's relations, his brothers and all those relations who I still keep in touch with who live…near Derby. And they had an ice cream business, a grocery business, a fish and chip business and I used to go and spend six weeks, you know I used to go back with them. This is what I mean. I had a family closeness right from the very beginning.
>
> (Jennie)

She also invoked the metaphor of family when talking about her workmates and her church community. Firstly her workmates: 'they're all, well there's something about a mill…that you're all as a family, joined together somehow; you're all friends'. And then describing her church friends: 'we're a family at church.'

Mags, whilst occasionally challenging this ideology of the family, suggested that she had been:

> …lucky as regards family. (P. 'Lucky' is an interesting word to use, why were you 'lucky'?) Well they never left me out. They'd always look after me. And they always have.

She may of course have been comparing herself with other disabled children she met at the Crippled Children's Home, who were not so lucky with their families. After all, her family did not abandon her even if they had low expectations of her life chances (see Chapter 8).

Eunice too spoke often of the importance of the institution of the family as a naturally supportive environment. As a committed Christian she regarded the family unit as important and considered older women who did not have a supportive family to have been at a disadvantage, particularly widows who do not have children: 'I really do think when there are just two of you it must be more difficult than when you've got a family.'

Underpinning Farzana's story were strong cultural issues concerning the family. As a Muslim woman, the family was the source of her identity, support, strength and pride. She described herself in terms of her role firstly as a daughter, then a wife and subsequently a widow and a mother. With reference to her children she said with pride: 'They are good children; they have never given me any trouble.'

Occasionally, within the sub-plot there was a dissenting voice. Patricia, for example, felt able to question the ideology of the family when talking of her own difficult childhood, where the family certainly was not a place of either warmth or security. However, this only served to highlight the contrast between her own childhood and that of her daughter, who is served by a good mother.

Unsurprisingly, a number of types of family relationship were discernable amongst the women in the study. These form the sub-plots of: interdependence; family as friends; 'a small but very close family'; dependence; and 'not close'. I discuss each of these in turn.

*Interdependence*

In 1981, Jean and her increasingly disabled husband moved to purpose built accommodation. Geographically, they moved away from their family but Jean did not consider this to have been problematic in terms of maintaining relationships: 'it made no difference us moving here in terms of closeness. They all had cars. We still kept in touch regularly.' Jean had continued to maintain regular contact with her family, often providing as well as receiving practical help. A good example of this reciprocity was her annual visit to Blackpool. For a number of years: 'while I've still got my health,' Jean has spent a week at her son's house looking after his mother-in-law who has Alzheimer's Disease As a result of this, her son and his wife have been able to take a holiday. The family in turn have continued to keep an eye on her and Jean described this relationship as close. However, she stressed the importance of leading separate lives and private space. Above all, generational difference was to be respected:

> You can be too far away, but you can be too near, on both sides. As long as I'm within a distance that I can get there if they want me or they can get to me…its important to have friends of your own age as well as family. Different generations don't mix …their outlooks are different.
>
> (Jean)

Jennie's relationship with her family, of closeness but interdependence, had a precedent. Just as her own mother had helped her, she too has shared the child-care with her daughters:

> (My mother and I) We both worked separate shifts, so that she was able to look after the children when I wasn't here … and my dad used to do things for us as well…But it was mainly my mum.
>
> (Jennie)

She had been used to sharing her house with different generations of her family both before her husband died and since. One daughter has lived with her and she has shared the care of a grandson with another daughter. Two other grandchildren have lived with her at different times and one granddaughter continued to use Jennie's house as her main base when she was home from university. At the time of our meeting, Jennie had been to stay with her daughter and son in law to provide care after her daughter's hysterectomy. Geographically, she was now distanced from a number of members of her family but they were still:

> Very close … they think a lot about me, they make sure I'm alright; even my grandchildren phone me up two or three times a week.
>
> (Jennie)

Two of Farzana's sons, her two daughters-in-law and three grandchildren shared her home. The daughters in law managed the cooking, looked after the house and cared for their children. The rest of her family lived nearby and were regular visitors: 'I have many grandchildren. It's very nice because they come to visit me'. Although no longer active in the household, Farzana was still consulted on domestic issues and had a status that was openly acknowledged by her family. Furthermore, despite being more physically dependent on her family for excursions outside the home, there were nonetheless many continuities surrounding family relationships. She had supported her family and they in turn now provided support to her. Her son regularly drove her to the mosque and her daughter took her shopping.

*Family as friends*

Some family relationships were framed as 'friendship' or 'companionship'. Joan, for example, has a history of mutual interests with her daughter that had got better over the years. Both before and since becoming a widow, Joan had been on holiday with her daughter and son in law and they all shared a lifelong passion for and participation in amateur dramatics. She had looked after two grandchildren when they were younger, in order to provide her daughter and son in law with time for themselves and this was reciprocated in numerous ways, such as help with major jobs in the house. This worked well precisely because it was a reciprocal arrangement. A number of years ago Joan, her daughter and son in law bought a canal boat and spent most weekends on the boat, working together as well as enjoying themselves. This had been particularly helpful and supportive in the early days of widowhood:

> (Having the boat together) was lovely. Although we were all really sick at heart because of dad, we loved going to the boat.... My son in law would get off work early and we'd get off to the boat, get it all laid out, then we'd go up to Lymm and do the weekend shopping and we'd go back to the boat with this shopping. It just filled all our time; it was marvellous.
>
> (Joan)

Her relationship with her family continued to be one of give and take. For example, Joan had become both friend and confidante to her grandchildren, who are now students. She had recently moved into what she described as 'a granny flat' attached to her daughter's house: she certainly did not view herself as dependent on her family, but rather actively welcomed the living arrangements as being convenient for all concerned.

Elizabeth described her family as her friends. Her daughters are both companions and confidantes: 'I get friendship from my family and I think I can share things with my family too'. She shared specific interests with her two daughters with whom she regularly visited craft shows, embroidery exhibitions and gardens. This type of relationship was not new for Elizabeth. Indeed, friendship with family members had been an important part of her married life. Her husband had a close relationship with his brothers and although they had little time for a social life, they did go out for meals and visits with his family: 'we were never without somewhere to go and we still do. I've got two sisters in law who I go out with now.'

Eunice too recognised the significance of a close family, particularly grown up children, as a source of friendship and acknowledged that lack of family might be problematic. Her daughter lived some distance away near Plymouth, but they regularly visited each other and because they had always shared similar interests often took short holiday breaks together. They had recently been for a long weekend in the Lake District where they spent time looking at gardens. This family friendship also extended to Eunice's brother, who was a widower. They shared lunch once a week and took turns to cook Sunday dinner. Eunice's close relationship with her parents and particularly with her mother, had certainly been replicated in her current family relationships.

Edith and Mags both described their relationship with their sisters as 'like friends'. Edith and her husband had no children but she was one of a large family. She described her family as very close and gave as an example of this the way that all the sisters had taken turns to care for their mother and brother, when they were terminally ill. However, she was particularly close to one sister who had always been single. This relationship preceded Edith's widowhood; indeed, she and her husband went on holidays abroad with her sister and often shared social activities. They had always provided companionship and emotional support for each other:

> We used to have lovely holidays. Even when Donald was alive, Miriam (sister) used to come too. Even though Donald and I had no family we weren't ones for living just for each other. And Donald knew that Miriam was my special sister.
>
> (Edith)

Mags too, had always had a special relationship with her sister. Even though the relationship started as one of duty, (Cissy and her husband had promised their mum that because of Mags' disability they would always take care of her) it eventually became one which was characterised by reciprocity and friendship. Before her marriage Mags had lived with Cissy and her brother in law and although there was a temporary rift when she first went to live with her husband-to-be, they soon sorted out their differences and remained close. They even bought a caravan together and regularly went away as couples:

> Jim and I never went anywhere without them. We bought a caravan. Cissy and I had an endowment and we bought this caravan. It was only on a farm, there was nothing there, but it was a base where we could get out from, near Burnley. We used to go there every weekend. We never went away without them. And then when Charles (her sister's husband) was bad with his arthritis, well we able to help him. We had some good times.
>
> (Mags)

Mags was proud of the relationship she had with her sister and demonstrated that, within the obligations of family, it is possible to be both sister and friend.

*A small but very close family.*

One family relationship stood out as distinct from the others. It was one in which there were particularly strong female bonds. Although Evelyn and her husband had no children of their own, she had been very involved with the upbringing of her niece, whom she described as: 'like a daughter'. Evelyn's only sister had long-term mental health problems and was often unable to care for her daughter. As a consequence of this, Evelyn and her mother, who herself had one sister who shared the family house, often had sole charge of her niece. With the exception of Evelyn's brother-in-law there had been no real male presence in her family of origin and the three generations of women had been a very self-supporting female group.

Such strong female bonds had provided her with a great sense of continuity and security in her life. She identified herself as a good family member and had confidence that this will be reciprocated. After the deaths of her mother, her aunt and her sister, Evelyn and her niece developed an even stronger bond. Indeed, the primary reason for Evelyn moving back to Stockport, when she was no longer able to look after herself, was to be near to her niece. In recent years the two women had spent a lot of time together; the niece regularly visited her in the sheltered housing complex and Evelyn often spent weekends at her niece's house.

*Dependence*

A relationship of dependence on family was one in which there had been and continued to be a lack of reciprocity, an unequal balance of power. The social self relied heavily on significant others within the family for both participation and support.

Throughout her life course, Patricia's source of identity had been that of the good mother, and the focus of her life the home in which that could take place. This was in stark contrast to her family of origin, which she described as 'nothing to be proud of'. Her social life had centred on her family but it was one in which she was dependent. She had relied on her husband to take her out shopping and on outings and relied on her daughter and younger sister for friendship. The relationship with her sister was still uneasy and Patricia contended that her sister only visited: 'out of duty'. Patricia's relationship with her daughter, who was in her early forties, unmarried and living away from home, was still the focal point of her social world. She wanted to remain the good mother but, increasingly, she felt that the roles were being reversed. Her main source of identity, support and companionship came from her daughter even though she recognised that this created pressure and tension:

> She takes on a lot of responsibility for me. She worries about me and I worry about her. That's the trouble, there's only two of us now.
>
> (Patricia)

Patricia had become totally dependent on both her daughter and her sister for practical, social and emotional support and this was proving to be increasingly problematic for her.

*A lack of closeness*

Whilst still subscribing to the centrality of family, there was nonetheless an acknowledgement by some women that not all have a history of close relationships with their families.

Betty was perhaps the most explicit in describing this lack of closeness. She had spent her school years away from her family and accepted that as a consequence family ties were not strong. As her own children have grown up, Betty has felt increasingly distanced from them:

> They've all got on with their own lives …possibly we're not close, we're not a very close family. When their children were little I used to see a bit more of them then …but you see they've got other things to do and I do other things.
>
> (Betty)

She considered that she no longer had much in common with her own family, suggesting that they regarded themselves as having moved up in the world. Instead, she had found herself welcomed into the family of her best friend and neighbour: 'I'm an extraneous Auntie. I do feel very much part of their family. I go to most of the family parties and gatherings.' Betty was also quite close to her brother, who had been her husband's best friend. They went out together for meals, usually once a month: 'He pays; he's got more money than me!' They were companions rather than confidants, who had fun together, laughing about getting old. At other times she sought his advice concerning money.

Family did not feature significantly in Bee's story, although the centrality of family in the lives of women was acknowledged. For example, she described her relationship with her stepson, who had caused many problems between herself and her husband, as: '…love/ hate, he was very clever but he got involved with drink and drugs in Singapore and eventually he committed suicide.' Although her stepson had been married with children, Bee had lost contact with his family and felt deprived of a relationship with grandchildren, which she conceded was important to women. She described her relationship with her own brothers and sisters as: '…mixed. I was one of five children. I seem to have become the most successful of all the children.' There was, she reflected, resentment about her success and she was aware of the gulf in social class between herself and her siblings. Bee's relationship with her mother had become very strained:

> My mother is a pain! I think she thought that when I was widowed she would move in here but it was not to be, I have my own life.
>
> (Bee)

However, she recognised a moral obligation to family, supporting her mother financially and ensuring that her care needs were met. She was fond of two nieces, for whom she also provided financially.

*Summary*

Whilst embracing a variety of family relationships, this narrative situates a woman's social identity within both the ideology and the reality of family life. This has drawn attention to the complexity and history of family relationships and the centrality of these in women's lives.

## Conclusion

In this chapter I have examined the social world of older widows over the life course via four narratives of 'Me and My Social World' and demonstrated that a variety of complex relationships have existed with friends, family and formal organisations, in which older widows have confirmed their identity over the life course. Relationship skills and styles have been developed, change has been managed with or without the support of significant others.

As with other parts of their lives, women's social worlds have been highly gendered throughout their life course. That some women are more skilled and more connected in social relationships has become apparent as the narratives unfold: these are commonalities and differences that are taken into widowhood. Alongside 'Me, Myself' and History and Me' yet another piece has been added to the jigsaw of later life widowhood.

| Me, Myself | History and Me |
|---|---|
| *High Self-Esteem*<br>feeling secure<br>•   a strong value base<br>•   self-confidence<br>•   learning from experience<br>•   independence<br>•   regrets for others | *Belonging to a Generation*<br>•  difficult times for some<br>•  the War years<br>•  changing times |
| *Fluctuating Self-Esteem*<br>•   ambition versus 'I might have'<br>•   becoming 'someone else'<br>•   a bit of a rebel<br>•   pride | *Gendered Lives*<br>•  education<br>•  becoming a wife<br>•  a woman's place is in the home<br>•  working lives<br>•  breaking the rules |
| *Low Self-Esteem*<br>•   powerlessness<br>•   a lack of self-confidence lonely<br>•   failing to live up to expectations<br>•   always being grateful<br>•   no individuality | |

**Me and My Social World**

*Friends matter*
- my friends are part of my life, the 'social me'
- the constituents of friendship
- friend-makers
- it must be awful not to have friends
- significant female friendships over the life course
- restrictions on friendship

*No friends of my own*
- no need for friendship
- no time for friends
- I don't know how to make friends
- a 'social life' but no real friends
- full time employment

*A 'joiner-in'*
- proud to be a 'joiner-in'

| |
|---|
| • managing change<br>• not joining in |
| *Family first*<br>• an ideology of the family<br>• interdependence<br>• family as friends<br>• a small but very close family<br>• dependence |

**Figure 10.7   Me, Myself; History and Me; Me and My Social World**

In the next chapter, I explore the final piece, that is 'Me, Now'. I examine the continuities and discontinuities that characterise these women's current experience.

# Chapter 11

# Me Now

**Introduction**

In the literature reviewed at the beginning of this book, I demonstrated that the overwhelming image of later life widowhood has been one of loneliness and loss. I then argued that this was a restrictive, one-dimensional image that took no account of either individual or collective biography. I have suggested instead a more complex, multi-dimensional model of widowhood grounded in individual and collective biography and comprising numerous components. In this final part of what I have described in previous chapters as a jigsaw, I further challenge the uniformity of a one-dimensional image of later life widowhood, by exploring the multiple narratives emerging from the stories each participant told about her life now, as an older widow. As in previous chapters, I explore both the subjective experience and the factors that contribute to identity in later life widowhood and, where appropriate, links are made to previous chapters.

Analysis of the data highlighted the multiple narratives, summarised below in Figure 11.1:

| |
|---|
| • Loneliness and despair |
| • Getting on with your life |
| • A transition |

**Figure 11.1  Multiple narratives of Me Now**

Each woman strongly articulated one of the narratives but within each individual story, links were sometimes made with another narrative. The experience of later life widowhood is both fluid and complex. For example, whilst Mags acknowledged that she had both got on with her life and tried to live it to the full, she sometimes despaired concerning her health, that there was little to look forward to. Eunice has changed in many positive ways in the years since becoming a widow but, occasionally, she had days when she was lonely and felt that life was unfair. The three narratives therefore are not fixed categories, but are points on a spectrum ranging from a narrative of loss and decline to one of growth and change. Nonetheless, there was a predominant narrative in each woman's story:

| |
|---|
| • *Loneliness and despair*<br>Dorothy[1]; Patricia; Vera |
| • *Getting on with your life*<br>Bee; Betty; Elizabeth; Evelyn; Farzana; Joan; Katherine; Mags |
| • *A transition*<br>Doris; Dorothy; Edith; Ellen; Eunice; Jean; Jennie; Pat; Phyllis; Sylvia |

**Figure 11.2  Locating the participants within the narratives of Me Now**

I now discuss in detail the three narratives arising from Me, Now.

**Loneliness and despair**

This narrative conforms to the popular image of later life widowhood, one in which the older widow is portrayed as a passive victim of circumstance. Both old age and the death of a spouse have conspired to create a situation in which life is often intolerable. The following sub-plots are discussed:

| |
|---|
| • Loneliness |
| • Loss of confidence |
| • Someone missing |
| • They don't understand |
| • Being different |
| • Little pleasure from life |
| • The future is bleak |

**Figure 11.3  Loneliness and despair**

*Loneliness*

Loneliness predominates in this narrative. Loneliness is qualitatively different from aloneness, which appears in other narratives, in that it is both negative and

---

[1] At our first interview, Dorothy's story was initially predominantly a narrative of loneliness and despair. She became quite distressed and talked off-tape of considerable unhappiness during her married life disclosing secrets not previously shared. This information was therefore not included as data. At our second interview, one month later, she seemed surprisingly relaxed, and was intent on looking forward and seizing some of the opportunities which widowhood seemed to be offering her. She strongly articulated the view that telling her story had been both helpful and therapeutic. I discuss this process further in the next chapter.

destructive. It leaves an older widow feeling isolated and separated in some way from the rest of the world. Loneliness and sadness sit side by side.

For Patricia, participation in the study provided an opportunity to relieve her feelings of loneliness. As an older widow, she often felt lonely but she also acknowledged in the course of telling her story that throughout her life she had been lonely. She had rejected the counselling offered in the aftermath of her husband's death, finding it unhelpful and intrusive, but she welcomed the opportunity to tell her story for the purposes of a research study. On each occasion (two interviews and one feedback session), she expressed her enjoyment at the opportunity to talk. I discuss her feelings about reading her story in Chapter 13 but suffice to say here that she found the experience quite harrowing, perhaps because her feelings of isolation were so explicit. For example:

> I don't go out much now. I get very little pleasure from life. You know, I rarely see anybody and I get so lonely. Some days the only one I talk to is Daisy (her dog). So often I just feel 'down'.
>
> (Patricia)

No longer feeling useful and instead being dependent on others compounded this isolation. Dependency was an undesirable state signalling reliance on her daughter and to a lesser degree her sister, as discussed in the previous chapter. Looking after others, just as she did earlier on in her life, was the preferred state:

> She (sister) tries to do little things for me, and at one time she took me out more than she does now. But then again I don't walk terribly well now so I think I can be a bit of a burden to people. My life has changed, I feel I've got nobody to look after ... well I've always had somebody here, and even when my mother was around, well I didn't do my mother's work or anything like that, I did bits of decorating for her and you know I would do lots of jobs for her ... so I miss them all. And I think that gets me more than anything the loneliness, and not having somebody come in for a meal, to do things for, I mean that's what I used to do ...
>
> (Patricia)

Patricia also identified ill health and lack of money as contributory to her loneliness in later life:

> What can I say? I really don't go anywhere. I don't go out much. There are three reasons really. Because I can't get there quickly, everywhere I go I've got to go on a bus, and that gets on your nerves after a while. I can't afford to go out, I've no money to go out and I just think I can't do that anymore, and I've really nobody to go with. As I say there are those factors that keep me in.

Vera too described herself as isolated and lonely, acknowledging that although she enjoyed her own company, she was afraid of meeting others. Furthermore, a fear of dependence made her fiercely independent: 'My independence is very important to me. I don't want to have to rely on others'. She too identified poor health as prohibiting many opportunities for joining in. She would have liked to join a sports club or a keep fit class, but felt unable to do so. It is interesting to note the subjectivity associated with health. Poor health features in other narratives, explored later in this chapter, but instead of being prohibitive, as it is in this narrative, it is a restricting, sometimes irritating, factor which needs to be overcome. By contrast, the perception of ill health in the current narrative is that it is prohibitive to participation and thus is a major contributor to loneliness.

Dorothy struggled between what she perceived to be independence and dependence. She desperately wanted to be independent and cited the example of one of her sons who had recently made a home for his mother in law in a part of his house; this certainly was not an option she favoured:

> I don't want to live with any of my sons. I don't want to move in, I want to shut my own door, have my own independence.
>
> (Dorothy)

However, she also acknowledged that sometimes her loneliness was unbearable and she wished to see more of her sons:

> I am so disappointed they don't come more often ...Sometimes I get very, very lonely and I get so depressed, I really have to shake myself out of it, but it's so difficult.
>
> (Dorothy)

Independence, as with poor health, also features in other narratives of Me, Now. However, it needs to be noted that the meaning attributed to independence in the current narrative is 'not having to rely on others'. This is in stark contrast to some of the women in other narratives who experience independence as interdependence, and thus relying on others some of the time is part of the package. I explore this further later on in this chapter.

*Loss of confidence*

The literature confirmed that many women experience a temporary loss of confidence when they are first widowed. However, this narrative speaks of a loss of confidence that increases rather than subsides as the years progress, with both age and widowhood held to be responsible. For example:

> Being widowed saps all your confidence. It has mine ... and it still hasn't come back.
>
> (Vera)

> I don't feel as confident as I was but then again I'm getting older. I've always lacked confidence but that is worse now. Probably because of circumstances ... and I don't get out as I've said to you and I think that takes a lot of your confidence when you don't go out. I've always been shy and lacking in confidence, but you get more within yourself when you are on your own ...
>
> (Patricia)

A lack, or in some instances, a loss of spiritual belief contributed to this feeling. In recent times, Vera had lost the sense of purpose that a spiritual belief used to give her:

> I used to be very religious but I had started thinking more and more about it. I started thinking about things that were happening and then when my husband was taken ill, I just could not come to terms with what had happened. Since then there is nothing that I've got, that I could hold on to. It went completely and it's never come back. I'm quite envious of people who can return to religion.
>
> (Vera)

Vera was very aware that her local church may well have provided an avenue for increased social contact but did not regard this as a worthy reason for attending:

> I wouldn't go to church just because friends did, it would have to be for religious reasons. So that's why I haven't met up with a lot of people I used to know.
>
> (Vera)

She identified the difficulty of doing things on her own and not having the confidence to ask someone, for example one of her co-volunteers, to share an activity with her:

> … now that's something that's hard to do on your own, to go into places and find out about things. Some people have the confidence to do it but I don't, not without a friend. I still find it difficult to go to places on my own.
>
> (Vera)

Dorothy understood this feeling only too well:

> I still lack a lot of confidence, there are lots of things I won't do. I won't go in a café on my own, no way. I've always gone everywhere with Roy or the boys, I can't do it now.

The subjective experience of these women was often at odds with how they were perceived by others. Despite their vivid descriptions of a lack of confidence, both Vera and Dorothy led very busy lives, exhibiting to others both competence and confidence. Vera, for example, has worked at a volunteer job shop, where her skills were highly valued. Dorothy volunteered at the school where she had previously worked as a dinner lady and had recently started paid work at a playgroup:

> I've got a regular job now at a playgroup in the village on a Friday morning. I just went in there voluntary and she asked me last week if I want to take it over permanently. I love children. I go over here (to the school) on a Monday to the juniors and I listen to the children reading for an hour and a half, and on a Thursday I go to the Infants School and teach the 5-7s to bake. I love being with children.
>
> (Dorothy)

For both of them, having a busy life was an important routine that helped them to feel some semblance of control, but in reality disguised a lack of confidence and low self-esteem. As with poor health and independence, subjective feelings were paramount in expressing the narrative.

Patricia, who experienced very little control over her life, so fiercely feared letting go of the little bit of control she still has, that she rejected possibilities for decreasing her loneliness. For example, she has considered the possibility of returning to church when encouraged by a neighbour:

> ... she tried to get me to go back. I'm a Catholic, a lapsed Catholic. But I said I couldn't walk all the way down there and back, its right down the bottom of the road. And I don't know whether I want to or not, I used to say I would but then I don't know ...I thought I would like to go back to the church from the religious side, but the only trouble is with Catholics, they stick together and once they get their claws into you, as I say, they try to run your life and I want none of that. So I never went back. I went in once with the couple next door, that was last Christmas.
>
> (Patricia)

Furthermore, Patricia was a very talented needlewoman, making and selling a whole variety of craft items. Her daughter had encouraged her to sell to other businesses as a way of extending her networks, but Patricia had been reluctant to follow up this suggestion, not wishing to be put under pressure and, more importantly, not wanting to be exposed to potential criticism that she feared would decrease her confidence even further: 'Oh no, if anybody said to me "this is how you do this" or "I want you to do it this way" ... I'd say, oh the hell with that, I'll do it the way I know and the way I want to do it!'

*Someone/something missing in life*

A feeling of incompleteness or of something or someone missing is expressed throughout this narrative of loneliness and despair. As with loss of confidence, this feeling of incompleteness is widely reported in the literature on the early days of bereavement and the women in the study were no exception. Betty for example, described her feelings when she was initially bereaved: 'You feel as though, it's as though half has been chopped off you... yes and it's all raw down one side.' However, this sub-plot expresses that feeling of incompleteness as a part of the regular, ongoing experience of later life widowhood. For example:

> Your everyday life is different, like getting a meal ready and there's nobody, I mean I had somebody here all day and it's that silence, there's nobody else to talk to, there's nobody. I mean after five years I still sort of think, gosh, there's nobody else to say anything. I mean for instance when I was doing that decorating, he would have popped in and out all the time and said, 'Come on, leave it now, have a rest now, have a cup of tea' ... so that is very, very different. There's that something missing ...
>
> (Patricia)

> I think this is one of my main difficulties, functioning as an individual, especially if you've been with someone for thirty or so years. I used to be able to join in conversations with anyone but that was when my husband was there. It's still like there is someone missing. I still find that even now, going to my sons. I won't go unless they invite me. I won't say I'm coming; I'll wait for them to invite me. Perhaps that is confidence again as well. In my own mind I still need someone to push me …
>
> (Vera)

Dorothy felt the incompleteness to the extent that she was no longer really comfortable in her own home:

> I can't sit in the house on my own really. I do try the odd times to stay in and I do my work, but not like I used to when Roy was here. There doesn't seem to be any point now.

However, unlike some of the others Dorothy had a strategy for dealing with these feelings which gave her some comfort:

> I still think of things he said. I went to try on a dress from my friend's catalogue. It was a black dress with little flowers on it and it fitted lovely. And I could hear Roy saying, 'Don't put that on, it's black. I don't like you in dark colours'. There are things I don't do because of what he said, I still think of things he'd say. I sometimes think he's here and I dream about him a lot; if I'm not well I talk to his photograph.

*They don't understand*

Alongside the feeling of incompleteness in this narrative there is also a strong sense of disappointment with other family relationships, particularly with sons, who seem either unwilling or unable to comprehend their mother's feelings.

Vera had three sons who all lived a considerable distance from her. It had been with the strong encouragement of her sons that she made what she subsequently acknowledged was a very hasty move back to Stockport within six months of her husband's death. At that time, her sons were living away from home and unanimously agreed that she should return to Stockport where she had spent her early years, and the place where she had lived the longest. Other than that initial encouragement, little ongoing practical or emotional support had been offered by her sons, either in the early days of her bereavement or now:

> Craig was at university and I found that I didn't get the help. I didn't have anyone to discuss things with and I think that saps your confidence. My other two sons were working and they didn't seem to understand, or they cut their minds off I think.
>
> (Vera)

Despite the arrival of grandchildren her sons were still peripheral in her life and this continued to sadden Vera, particularly because she would have liked the opportunity to be a more active grandmother. She considered her sons to lack understanding of the difficulties she has experienced as a widow and how hard it has been to re-engage. For example, her son in Paris had urged her to join an evening class to learn French and cannot understand how difficult this has been for her to do on her own. Whilst she understood that they would be around for emergencies, this had been little comfort.

Dorothy also wished that her sons and their families would feature more strongly in her life. As a result of the break up of one son's first marriage, she had completely lost contact with her grandchildren. In some ways her experience was similar to that of Vera. One son in particular often expressed his frustration with her obvious dissatisfaction with life. Dorothy recounted the story of how he used to telephone her and ask how she was:

> I used to say, 'Not so good'. But he would say, 'That's what you always say'. So now I say, 'I'm fine', even if I'm not. But we don't speak as often now.
>
> (Dorothy)

She was no longer as close to this son as she had been when her husband was alive, but recognized that: '…perhaps he was closer to his dad than me.'

Edith's disappointment by contrast had been with her siblings. Although her family have been very close in many ways, pulling together in times of family crises, she felt that they had never really understood how difficult the early days of widowhood had been for her. She wishes they would be more supportive when she needs them:

> I had a breakdown; they didn't really understand. Do you know Pat, I think they were embarrassed. I would like the support from my family.
>
> (Edith)

*Being different*

Within this narrative of loneliness and despair there is a strong feeling of not being like other women. Patricia and Vera both espoused the view that they were different from other older women. Given that they both knew that older women predominate in later life, they also recognised that this got in the way of developing potential friendships and certainly increased their isolation.

Vera had spent a large part of her life in a predominantly male world, that of the RAF, and had few female friends during that time:

> I always got on a lot better with men than with women. That is probably because I've got three sons, my husband, and in the officers' mess it was mainly men. I was always in a man's environment, I was always talking to men and very few women. And I find that is a difficulty. I now have to re-do that as a widow. I have to rebuild my life, it cannot stay the same. But I find it difficult to talk to women about my interests, like sport. Yet I don't want to get married again …
>
> (Vera)

In the following story, which she recounted during her second interview, she acknowledged her own ageist and sexist attitudes:

> Before my husband died, we went on holiday with a couple of friends. She was about eight years younger than me, but her husband was the same age as us. We were neighbours, we'd been going about together for years. We were at Blackpool one year ...as we were standing near the hotel, where we were staying, there were some coaches and a whole lot of women on their own got off that coach and Jenny stood there and said, 'Vera, do you think that in ten years time we'll be doing that?' And I'm now doing it. And every time (when I go away on holiday with Age Concern), I think of Jenny and what she said. All of those women on their own, not a man in sight. She was horrified that it might be us. I was in my late forties and I felt the same although I still feel like it now, and I think its your children's view ... I find it very sad.
>
> (Vera)

Vera had been unable to change her view that the male world she used to belong to was in many ways better and therefore the female world that is now open to her is inferior by comparison.

> I think I'm a bit on my guard with women. My sister and I never really got on, I'm a bit wary. I only have had three really close friends, one in New Zealand, one who died last year and my other school friend. It makes it difficult to extend friendships, I feel much easier with men. I don't think I'll change now.
>
> (Vera)

Patricia made many references to differences between herself and other women, for example referring to a neighbour who has tried to befriend her:

> As I say, with Josie, its alright going with Josie, I've been twice but she can walk quicker than me and her taste is not mine so...I did it twice but she's not like me at all... I've only actually been out shopping with her twice but there again we are very different, very different you see...she likes to go dancing but then again the dancing they like is so different, they weren't as serious as I was. I mean, my hubbie, as I told you, was a teacher, so they weren't as serious as me and she's asked me to go with her but they do this modern sequence, which I'm not interested in, and then she goes to this line dancing which I wouldn't do.
>
> (Patricia)

She considered that she had little in common with other older women and certainly did not identify with them:

> ... oh no, I'm not that type. I don't know about those clubs, it's not for me, all those old people, I can just see them all, all these old ladies dancing together, but that's not for me, no, no, I'm not going to go to dancing. If I'm going to dance it's with a partner, a proper partner, a man. So that's where I'm different you see.
>
> (Patricia)

So, even though it had proved problematic in terms of developing relationships in later life, there was a strongly held belief in this narrative, that the company of women is qualitatively inferior to the company of men. Moreover, criticism of other women was both explicit and implicit in the stories:

> I would never dance with another woman, none of them can take a gent off properly, not at all. And I still won't go out even to the shops for a loaf without making sure my hair is all right, putting a bit of lipstick on... not like some older women. That will never change. I don't care how old I get...I'll never be a sweet old lady, I mean I don't think I'll ever let myself go in that respect, even though there's no-one to see you. You see some women...I mean my husband was keen on how you looked.
>
> (Patricia)

### Little pleasure from life

The overwhelming feeling that emerges from the narrative of 'Loneliness and despair' is that overall there is little pleasure to be gained from life as an older widow. These women rejected as poor compensation the factors that other women, whose stories encompassed a different narrative, judge as positive aspects of widowhood.

Patricia, for example, talked with both pleasure and pride about her sewing and decorating skills. In recent years, she had taken up craftwork, now an important part of her life:

> I do try hard. I've got a little room, the little bedroom upstairs; I've had that turned into a workroom. So I can close the door and I get carried away up there, go up there for hours. It gives me great pleasure. I've been doing this for about five years now, since my husband died. I do get pleasure from making things. I mean I've had people buy things off me to send to Hong Kong for presents. One's gone to Belgium, one's gone to Geneva, Holland. Now isn't that something? I like to decorate too...I mean I've started to do a bit of painting in there, in the kitchen, yesterday. Its just something to do, I'm going to do a bit of painting over the weekend...I can't just sit here, I have to be doing something.
>
> (Patricia)

However, this was countered with: 'That's all I do get pleasure from, there's not much left these days.'

Dorothy echoed these sentiments:

> I do all these things but I put a front on when I go out. I mean I enjoy holidays with these friends I've got but I still think I wish I was with Roy. Nothing makes that better. I mean I laugh and joke and when we went to book this holiday with Joan up the road, the lady said 'is there any special request?' and I just said, 'oh, yes two young gentlemen', just joking. But I didn't mean it.

Vera too suggested that she goes through the motions of making the best of her life as a widow:

> I spend a lot more time reading now than I did when my husband was alive, we were out such a lot. I drive a lot more than I did then, he would always do the driving. I see a lot more of the country than I did and I do the things I like doing, I think I look at places more, the architecture... And of course my independence is very important. I feel that I am in charge of what I want to do...if I want to go to bed at 7:00 at night, I can do. If I want to go to the end of the earth I can do. If I want to go and buy up Marks and Spencer I can do. I've nobody else to say 'can I?' to. I'm in the fortunate position of having money to make choices. I would miss this after all these years (if I had to give it up).

But, relatively speaking, these changes were insignificant. Vera was unhappy with her life and the person she had become. Even when talking about her new independence and the choices she was now able to make, she finished with the proviso: 'perhaps that is wrong.' Through her loneliness as a widow, she had become what she described as very self-centred and self-preoccupied:

> Sometimes, I've got so self-centred about it that when the boys say they are coming home, I think 'oh, no, I've got to get a meal ready' ... I think you do get very selfish, you get that if you don't want to go somewhere or do something, you don't have to ...My life is so different now.
>
> (Vera)

### The future is bleak

Not surprisingly, given that the compensations of life now are minimal, the future is seen as bleak. Apart from general concerns about her future, Vera worried about what would happen when she can no longer manage her voluntary work, her lifeline into the community and the place where she was both appreciated and validated:

> My voluntary work has helped me to develop things I haven't done before but what will happen when I can't do it anymore? That will be a blow when I can't do that.
>
> (Vera)

She was not looking forward to the future because life would be even more difficult than it currently was. Reflecting on her life now, she said: 'It's all so depressing'.

Patricia, too, was not optimistic about the future. She was disappointed that her only daughter, now forty, had neither married nor had any children. If there were grandchildren, she could have seen a future through them:

> When Wendy and I get together we get a bit, how can I say, a bit morbid if you like, about the future. She gets upset because she's not married and says: 'I've even denied you your grandchildren', because I'd have adored grandchildren, I love children... There's not much to look forward to these days is there? (Patricia)

Interestingly, at our first meeting Dorothy too saw the future as bleak and acknowledged that she found it extremely difficult to look forward. However, the telling of her story was an extremely positive experience for her, and at our second meeting Dorothy acknowledged that as a result of reviewing her life with an interested listener, she was then better able to look forward. It was the first time in her life she had told her story and telling it had enabled her to feel more positive about life now and even the future.

> I felt much better actually. I got it off my chest. I enjoyed reminiscing to someone who had not heard it before…and I felt such a lot better after. I did think a lot about it after you'd gone. And I seem to have a lot more energy since I did that. I think it was telling the story out loud. I mean, the family, well its natural, they know all about my past life and I don't think they want to hear all about my time in the past. They say to live for the future, which I try to do now…being able to tell you, well, it was quite a relief and I enjoyed talking about myself. I have to take life as it comes now. I've even booked for Cliff Richard in May. Yes, I'm looking forward.
>
> (Dorothy)

I reflect in more detail on the research process, and the effects of participating in the research, in Chapter 13.

By way of contrast, other women in the study talked about their fears for the future but not within a narrative of 'Loneliness and despair'. Phyllis, for example, had deteriorating eyesight and problems with her hip that impact on her daily activities. These activities were such an important part of her daily living that she sometimes worries about what she will do if she is no longer able to do them:

> I have my special glasses but my eyes ache. Jean's been very good, all my friends have but I can't knit now, I can't watch television much anymore. If I go shopping I can't see the prices. It annoys me. I'm too independent, I've always had to do things for myself, and it's hard to ask for help. I can't do a lot of things and I do sometimes worry about the future.
>
> (Phyllis)

Nonetheless, she did not allow herself to indulge these fears for too long: 'it's taken me a long time to get over it, I'm really only just getting used to it but I know I'll cope, I always do.'

*A cautionary word*

I suggested earlier that narratives are fluid. Other women in the study sometimes invoked the narrative of 'Loneliness and despair' when all was not well. For example, a number of the women expressed the view that when they felt under par, or exposed as 'partner-less', then it was all too easy to attribute fleeting feelings of despair and loneliness to widowhood. Eunice, for example, spoke for the many:

> I feel stronger now unless something comes along and you're a bit under par or you don't feel well. You can sail along. I had an operation two years ago and it just felt strange that there was nobody here, and every friend that I knew seemed

to be on holiday. And I felt so vulnerable. My brother was here and he took me to the hospital and he dropped me at reception and he said, 'Will you be alright now?' All the other women had a husband, or someone sitting there...when you've had a husband, who you are 'number one' to, you miss that. I felt I had no one to look after me. So you see, you sail along and you are fine but there are days when you feel vulnerable.

(Eunice)

However, she also acknowledged that when you are married, you might have those feelings of vulnerability but attribute them to something else that is happening in your life. As a widow, it is sometimes all too easy to attribute every mishap to widowhood.

*Summary*

This narrative then speaks of an unrelenting unhappiness, and attributes that unhappiness to widowhood. This is not the same as either expressing regrets about a husband's death, or acknowledging what is missed about married life. Eunice for example, acknowledged: 'You miss the companionship...we should have been enjoying life together and whilst I'm alright financially I'd have much rather had Laurie with me and shared things together.' Bee missed both the conversations she used to have with her husband and her shared, if often unsaid memories and for Pat, the physical and sexual aspects of married life that she enjoyed, were no longer fulfilled. This narrative speaks not just of regrets but also of a life to be endured and a joyless future.

## Getting on with your life

Paramount in this second narrative thread is stoicism, exemplified as the acceptance of the inevitable. Following on from that is a desire to get on with life. It is underpinned by continuities of positive relationships or roles, which have eased this process. The women who voiced this narrative, have given themselves permission to get on with their lives. Having done their best for their husbands, they could see some benefits and advantages to their lives now. I discuss the following sub-plots within this overarching narrative; summarized below in Figure 11.4

| |
|---|
| • Accepting the inevitable |
| • Good memories and few regrets |
| • Aloneness |
| • Finances |
| • Health |
| • Validation by others |
| • Keeping busy |
| • The future: one day at a time |

**Figure 11.4  Getting on with your life**

*Accepting the inevitable*

Accepting the inevitable is paramount in this narrative of 'Getting on with your life'. For example:

> Life goes on and you must get on with it; you have to make the most of it ...
>
> (Evelyn)

> I don't make my life a misery, life is for living ...
>
> (Ellen)

> I got my life back together again after my husband died. You have to, dear ...
>
> (Joan)

As far as Joan was concerned, there was never any alternative to getting her life back together. Just as her stoicism enabled her to manage previous disruptions, so it would get her through bereavement and allow her to get on with her life.

Sylvia initially needed some help to get her life back together again. She joined a bereavement group, which she found both supportive and validating; there were people there, mainly women, who could understand her feelings. However, she soon grew out of this group and needed to get on with her life:

> After six months, I thought 'this is stupid, you're letting yourself go'. I was sixty then, I'd had my sixtieth birthday and I thought, 'Who's going to look after you, if you're ill' because I knew I was going to be. I didn't eat properly. I'd stopped cooking. I'd stick things in the microwave and sit in front of the telly and watch things I've never watched before or since. I knew they had this sequence dancing at Woodley on a Monday afternoon, so I thought 'Get ready and go'. And do you know I began to look forward to going ...
>
> (Sylvia)

Farzana's faith has enabled her to accept the inevitable, just as her faith had enabled her to both accept and manage other changes in her life:

> At first it all seems very different but you get used to being a widow and having all the responsibility. I put my trust in Allah.
>
> (Farzana)

She accepted that what has happened, had happened for a reason and therefore she must get on with her life.

Interestingly, several women had talked beforehand with their spouses about the fact that one of them would die before the other. Katherine for example, had taught her husband how to cook for himself and he had shown her how to change a fuse and do other minor jobs around the house:

> You can't live forever, both of you, not unless you commit suicide together...there

was always an understanding that one of us would go before the other, you've not got to sit down and weep for the rest of your life.

(Katherine)

## Good memories

Having good memories seemed to help the process of getting on with life. Bee for example, was convinced that such memories have helped her to accept the inevitable and deal with the present. She spoke for a number of the women:

> You put on a brave face and say to yourself, 'right you've got to make a new life for yourself and get on with it.' You've got your memories, wonderful memories. I have a memory case of Harold with all the photographs he loved and all the letters…and I take it out and I read them and it gives me comfort, lovely.

(Bee)

Of significance is that these memories contained few regrets. It is noteworthy, that this was in stark contrast with Dorothy and Patricia who both spoke of unhappy memories and unresolved problems. Bee on the other hand was confident that she did her best for Harold and this too enables her to get on with her life:

> When he was poorly, it was no problem to me. I used to put him in the car and take him out. I got a disabled badge and a wheelchair; but he was frustrated, that was the worst part, the frustration…but I have the satisfaction of doing the best I could for him, that was the main thing. And do you know, that really helps me now, knowing that.

(Bee)

## Aloneness

Aloneness is a very different state of being than loneliness. In this narrative of 'Getting on with life', aloneness is equated with a positive state of being on one's own. Bereavement was a time of loneliness but, as the inevitable becomes accepted, aloneness is construed as a positive feature of daily living. Widowhood offers some women their first opportunity for solo living. As such it is a completely new experience and one which is to be valued. Evelyn for example, expressed contentment with her current life: 'I'm very content with my life now. I wouldn't worry if I didn't see anybody all day.'

For those women for whom life had been dominated by domestic or caring responsibilities, aloneness was potentially an opportunity. Jean, for example, talked of the freedom that comes from being alone compared with marriage and family life:

> There's a lot of freedom when you are on your own. You can just please yourself. I like my own company; I'm never lonely. In fact I like my own company as much as I like being with other people.

She provided a vivid example of a Sunday when she pleased herself, and reflected on the benefits of living alone:

> Sunday morning I went to church but I didn't really speak to anyone. It was a lovely morning and I thought when I came back, I'd take myself off for a walk around the park before lunch. When I came out of church it had got so windy, it was so cold. So I came home and thought, 'blow the walk', I'm not bothering. So I made myself a cup of coffee and didn't have any lunch until about 2: 0 clock. In fact I did this the opposite way about. I've never done this before. I had something cooked at teatime, about 6 pm. Normally I have a cooked lunch at lunchtime on a Sunday so I don't have to do anything in the afternoons. I can watch television or whatever, but I don't know, for some reason I decided to do it different, I didn't feel hungry. When you are in a family, you eat even when you aren't hungry because you have to make it. We used to have four meals a day. I must admit, it's much easier on your own. You can have what you want when you want it and if you don't want to you don't have to. I've given up having supper but sometimes I wake in the middle of the night. And then I get up and make myself a drink, get a biscuit. Sometimes I make myself a piece of toast and I get back into bed. Sometimes I go to sleep, sometimes I don't. I don't mind, I just please myself.
>
> (Jean)

Aloneness then is associated with the freedoms of pleasing oneself, making choices and changing one's mind. This is in stark contrast to married life, where such freedoms were often not available.

For others, such as Doris and Elizabeth, aloneness had been a feature of their lives and, as such, not to be feared now they are widowed:

> I don't mind my own company at all. I quite like being alone but then I always have. People bob in and out here (her room in a residential care home) but I like my privacy.
>
> (Doris)

> I don't think (being alone) worried me unduly. I just carried on. If I felt I wanted to go out, I'd take myself into Stockport or something on the train. I think I've always been able to cope with my own company. I can do things on my own.
>
> (Elizabeth)

Aloneness therefore is not destructive in the way that loneliness can be. Instead, it is a pleasant state of being in which choices can be exercised.

*Enough money*

Being financially sound, or at the very least being satisfied that there is enough money to get by, was deemed to be integral to getting on with life. Some women identified themselves as 'well off'. Eunice feels that she had been well looked after and Vera too acknowledged that had this not been the case then her life would have been even worse than it was. Notably, Bee attributed her ability to get on with her life to her financial security:

It's made a lot of difference (having money); it would be no use me saying it hasn't. At the beginning I was very, very careful. Because I've always had to appreciate money, even when Harold was in business I was careful. So when I became independent, well I became independent when we sold the business, so even if Harold hadn't left me any money I would have been all right. But anyway, he did leave me money and John, my financial adviser, says you have to enjoy everything you want...but at first I was very careful, I think that is something that is born in you. But now, I can do what I want and that's why I'm going on this trip on Concorde and the QE2 in the autumn. And it's so exciting! But I don't know what my next adventure will be ...

(Bee)

Pat echoed the view that being financially sound has certainly helped rather than hindered her capacity to make choices and get on with the way she wanted to run her life:

I feel as though I am very lucky. I've got an income (from the family business), it's a good feeling because within reason, if I want anything I can go out and get it. I can go on my holidays. It makes such a difference being financially secure.

(Pat)

However, being 'well off' is not a determining feature of this narrative. Some of the women expressed the view that although they have very little money as widows, they want for nothing. Katherine for example was entirely dependent on her pension and housing benefit and had little to spare. Nonetheless, as she so strongly articulated throughout the interview, she had every intention of getting on with her life. Lack of money was not going to prevent her meeting her friends and attending weekly dances.

Betty's determination to get on with her life and do what she wanted to do, despite having only a state pension, had led her to seek employment as a cleaner. This was despite suffering from arthritis and some days not feeling well. She recognised that her low income now had resulted from her inability to build up a pension earlier on in life, despite lifelong paid work, but acknowledged that she has to deal with the here and now:

I do it for the money. It keeps my car on the road and I can afford to keep the house up and it keeps me independent. And of course, I can go out to the theatre, not the professional theatre. You see, I never built up a pension, there just wasn't the money...but it doesn't stop me. I'll keep on working as long as I can.

(Betty)

So, although having a good income enabled some of the women to get on with life, the lack of a good income did not appear to be a hindrance. Subjective feelings about managing were of paramount importance.

*Managing Health*

In this narrative of 'Getting on with your life', health was dealt with in very much the same way as finances; that is, it is there to be managed. If you have good health, you should be grateful and if your health is poor, then you just have to deal with it.

Those with good health were very grateful that their health is good, especially compared to the health of friends. For example, according to Katherine: 'I want to stay as I am, healthy as I am at my age and not being full of ailments as a lot of people are.'

Taking precautionary measures wherever possible was integral to managing. Pat for example, acknowledged the importance of good health and tried to keep herself well. She had already anticipated the probability of a hip replacement, so attended a slimming club and a keep fit class to keep her weight down. In addition: 'I walk a lot, I think its good for you, no health wise I'm quite fit. I'm in BUPA so if I want anything, if I need anything, I've been paying that for years' (Pat).

Those with poor health found it restricting but not inhibiting and thus had adapted accordingly. For example, although Evelyn's sight was failing and she had both osteoporosis and a heart condition, her discussion of her health was in terms of what she was able to do, rather than what she was not able to do. She stressed the continuities between her life now and in the past, and identified the strategies she had employed to maintain these continuities to lead her life the way she wished to lead it:

> I spend most of my time here now, I don't move about as well. I enjoy knitting and reading. I knit for myself, not for anyone else, in case I make mistakes. And I do now! I've always enjoyed knitting; I've done it all my life. My mother taught me, the first thing I knitted was Grandad's garters. My eyes are beating me a bit at the moment, that's the problem with reading too. I'm not keen on the television but I like the wireless. I listen to Radio 2; I like the music and the interviews. I've been listening tonight to Roy Hattersley; he's an interesting man. And I listen to tapes; my niece's husband recorded all my old records for me. I like listening to Perry Como and I love listening to music played on the cello. I used to go to the Theatre Royal in Nottingham to listen to music…my mother used to take me. And in Blackpool we used to go to the theatre. I don't go to the theatre now, but I listen to the music. Sometimes I listen to Radio 4 and I enjoy the plays.
>
> (Evelyn)

Elizabeth too observed that she had good days and 'not so good' days:

> I can't see as well now and I can't do as many things. I've got polymyalgic rheumatism and I'm on steroids. About once a month it seems to flare up again and it always seems to be the same weekend …it was this weekend …I've got a stiff hand today and my legs ache. So, with my eyes not being so good it means I can't knit. But it doesn't stop me getting out, I went to the library yesterday; I get

> big-print books. My knitting will have to wait for a good day. I don't let it get me
> down. I get on with what I can.
>
> (Elizabeth)

Objectively, Doris's health was poor and she acknowledged that she had recently begun to weigh up more carefully what could reasonably be managed. However, she was determined not to stop altogether:

> I don't go out at all now…I'm aching and my arthritis is spreading. (If I go out) I
> like to know where I am going and I like to know that I can cope, know where the
> loo is, that sort of thing. That's why I wouldn't go on that committee for Age
> Concern. But I do things here you see, I'm on the residents' committee here and
> I'm very involved, that sort of thing. I suppose I feel safe here, I know what's
> what.
>
> (Doris)

Good health therefore made getting on with life easier, but poor health was certainly not a valid reason for opting out.

### Validation by others

Being valued as a person by significant others is important. Bee, in particular, has been enabled to get on with her life by the comments and actions of friends. She had particularly appreciated comments made after her husband's death concerning her care of him throughout his life and especially when he was ill:

> He was so well respected but they all say 'Thanks to you Bee, you looked after
> him so well, he'd nothing to worry about, you were always a good wife.'
>
> (Bee)

She clearly felt valued by her friends. During our second interview Bee had just returned from a one month visit to the United States and commented on her friends' reactions on her return:

> Quite honestly Pat, since I've come back they've been on the phone. And it's quite
> upsetting really, because Mary said to me 'Oh I have missed you, oh I do want
> you back'. And Joan, who lost her husband, has said the same thing, 'I do love
> you and I want you back and when are we out' and so on. I'm going out tonight
> and that's just how it's been, and I'm going to a party on Sunday. It's lovely when
> you are missed.
>
> (Bee)

Validation can come from a variety of sources. In addition to positive relationships with her family, Mags felt validated by the staff at the residential care home and they made her feel special:

I know I can't manage to look after myself and my niece can't, but it's not so bad here and I've come to the conclusion that if I can't go home, I don't want to be anywhere else and here they treat me like a friend. The girls spend a lot of time in here, they tell me things, and they know they can trust me. I like that.

(Mags)

Vera had found some compensation being with other widows and widowers. Indeed, the only time she felt validated in her life now was at the self-help group, which she had helped to form. The only people who really understood her feelings were: 'the people who are in the same situation as me, the people I've met at the club'. However, even here she did not feel entirely at ease, feeling that she is different even from those who understood and respected her feelings of loss.

*Keeping busy*

Keeping busy and structuring one's time was construed positively in this narrative of 'Getting on with your life', whereas in the narrative of 'Loneliness and despair' routine and structure was seen by the women involved as an attempt to both gain some control and cover-up low self-esteem and lack of confidence. In the current narrative, there is a strong feeling that being busy is essential to getting on with one's life. Phyllis seemed to sum this up for many of the women, with the following words: 'Life's what you make it. I like to be doing something, I like to be busy'.

Elizabeth also liked to organise her week, just as she had always done.

I like to have something happening every day …I don't like a day when I haven't something in view. So I do my work and what-have-you and then if I haven't got anything else to do, I take myself off into the village, to the library and sit there for a while and walk back. I went to the library yesterday. This week I've had marmalade oranges and I've already made one lot of marmalade. That's two days work.

(Elizabeth)

Katherine's week revolved around activities with friends and neighbours and enjoying herself as much as possible. She identified keeping busy as a major feature of getting on with life as a widow; those who do not keep busy spend too much time worrying and that way lay a life of misery. This came easy to her: 'I'm adaptable and you see I've not moved from my friends, I still keep in contact with all my friends …and there is so much going on here.'

*The future*

The emphasis in this narrative is on getting on with life but there is little discussion about the future, more a feeling of life is to be lived now. Bee for example, was only too aware that she was at a crossroads, trying to look forward but wanting to live for the here and now. She was enjoying being courted and described her transatlantic relationship as: 'just like being in the forces'. However she was comfortable with the continuities in her life and rather fearful of possible discontinuities. She envisaged a long life ahead of her, but the deaths of a number of close friends, as well as her husband, had caused her to reflect on her life:

> God, you have to make the most out of life while you can…I'm just happy to be as I am. I'm getting a lot of excitement out of my life…I never think of ageing; I enjoy life.
>
> (Bee)

However, there was recognition by some of the women of time moving on. The process of getting older and the resultant changes were stark reminders. Farzana for example, suggested that most of the changes in her life had come about as a result of getting older, rather than becoming widowed:

> My life is very different now, but I was much younger when my husband was alive. I don't feel my life is different because I'm a widow, but because I am older now and my children have grown up.
>
> (Farzana)

Betty did not relish the prospect of getting older, fearing that she would lose her independence, but she dealt with this by sharing her feelings with close friends:

> I've got to 72 and there's not really much going for me now. I'm getting very near the edge of the cliff. All sorts of things get you down as you get older. I talk about it every Monday night (after the Drama group). This gentleman, Johnny, he sent me a card on my birthday and it said 'On your birthday, I just want you to remember one thing…' and then you turn it over and it says, 'and if you do, you've done very well'! (laughs) Oh, the memory, you think, 'oh I can't remember the name of it' but you can remember things that happened years ago.
>
> (Betty)

Sharing fears and feelings with others about the future, is yet another strategy employed in 'Getting on with your life'.

*Summary*

This narrative of getting on with life generally expresses satisfaction with life now, sometimes muted but at other times more enthusiastically. It is a narrative in which continuities abound. Many of the women who voiced this narrative have been strong individuals all their life and widowhood is a continuation of that life. They spend time with the friends who have been important to them throughout their lives and they are secure in other relationships. They have often continued to live in the same house or district that they shared with their husbands. Family relationships, whether weak or strong, have been maintained.

## A transition

The third and final narrative of transition is about change; the change that has occurred through the process of becoming and being an older widow. The women who voice this narrative acknowledged that, although they certainly did not choose to become widows, they have changed within themselves from the women they were as wives. They both welcome and value these changes. Widowhood is thus construed as a transition in older women's lives and encompasses the following sub-plots, summarised below in Figure 11.5:

| |
| --- |
| • New self awareness |
| • Putting me first |
| • Freedom from |
| • New relationships |
| • Interdependence |
| • New interests/ new opportunities/ new skills |
| • Looking forward |

**Figure 11.5 A transition**

*New self awareness*

An important part of this transition was growing self-awareness and insight. Taken for granted assumptions have been reflected upon and even challenged. After a period of bereavement Eunice, for example, confirmed that she had moved into another phase of her life and with it had gained a new perspective. Acknowledging the importance of time as a healer, she identified greater self-knowledge and self-awareness:

> Material things are not so important now. Whereas you might have been upset because a vase was broken, you really put things into perspective. People matter and I know when the car was damaged, I can remember being very shocked after the break in, my car was broken into. And I was very shocked...but you do get it into perspective, because you realise that you are not hurt and it is a material thing. I think you get things in perspective, you sort out what's important and you realise that life is never the same, it can never be the same but you are strengthened. I think I am able to understand how people feel and I feel I can comfort people who've lost anyone, not to be afraid of letting them talk to me.
>
> (Eunice)

In between our two meetings, she had taken time to consider the diversity of experience in widowhood:

> There are four of us, who go away. We are all widows and we are all different. One friend didn't have a particularly good relationship with her husband at the end, and one friend lost her husband on Boxing Day. There is one woman who is still terribly miserable when I meet her and she lost her husband about the same time and she gives me a hug and says, 'How are you, it's very difficult isn't it?' And I don't feel like that at all, you can see it all over her face. But she has a very bad relationship with her daughter; we are all very different even though we are widows.
>
> (Eunice)

She had found herself reflecting a lot more recently, perhaps because it was a time in her life when it was sanctioned, as well as having both the space and the opportunity to do so.

Jennie too acknowledged that she had found herself reflecting on issues that she had previously accepted. She was in a new phase of her life in which friends, who had always been important, are now truly valued:

> I have a new life here. I have my friends and I'm still healthy. I'm as close to my friends as I am to my family. I feel as though I've been given new chances...I can do so many things on my own or with friends. I can do things I didn't think I could do.
>
> (Jennie)

Jennie's very strong religious beliefs had given her further strength.

> You've not got to be miserable...and well I think more or less it's your determination to do things and there again, I say being a Christian, whatever I've done I think the Lord has helped.
>
> (Jennie)

As a result of experiencing the initial trauma of bereavement and its toll on her well-being, Edith had a greater self awareness and with it a new confidence:

> At one time I never would have said what I feel, but I accept more now. I don't think anything could hurt me as much as that. Now I can do things myself and I get such a kick out of it...organising a holiday for my friends and myself. I'll try anything now, but I never used to be like that. I have patience that I never had before. I can even encourage other people now. I think I'm more accepting and I'm much stronger. I've grown a lot. You don't ever get over it, but each time you achieve something you cope better and each time it gets better. Do you know, I watch a lot more now.
>
> (Edith)

Edith was very proud of her own achievements and wanted to talk about them:

> We went to Canada for three weeks. It was so exciting. I was going in a different direction from anywhere I'd ever been. And I planned it all myself!

Like Eunice, she had developed greater empathy and understanding than she did in the past, which she was able to use to support others:

> There's this lad who I work for, he lost his mum at Christmas and he's going through a phase of being nasty. And I talked to him about it and he said he missed his mum. So we talked about it. People used to ignore me and not talk about Donald at all. It's important to talk, not to bottle it up. So I have learned a lot and I can help him.
>
> (Edith)

In widowhood, Doris has had the opportunity to please herself for the first time since before she was married. Instead of always subjugating her own views and feelings to those of a domineering husband, she was able to put herself first and do what she wanted, when she wanted. This was a complete reversal of how she had lived her life and the first time she had either really acknowledged feelings of injustice, or felt able to respond to them:

> I thought, well I'm not staying here (in the marital home), I'm going to move. It could have been done before but he wouldn't. He was very stubborn. If he didn't want to do something, he wouldn't. So as soon as he died, I felt I could please myself. It was the first time in my life that I could please myself. After he died I had the freedom to put the house on the market...I knew I wouldn't stay there. I longed to get out of it because he wouldn't spend the money on it. I thought I'd go where I can pay to be looked after and not depend on people and I'm very independent here. Since he died and since I've become more disabled, it mattered to try to be more independent, to make choices, to make my own judgements. Because whatever I said, you know such as holidays, he'd say 'Oh no, you wouldn't like it there, we'll go somewhere else'...and do you know, I'd give in for peace, I hate arguments.
>
> (Doris)

Sylvia had recently met a new partner and had begun to reflect on her married life. Consequent on her newly increased self-awareness, she expected something more from the current relationship and acknowledged that she anticipated more equality:

> I really am very, very happy again and I love him very, very much. But it's a different type of love that I had for John. I loved him but it wasn't passion, not like I feel for James. I think a lot of what I had for John was gratitude because when I brought Susan home I expected to be on my own for the rest of my life.
>
> (Sylvia)

In this narrative then, becoming and being a widow has provided an opportunity, perhaps the first opportunity, and the time and the space, for some women to think more deeply about themselves and thus become more aware of their own needs and feelings.

*Putting myself first*

This narrative of transition is also one that not only recognizes the important move from 'we' to 'I' but also explicitly speaks as 'I'. There was a period of time for some in which this move took place. Eunice for example, found that when she was first widowed it was difficult being 'one person' but acknowledged that gradually you become 'one'. She has gained confidence and learnt new skills, particularly in coping with financial matters, the area of domestic life which had been the responsibility of her husband:

> I coped and I managed and now on finances and other things like that I've become my own boss and I have all my affairs sorted into files and that sort of thing. It's 'my' way of doing things. I'm my own boss now I suppose.
>
> (Eunice)

For Phyllis however, the move had been quite deliberate; widowhood has been a time of starting again as an individual. Having been in business with her husband all her life running a public house, she had been one part of both a professional and personal partnership:

> I knew that when I moved here I had to make a new life for myself. It had to be 'my' life. If my husband had been alive, life would have been very different. I think we would have vegetated in the village where we lived.
>
> (Phyllis)

The role of others in confirming the move from 'we' to 'I' has also been significant. Edith was very pleased that people now accept her as Edith, rather than one part of 'Donald and Edith'. This was in stark contrast to how Edith felt in the early days of widowhood (see Chapter 10):

> That's really important, people accepting me as Edith. It's a big thing, you don't forget some of your old friends, but of all the friends I've made, and believe me I've got a lot of new friends, they accept me as 'me', as Edith.

Sylvia too perceived that previously she had only ever seen herself in relation to others, as part of 'we' rather than 'I', an individual with needs but in widowhood it was different:

> I'd spent years seeming to do what other people wanted me to do. I know its no fault of theirs, I always seemed to give in. If he wanted to do something or go somewhere that I didn't, well I'd go along with it. So I thought, I'm going to do what I want to do now and that's how it is in my relationship with James.
>
> (Sylvia)

Her daughter has objected to her mother's new relationship and has ceased all contact. After initial sadness over this, Sylvia wanted to get on with her life, meet her own needs and not feel that she has to any longer please or appease others, as she had done in the past. She identified this as a major change in herself.

Opportunities to be an individual were scarce in Doris's married life. Although in her head she had always felt independent, she went along with what her husband wanted. Now she was able to show others, as well as herself, that she is 'I' rather than we:

> I'm handling all my own money now, which is nice. It costs a lot to live here for the rest of my life. The boys know there won't be much left if I live for a long time (laughs). I have a financial adviser from the bank to help me make the money last as long as I can. I quite enjoyed that side of things, making my own decisions and selling the bungalow ... I had sixty years of married life and I felt I'd had enough. It's so good to be 'me'! For the first time in my life I'm doing what I want and it's so nice. And that is liberating ... and at my age as well.
>
> (Doris)

'I' acknowledges wholeness whereas 'we' implies half of a relationship in which the other partner is absent; this narrative of transition is definitely that of 'I'.

### *Freedom in/independence from*

This narrative also speaks positively of gaining independence or finding freedom in widowhood as a result of becoming 'I'. This was unlikely to have occurred in marriage. This is different to the narrative of 'getting on with your life' in which independence, which may have been a feature of married life, continued into widowhood. It is also in stark contrast to the narrative of loneliness and despair in which freedom and independence are negatively construed and equated with loneliness and 'selfishness'.

Pat for example, talked confidently about the independence she has gained. She enjoyed not having to consider the needs of another person, as well as having the freedom of being a single person:

> Even though you are on your own, you get a certain independence that you really don't want to lose. It's not just the independence of being able to do what you want when you want, which you can do, it's the thought of having someone to rely on you to be there and having to come home. I just wouldn't want to be bothered with looking after somebody, because I've spent my life looking after somebody...you don't want to be responsible for someone again.
>
> (Pat)

Ellen echoed these feelings, recognising that in widowhood she had gained 'freedom' for the first time in a gendered life:

> ... now I'm a freelance. I can shut the door when I want and open the door when I want ... (freedom) is very important to me. I just feel I've never had freedom. I mean, even from joining the army, from being in school and to then going in the army at 17 and a half, you were under the control of people, then you get married and you're under control, then you have children and you're under control, and so forth. Right the way through. And so I've never really had freedom. It's the first freedom I've ever really had and that's why I think I enjoy it...I really like the freedom, I've never had it ... and I love it.
>
> (Ellen)

More specifically, others have discovered a certain freedom in some aspects of daily living. Again, the context was that of gendered lives. For example:

> One thing I enjoy when I go to bed at night, I always have a book to read and sometimes I read until my eyes are nearly closing, until midnight. Well, clearly I couldn't have done that before. I would have read until Laurie went to bed. I can watch whatever television programmes I want, even if they're late. Yes, there is a certain freedom and it does get a lot easier, even though some people say it gets harder ...and its no disrespect to your partner to feel that.
>
> (Eunice)

This narrative then speaks of the freedom of independence, acquired alongside newly gained confidence. It is tinged neither with guilt, nor with self-deprecation. Moreover, it is not necessarily disrespectful of the deceased spouse and for some women this was very important. This is reflected in other aspects of the narrative.

*New relationships*

As a result of both personal change and opportunities, new relationships are construed as possible within this narrative of transition.

*Best friends*

For many of the current generation of older women, the roles of wife and best friend were incompatible. She may have had a best friend when she was a girl, but once a woman became a wife her first loyalty was to her husband and then her family. Jennie for example, insisted that women did not have best friends when they were married. Widowhood for some women had provided an opportunity for such friendships to be re-kindled and much pleasure may be gained from having a best friend. Jean and Phyllis described each other as best friends. Having met as older widows, they discovered a lot in common and provided companionship, emotional support and time for each other:

> We like a lot of the same things. We've both taken up this dancing and we like to go to the club. We like to go shopping together and we don't worry too much about money...we share a lot of interests and we both like people who are straight

and above board…it's very nice when you've got a friend, a real genuine friend.

(Jean)

You know, I don't do many things now without Jean. We do most things together …it's nice to have one special friend to share things with… you need that.

(Phyllis)

Jean illustrated their time together:

Phyllis was here for lunch and then she went home. We often do that Tuesdays and Fridays as well. We go for a walk and then sometimes go for a pub lunch. We have toasties and sometimes I have a coffee and Phyllis has a half of bitter …friendship matters to me. I want to be a proper friend to people and I want the same in return. Friendship is about trust and respect and love.

It's very nice when you've got a friend, a real friend … we like a lot of the same things, we share a lot of interests. They (friends) are very important. If you are feeling down in the dumps, bothered about anything you can call or get on the phone to Phyllis … it's so important to have friends of your own age. And when we get together, we talk about all sorts of things. Families; things that are going on at the club; news and of course gossip (laughs) ... We always find something to talk about.

(Jean)

As a widow Evelyn had developed a close friendship with a woman, also widowed, whom she had previously known as part of a couple:

I'd never really had a good lady friend until Jenny. I was very close to her. Although we were neighbours we didn't really get to know each other until our husbands died. We used to go out together as couples before that; as couples, but not as real friends.

(Evelyn)

In widowhood Evelyn had the time to develop friendships, deriving considerable pleasure from such opportunities.
Elizabeth recounted a similar experience:

She's become one of my best friends since our husbands died. I've gone to her or she's come to me and we've gone on holiday together. When we are together, we talk a lot, about silly things…no, not really. We do laugh a lot, that's true, but we talk about serious things as well. I'm like a girl again, not an old lady. We are very good for each other.

(Elizabeth)

Both Elizabeth and Evelyn acknowledged the difficulties of having close female friends when they were still married. For both of them working life and married life excluded a wider social world. Then in retirement, their couple status seemed exclusive of other relationships. It was only in widowhood that they had been able to discover the joys of 'best friends'.

Dorothy's relationship with her close friends was companionable, doing things together, but also offered her the chance to share feelings and worries, a level of intimacy not available from her sons. She shared confidences with one friend in particular:

> When we were on holiday last year, we went to Malta and we'd had a drink or two, and we went to bed. At two in the morning she got up and she was very upset...and I said, 'Are you alright Joan?' Then we sat on the balcony and she started to tell me about her husband and I poured out my story (Dorothy and her husband had had problems which she asked not to be part of her transcript). So we'd got something in common. It felt good to be sharing things like that with a friend.
>
> (Dorothy)

She was able to talk to her female friends in a way that she was never able to talk to her husband, who criticized her for: 'keeping myself to myself'.

*The friendship of other widows*

The friendship of other widows was valued; they understood, had time for each other and mutually provided companionship, affection and support. According to Ellen: 'You do sort of cling to one another, people who are on their own rather than go to a couple ... I do think that is so'.

When she was first bereaved, Dorothy had found weekends to be very lonely, whereas now she spent most weekends with her widowed friends:

> I used to find weekends very lonely. Fortunately, I've got a very good friend that I go to every other Sunday, well I see her every Sunday. Once a fortnight we go to her Auntie's, she's 98, and we do little jobs for her and we sit and chat while Auntie has a sleep. And on the other Sunday I go to her house and have Sunday dinner. It gets me out of the house on a Sunday, you see. Saturday I go to Hyde with another good friend who's recently lost her husband. Three of my friends are widowed, the one I go shopping and swimming with. I'm going away with her and this one on Sunday; she's been on her own for 15 years. And then there's Joan over the back here, I think its two years since her husband died.
>
> (Dorothy)

Dorothy has found these women to be a source of support and companionship. They had been more understanding of her feelings than her sons and more time was now spent with these friends than with family.

Pat, who was widowed in her late forties, has found that that in later life the society of widows has opened up a new social world for her. As a younger widow with teenage children, she was extremely isolated. She had few remaining couple friends and even fewer female friends. Furthermore, she was perceived as a threat by other wives and there seemed to be few opportunities to meet younger women like herself. This was perfectly explicable in a gendered, couple-oriented society:

> Well you go out as a couple, don't you? My husband and I went out as a couple; we went out with other couples. We wouldn't have dreamt of asking a single woman out for an evening.
>
> (Pat)

However, in her late sixties, she has found that she is no longer unusual. She was now part of a friendship group consisting mainly of widows in their sixties, seventies and eighties. Socially and geographically, she was now surrounded by similar others:

> I've got friends now, quite a lot. I don't think I've ever had so many women friends … all my friends of my age had husbands. Now of course there's Jennie, every Thursday four of us get together for a coffee, there's all the people I've met through the church, we go out for meals … and I've joined the Women's Guild, I've got friends there. And there's six of us go on holiday every year. And we're all widows.
>
> (Pat)

When Betty's neighbour was widowed, they started to share social activities. This enabled a deeper friendship to develop and they have long ceased being just neighbours and have become friends:

> Although she was my neighbour, we were not friends; we were acquaintances, after all she had her husband … but when she was widowed, we started doing things together from time to time and over the years we've become very friendly. Now we hardly go anywhere without each other.
>
> (Betty)

Betty confirmed that for many women, their primary relationship is with their husband; more often than not this relationship is all consuming and exclusive of other relationships. Only when that relationship is terminated by the husband's death can other friendships begin to flourish.

*Loss of couple friends*

The increased number and quality of friendships with other women had been paralleled by a decrease in friendship with couple friends:

> I found and I think a lot of women do, that the joint friends tend to disappear when you become a widow, because … well I don't know why but they do … we used to go out every Sunday night together (with one couple) but that stopped.
>
> (Betty)

Eunice had already been advised of the potential loss of couple friends by other widows when, the year after her husband died, she went on a Saga holiday to Exeter University. She met a number of other widows, who told her: *'You'll find all the friends who you've had as couples, they'll drop you'*. Although she had been sceptical about these comments at the time, she has since found them to have some truth:

> There is something in it because some married friends don't contact me ... when I'd gone back to church and in the pews people have been sitting together and I have found that with couples you can be left out.
>
> (Eunice)

Edith confirmed that she had been ostracised by her couple friends and that it had been extremely painful:

> I thought I had friends at my previous house. When my husband was alive, it was all Donald and Edith this and that, but it was amazing when he died they didn't want to know me, they were all still couples. I think that's awful. Some very, very close friends of ours, they live in Scotland and whenever they wanted to visit Manchester, to visit other family, it was only ever us they would stay with, they never went anywhere else. They rang me up a year after Donald's death and said they were in the area and could they call and see me. I said, where are you staying and they said with some cousin. It was awful, they were so different with me and well, I could never be the same with them, it's awful really.
>
> (Edith)

As Joan illustrated, it came as quite a shock to find that one reason for this might be that widows are perceived as a threat:

> One thing you're very conscious of, husbands and wives, the wife might think you want their husbands. Well it was a terrible surprise, it really was. Particularly with one lady, she sort of kept grabbing him by the arm, as if I was going to grab him too. And that was the last thing I wanted.
>
> (Joan)

However, it was important not to generalize as Ellen confirmed:

> Two of my dearest friends now, well he went to school with Joe, and his wife Betty worked with Joe's sister, so they became great friends of ours. When Joe died, if I wanted anything he'd always come down and say I'll come and fix things in the house for you and I go to their house now.
>
> (Ellen)

She suggested that the loss of couple friends was not entirely about intended exclusion but rather single women excluding themselves because of anticipated discomfort. If you had a female friend, you did not feel in the way:

> I don't think its the married people, I think its the people who are single, they think they are intruding ... they think they are getting in the way. Because I feel that sometimes, I feel more alone in a crowd. When you go somewhere and there are twos, husband and wife, you don't know whether to tag on to them or to sit down. So Dorothy and I, well we're OK together.
>
> (Ellen)

*No wish to remarry*

Although changing relationships are part of this narrative, remarriage does not really appear on the agenda. This is as a result of positive reflection rather than resignation. Although some women missed the company of men, these older widows did not generally see themselves becoming part of a married couple again. Jennie, for example, reflected on how she has turned down a proposal of marriage:

> I've had an offer, a professor from the university, we'd been married about the same length of time and been widowed. But I didn't want to; marriage ties you down. I wouldn't want that again. Now, if I want to ring a friend to do something I can. I've a lot of freedom now. Marriage restricts you even if you have a happy marriage, and that's how it should be. If you marry someone it's because you want to be together. He's married now and I'm friends with his new wife. Ada asks me if I feel I missed my chance. They go on holiday three times a year and he's building her a new bungalow, but I don't feel I have. It's not what I want. Sometimes I miss having someone to do jobs around the house, gardening and plumbing, but I have neighbours who do jobs for me. I do all my own decorating, I have high ladders, and I do my own papering and painting.
>
> (Jennie)

Eunice too has given this careful consideration:

> I've missed male company. I mean some people actually approach dating agencies but I've never done that. I wouldn't want to marry again; I'd be quite happy 'living in sin' I think or just having a friendship with someone. I mean, nowadays if I want to cook a full meal for myself I can, but Laurie enjoyed his food and it would always have to be a proper meal for him and I don't think I'd want to do that again.

There was general agreement that it was most probably different for widowers. Betty speaks for many of the women when she says:

> A lot of men marry don't they? They need someone to lean on; they can't manage on their own. Some of them can but many can't. You see; I can manage.

It is interesting to note that so many of the women who voice this narrative of transition are reluctant to undertake another relationship in which there is a risk that they might either become dependent on their partner or have a partner dependent on them. For example:

> I would like a man to be friendly with. I've joined a 'singles club' in Stockport. It's just for people who are on their own to meet and have a friendly evening and it's for my age group more or less. It's nice to have a conversation with a man, it's different than women's conversations all the time. I wouldn't mind somebody to go with for a meal or something like that, but I'd never get married again. I couldn't be bothered with all the washing, and I think if you get married young,

well you're used to each other's ways. Whereas when you're older, you're very set in your ways and it would be difficult I think to learn to live with somebody again. And you also, even though you are on your own you do get a certain independence that you really don't want to lose either. If you like going somewhere you can go and you don't have to rush back.

(Pat)

Even those women who had embarked on new relationships with male partners have thought about the changes in themselves, and the consequences of those changes on new relationships. Phyllis, for example, has a man friend who lives in the same block of flats as her, and whom she describes as a companion:

We share the same interests. We like the same music, we both like to go walking in Derbyshire. He sometimes comes here of an evening. At the moment I'm having the best of both worlds. It would be a big thing. Now I can pick and choose when I go out and I don't think I could with a man. I'm quite happy and content. We've been walking today along the canal. I like my independence. I had two years on my own before I went to live with John and my grandson and I've been here four years now. I don't think I want to give it up again.

(Phyllis)

*New interests/ new opportunities/new skills*

New opportunities or interests, as well as new friends, have been embraced with enthusiasm and confidence. And so often these were interests not previously shared with a spouse. Jean and Phyllis discovered a shared passion for dancing when they met at the local Senior Citizens Club. Both of them had danced before they married, but their husbands had not been interested:

Albert couldn't dance; he had two left feet. Phyllis and I met at the club (the local Senior Citizens' club) and it all started when we went to Jersey, they do modern sequence dancing there. So we had a word with the chairman and discovered that if we could get 25 to 30 people interested we could start a class…it's been going six years now. The dancing club is mainly women…Phyllis and I dance together, she can take the gent's part. We dance with other people too, but I can only take the lady's part…all of my friends dance at the club. We dance at the Holy Spirit as well, the music is nice and sometimes we sing along with it.

(Jean)

They have also begun to travel to foreign places together on holiday; although neither of them had regular holidays with their husbands.

Jennie has undertaken new challenges in widowhood that were prohibited in the last years of her marriage, when caring responsibilities dominated. She has finally allowed herself the time to learn new skills. For example, she had learnt to swim and after she had proved to herself that she was able to swim adequately, she went paragliding on holiday.

A number of women talk about taking on roles previously occupied by their husbands. Eunice for example, had decided not to rely on the services of an accountant but instead to do her own books. Edith embarked on selling her bungalow and buying and then furnishing a flat. She always deferred to her husband's taste in décor during her married life, but she was now determined to have a go herself:

> I've never done anything like that before; I had all the bedrooms fitted. I had to get rid of my furniture and buy all new furniture, apart from the unit and the rug that Donald had bought. Now I can buy things that are my taste. My bedroom would not have been to Donald's taste. It's not that I never liked the things he liked, but he would never have had the bedroom like this.
>
> (Edith)

When she was first widowed, Edith recognized that she would have to make a number of changes in her life and joined a local volunteer group. Volunteering has been her turning point, enabling her to meet people and learn new skills. Encouraged by this, she has also begun casual work on the local market, selling kitchen goods. She reflected on what her husband might have thought of 'Edith now':

> I don't know, sometimes like when I'm on the market, I can't go dressed up, I think, if Donald could see me now, he'd either say 'poor Edith' or he'd say 'good on you Edith, I'm proud of you'. I think it would be the latter. I never would have done that before.
>
> (Edith)

## Looking forward

Within this narrative of transition, there is a vision of a future that is to be embraced with both realism and dreams. Jennie was aware of the differences between her life now and how her life might have been. With John's increasing disability and need for care, her future seemed to be very bleak; indeed, she had found it hard to look forward with confidence. She no longer feared for the future but was excited about the possibilities. Nonetheless, she was aware that this might change as she got older:

> As long as I can look after myself, I want to stay here. You can't impose on your family. I've told them, if I can't look after myself, you must put me in a home. I am not afraid of the future. I have my friends and my life here, and I spend a lot of time at the church, it's such an important part of my life.
>
> (Jennie)

Jean too wished to carry on enjoying her life and meeting new friends. Widowhood has been a time of such rapid personal change for her and she wished it to continue in this way as long as her health permitted:

The time will come when I can't do things for myself and I shall have to be ready to ask for help. But I'm not fearful. Our Jean will see to that and the family, I have nothing to be afraid of.

(Jean)

Edith and Pat both had dreams of travelling to foreign places. Edith was still trying to decide whether she wanted to move to Canada or, at the very least, plan another holiday there. She is torn between the continuities, her links to her family and the desire for new adventures:

I have my dreams Pat. I've thought of selling this flat and going back to Canada, many times. If I could sell this flat, I'd lead a 'life of Riley!' I might do it you know. That would surprise my family!

(Edith)

Pat dreamed of visiting exotic places but had not yet found a kindred spirit to accompany her so for the time being she has compromised, contenting herself with visiting the places her friends wish to visit. This has not stopped her dreaming:

My brother is going to the Far East. I am so envious. I've asked my friends but they say: 'No, let's go to Switzerland, or Austria' and we get out the brochures and start planning. But I'd love to go somewhere like Vietnam or Thailand. But I wouldn't go on my own, no I couldn't, but I'd like to…we'll see.

(Pat)

In widowhood, Ellen has begun to look forward, perhaps for the first time in her life. For most of her married life, she had lived for the here and now. This was not a problem at the time, but she recognised a difference in the new Ellen. She was very secure in a web of relationships and looked forward to an equally secure future. Like Jenny, she has made comparisons with her life as a carer and the possibilities for the future:

When we went away, we had to fix somewhere because it was flat, it was a case of finding somewhere because of the wheelchair, because of the pushing. I mean okay, we had a good time, we went to London, because I couldn't do it up hills, so we used to have to pick and choose where we went. But now, it's a case of if I fancy going I can. I've not been abroad, I've no inkling of going abroad, no inkling at all. If I won any money, my idea, it sounds daft, is to get on a train here and get a train anywhere to go right the way round Great Britain. And the one particular place I'd like to go is the Hebrides. I see pictures and I think its fabulous…yes, I'd love to go. You know if I won any money, that's where I'd go…I wish they'd bring out a thingy… for travel, for cheap travel right the way round in a year, so you could pick your time and go. Before you were limited where you could go, but now I'm a freelance.

(Ellen)

*Summary*

This narrative of transition comprises change, positive change, which incorporates the possibility of a future to be enthusiastically embraced. This is not about loneliness, nor is it about 'getting on with life' as it has always been lived. It is about a new life in widowhood, a new phase in the life course. Life 'now' has been reflected upon and it has been found to be very different from life as a wife. The women who voice this narrative are enmeshed in networks and relationships, are self-aware and very comfortable with the person they are now.

## Conclusion

In this chapter I have presented three narratives of Me Now. Each narrative embraces a variety of stories and between them they encompass a spectrum which ranges from misery and regret at one end right through to opportunity and change at the other. I have thus assembled the final part of the jig-saw of later life widowhood. This now comprises multiple narratives of:

- Me, Myself
- History and Me
- Me and My Social World
- Me, Now.

In the next chapter I bring these narratives together and argue that without cognisance of all these multiple narratives and their sub-plots, we cannot begin to make sense of older widows' lives.

# Chapter 12

# Multiple Narratives of Later Life Widowhood

## Introduction

In this chapter, I bring together and discuss further the multiple narratives emerging from my analysis of older widows' stories presented in the previous four chapters. I argue that without an understanding of the multiple and complex narratives of older women's lives, we are in danger of misinterpreting their current experience by subscribing to the dominant, one-dimensional narrative of later life widowhood as a time of loneliness, ill health and misery. Indeed, we ignore the impact of major continuities in older women's lives and focus instead on the discontinuities. By contrast, we only become aware of the subjectivity of the continuities when we engage with these multiple narratives. I go on to argue that although multiple narratives are not predictive, they certainly enable us to better understand the totality of the current experience, and the hidden lives therein. I further suggest that such an understanding also enables older women themselves to make better sense of that experience. I argue for an acceptance of the fluidity of older widows' multiple narratives: as Eunice said, there are days, or circumstances which conspire to make her feel sorry for herself and you think: 'poor me, I'm a widow' (the objective and the subjective come together), but that is not how she feels most of the time. Her major narrative is that of widowhood as a transition but there are times when she dips into widowhood as a time of loneliness and despair. I also acknowledge that both age and gender are integral to older widows' multiple narratives.

## Revisiting the life stories of older widows

At this point, it is useful to recap. Analysis of the twenty stories identified four 'parts' (Atkinson, 1998). Each 'part' contained a number of overarching narratives, within which there were a number of what I have termed 'sub-plots'. Whereas the order of my findings' chapters reflected a 'looking back in order to understand the present', my focus in this chapter is 'to understand the present'. Consequently, the order in which I now discuss the multiple narratives reflects this emphasis by beginning with 'Me, Now':

- 'Me, Now' consists of three narratives, which speak of the current experience of later life widowhood. They comprise: 'Loneliness and despair'; 'Getting on with your life'; and 'A transition'. They thus encompass a spectrum which ranges from 'misery and regret', to 'life goes on', to 'opportunity and change'. These narratives are invoked to explore 'the woman I am now' five or more years on, and are often used to compare and contrast the present with the immediate aftermath of the death of a spouse.

- 'Me, Myself' consists of three narratives of personal identity, which older widows use to describe themselves over the life course. These narratives comprise: 'High self-esteem'; 'Fluctuating self-esteem'; and 'Low self-esteem'. They locate the experience of later life widowhood within personal biography, and each one includes a number of sub-plots, which contribute to the narrative.

- 'History and Me' encompasses two powerful narratives of a collective past which because they have both sculpted and structured the lives of all these women, contribute to the present, to 'Me, Now'. These narratives of a collective past, comprising 'Belonging to a generation' and 'Gendered lives' highlight both change and stability, during which women were expected to adjust and adapt to challenges and restrictions. The interplay between the past and the present in terms of women's lives is an important part of the overall story of later life widowhood, with reference to historical location often being called upon to make sense of the present.

- 'Me and My Social World' comprises four narratives of social identity: 'Friends have always mattered to me'; 'I've never really had friends of my own'; 'I've always been a joiner-in'; 'I've always put my family first'. Each narrative locates the connections older widows have had (or not had) with others over the life course, identifying the relationships that have been developed, and the skills that have been practised. These narratives, to a greater or lesser degree, confirm the role, the centrality and the history of a variety of social networks in older widows' lives.

I summarise below in Figure 12.1 the diverse multiple narratives, and equally diverse sub-plots, which have been developed from my analysis of the four parts of the biographical interviews: Me, Myself; History and Me; Me and My Social World; Me, Now.

| Me Now | Me, Myself | History and Me | Me and My Social World |
|---|---|---|---|
| *Loneliness and despair* <br> • loneliness <br> • loss of confidence <br> • someone/ something missing <br> • they don't understand <br> • being different <br> • little pleasure from life <br> • the future is bleak | *High self-esteem* <br> • feeling secure <br> • a strong value base <br> • self-confidence <br> • learning from experience <br> • independence <br> • regrets for others | *Belonging to a generation* <br> • difficult times for some <br> • the War years <br> • changing times | *Friends matter* <br> • my friends are part of my life, the 'social me' <br> • the constituents of friendship <br> • friend-makers <br> • it must be awful not to have friends <br> • significant female friendships over the life course <br> • restrictions on friendship |
| *Getting on with your life* <br> • accepting the inevitable <br> • good memories and few regrets <br> • aloneness <br> • finances <br> • health <br> • validation by others <br> • keeping busy | *Fluctuating self-esteem* <br> • ambition versus 'I might have' <br> • becoming 'someone else' <br> • a bit of a rebel <br> • pride | *Gendered lives* <br> • education <br> • becoming a wife <br> • a woman's place is in the home <br> • working lives <br> • breaking the rules | *No friends of my own* <br> • no need for friendship <br> • no time for friends <br> • I don't know how to make friends <br> • a 'social life' but no real friends <br> • full-time employment |
| *A transition* <br> • a new self-awareness <br> • putting myself first <br> • freedom from <br> • new relationships | *Low self esteem* <br> • powerlessness <br> • a lack of self-confidence <br> • lonely <br> • failing to live up to expectations <br> • always being | | *A 'joiner-in'* <br> • proud to be a 'joiner-in' <br> • managing change <br> • not joining in |

| | | | |
|---|---|---|---|
| • new interests/ opportunities/ skills <br> • looking forward | • grateful <br> • no individuality | | |
| | | | *Family first* <br> • an ideology of the family <br> • interdependence <br> • family as friends <br> • a small but very close family <br> • dependence |

**Figure 12.1  Multiple narratives and sub-plots of later life widowhood**

**The concept of 'multiple narratives': furthering our understanding of the objective and subjective experience of later life widowhood**

In order to explore the objective experience of later life widowhood, I return initially to issues raised in the literature review chapters. I then go on to discuss the implications of findings from the current study concerning the subjective experience of later life widowhood and the way in which both of the 'objective' and the 'subjective' contribute to the overall 'lived' experience.

*Becoming and being an older widow: the objective experience*

I argued in Chapter 2 that the objective experience of 'becoming and being an older widow', or to put it another way, the dominant narrative of later life widowhood as portrayed in the literature is one of pathology, homogeneity and discontinuity (Marris, 1958; Torrie, 1975; Adlersberg and Thorne, 1992). Indeed, the death of a spouse is considered to be one of the most stressful of role transitions (Holmes and Rahe, 1967; Parkes, 1986). I went on to suggest that this picture had arisen as a result of the following: merging 'widowhood' with 'bereavement' (Vachon, 1976; Pearlin, 1980; Bennett and Morgan, 1992); pre-occupation with the 'problems' of older women (Gibson, 1996); a combination of ageism and sexism (Reinharz, 1986; Bernard et al, 2000); and neglect of individual and collective biography (Anderson et al, 1987; Andrews, 1991; Berger Gluck and Patai, 1991; Bornat, 1993; Davidson, 1999).

I reviewed evidence to suggest that older women may internalise this objective experience (Adlersberg and Thorne, 1992; Jones Porter, 1995) and therefore find it difficult to give expression to any other experience of widowhood.

I discussed in detail 'the move from we to I' (Havighurst, 1972; Lofland, 1982; Lopata, 1979; Parkes and Weiss, 1983; Silverman, 1987; Hansson and Remondet, 1988; Martin Matthews, 1991; Davidson, 1999) and postulated that there were a variety of ways in which women manage this move, depending on a number of factors: self-identity (Lopata, 1973; Lieberman, 1996; Martin Matthews, 1991; Van Den Hoonaard, 1997); generation and history (Brabon, and Summerfield 1987; Summerfield, 1989; Walker, 1990; Bornat, 1993; Davidson, 1999; Rowbotham, 1999; Sokoloff, 1999); marital relationship (Lopata, 1973; Martin Matthews, 1991 Wortman and Silver, 1993; Lieberman, 1996); age (Neugarten et al, 1965, 1973; Matthews, 1979; O'Bryant, 1989; Martin Matthews, 1991; Pickard, 1994; Andrews, 1999; Davidson, 1999); gender (Stroebe and Stroebe, 1987; Allen, 1989; Martin Matthews, 1991; Arber and Ginn, 1991, 1995; Bernard and Meade, 1993; Bornat, 1993; Jones Porter, 1995; Stevens, 1995; Gibson, 1996; Davidson, 1999; Bernard et al, 2000; Machin, 2000); and 'view of the world' (Allen, 1989; Coleman, 1995; Ruth and Oberg, 1996).

I argued that contrary to popular stereotyping which structures later life widowhood as a time of vulnerability, both 'age' and 'gender' might be construed as assets. I further suggested that we know very little about how older women themselves make sense of the experience of widowhood nor do we really understand the impact of individual and collective biography on that subjective experience.

*The social world of older widows: the objective experience*

In Chapter 3, I argued, with reference to a number of researchers (Morgan, 1989; Martin Matthews, 1991; Morgan et al, 1997) that this dominant narrative of later life widowhood as one of pathology, homogeneity and discontinuity is further reinforced in the literature on the social world of older widows (Lopata, 1973; Ferraro, 1984; O'Brien, 1985; Ferraro et al, 1994), with older widows' relationships with others usually being framed in terms of 'support'. This literature comprises two distinct areas: 'support' and 'participation'.

The 'support' literature has focused particularly on 'type' and 'timing' of support available to older widows (Bankoff, 1983; Jacobson, 1986; Roberto and Scott, 1986; Martin Matthews, 1991; Morgan et al, 1997) whereas the 'participation' literature (Atchley, 1975; Arling, 1976; Dickens and Pearlman, 1981; Jerrome, 1981; Ferraro, 1984; Babchuk and Anderson, 1989; Martin Matthews, 1991; Pickard, 1994; Adams, 1995; Lieberman, 1996) has emphasised the importance of continuities. However, the continuities referred to have generally comprised those from life just before widowhood. It is rare to see either 'support' or 'participation' located within individual and collective biographies. Network changes have been noted, but with reference to widowhood rather than life course. One dissenting voice, whose work has been greatly influential on the current study, is Matthews (1979) who has demonstrated a range of different ways of 'doing' friendship and family relationships over the life course and the impact this then has on women's relationships in later life. I went on to suggest that in-depth explorations of smaller samples of older widows would permit greater discussion of the quality, as well as the quantity of relationships, over the life course, and would perhaps provide some insight into how older widows make use of the skills they have developed and the relationships they have made over the life course.

### The subjective and the objective reality of later life widowhood

In my findings chapters, I have provided numerous examples to demonstrate the importance of understanding the subjective, as well as the objective, experience of widowhood, and the narratives that underpin this experience. Using evidence from the life stories, I have argued the importance of recognising that the same seemingly objective situation or circumstance may be experienced subjectively differently. For example, ill health is perceived by Patricia as a barrier to participation, but objectively worse ill-health is perceived by Doris, Elizabeth and Katherine as a mountain to be climbed. Living alone is synonymous with loneliness for some women but, for others, the same state of aloneness is viewed as an opportunity for time to oneself. Clearly both the objective and the subjective experience contribute to the overall lived experience, but without engaging with older widows' narratives it is difficult to understand in what way this occurs. Having knowledge of the multiple narratives underpinning older widows' lives, enables us to make sense of both their subjective and their objective reality and thus better understand their experience.

### The subjective experience of later life widowhood

Older women have to deal with the objective experience of widowhood: a dominant narrative of widowhood as pathology, homogeneity and discontinuity, on a daily basis, but how much it really impacts on them will be tempered by their subjective experience and the multiple narratives underpinning that experience. The findings from the study demonstrate that the current management of daily living ('how I feel about living alone'; 'how I feel about not having money'; 'how I feel about my health'; 'how I feel about the loss of couple friends'; 'the response of family and friends to me as an older widow') will mainly depend on the narratives of 'me', 'history', 'social world' and 'now'.

It is evident from this study that for some older widows, both age and gender are clearly assets upon which they draw in widowhood - those women who make new friends in widowhood via a 'community of widows', the freedom to be who you want and do what you want, and so on. The multiple narratives of these women enable them to engage with similar others, to make the most of opportunities that are presented to them, especially those which may have been impossible when they were younger and married. As I demonstrated in Chapter 11, even widowhood combined with very old age and impending frailty may not be a disadvantage. Doris, for example, at 81 years of age is extremely frail and no longer able to care for herself, but her narrative spoke with excitement of widowhood as transition. Widowhood has provided her with opportunities not available to her earlier on in her life course. However, for some older widows, particularly women such as Patricia and Vera, age and gender are clearly disadvantageous: old age is fearful, bringing with it further isolation and ill health and for a woman who feels ill at ease with other women, it is certainly not an asset to find herself in a world inhabited mainly by older women.

As I demonstrated in Chapters 8-11, how an older widow interacts with others, and vice versa, depends largely on skills and relationships developed over the life course and how she 'understands' relationships with others. At the same time, she may also have to contend with the ageist and sexist prejudice of others who may also problematise widowhood. How she manages such negative attitudes will depend on her multiple narratives, in particular, her self-esteem and the skills in relationship building she has developed over the life course.

Katherine for example, had no time for people who try to put her down and dealth with them accordingly. She had a confidence that had spanned her life course (a narrative of 'High self-esteem'). She had always been a 'friendmaker', indeed friends have been an integral part of her life. Her husband, and subsequently her family, had endorsed this (a narrative of 'Friends matter'). Now in widowhood, she has found it very easy to make new friends, as well as maintaining old friendships, and espoused the view that there was both safety and power in numbers! She acknowledged her old age and was proud of it. Her relationship with her family has never been one of dependence, and even though her health was no longer good, prompting increasing reliance on others, she did not regard this as problematic. Her narrative of 'Getting on with your life' embraced all aspects of her relationships with others.

Alternatively Vera, who has always had a low opinion of herself (a narrative of 'Low self-esteem') was very sensitive to the negative imagery of later life widowhood and the negative comments of others about older widows. Indeed she was only too aware that she herself had made such remarks in the past, and had never really had a close female friend (a narrative of 'No friends of my own'). As an older widow, she was fearful of asking her family for support because she did not want to be seen as not managing; she did not want to conform to what she perceived to be a negative stereotype (widowhood as a time of 'Loneliness and despair').

*Fluidity*

The way in which the 'objective' and 'subjective' experiences of widowhood are interlinked is also reflected in the fluidity of older widows' narratives, particularly that of 'Me, Now'. I demonstrated in Chapter 11, that there are occasions when a different narrative is articulated from the dominant, personal narrative. We all have days when life is difficult, and we may forcefully express that view to anyone who is prepared to listen to us. However, if we belong to a group who are stigmatised in the way that older widows are (Matthews, 1979), those 'bad days' are more likely to be seen as the norm. To put it differently, if that narrative conforms to the popular narrative of widowhood, it is more likely to be heard and confirmed- your days are difficult because you are an older widow **not** your days are difficult because we all have difficult days. Therefore it is important that we listen carefully to what older widows tell us about their lives and engage critically with their multiple narratives.

*Hidden lives: re-conceptualising older widows' lives through multiple narratives*

I now focus my discussion on the continuities and discontinuities that older women bring to later life and the way in which older women make use of those to make sense of 'who' they are in later life widowhood.

In Chapter 2 and 3, and more specifically in Chapter 4, I put forward the view that no single theoretical perspective will suffice if we are to really understand the experience of later life widowhood. I acknowledged that there are both benefits (Neugarten et al, 1965, 1973; Ferraro, 1984; Antonnucci, 1985; Martin Matthews, 1991; Sheehy, 1996) and limitations (Cummings and Henry, 1961; Blau, 1973; Lopata, 1973, 1996; Lieberman, 1996) of traditional ways of constructing widowhood. I then argued that it is possible to re-conceptualise later life widowhood by situating it within a feminist life course perspective, which draws on the disciplines associated with gerontology and feminism (Gibson, 1996; Reinharz, 1986; Giele and Elder, 1999; Bernard et al, 2000). I suggested that this allows us to situate older widows' lives within a framework of being 'old' and 'female', and the lifelong structured nature of that framework, to entertain the possibility of growth and change and to permit the focus of attention to be on the totality of older widows' experience.

I now argue that the concept of multiple narratives, derived from my study of older widows' life stories, is a useful tool with which to re-conceptualise, analyse and understand older widows' lives within a feminist life course perspective. Whilst acknowledging fluidity, it is possible to identify through those narratives the continuities and discontinuities that older women bring to later life widowhood, depending on their individual and collective biographies. The balance of continuities and discontinuities will vary considerably, and there will be both diversity and similarities in their experience. There may for example, as I have derived from my analysis, be collective narratives of 'gendered lives' and 'belonging to a generation', but diverse narratives of self, social world and widowhood. The structured nature of older widows' lives, as articulated within the narratives of 'History and Me', becomes an integral part of the analysis of the current experience. So too does the acknowledgement of a possibility of growth and change, continuity or decline as articulated in the three narratives of 'Me, Now'.

These narratives cannot predict the experience of later life widowhood. On the contrary, by situating the experience within the female life course, the narratives offer a way of looking back and thus deepening our understanding of the social reality experienced by older widows. More importantly, they offer us a tool with which to unlock the hidden lives of older widows, which because they are lived in the private rather than the public sphere, are rarely heard and certainly not valued. So often, the stories ordinary women have to tell about their lives become submerged and their lives appear to be more one dimensional, and thus less diverse, than they actually are. Even worse, they are rendered invisible (Bernard and Meade, 1993; Gibson, 1996). The concept of multiple narratives challenges this view and reveals the complexities underpinning older widows' lives, lives that are rich in individual and collective history and relationships with others. Forster (1998) for example has illustrated such complexities in relation to the history of generations of women in her own family and thus gains better understanding of both her mother and her grandmother. She argued that without knowledge of the complexities of family history, and the relationships that have been part of that history, she could have no real understanding of the subjective experience of both her mother and her grandmother. Perhaps even more problematic are the incorrect assumptions that are made, and the stereotypes that are engaged with, without such knowledge. Dominant, public narratives about women's lives are believed, erroneously, rather than older women's own narratives. And yet, older women themselves as experts in their own history employ these narratives, and the continuities and discontinuities therein, to make sense of 'who' they are in later life widowhood. They may not employ such 'academic' terminology but, as my study has demonstrated, they often make use of the past to understand their present.

I now exemplify this by going right back to the stories of the older widows who have participated in my study, and from whose experience the concept of multiple narratives has been derived.

**Revisiting multiple narratives of 'Me Now'**

Several women's stories have been chosen to demonstrate the range of multiple narratives of later life widowhood that exist, but any of the women's stories would equally have demonstrated the range of possibilities. They all reflect both the hidden nature and the complexity of the multiple narratives that underpin later life widowhood.

*Widowhood as a time of loneliness and despair*

I argued earlier that the dominant narrative of later life widowhood as portrayed in the literature is one of: pathology, homogeneity and discontinuity. And yet, in my study, the life stories of only three women encompassed a not too dissimilar narrative of *Loneliness and despair*. It is interesting to note their many commonalities. For example, Patricia, Vera and Dorothy all confirmed a lack of confidence and self-belief that had followed them through the life course: a narrative of 'Low self-esteem'. None of them could remember there being much love around at home when they were growing up, and all three confided that they find it hard to show affection to others.

In one way or another, they all acknowledged that the Second World War had impacted on their lives in some way, and identified themselves with a particular generation of women whose lives had been affected by the times during which they lived: a narrative of 'Belonging to a generation'. All three women described how they devoted themselves to the roles of wife and mother, to the exclusion of other roles, and followed their husband's lead in decisions affecting the household: a narrative of 'Gendered lives'. For each woman, the role of 'good mother' was particularly important, reflecting perhaps their individual determination to do better by their children than they felt had been done to them.

Neither Patricia nor Vera had a history of close friends, and both women acknowledged feelings of unease with other women. Patricia, for example, has never had a friend of her own and did not really know 'how' to make friends. Dorothy had enjoyed the company of friends when her boys were young but really had little time for friends outside of family life: 'No friends of my own'. Unlike Patricia and Vera, Dorothy enjoyed the company of other women and was saddened when circumstances meant that she could not maintain her friendship with ex-neighbours. All three women were disappointed by what they believed was their families' reluctance to either understand or hear their current feelings. This was in stark contrast to the time and energy they had lavished on their families for many years: a narrative of 'Family first'.

All three women spoke of widowhood as a time in which loneliness was predominant. Patricia and Vera in particular, construed themselves as 'not liking' and 'being different' from other women, which had proved to be problematic in a world of older women. Vera had tried very hard to mix with other women through her voluntary work, but her subjective experience was still that of feeling isolated. Dorothy was still uncertain about her feelings about 'becoming and being an older widow' and about widowhood, and her story fluctuated between two narratives: 'Widowhood as loneliness and despair' and 'Widowhood as a transition'. Although at our first interview she was embracing the former, at our second interview she was embracing the latter, talking positively about her future and the possibilities it offered. I argue in the next chapter that the process of life story telling has clearly been helpful for her.

*Widowhood as a time of getting on with your life*

Of utmost importance, within this narrative, were the continuities that Bee, Betty, Elizabeth, Evelyn, Farzana, Joan, Katherine, and Mags had brought to later life widowhood. These continuities had enabled them to 'get on' with their lives. They experienced some changes in widowhood, but these were far outweighed by the continuities. However, as with 'Widowhood as a time of loneliness and despair', the routes each woman had travelled through to this dominant personal narrative varied considerably.

Bee for example, prided herself on always having known what she wanted out of life and generally having self-confidence, but acknowledged that she had not always felt good about herself. She has had a number of major disappointments during her life, which have left her self esteem not completely intact: a narrative of 'Fluctuating self-esteem'. Like so many of her contemporaries, her family experienced considerable hardship before the Second World War, and she was determined it would not happen to her: 'difficult times for some'. She fell in love with and married a very wealthy man, her senior by nearly thirty years, and knew that she would never be poor again. She became the good wife, who did not work outside the house, and whose life was focused on her husband: narratives of 'Belonging to a generation' and 'Gendered lives'. She was not close to her family and acknowledged that she never really had been but, for all of her married life, she has had a circle of friends with whom she and her husband socialised regularly, and who could also be relied upon for support. Her story was interspersed throughout with references to friends: 'My friends are part of my life, the "social me", to the point where she was unable to imagine her life without these friends: 'Friends matter.' Bee, unusually amongst all of the twenty women, still had most of her 'couple' friends, as well as some widowed female friends. She continued to play golf and bridge, attended dinner parties, and moved within the same social circle where she was both valued and validated. Despite a current relationship with an American man much closer to her own age, which suggested the possibility of change, the continuities in her life dominated, and her life was similar in many ways to the life she had lived for many years. It may of course change if Bee were to decide that new possibilities are better than the safer, more predictable, continuities that have been so fundamental to her past and current life. Whichever course she might choose to take her focus will continue to be to get on with life. As a footnote to her story it is interesting to note that despite strong continuities and the validation that came from those continuities, Bee had noted the negative connotations of her widowed status ensured that she was thought of 'objectively' by some (albeit a small number) of her social circle, as: 'poor Bee'.

Elizabeth described herself as always having had a strong sense of autonomy and a self-confidence: a narrative of 'High self-esteem'. She was very aware of belonging to a particular generation, and vividly described her life during the Thirties when she was 'in-service', and during the Second World War when, for four years she and her first daughter lived alone: a narrative of 'Belonging to a generation'. She too embraced the role of the good wife and mother and followed her husband's wishes, when he wanted to buy a bakery: a narrative of 'Gendered lives'. Nonetheless, she still had a strong sense of her own autonomy. Unlike many of her contemporaries, Elizabeth had undertaken paid work for most of her married life, latterly in the bakery, as well as bringing up three children. Her life had always been busy. As a result there had been little time or opportunity to develop a circle of friends, and her social world had comprised mainly the extended family: 'No time for friends' and 'Family first.' She described herself as not a joiner-in, neither in the past nor in the present. In widowhood, Elizabeth's social world still consisted of family: indeed, she indicated that her daughters and their children were more like friends than family. One major change in widowhood has been the development of a friendship with another widow, whom she had first met when they were both on holiday with their husbands. They have gone from being acquaintances to being best friends, gaining considerable pleasure and having fun, as the friendship has developed. However, despite this significant change, Elizabeth's predominant narrative was that of continuity: 'Getting on with your life'. The autonomy present in her earlier years, had enabled her to continue with her life, maintaining the friendship of family members, relationships based on reciprocity, and enjoying living alone in her own home where she kept herself busy: 'I've always been independent I think'.

My final example in this section is Farzana, whose faith has guided her throughout her life. Farzana described herself as having a self-confidence that came from knowing her place in the world: a narrative of 'High self -esteem'. Married from an early age, her life has been highly gendered and she has devoted herself to the roles of good wife and mother: a narrative of 'Gendered lives'. Indeed, alongside her faith, the continuity of her narrative of gender had enabled her to manage major changes. She has had few friends, indeed she was adamant that she has never really needed friends, and her life has continued to be centred on her immediate family, her immediate neighbourhood and the mosque: 'Family first'. She continued to live in her own house, along with two of her sons and their families, and articulated the view that her life had not changed much as a result of becoming a widow. Other changes have taken place, for example her health was not so good and she was very aware of getting older, but these had not been precipitated by widowhood: 'Getting on with your life'.

### Widowhood as 'a transition'

For Doris, Edith, Ellen, Eunice, Jean, Jennie, Pat, Phyllis and Sylvia, the major narrative of 'Me, now' was that of widowhood as a transition. However the multiple narratives underpinning their understanding of the present, are both complex and varied, and the way in which 'the pieces' fit together differed for each of them.

Doris, for example told of a rebellious 'self' that, once the gloss of early marriage had started to fade, gradually became submerged in her marriage to a very 'controlling' husband: a narrative of 'Fluctuating self esteem'. Her life had been highly gendered: she was the good wife and mother as expected of women of her generation, had no income of her own and very little opportunity to make choices: a narrative of 'Gendered lives' and 'Belonging to a generation'. She had some daytime friends, usually neighbours, who were much older than her, but her social world consisted mainly of her husband and sons, and most of her social life revolved around her husband's business world: 'No friends of my own'. As her husband became ill, she dreaded being his carer: 'he would have been such an awful patient', but knew that she would have to take on that role because that was what she had always done. For Doris, widowhood has been a blessed relief, and a time of real opportunity when, for the first time since she was a teenager, she was able to take decisions based on her own choices and wishes: widowhood is 'A transition'.

Jean by contrast described herself as a woman who always had a lot of confidence and self assurance: a narrative of 'High self-esteem'. She was extremely proud of her lifelong independence and was very aware of the place of generation and gender in her life. During the war years, when her husband was away at sea, she worked in a munitions factory, whilst trying to look after her young family. When she became pregnant before marriage, she felt the full weight of censure from her father in particular, and others in general, towards girls who 'broke the rules'. She has always done 'women's work'. When her children were growing up economic necessity, and her husband's increasing disability, demanded that she juggle family and work, but she still managed to put her family first. This left little time for friendships although she always knew she was a sociable woman, who liked to join-in: narratives of 'No time for friends'; 'Family first'; and 'A joiner-in'. Widowhood for Jean has been a time of opportunity and fulfilment. She has had the opportunity to develop friendships with other women, including a 'best friend' for the first time since her girlhood, 'join-in' new interests and enjoy 'aloneness'. For her widowhood has been a transition and a time to put herself 'first'. Others recognise Jean as a very busy woman, a continuity from a life of busyness, but what they might not see is an older women participating and 'joining in' in ways that had been impossible for her earlier on in the life course. She was now having fun and looking forward to the future with excitement!

Sylvia described herself as always having lacked confidence and felt 'grateful' or 'beholden' to others: a narrative of 'Low self-esteem'. She was very aware of the impact of both generation and in particular, gender on her life. As a girl she had had a taste of grammar school education but had been thwarted once her mother could no longer afford the uniform. Had she been a boy, the money would have been found from somewhere. She 'broke the rules', firstly by becoming pregnant as a teenager and secondly by keeping her baby and not marrying the father. The latter had required considerable strength and determination and she had little opportunity for friendship: 'No friends of my own'. When she had married in her early twenties, she was so grateful that she devoted her time and energy to her family, which subsequently included another child, and to her mother who came to live with her: 'Family first'. Sylvia lost both her husband and her mother within six months of each other, and found herself initially plunged into despair. After this initial period of severe grief, she had drawn on an inner strength and determination that had served her well as a teenage single mother, and she started to socialise with others. She began to learn how to enjoy having time for herself, something she had never had before. She discovered that she had social skills that had previously been dormant. She now had another partner, for whom she had love rather than gratitude, and recognised that her later life widowhood has been a period of change, that beheld a future: 'A transition'.

## A three dimensional jig-saw

In Chapters 8 to 11, I used the metaphor of a 'jigsaw'. However, perhaps a three-dimensional jigsaw, one in which all the different pieces can be turned round and put together in a variety of ways, is a more fitting metaphor. The way in which these pieces are put together will portray, at any one time, the picture, or the story, that is both experienced and presented. In other words, there are many different images, which emerge from the jigsaw; we cannot truly understand them without first assembling all the parts (the narratives), and the individual components (sub-plots) of those parts. No one element is more or less important than another; it is the way in which they all fit together which creates the individual experience.

In this chapter, I have argued for a concept of multiple narratives as a way of better understanding the experience of later life widowhood I have demonstrated that the 'objective' experience, in other words the dominant public narrative, of later life widowhood is one which incorporates pathology, homogeneity and discontinuity. How older widows manage that objective experience is I have argued, heavily dependent on their subjective experience, which in turn is grounded in their multiple narratives and the sub-plots making up those narratives.

It would be so easy for example to identify the unhappiness of those women whose life stories encompass a narrative of widowhood as loneliness and despair, as solely due to widowhood. Objectively they all conform to the popular, public narrative of later life widowhood: they are old, female, widowed and lonely. However, by understanding their multiple narratives, we can see that the roots of their unhappiness and loneliness lie in the stories they tell about other parts of their lives, a combination of: lifelong low self-esteem; a lack of social identity; feeling different from, and suspicious of, other women; a life structured by gender and generation; a dependence on family over the life course. This is so important as Jones-Porter (1995) reminds us. We need to get beyond the 'objective' and start to understand the world that older widows actually experience. Telling Patricia, as her daughter and sister have done on a regular basis, that all she needed to do was to 'make friends' takes no account of her narratives of 'Me, Myself', 'History and Me' and 'Me and My Social World'. As I demonstrated in Chapters 8-10, Patricia's lack of confidence, and poor friendship skills, were rooted in her life course. Widowhood only served to emphasise her loneliness and isolation to others; she has always been aware of her subjective experience. Vera kept herself busy, encouraged by others, meeting and working with other women, but her subjective experience as identified through her narratives, told the story of a woman who was really lacking in confidence and was unhappy in the world of women. She has not lived in such a world for many years and finds it wanting.

By contrast, an objective observer would describe Doris's life as very difficult. She was in poor health, with few friends, lived in a room in a residential care home and relied heavily on the support of care staff to meet her personal needs. How wrong they would be. Doris spoke of widowhood as 'liberation'. Without an awareness of the pieces (the narratives) of the jig-saw and the way in which these pieces are turned round (the sub-plots) we can have no real understanding of Doris's current experience as an older widow. Indeed, it would be so easy to construe her situation in terms of 'sadness', 'loneliness' and 'isolation' instead of a woman who for the first time in her life has gained the freedom to make her own decisions. As Martin Matthews' (1991) study of older widows emphasised, understanding older widows' interaction with the world around them provides us with a much better understanding of their current experience - and it may not always be as it seems.

Furthermore, an unknowing observer might perceive Sylvia as an old woman lucky enough to have found herself a male partner, a rarity in later life, and in doing so removed the stigma associated with being an older widow. What this unknowing observer would not know is that for Sylvia, widowhood has been a time of opportunity in which for the first time, she has found both love and friendship, and the capacity to have a relationship based on reciprocity. She could not know what the future held, but she was certainly looking forward to it. Engaging with the subjective, as well as the objective reality of older widows via their multiple narratives, therefore, enables us to go beyond the stereotypes of later life widowhood and challenge the myths that have developed (Lopata, 1996; Chambers 2000). Otherwise we are in danger, of only seeing the negative aspects of later life widowhood and thus contributing to the 'problematisation' of older women (Gibson, 1996).

I have also argued that the continuities which older women bring to later life widowhood are positive and negative, as well as diverse, and this has implications for the way in which they manage discontinuities. Some women actively embrace the discontinuities of later life widowhood and subscribe to a narrative of widowhood as a transition. There are several explanations for this transition. The way in which women's lives have been structured at a particular historical time, for example in terms of education, family and employment roles, has determined the possibilities available to them. Some women have willingly embraced those roles with, or without, an awareness of the structured nature of their lives. Others, such as Doris, have assumed their roles, under sufferance. Widowhood may provide the first opportunity to challenge those roles. However, in order for that to happen, older women must want or need and feel able to embrace that opportunity. They may draw on skills, opportunities and resources located within their personal and collective biography, previous relationships with others and a realisation that life does not have to be as it always has been. Serendipity may also play a part: for example meeting a new friend or partner with whom to embrace new roles and opportunities. For some women, there may be a realisation that for the first time in their lives they have the potential to be individuals, and this can be both exciting and daunting (Martin Matthews, 1991; Van Den Hoonaard, 1997, 2001; Davidson, 1999). For yet more women, widowhood might provide the first opportunity in many years to 'play': after all, family life can be a serious business (Sheehy, 1997). New skills, new interests, revisiting old interests are all possibilities (Lieberman, 1996). However, what is very clear is that each woman's own personal narratives of self, history and social world, will be fundamental to her engagement with those opportunities, and to her own narrative of her current experience. Furthermore, we can only understand that narrative of 'Me, Now' by reflecting back over the other threads of her biographical narratives (Bornat, 1993). As I argued earlier on in this chapter, an objective appraisal will not suffice. It may be the opportunity to challenge previously socially structured lives that impels older widows, or the potential to embrace new roles and responsibilities.

For other women the lifelong continuities they bring to later life widowhood, continuities of self, relationships, place or belief enable them to successfully manage the discontinuities of their new status as widow and get on with their lives in the way that they always have: previous experience, both personal and as a generation, has taught them that major life changes can be successfully mastered. As Matthews (1979) has reminded us, we need to take account of those 'turnings' at earlier points in the life course in order to better understand the present. These women subscribe to a narrative of widowhood as a time when you just have to get on with your life. Continuities underpin this narrative, whether it is continuity of self, relationships, place or belief. That is not to say that changes have not taken place, nor that there have not been any difficulties, but rather they are perhaps less influential than the continuities, which inform the current subjective experience. These women lead their life from day to day, with little looking forward to the future, knowing that they will manage, just as they have always managed. They may possibly be perceived negatively as 'older widows', but their continuities enable them to manage both ageism and sexism.

However, there is a group of women for whom the continuities which they bring to later life widowhood, are both unhelpful and disabling in the face of the discontinuities of widowhood itself (Matthews, 1979). These continuities include a combination of: lifelong low self-esteem; a lack of social identity; feeling 'different' from, and suspicious of, other women; a life structured by gender and generation; a dependence on family over the life course. The discontinuities and disruption of widowhood further compound the difficulties brought about by these continuities and make life even more intolerable. Widowhood for these women is encapsulated in a narrative of loneliness and despair.

Older widows make sense of 'who' they are in later life widowhood by drawing on their personal, social and collective identity over the life course. Their multiple narratives of: Me, Myself, Me and My Social World, and History and Me all reveal aspects of previously hidden lives that contribute to the narratives of Me, Now. I discuss the process of giving voice to these narratives in the next chapter, but what becomes apparent in the revealing of these hidden lives is that older widows draw on a range of experiences derived from their multiple narratives, and the sub-plots within those narratives, in order to make sense of who they are in later life widowhood. In doing so, they are continually integrating the past and the present, practising what I highlighted in Chapter 4 as the 'reflexivity' of the self (Giddens, 1991; Phillipson, 1998; Thomas, 1999). Furthermore, the women in the study had a real sense of the 'public' versus 'private' nature of their lives, and the way in which their lives, largely played out in the private sphere have been hidden (Reinharz, 1986; Berger Gluck and Patai, 1991; Giles, 1995; Stevens, 1995). In practising the 'reflexivity of the self' they were thus drawing on both the subjective (private) and the objective (public) in order to make sense of their current experience. The participants in the study all had an acute awareness of both 'age' and 'gender' as integral to their multiple narratives. 'Age' in terms of both belonging to a particular generation and also 'personal' ageing, and 'gender' as a social construction over the life course, combining with age in recent years. For some, these were positive constructs, but for others less so. As several commentators demonstrate with reference to age (for example: Johnson, 1978; Ruth and Oberg, 1996) and gender (Bernard and Meade, 1993; Bornat, 1993; Bernard at al, 2000) older people make sense of 'who' they are via biography and I have demonstrated that 'generation' is integral to the collective nature of that biography (Riley, 1973; Giele and Elder, 1998). Multiple narratives, derived from older widows' life stories, and grounded in their personal and collective history, will not only inform older widows' management of day to day encounters but also current negative societal images and stereotypes (Andrews, 1991, 1999; Bytheway, 1995; Gibson, 1996). How each woman then makes sense of that experience will also be rooted in her own multiple narratives.

It is important to acknowledge the fluidity of these multiple narratives, and the influence of the dominant pathological narrative that makes it all to easy to attribute any of the problems encountered by older widows to 'widowhood' rather than to life in general. I have contended that the way in which older women make sense of life as an older widow can only really be understood in relation to older widows' own dominant narratives and the complexity of sub-plots contained within those narratives.

## Conclusion

In this chapter, I have argued that the concept of multiple narratives is an extremely useful tool for employing a feminist life course perspective on later life widowhood, in that it not only enables us to identify both the continuities and discontinuities which women bring to later life but also engages with the structured nature of women's lives throughout the life course, within a patriarchal society. Furthermore it is only by employing such an approach that we are able to access the 'hidden' lives of older widows via their multiple narratives, and thus begin to hear their voices. And yet, because older widows are a stigmatised group, they have so little opportunity to make explicit the complexities of their lives. Indeed, they may start off their story as Joan did with: 'I can't imagine my life will be very interesting to you'. In making sense of their daily lives, however, they are drawing on these individual and collective narratives. The feminist life story interview clearly provides an explicit format for that process of 'making sense' to take place, an issue I discuss in more detail in Chapter 13.

In the next chapter therefore I move away from a focus on the content of the women's stories and return instead to the process of the research. I explore the way in which the women told their stories, the way the research process developed and the women's reflections on that process. I then reflect, finally, on my own role in the process of collecting the life stories.

# Chapter 13

# Reflecting

## Introduction

In Chapter 6, I outlined the process of the fieldwork for the study and described my attempts to adhere to feminist research practice in my use of a biographical method of research, as a way of both reaching and hearing the voices of older widows. The inclusion of such detailed information in the book is I argued fundamental to understanding the generation of such sensitive data, data that would not have been available had I not paid attention to the process of the research. The research literature, discussed in Chapter 5, stressed the interactive and collaborative nature of feminist biographical research practice and also acknowledged the importance of power issues affecting this collaboration (Bornat, 1993; Standing, 1998). In addition the lingering reflections for both the person telling the story and the person who is listening to that story were noted (Opie, 1992; Yow, 1994). Feminist research practice makes these reflections explicit and incorporates them in to the research process (Oakley, 1981). Indeed, the data and consequent knowledge emerging from feminist research is a product of this practice (Harding, 1987). Fundamental to feminist research practice therefore, both as a result of reflection and participation, as well as the generation of data, is the potential for change for all those involved in the process (Kelly, 1988; Kelly et al, 1994).

From the beginning of the study, I was explicit with all participants concerning my interest in the research process as well as the emerging content. I described in Chapter 6 how I set about that process. I anticipated that in addition to being sensitive to the feelings of the participants there was potential for me be affected to a greater or lesser extent as a result of my decision to become an active, rather than passive, participant in the generation of data. I also described in Chapter 6 how I recorded my feelings in a field diary and how, in the second interview, as well as checking the content of the transcription, I explored with each woman her reflections on the interview, her feelings both during and after the interview, and how she felt when reading the transcript. This chapter picks up that discussion and critically reflects on the process of the research. Firstly, by discussing my own role in the research process via an analysis of my field diary. And secondly, by analysing what the women had to say about telling their story: what I have chosen to call, 'Me telling my story'. For the reader, this candid discussion presents a rare opportunity to gain an insight into the sometimes, difficult and messy process of carrying out fieldwork.

**Reflections on the research process - my voice**

As I discussed in Chapters 5 and 6, I committed myself to feminist research practice. I outlined in those chapters how I was actively seeking subjectivity and I acknowledged my own powerful role in eliciting that subjectivity. I recognised both commonalities and differences between myself, and the women, and between the women themselves. I stressed, with reference to other feminist researchers, that I am interested in listening to women's voices (Berger Gluck and Patai, 1991). I argued that feminist inquiry is a way of both enabling the voices of older widows to be heard and exploring the experience of later life widowhood. Fundamental to feminist research practice is both reflexivity and the potential for change (Oakley, 1981; Reinharz, 1991; Opie, 1992;).

In line with feminist research practice, I acknowledged my own role in the generation of data (Oakley, 1981). My field diary recorded how I managed this process, and the feelings that accompanied it. It enabled me to reflect on my own role, and thereby build in the potential for change. It also situated me clearly within the research process as both participant and researcher. This built reflexivity into each stage of the research, which then informed subsequent stages. I note elsewhere in this thesis that the diary was both an academic tool and a safety valve for me the researcher- it was thus a tool for analysis but also enabled me to have a site for my feelings. As described in Chapter 6, I then subjected the field diary to analysis. I now present a discussion of that analysis with reference to the following issues: my practice; my feelings; power relationships; reciprocity and collaboration; gendered scripts; ethics.

*My practice*

Having recognised from the very beginning that I was integral to the generation of data, I knew that I had to be sensitive to my research practice. Thus it was important to learn from each interview. The field diary provides a record of my interviewing practice and skills. For example, before my first pilot interview I noted:

> Have arranged an appointment for this evening at 7:30. I feel really nervous - will I be able to sit back and let J talk about her life? What about silences?

Subsequent to the interview, I recorded:

> I tried so hard to listen but sometimes intervened inappropriately. I feel that I am not always picking up leads. I need to slow down, risk silences and stay with the story which I am being told. Perhaps I'll get better at this?

Some interviews were more difficult than others and my field diary reflected this. My interview with Elizabeth for example was initially quite tense. I had met her on several occasions previously through her daughter but I did not really know her well:

> Knowing E a little already wasn't necessarily helpful. All very stilted at first whilst we negotiated roles - was I here for a chat as a friend of L (daughter) or as a researcher? … Worked hard to demonstrate my interest and focused on E rather than our different but mutual relationship with L. Used 'active listening' skills and made sure the interview went at E's pace, and was led by E. As her story unfolded it became easier and we were able to relate to each other as two women who were constructing a story together rather than two women brought together by a third person.

As the field diary records, I did not want to go into 'passive researcher' mode but, on the other hand, I wanted the interview to be more than a 'friendly chat'. I knew that I must both gain the confidence of individual women but also focus on collecting data. As I indicated in Chapter 6, with reference to Mason (1997), this at times seemed like an impossible task. By continually reflecting on my practice, however, I found that with each interview my skills as an interviewer developed. For example, I was able to better pace the interviews and manage silences, and I became more practised in follow-up questions. In truth, I became less anxious! After my second interview with Eunice, I wrote:

> I now really understand what the literature is saying about listening 'in stereo' and feel I am doing just that. Each interview has informed the next and I now feel so confident with my skills. This sounds arrogant but I guess it is a measure of how far I have moved from the very first interview. Still a lot to learn and new situations to manage but my reflection has paid off.

On several occasions in the field diary, I made reference to 'external factors' influencing both my practice and, potentially, the unfolding story. I make note of these here to, firstly, exemplify the flexibility and sensitivity that was integral to my research practice and, secondly, to demonstrate the interactive nature of the research relationship developed with the participants. For example, when I visited Edith for the second time she was initially very agitated as a result of a recent burglary:

> Edith was burgled last week and was cross that this had undermined her confidence. At first this felt difficult, she was very preoccupied with what she had been through but was insistent that she wanted to carry on with the interview and follow up our last conversation. She needed to talk about her feelings first so I took my time and spent quite a lot of time listening to her anger. She didn't want the tape recorder on at this point, but wanted reassurance that most people would feel as she does and it wasn't just because she was a widow. When she was ready I switched the tape recorder on. My role then? Prompting, encouraging, more directive this time? Referred back to what she had said last time, referring back was necessary to focus the interview and to develop the closeness of the first interview. Very active listening and exploring. Hard work but paid off; she began to relax and talk about her life 'now', her new interests in music, crafts, amateur dramatics …Said she was pleased to do the interview, she liked talking about her life now, felt she had 'grown' in widowhood and was determined not to let the burglary get her down.

As the field diary records, I needed to take my time and be prepared to let Edith express her feelings. I needed to forget my research agenda for a while and actively demonstrate my empathy, share her crossness and listen. I knew I had the skills to do this and so drew on previous experience. Having ascertained that she did want to carry on with the interview, I then had to have the sensitivity to know when it was appropriate to shift the focus of our discussion back to our first meeting, and then having done so adopt a strategy to maintain this. Flexibility was required, but so too was an understanding of both her strength of feeling and her need for reassurance.

My second example demonstrates sensitivity but also highlights my flexibility in the face of a potential data collection catastrophe! I was visiting Jennie for the second time and called at her house at the time we had arranged. My field diary records:

> Jennie quite agitated when I arrived; it was to do with a family matter and she became tearful. Spent a while discussing this, I knew something of the history and so was aware of its importance to J. Actively listened and empathised, and didn't set up the tape recorder until J felt more settled. Interview went well, J more thoughtful this time, less descriptive more reflective on her current life and circumstances; she had clearly been thinking through a number of things since our last meeting … I was very aware having listened to the previous tape of my interview with J that I was very repetitive in my responses- I had said 'right' in every tone possible- so I tried very hard to concentrate and vary my verbal prompts and response. Acutely aware of my body language. At the end of the interview J went to make a cup of tea. Suddenly became aware that the tape player was not working and I became quite agitated. Imagine my horror when I got home and found that nothing had recorded from such a detailed and thoughtful discussion. I immediately wrote down as much as I could remember and I will go back to J to review this, go over the discussion again. A salutary lesson- I was so preoccupied with J's distress at the beginning that I didn't do my usual checks. I had taken an extension lead from home but it transpired that there was no fuse in it. How many times have advised students to check and re-check their equipment?

My learning curve at this point was extremely steep; I needed to hold my nerve and return to Jennie with my notes, and explain what had happened. I felt extremely incompetent but, together, we managed to salvage the situation, re-visiting the story. In terms of the story which was eventually generated and confirmed, Jennie had several opportunities to check and re-check and she was extremely pleased with the end result. I feel certain that she felt herself to be the expert partner in this exercise. In terms of my practice, I made sure that this sobering experience never happened again.

*My feelings*

So much of what I was listening to as the women told me their stories was emotionally charged, particularly as each woman recalled how she had felt around the time of her husband's death. My field diary records these emotions. For example, after my first visit to Edith I wrote:

> A woman for whom life fell apart and who had 'rebuilt'. Desperate to tell me her story, became very tearful when remembering but was so positive about 'now'... How did I feel? Very sad at her tears, enjoyed sharing her excitement of 'now'. Edith was clearly very pleased to tell her story to an interested listener but still a tremendous tug at my emotions. Came away feeling exhausted and wondering if I can really manage this. Glad to write my feelings down.

I became aware of how privileged I was that the participants felt able to relate their innermost feelings with me but was also very aware of the responsibility that incurred (Bornat 1993). Sharing those feelings with them was clearly an important part of the research process and one I was extremely careful not to abuse. Moreover, it was fundamental to understanding their narratives. On more than one occasion I openly cried with the woman as she told me her story. I recorded in my diary after my visit to Eunice:

> Eunice talked about the untimely death of her daughter, which prompted painful memories of the untimely death of my mum at a young age; we both cried together and shared our feelings with each other. We were then able to go on to talk about 'timely' deaths and how different they are. This felt more like two people sharing painful feelings than 'research' - I hadn't expected to feel like this at this point in the research but I guess it means that I am still very sensitive to the powerful emotions which are being generated and this means that Eunice was able to share her story with me in a way that she might not otherwise have done.

Being sensitive to, and sharing emotions, enabled me to enter into the story being told and there is no doubt in my mind that it also furthered the telling of that story. Without that empathy, many previously untold stories and thoughts would not have been related. However, it was not without some cost to myself, and my feelings.

So often my field diary records exhaustion or tiredness either after or during an interview. For example, early on in my data collection, I timetabled a number of interviews closely together and this proved to be difficult. My diary records:

> Difficult interview, both tired, didn't sparkle, J quite reticent. One or two moments where J's intolerance of those who didn't cope was revealed. Perhaps I found that more difficult because I was tired? Are there times when you (the researcher) need to have confidence to call a halt to the interview? Balance this against fixed timetable and time spent?

I learnt from that early experience that if I was to be effective in generating sensitive data that I needed to pace my interviews. Indeed, I needed to acknowledge the powerful effect the research was having on my emotions. Leaving sufficient space between interviews allowed time for both recovery and reflection before embarking on the next set of interviews.

*Power*

As I described in Chapter 6, I was very aware of the need to pay attention to power issues, both as a result of my commitment to feminist research practice but also as a result of my own value base. Pragmatically, I knew that adverse power relations would also impact on the telling of the story and thus the generation of data. I went to great lengths as described in Chapter 6, to ensure that each interview was a meaningful experience for all parties. However, I still had to make sure that by saying 'they got something out of it too' I was not masking other issues (Yow, 1994). I understood that power relationships would affect both the content and the process of the research, including the women's feedback. My field diary records my awareness and the way in which I tried to address what I recognised as an inherent power imbalance (Bornat, 1993; Standing, 1998). For example, quite early on in the data gathering process it was apparent that the prospect of the interview was daunting for some women; most of them had never participated in research before, never mind being the focus of the research. Although they had spoken with me over the telephone, where I had sought to explain and reassure, there was clearly apprehension both about meeting me and participating in the research:

> Interview with El who seemed initially quite nervous but couldn't stop talking- almost as though she had been rehearsing what she was going to say and needed to say it straight away ...

I responded very positively:

> Very positive body language, lots of smiles and nods, lots of eye contact, constantly reassured and reminded El that there was no right or wrong answer, she was the expert in her story and she relaxed. In addition, my genuine enthusiasm for and interest in her story enabled her proceed. She then went on to demonstrate that she had given a lot of thought to her current situation and was pleased to be sharing her story with me.

So many of the women demonstrated both their anticipation and sense of occasion at participating in my research, through discussions with family, by dressing-up for the interview and by preparing refreshments. For example, my visit to Farzana had been discussed with her sons who had supported her participation and her daughters-in-law who had prepared teas, samosas and sweetmeats for us to share at the end of the interview. Joan's daughter had helped her to prepare a tray of tea and biscuits, and Mags had arranged with the residential home for us both to be served coffee in her room. However, I was sometimes left with mixed feelings about why this was happening. It was a powerful reminder to me of how the women perceived me, a younger, academic coming into their homes. My diary records my visit to Farzana thus:

The 'social' part of our meeting was very relaxed. Farzana seemed very eager to show me hospitality and had obviously prepared for the occasion. Her daughter-in-law brought in several trays of delicious food and we all 'chatted' together, while we ate and drank. I am always overwhelmed by the kindness of the women I am meeting but I sometimes feel very conscious of being treated as 'an important visitor'. There are also gender/generation issues here I think - rules of engagement with other women perhaps. My mother-in-law would do the same. It's the 'private' becoming 'public' I suppose. And something about me being 'important'. Perhaps I need to relax about this and just accept?

There are a number of possible explanations to my questions. Narratives of gender and generation were being played out in the form of hospitality to be offered to an important visitor who had entered the private domestic world, and to 'dress up' for the occasion and offer refreshments was entirely appropriate behaviour for those narratives. In addition, the 'private' was becoming 'public' as the stories were shared with me. These social ceremonies seemed to be crucial in enabling those stories to be told and celebrated.

I respected the fact that I was in another woman's home and therefore I was on **her** territory. As I discussed in Chapter 6, I felt this was advantageous to each woman; she had chosen where the interview would take place, she was on home territory and I was the visitor. As such, I was to abide by house rules. I note several occasions where this was apparent. For example:

It was sometimes difficult to make eye contact because of the way K had positioned the chairs and because the TV remained on during the interview, thankfully with the sound turned off. K wanted to keep an eye on her TV screen which was screening pictures from the CCTV camera outside the apartments. I found it very distracting and I ended up sitting sideways to try to maintain eye contact, which was so uncomfortable! K said she always kept the CCTV camera on her TV if she wasn't watching a programme. It helped her to know who was coming and going.

Katherine made it very clear that the television always stayed on when she had visitors and I was to be no exception; she was very practised at maintaining a conversation whilst keeping one eye on the television screen (and making the odd comment about who had a visitor) and I just had to adapt.

On another occasion, the interview took place in the presence of the woman's dog, which growled at me every time I moved. I am rather nervous of dogs but was very aware that the dog's presence reassured the woman. Indeed, the dog provided a starting point to the discussion and enabled her to overcome her initial nervousness.:

Interview with P (contact made via a friend who is friendly with P's daughter). Was rather alarmed by her barking dog who seemed to need to make sure I was a friend. This required considerable skill and tolerance on my part. I needed to reassure P that I would be interested in her story; we did a lot of talking around the research first, interspersed with talk about and to the dog - this seemed to help P to relax although I felt really nervous of the dog!

I have not yet come across any advice in research text suggesting the involvement of a pet in the discussion, but it seemed to be successful! After a while, Patricia felt able to encourage the dog to sleep in its basket in another room and so we were both able to relax into the interview.

Several women took great pride in giving me a tour of the house. Edith showed me the bedroom she had recently decorated. Dorothy took me into her garden to show me roses given to her as a retirement gift. Patricia took me up to her sewing room to show me the craftwork she had been doing. On my second visit, she took pride in showing off the decorating she had done since my first visit. On each occasion I actively demonstrated my interest and gratitude for this sharing of their 'private' world.

As highlighted in Chapter 6, I took seriously issues of difference; at times this was more difficult than I had anticipated. For example, the use of an interpreter was an acknowledgement of Farzana's need to tell her story in her own language. I ensured that our differences of ethnicity and age were respected throughout the whole process; we met together the day before, the ethics of the research were discussed through the interpreter, and we were able to clarify any areas of difficulty or ambiguity. Ethical issues were raised and confirmed again at the beginning of the interview that took place the next day. However, although the participation of the interpreter was a positive choice, it did rather change the structure of the interview. It meant that the telling of the life story became a more public event and felt less like the private 'conversation with a purpose' of the other interviews. During the course of the interview, it became apparent that the interpreter, no doubt because of her familiarity with both of us, went beyond interpreter role and was both encouraging the older woman to expand her story and raising other issues in her questioning. At times Farzana seemed quite resistant to this. The interpreter confirmed this after the interview had taken place, and acknowledged that she would have been better confining herself to translating my questions. My reflective diary, written after that interview, recorded my own discomfort:

> I felt very uncomfortable during this interview. Why? F was very nervous, polite and offered to tell me her story but my lack of experience of using an interpreter, and M (the interpreter) going beyond the scope of her role, meant that the interview was very stilted and at times I felt 'outside' the conversation. There were long gaps, and I struggled to ask follow-up questions. Was this because I felt less powerful? I am sure that when I listen to the tape I will hear myself getting more nervous as the interview progressed. It certainly felt that way during the interview. When we turned off the tape and F's daughter brought us some tea and snacks, F started to talk to me directly about her life as a widow, although she is not very confident at using English. This felt much better (for me?) but we were limited by the lack of a common language. There might also be issues here, despite/ in addition to the role of the intermediary, about a younger white woman interviewing an older black woman and assumptions that we were both (consciously or unconsciously/ correctly or incorrectly) making.

It has to be acknowledged that despite my feelings of unease about what I perceived to be the awkwardness of the interview Farzana expressed to me her satisfaction at telling the story and talking about the responsibilities she had gained in widowhood.

So how successful were my attempts to address the inherent power differentials? There was differential impact depending on a number of factors: how each woman perceived me; how she perceived herself; our degree of difference; and the interpersonal relationship that was developed. As I acknowledged in Chapter 6, there were a number of occasions when I certainly felt the least powerful partner in the research relationship. I recognise that on one occasion I found myself particularly overawed by my surroundings, and the expectations placed on me by one of the women. My second visit to Vera was another such occasion:

> V seems to have an overwhelming feeling of resignation to her lot but also very controlled about this, very self-aware. Came away feeling quite powerless - felt I wanted to offer her something but didn't know what. This is the first interview where I have felt at such a loss.

Although this was a specific feeling on my part, it does indicate my recognition of the dynamics of the interactions taking place and that what I perceived to be an inherent power imbalance in my favour was not always the case. It was so important to recognise this as I transcribed the stories and then subsequently analysed the data. Giving back the transcription and having the subsequent discussion of content and process provided an opportunity to raise any such issues.

As for the impact of power on the stories which were unfolding, this again will have been differential and one factor amongst many. It is important to remember that I was not searching for an objective 'truth', but rather I was seeking a subjective narrative underpinned by biography (Harding, 1987). What each woman chose to tell me was individual and will have been influenced by power, alongside the other influences already discussed: my practice, our relationship, our feelings (Skeggs, 1995). What I tried to do was to minimise our power differential in order for each woman to feel able to tell me her story whilst recognising that I could not completely remove such difference. It would be foolish to pretend that there is only one story to be told; each story will have been selective and was the story told to me within a research relationship at a particular point in time (Skeggs, 1995). However, I would argue that the stories, and the multiple narratives and sub-plots which emerged from those stories, were ones that may not have emerged had I not paid attention to power issues and had I not been both sensitive to, and pro-active about, the potential barriers of power differentials.

I both recognised and took responsibility for my power and expertise when it came to data analysis. I raised this issue in Chapter 5, when discussing the beginnings of the study. I had originally anticipated that the women would be involved in the analysis of their stories. However, it became very apparent in those early days, supported by feminist research literature (Berger Gluck and Patai, 1991; Kelly et al, 1994), that this might not be either feasible or desirable. Three of the women were subsequently involved in an informal discussion of the 'multiple narratives' that emerged, but they had no responsibility for analysis (Maynard, 1994). Following Mason's (1997) recommendations, I still paid attention to ethical considerations in both the analysis and the presentation of data. For example, in Chapters 7-11 I have honoured my commitments about confidentiality and privacy and acted in the spirit of the informed consent that I received. I took great consideration in analysing the stories to maintain the integrity of the women and to present their stories in the spirit in which they were given. Nonetheless, I initiated the study, including the selection of particular academic frameworks, and the ultimate responsibility for the analysis was mine.

*Collaboration and reciprocity*

The interviews were deliberately collaborative in that I chose to be an active participant in the creation of the life stories, an experience that was both humbling and exciting. All of the women were very open and, in turn, I too tried to be as open as possible. I was particularly struck by the number of women who said it was the first time they were able to tell their story to an eager listener and this in turn encouraged me to respond to each of them in an honest and respectful manner. My field diary records my feelings after visiting Evelyn for the second time:

> Evelyn was very pensive, very calmly talking about her life before and after Sidney's death ... atmosphere of contentment ... Again I had that overwhelming feeling that I was so privileged to be sharing her thoughts and her story.

I became acutely aware of the hidden nature of these women's lives and the lack of opportunity to share stories of private and public lives. Both gender and generation had conspired to silence their voices. So many of the women talked at great length about their lives, inviting me to participate in their stories, asking questions about my life, comparing and contrasting my life with theirs and sharing experience as women. The following examples are extracts from the field diary: 'Edith was desperate to tell me her story'; 'Patricia wanted to share her story with me'; 'Elizabeth invited comparisons with the opportunities for young women of her generation with the opportunities available for L (her daughter) and me'; Katherine corrected me when I got something wrong or made an incorrect assumption but it felt very comfortable'; and so on. On another occasion, Farzana invited me into another room to show me her husband's portrait that was in pride of place alongside photographs of her children and grandchildren. She then asked me to tell her about my family. I managed to produce some small photographs I have, and told her something about my three daughters. In sharing these details of our respective family lives we were exploring our commonalities (Miller, 1991; Neysmith, 1995); we were both aware of our differences of age, generation, ethnicity, religion and culture (Andrews, 1991) but we had shared roles of wife and mother that on this occasion seemed to offer us a common language. Ellen also made reference to our shared experience of having three children with phrases such as 'you'll remember this', in reference to position in family. I was thus actively invited to participate in these discussions and so often the stories prompted memories of my own, particularly when allusions were made to our commonalities: gender, being a wife, being a mother, juggling work and family. These commonalities did not negate our very real differences but, alongside my explicit willingness to be a co-participant, enabled a collaboration to develop that otherwise might not have done.

However, active participation on my part did not necessarily promote harmony! Occasionally a woman made a judgemental remark and invited me to share her feelings and opinions. This was not always easy particularly when it challenged my own values. For example, my field diary recorded that one participant was making less than generous comments about another woman. Yet another made disparaging remarks about working class women and invited my agreement. I felt challenged by each of these situations but also recognised each woman's own value base. Therefore, I tried to reply honestly, whilst acknowledging her values. There is a need to be open and honest but not judgmental. The situation would have been more difficult if a participant had openly expressed racist or sexist views. Although this situation did not arise, my stance is clear: whilst I may not agree with the values expressed, I have to acknowledge they are the values of the person being interviewed. Nonetheless, if I am asked a direct question or I am invited to agree with an opinion I will express my own views.

*Gendered scripts*

As a result of this collaboration, and my active participation in the research process, 'woman to woman' stories began to unfold, with clearly gendered scripts: that is the culturally and socially constructed scripts, that women both consciously and unconsciously adopt to tell their stories (Sangster, 1994; Ray, 2000). Ray (2000: 77), drawing on feminist literary criticism has demonstrated that the female 'self' represented in female autobiography is often self-effacing, oriented to private life, is likely to foreground relationships and subjective states over accomplishments and be anecdotal. According to Sangster (1994), a feminist historian, women's narratives are likely to be characterised by understatements and avoidance of the first person. Knowing this, and armed with my academic frameworks, I felt able to ask questions in order to explore further those understatements and to encourage my co-participants to move beyond their prescribed cultural scripts.

Citing a woman in a senior's writing group, Ray (2000: 78) noted that men tell us about themselves, rather than revealing themselves through gendered scripts. The participants in the current study told their stories in terms of relationships with others, and feelings, rather than factual detail; indeed they often used their own family relationships as markers of historical time rather than remembering specific dates. At the same time as I was encouraging these women to go beyond their culturally prescribed scripts by making use of my academic knowledge, I also found myself responding to those stories in similar terms; rather than probing for more factual, so-called objective information. I actively sought out the subjective experience and I was encouraging the anecdotal, the discussion of relationships and feelings. These gendered scripts resonated with me both personally and professionally and enabled me to bring to the surface the stories of the hidden lives of these twenty women.

*A note on ethics*

I have tried throughout to adhere to a stated code of ethics. However, I became aware with each set of interviews I carried out that the very intimacy and collaboration I sought from the interview relationship had the potential to make the interviewee more open and self revealing than she might have been in a more formal relationship. For example, one woman asked for the tape recorder to be switched off whilst she shared a secret with me; she did not want it to be part of the data but she wanted me to understand some of her unresolved feelings about her husband. Another woman talked of her husband's infidelity. Indeed, so many of the women opened up large parts of their lives to me.

I noted in Chapter 6 that feminist research literature has recommended caution about encouraging intimacy (Stacey, 1991 for example), urging us to ensure we do not misuse it. On each occasion I took great care to seek informed consent, set boundaries and clarify my role, using my field diary to reflect on how successful or otherwise I had been. Each woman had the opportunity to change what she had said, to clarify or to add to her transcript. I left a contact telephone number and address for each woman to contact me should she wish to withdraw, make changes and so on. Two women did contact me after the interviews had been concluded, both of them to say how much they had enjoyed participating in the research, one of them to contribute some further information. I feel confident that my research was as ethical as it possibly could have been given that according to at least one feminist writer that it is not possible to carry out totally ethical research in an unethical world (Patai, 1991).

*Summary*

So far I have reflected on my own role in the research process and have acknowledged that I was integral to both the dynamics of the interviews and the generation of data. I have demonstrated the way in which I reflected on that role during the process of data collection and how, as a consequence, each interview informed the next. However there were twenty other players, whose views on participating in the research process I actively sought. At this point therefore I turn to my co-participants to present an analysis of their reflections on the research process.

## Me telling my story

Sixteen of the women welcomed a second interview and most were eager to talk not just about the content of transcripts but also the process of participating in the research. Initially I made notes during the discussions but, latterly, I used a tape recorder. This section of the chapter analyses those discussions in relation to feminist research practice by exploring the following themes: validation; making sense; reflection; the potential for growth; and concerns. At the end of this section, I discuss how one of the women found the process quite painful and then speculate as to why some of the women who participated in the second interview were reluctant to reflect on the process of the research. Finally, I consider why others did not wish to take up the opportunity of the second interview.

*Validation*

Feminist life story literature has suggested that the process of telling one's story to another offers validation. In giving a life story the interviewee has the opportunity to make sense of scattered events by telling that story to an eager listener. According to Yow (1994: 117) this validation is particularly important to people who are devalued, such as older women. Joan's first comments when I returned for the second interview were that hers had seemed quite a sad story. In asking her to discuss this further it transpired that after reading it herself, she had shown it to her daughter who had said: 'Oh mummy what a sad story, couldn't you have said something more cheerful'. However, after further discussion and reflection, Joan was then able to say: 'Well, whatever my daughter says, it made me feel stronger because I thought, well I did do that'.

Sylvia was validated through the process of telling her story and reading her transcript:

> I quite enjoyed it, it helped me; it seemed to relieve me, I've never talked to anybody like this before, well you don't. It was absolute relief to tell you. And I thought, well I've always got that now, when I'm on my own I can sit and read it, realise what... well it seemed easy to talk to you, things came back that I thought I'd put to the back of my mind, I was able to put in place.

Dorothy too found the experience to be positive: 'I thought it was great, the fact that I could say it how I wanted to say it and what I wanted to say'.

For each woman, the process of telling her life story and situating widowhood within that story, in her own way and at her own pace, was to a greater or lesser extent a validating experience. The amount of actual change that took place was clearly individual but to be able to tell one's story to an interested listener was both positive and meaningful (Opie, 1992). On one occasion, I was at Jean's home when her daughter telephoned. I heard Jean say: 'I can't talk now, Pat's here with her tape recorder listening to me and I can talk as much as I want (laughs). She doesn't tell me she's heard it all before.' Although Jean was being playful, her comments nonetheless suggested that it was a rare opportunity for an older woman to be able to tell her story, without fear of censure from others. No wonder so many of the women enthusiastically shared their stories, stories that have been hidden not only from the public sphere but also within the more private world of the family.

*Making sense*

In the telling, the narrator creates a story that gives her life meaning and makes sense of things that happened (Opie, 1992; Yow, 1994).
For Doris, the process was:

> ... very interesting really. It brought back memories. I enjoyed doing the interview, its nice to be able to talk about yourself, you don't, well I don't normally talk about myself or my past to anybody because they're not interested/ I was very relieved that my husband went as quickly as he did. He would have been a terrible patient, it would have been dreadful, he would have been so demanding ... I thought it (the transcript) was all very good...

It becomes a way of understanding anew some of the things that happened and a way of accepting some of the things that hurt; this is comparable with Butler's (1980) Life Review. For example, Sylvia says:

> (telling my story) ...prompted memories.... I was grateful to John. I don't think I really loved him. I think it was gratitude. I loved him but it wasn't passion, not like I feel for James (her new partner). Well in a way, it was a relief (to tell my story). Because you see, well there are parts I wouldn't like James to read because he might think, well it might hurt him, but it was a relief. There are certain things I can't say to him ... and not to my family either.

Talking about her past life, in the context of her present, enabled Joan to sort things out which had been troubling her:

> I enjoyed it very much. Thank you for giving me the privilege of doing it. These things, when you get to my age, they're all on your mind and you can't really talk about it because people just say, oh I've heard that before...you sort them out...

Here Joan was articulating the views of a number of the women: telling one's story to a non-judgemental and interested listener who is not denying the subjective experience but instead is actively engaging with that story enables the storyteller to begin to make sense of her life. As such, she is able to verbalise some of the more troubling parts and to give that life some meaning.

*Reflection*

A number of women used the time between the two interviews to reflect on their story or to remember. So often I was met at the second interview with the following sentiments: 'I have been thinking' or 'Since we last met I've remembered …' For example, an extract from the field diary recorded that on my second visit to Elizabeth:

> Elizabeth asked me to read the transcript out to her … she listened attentively and asked no questions. Only when I stopped did she say that she had been thinking about what we had been talking about and had come to the conclusion that living alone had made her more selfish …

This reflection had been helpful because it had helped her to sort out in her own mind why she sometimes felt resentful when her family visited unexpectedly or her grandson wanted to watch a different television programme from her; she had realised they were invading her precious time and space, something she had learned to value.

Bee too had been 'thinking'. In between the two interviews she had been to the United States of America to visit her new partner. During this time, she had reflected on what we had talked about together. In particular she had found herself thinking about what she had said about her relationship with her husband and her friends. She had valued our discussion because it enabled her to understand the importance for her of a shared history, something she did not have with her new partner. This was potentially an issue in her new relationship and one that she felt she would have to seriously consider.

For some women, participating in the life story interview enabled them to remember previously forgotten memories. Vera's memory of her own ridiculing of a group of older women in Blackpool many years ago (see Chapter 11) was prompted by our first interview. This memory had given her some insight into her own negative feelings about older women; she had been both surprised and saddened by this memory. She did not want to be one of those women whom she previously had ridiculed and yet, in her own eyes, she had joined their ranks.

*The potential for growth*

More than twenty years ago, when Oakley (1981) interviewed women in depth about their transition to motherhood, she questioned them about the effects of the project on them. She found that the experience was very positive for most of them and none of them judged that the interviewing had had a negative effect. In fact:

> Three fourths of the women said that being interviewed affected them and the three most common forms this influence took were in leading them to reflect on their experiences more than they would have done; in reducing the level of their anxiety, and/or reassuring them of their normality; and in giving a valuable outlet for the verbalisation of feelings.
>
> (Oakley, 1981: 50)

For the women who participated in the current study, the effects of participating have been equally differential. For some, the effects were minimal, others gained greater self-awareness and insight and yet, for others, a minority, the effects of participation were more far reaching.

Participating in the research had been an opportunity for Bee to reflect on her life at a time of possible change, and verify the more positive aspects of it. She welcomed this chance to reflect:

> Super, it was very natural. It was nice to talk about my life because I don't normally talk about (it). Well it's my life, that's what I thought this is my life.

The interview process enabled her to confirm her social identity and acknowledge its importance for her: indeed so much of her talk was about herself in relation to friends. The opportunity to read her transcript had increased her self-awareness of the role these friends still played in her life, and the importance of the many activities she shared with them:

> It made me realise that I would have to give up such a lot if I moved from here ... I don't know if I'm prepared to do that. After all, I have these lovely friends. That's the basis of it, I have these lovely friends. I've thought about it so much since we talked
>
> (Bee)

Joan identified that the telling of her story made her realise that there had been more in her life than she had initially acknowledged. Furthermore, the telling of her story had enabled her to put to rest some of the thoughts that had recently been troubling her, although she did have reservations about the process:

> I suppose it did (make me think), I suppose it did but it made me wish I could have done more. I was a little shocked seeing it all down on paper, like the wartime which I've never really discussed. It amazed me it came out like that, there were some terrifying parts of it, the wartime.... And I thought sometimes I shouldn't have said this or that...
>
> (Joan)

However, a few days later I received a card:

> A few lines to thank you for our conversations.... I think the transcript is excellent... thank you for the copy. I will keep it safe. I know my granddaughter will be pleased to read it  Best wishes, Joan

Having written about Dorothy in the previous chapter, I return to her in this chapter to discuss the process of her storytelling. It transpired that the life story interview had been both difficult and empowering for Dorothy. During our first interview, she told the story of a woman for whom life had been difficult and for whom widowhood was an exacerbation of those difficulties. During the telling of her story, she became quite upset and at one point requested I turn off the tape recorder. She then shared with me a secret about her marriage. We later switched the tape recorder back on again and she continued with her story. At the end of the interview, she said although it had been difficult at times, she was pleased to have had the opportunity to tell her story and she looked forward to receiving her transcript. At the second interview, which took place just before she flew off on holiday with her friend, she seemed much brighter and certainly more optimistic as she reflected on her participation in the study:

> I felt much better actually. It got it off my chest. I enjoyed ... reminiscing to someone who had not heard it before ... and I felt such a lot better after. I did think a lot about it after you'd gone. And I seem to have had a lot more energy since I did that. I think it was telling the story out loud. I mean the family, well its natural they know all about my past life and I don't think they want to hear all about my time in the past, they say to live for the future which I try to do now... being able to tell you, well it was quite a relief and I enjoyed talking about myself! ...I have to take life as it comes now. I've even booked for Cliff Richard in March. Yes, I'm looking forward
>
> (Dorothy)

Dorothy's major narrative shifted from one of despair to one that was beginning to speak of hope and a future to be embraced. I met Dorothy recently and her whole demeanour has changed. She talked with pride about losing weight and getting a new haircut. She again re-iterated that telling her story had been a 'turning point'; having the opportunity to tell her story, including the secrets, and saying it 'out loud' provided her with an opportunity to share the thoughts that had been preoccupying her, talk about her current experience and situate it within her life course. Although not intended as a therapeutic intervention, and I certainly cannot claim to have the skills necessary to undertake such an intervention, the outcome of participating in the research process had clearly been therapeutic. Not only has her life course experience been validated but the process has also provided her with an opportunity for growth.

For Patricia the process was slightly different. She enjoyed the social occasion, and the companionship that came from participating in the study, and certainly put considerable effort into preparing for my visits. After an initial nervousness, she relaxed and shared her life story enjoying the process. However, she was clearly unhappy with the transcript that had revealed her unhappiness and loneliness, and she did not initially want to keep it. Furthermore, she did not like the rambling nature of it and worried about her English. I had taken the view that although I would not initially 'tidy up' the transcripts, this could be negotiated during the second meeting (Skeggs, 1995; see also discussion on 'tidying up' in Chapter 5). I spent some time reassuring her about the appearance of the transcript, during which time we made some changes in order to improve the grammar. I was then able to encourage her to talk a bit more about the content. At the end of our final interview, she told me that she had enjoyed participating in the research and that it had been helpful for her. She also told me that she had decided that she might ask her doctor to refer her again to a counsellor since she now felt she might gain some benefit. I do not know if she did but I feel sure that participating in the study was ultimately a positive process, even though her 'gains' were perhaps less than some others.

*Concerns*

A small number of women expressed concerns either about remarks they had made about other people or the amount of personal information they had disclosed. Bee for example said at our second meeting, after she had read her transcript:

> This is me but I'm so concerned about the details... I thought gosh, you sound such an awful person.... (referring to what she had said about close friends who openly disapproved of a recent relationship she had developed with an American man) when I think about what I said about these women, friends of mine, saying they don't approve, I thought I can't say things like that.

After some negotiation, she made some changes that recognised these concerns. This was in accordance with my ethical stance, which clearly stated that no woman would be bound by what she had originally said, and that anything which was felt to be in any way untrue or undesirable by the woman concerned would be changed (Andrews, 1991; see also discussion in Chapter 6).

When she had read her transcript, Eunice too was troubled by remarks she had made about her brother and sister. Although unlike Bee, she decided she did not want changes made to her transcript:

> When I read the first page, I altered so many things and then I thought perhaps I don't need to do that. For instance when I said about my brother and my sister that I did better than them, I thought that's awful, did I say that?
>
> (Eunice)

She described the initial experience of reading her transcript as like 'seeing my soul bared' and it took some time before she felt able to look at it. She said: 'When I got down to it, it was fine but when I first saw it I thought gosh and I put it down and didn't want to read it'. But then she had found herself so absorbed in her own story to the point where she began to consider the possibility of building on her transcript and writing a more detailed life story herself at some point in the future. She has discussed her transcript with her daughter and has begun to reflect on the possibilities of leaving such a document as a legacy for her. She found herself thinking about questions she would have liked her parents to answer and how useful it would have been to have a written copy of their life stories:

> P. Is it a document you would look back on or is it something you want to discard?
> E. Actually, its made me think I would like one of these days to get down to writing something about my life, using that as a base because I think there are so many things I would have liked to have asked my parents that I didn't ask, so I would like to write something and I think I am a better writer than I am a conversationalist ... (in particular) the memories of my daughter are very painful, but if I were writing I would be able to write about it.

P. Who would you write your story for?

E. My children, especially my daughter, perhaps when I'm less mobile in the winter months.

I highlighted in Chapter 5, and earlier in this chapter, how a number of writers (for example Stacey 1991) have commented on the potential intensity of feminist interviews that often encourages women to disclose information or give expression to feelings that they have not always shared with others. It is so important that as feminist researchers we recognise this and engage in sensitive discussion that enables women to reflect on what they have said without us judging them, but also that they should not feel trapped by remarks they may have made in the intensity of the interview (Andrews, 1991).

## A negative experience?

Just one participant, Vera, found the life story interview to be quite painful and certainly did not enjoy reading her transcript. However, she was adamant that she had no regrets about participating in the study. To the contrary, she was at pains to ensure that I really understood just how difficult later life widowhood was, and that I passed this message on when I wrote up the study. Her agenda from the beginning was to tell me 'as it was' and she was not really interested in the process of the interview. I wrote in Chapter 5 about Coleman's (1986; 1996) work on reminiscence and how he has identified some people for whom reminiscing is never a positive experience. Vera may be one such person. She has recognised that her past is contributing to her present, and indeed she provided many examples as discussed in previous chapters, but she saw no need to engage with those issues when we discussed the process of the research.

## 'No reflection' on the process

So far, I have analysed the process of participating in the study to some degree in terms of active, meaningful discussion between individual women and myself, identifying both positive and negative experiences. However, despite my best attempts, discussions about the process of participating in the research were neither active nor meaningful, even with those participants who agreed to a second interview. Some of my discussions, such as those that took place with Katherine or Phyllis, were extremely superficial. They both thought I had conducted the interview well and that they had been given ample opportunity to tell their story. They both confirmed that I had been polite and interested but they did not really feel that they had much more to say about the process. Indeed, I was left with the feeling that they wondered why I was so concerned with their reflections! Both of these women were of course very engaged in a social world, with ample opportunities for discussion of both past and present with friends. It may be that the sharing of intimacies that took place in the life story interview meant less to them than it did, for example, to Dorothy or Patricia, for whom there were few opportunities to share.

In Chapter 6 I stated that four of the women declined to participate in a follow-up interview and I noted a number of reasons that were given either on the telephone or in writing: 'too busy'; 'going away'; 'get in touch when I have time'; and so on. Although no dissatisfaction was explicitly expressed, they were clear that they did not wish to participate any further, and that they were making a definite choice. I can only speculate as to their real reasons. There is no doubt that they had busy lives, but it might possibly be that they too could not understand why I wished them to comment on the process, reflecting either my lack of sufficient explanation or perhaps the inherent power imbalance resulting from our diverse statuses (see Chapter 6). Furthermore, I have to acknowledge that the wish to practise reflexive feminist research, underpinned as it is by my knowledge and academic background, is mine, and not that of my participants. Indeed, perhaps I should have been surprised that so many of the women agreed to reflect on the process of the research!

## Conclusion

In this chapter, I have critically reflected on the process of my own feminist research practice and sought to ascertain my success or otherwise in engaging the participants in the research study and consider the extent to which this resulted in change. I have discussed my own role in that collaboration and presented evidence from the women themselves about their role and the benefits, or otherwise, of participating in the study. Whilst acknowledging difference, I have argued for the centrality of our common gender in the joint enterprise of storytelling, an enterprise in which we were all active participants.

All of the women confirmed their pleasure at taking part and none of them judged that they had experienced any harm. For each woman, this had been her first experience both of participating in a research study and an in sharing her life story with anyone outside their family. (Indeed, most of the participants had not even shared a substantial part of that story with their family.) They all felt engaged in the telling of that story to me, the interested listener, and acknowledged that they had both the space and the time to say what they wanted to and to tell it in the way that they wanted to.

Although all the women welcomed the opportunity to participate in the enterprise, I recognise that the impact of this participation was differential. For some the gains were validation, the chance to make sense, a time for reflection, the chance to let others know 'how it really is' and, in two instances, a real opportunity to 'move on'; there were some concerns expressed but these were sensitively resolved by paying close attention to the ethics underpinning the research. For others though, participation in the research enterprise was both enjoyable and engaging, but incidental to their lives, a story to tell their friends and family but certainly not significant in either shaping or reshaping their lives.

It is important to remember that the women who participated in this research were not self-selecting, nor were they actively seeking personal change.

Unlike some other researchers (Summerfield, 1998) I chose not to put an advertisement in the local press inviting participation but instead, as I explained in Chapter 6, I chose a purposive approach to sampling. Consequently, the twenty co-participants did not seek me out to tell their stories but rather were invited to participate in the study. Indeed, once they had agreed, they were then encouraged to share their stories within a framework of feminist research practice, a framework chosen by me, the researcher. Thus, any 'gains' have to be evaluated within that context. Nonetheless, the responses of all the participants do seem to suggest that they were engaged in the process to a greater or lesser degree and, for some of them, this engagement brought about some change. It would seem therefore that a feminist, biographical approach to researching later life widowhood is able to engage older widows in the research process and has the potential, if not the certainty, of incorporating change.

# Chapter 14

# Conclusion

## Introduction

In this final chapter, in order to conclude this volume, I return to the starting point of my journey of exploration. I then note the limitations of the study and make recommendations for future research on later life widowhood. I conclude, where I began, on a personal note.

## Revisiting my 'beginnings'

My journey of exploration into later life widowhood began with my observations of older widows in my own neighbourhood and my quest for a greater understanding of their lives. Indeed, it was this quest that precipitated my hunch that there was much to discover. As I stated in my introduction, my overall aim was to investigate both the objective and subjective experience of later life widowhood through a review of the literature and by engaging older widows in a dialogue about their lives and the place of widowhood within those lives. Chapters 1-13 demonstrate to the reader my success, or otherwise, in achieving that aim. I have argued the case for a dominant public narrative of later life widowhood that socially constructs older widows' lives as a time of loneliness and decline. Indeed, I have provided evidence that both 'age' and 'gender' are construed as co-conspirators in this problematisation of older widows.

Older women's stories challenge this value-laden construction and point instead to a complexity of experience, rooted in individual and collective biographies rather than in later life widowhood itself. In order to understand how older widows manage their lives 'Now', it is vital that we listen to their stories and engage with the multiple narratives and the sub-plots underpinning those stories. Furthermore, although I have acknowledged that the schema I have developed is not predictive, I have nonetheless demonstrated that without an understanding of such a framework we can totally misconstrue and thus misinterpret older widows' current needs and aspirations. I have argued, in some detail, the case for a biographical method of research and analysis, underpinned by feminist research practice, as a way of eliciting those stories. Via an ethical and collaborative process of research I have represented the voices of the twenty participants. By situating later life widowhood within the female life course, a concept of multiple narratives has been employed as a way of uncovering the complex, but often hidden, lives of older widows. Both conceptually and methodologically, current understanding of the experience of later life widowhood has been developed. Moreover, it is possible to look at widowhood through a 'different lens' (Gibson, 1996) and hence uncover a multi-faceted experience that, because it is derived from biographical accounts, is recognisable to older widows themselves.

## Limitations

However, as with any study there are limitations that must be acknowledged. Firstly, as discussed in the previous chapter the multiple narratives derived from the biographical accounts of twenty older widows have been constructed within a particular historical location, at a particular point in time, within a set of particular circumstances and between two individuals. Furthermore, because the storyteller cannot possibly 'tell all', the story that is told is of necessity limited to those interactions. At each stage of the research process, selection has occurred: introducing the study; the sample; the way in which each women chose to tell her story and the content of those stories; the way in which I tuned into and responded to those stories; the biographical summaries; the narratives and sub-plots (Riesseman, 1993). This is further compounded by my interpretation of those narratives. As Rabinow and Sullivan (1987:12) have so succinctly noted, every text is 'plurivocal', that is open to several readings and several constructions. I have read the stories and then constructed and interpreted the narratives using my own theoretical and methodological frameworks. I acknowledge that there may be other constructions and interpretations. However, my intention was never to uncover an absolute truth that claimed to be the 'untold' story of later life widowhood, but rather to acknowledge that there are many ways of constructing experience, and that by engaging with older widows' stories we may gain greater understanding of the multiplicity of their experience.

Secondly, the concept of multiple narratives has been derived from the stories of twenty women and as such I acknowledge the need for caution in making generalisations about the multiple narratives of all older widows based on such a small sample. Furthermore, these women all belong to a particular generation and the lives of subsequent generations of older widows will be structured within different historical locations and contexts. However, what the study does highlight is the complexity of older widows' lives and the multiple narratives that emerge from a study of those lives. The narratives and sub-plots of other older widows may differ but what is certain is that those narratives and sub-plots will impact on older women's experience of later life widowhood, and will be crucial in both the meaning and management of that experience. So, whilst I acknowledge that the current study cannot claim to be representative, I nonetheless argue that the concept of multiple narratives that has emerged is a useful framework for understanding the experience of all older widows.

Thirdly, I have argued in Chapter 13 the advantages of a collaborative approach to the study of later life widowhood. However, I also acknowledge that there are disadvantages to such an approach. As an integral player in the production of my research data, I am nonetheless a product of my social and historical location and my subjectivity will inevitably be shaped by that location. I have tried to be explicit and 'come clean' about this by introducing reflexivity into my study, but I acknowledge that it is impossible to be totally objective about my own subjectivity.

Finally, because I was interested in older widows' subjectivity, I chose not to consult with others, such as family and friends, about the reality of the twenty women's representations. As such these realities could be challenged as being one-dimensional and insular or even untrue (Flick, 2000; Jovechelovitch and Bauer, 2000). However, my response to such a challenge is that because we know so little about the subjective experience of older widows, and so much about the so-called reality of later life widowhood as perceived by others, the subjective representations of older widows go some was to redressing the balance.

A biographical approach to later life widowhood therefore is not without its limitations but, on balance, these are outweighed by the developmental possibilities such an approach offers.

## And finally

In completing this study, and then writing it up in this volume, I have undergone a personal as well as an academic journey. Talking to older widows about their lives has inevitably made me consider the very real possibility that I too may become an older widow. As a result I have found myself reflecting on the biographical assets that are rooted in my personal and collective biography, the social networks I have developed over my life course and the skills I have practised in building relationships with family and friends. And I have emerged from that reflection with optimism. I have thus connected personally with the multiple narratives that have emerged from this study, a connection that has at times been painful but also liberating. It would seem that a feminist biographical approach to the study of later life widowhood has the potential to engage the researcher, and I hope the reader, as well as the other participants, and thus incorporate change.

# Bibliography

Adams, R.G. (1985), 'People would talk: normative barriers to cross sex friendships for elderly women', *The Gerontologist*, 25: 605-11.

Adams, R.G. (1987), 'Patterns of network change: a longitudinal study of friendships of elderly women', *The Gerontologist*, 27: 222-227.

Adams, R.G. and Blieszner, R. (eds) (1989), *Older Adult Friendship*, Newbury Park CA: Sage.

Adlersberg, M. and Thorne, S. (1992), 'Emerging from the chrysalis', *Journal of Gerontological Nursing*, 6: 4-8.

Age Concern (2000), *Statistics*, www.ace.org.uk.

Allan, G. (1989), *Friendship*, New York: Harvester Wheatsheaf.

Allan, G. and Adams, R.G. (1989), 'Ageing and the Structure of Friendship', in Adams, R.G. and Blieszner, R. (eds) (1989), *op. cit.*

Allen, K. (1989), *Single Women, Family Ties: Life histories of older women*, Newbury Park: CA: Sage.

Allport, G. (1942), *The Use of Personal Documents in Psychological Science*, New York: Social Science Research Council.

Anderson, K. and Jack, D. (1991), 'Learning to Listen', in Gluck, S.B. and Patai, D. (eds) (1991), *Women's Words: Feminist Practice of Oral History*, New York: Routledge and Chapman Hall.

Anderson, K., Armitage, S., Jack, D., Wittner, J. (1987), 'Beginning where we are: feminist methodology in oral history', *Oral History Review*, 57: 103-27.

Anderson, T.B. (1984), 'Widowhood as a life transition: its impact on kinship ties', *Journal of Marriage and the Family*, 46(1): 105-14.

Anderson, T.B. (1987), 'Widows in Urban Nebraska: their informal support systems', in Lopata, H.Z. (ed) (1987) *Widows Volume 2 North America*, Durham, NC: Duke University Press.

Andrews, M. (1991), *Lifetimes of Commitment*, Cambridge: Cambridge University Press.

Andrews, M. (1999), 'The seductiveness of agelessness', *Ageing and Society*, 19(3): 301-18

Antonovsky, A. (1979), *Stress, Health and Coping*, San Francisco, CA: Jossey Bass.

Antonucci, T.C. (1985), 'Personal characteristics, social support and social behaviour', in Binstock, R.H. and Shanas, E. (eds) (1985) *Handbook of Aging and the Social Sciences*, New York: Van Nostrand Reinhold.

Antonucci, T.C. (1994), 'A life span view of women's social relations', in Turner, B.F. and Troll, L.E. (eds) (1994), *Women Growing Older*, California: Sage.

Arber, S. (1993), 'Designing Samples', in Gilbert, N. (ed) (1993), *Researching Social Life*, London: Sage.

Arber, S. and Ginn, J. (1991), *Gender and Later Life*, London: Sage.

Arber, S. and Ginn, J. (eds) (1995), *Connecting Gender and Ageing*, Buckingham: Open University Press.

Arling, G. (1976), 'The elderly widow and her family, neighbours and friends', *Journal of Marriage and the Family*, November: 757-68.

Atchley, R.C. (1975), 'Dimensions of widowhood in later life', *The Gerontologist*, 29(2): 183-9.

Atkinson, D. (1997), *An Autobiographical Approach to Learning Disability*, Aldershot: Ashgate.

Atkinson, R. (1998), *The Life Story Interview*, California: Sage.

Babchuk, N. and Anderson, T.B. (1989), 'Older widows and married women, their intimates and their confidantes', *International Journal of Aging and Human Development*, 7: 67-86.

Balkwell, C. (1981), 'Transition to Widowhood: A Review of the Literature', *Family Relations*, 30(1): 117-127.

Baltes, P.B. and Baltes, M.M. (1990), *Successful Aging: Perspectives from the Behavioural Sciences*, Canada: Cambridge University Press.

Bankoff, E. (1983), 'Social support and adaptation to widowhood', *Journal of Marriage and the Family*, November: 827-39.

Bauer, M.W. and Gaskell, G. (eds) (2000), *Qualitative Researching with Text, Image and Sound*, London: Sage.

Beasley, C. (1999), *What is feminism?*, London: Sage.

Bennett, K. (1997), 'A longitudinal study of wellbeing in widowed women', *International Journal of Geriatric Psychiatry*, 12: 61-66.

Bennett, K. and Morgan, K. (1992), 'Health, social functioning and marital status: stability and change amongst recently widowed women', *International Journal of Geriatric Psychiatry*, 7(11): 813-817.

Bennett, K. and Vidal-Hall, S. (2000), 'Narratives of death: a qualitative study of widowhood in later life', *Ageing and Society*, 20(4): 413-28.

Bernard, M. and Meade, K. (eds) (1993), *Women Come of Age*, London: Edward Arnold.

Bernard, M., Phillips, J., Machin, L., Harding Davies, V. (eds) (2000), *Women Ageing: changing identities, challenging myths*, London: Routledge.

Beveridge, W. (1942), *Report of the Committee on Social Insurance and Allied Services*, London: HMSO.

Binstock, R.H. and Shanas, E. (eds) *Handbook of Ageing and the Social Sciences* (3$^{rd}$ edition) New York: Academic Press.

Birren, J.E., Kenyon, G.M., Ruth, J.C., Schroots, J.J.F. and Svensson, T. (eds) (1996), *Explorations in Adult Development*, New York: Springer Publishing.

Birren, J.E. (1996), 'Aging and Biography', in Birren, J.E. et al (eds) (1996), *op. cit.*

Blieszner, R. and Adams, R. (1998), 'Problems with friends in old age', *Journal of Aging Studies*, Fall: 223-41.

Blau, Z. (1961), 'Structural constraints on friendship in old age', *American Sociological Review*, 26: 429-39.

Blau, Z. (1973), *Old Age in a Changing Society*, New York: Franklin Watts.

Bloor, M. (1983), 'Notes on member validation', in Emerson, R. (ed) (1983), *Contemporary Field Research: a collection of readings*, Boston: Little Brown.

Bond, J., Coleman, P. and Peace, S.M. (eds) (1994), *Ageing in Society: an introduction to social gerontology*, London: Sage.

Bond, L.A. and Rosen, J.C. (eds) (1980), *Competence and Coping During Adulthood*, Hanover, New England: University Press of New England.

Bordo, S. (1990), 'Feminism, post-modernism, and gender-scepticism', in Nicholson, L. (ed) (1990) *Feminism/Post-modernism*, London: Routledge.

Bornat, J. (1993), 'Life Experience', in Bernard, M. and Meade, K. (eds) (1993), *op. cit.*

Bornat, J. (ed.) (1996), *Reminiscence Reviewed*, Buckingham: Open University Press.

Borland, K. (1991), 'That's not what I said', in Gluck, S.B. and Patai, D. (eds) (1991), *op. cit.*

Bowlby, J. (1953), *Child Care and the Growth of Love*, London: Pelican.

Bowlby, J. (1980), *Attachment and Loss*, New York: Basic Books.

Bowling, A. and Cartwright, A. (1982), *Life After A Death*, London: Tavistock Publishing.

Brabon, C. and Summerfield, P. (1987) *Out of the Cage: Women's Experience of Two World Wars*, London: Pandora.

Brandon Wallace, J. (1994), 'Life Stories', in Gubrium, J.F. and Sankar, A. (eds) (1994), *Qualitative Methods of Aging Research*, Thousand Oaks, California: Sage.

Browne, C.V. (1998), *Women, Feminism and Aging*, New York: Springer Press.

Buhler, C. (1935), *From Birth to Maturity*, London: Routledge.

Burgoyne, J., Ormerod, R. and Richards, M. (1987), *Divorce Matters*, Harmondsworth: Penguin.

Burman, E. (1989), *The Practice of Psychology by Feminists*, London: Sage.

Butler, A. (1990), 'Research ethics and older people', in Peace, S.M. (ed) (1990), *Researching Social Gerontology*, London: Sage.

Butler, R.N. (1980), 'The Life Review: an interpretation of reminiscence in the aged', *Psychiatry*, 26: 65-76.

Bytheway, B. (1995), *Ageism*, Buckingham: Open University.

Bytheway, B. (1996), 'The experience of later life', *Ageing and Society*, 16: 613-24.

Carver, V. and Liddiard, P. (eds) (1978), *An Ageing Population*, Sevenoaks: Hodder and Stoughton.

Cain, M. (1986), 'Realism, feminism, methodology and the law', *International Journal of Sociology of Law*, 14.

Caine, L. (1974), *Widow*, New York: William Morrow and Company.

Chamberlayne, P., Bornat, J. and Wengraf, T. (2000), *The Turn To Biographical Methods in Social Science*, London: Routledge.

Chambers, P. (1994), 'A biographical approach to widowhood', *Generations Review*, 4, 3: 8-12.

Chambers, P. (1998), 'Involving older women in the research process', *Generations Review*, 8(4): 6-8.

Chambers, P. (2000), 'Widowhood in Later Life', in Bernard, M. et al (eds) (2000), *op. cit.*

Chambers, P. and Pickard, J. (2002), 'Involving Older Members of the Lifetime Project in Research: a report of research in progress', *Education and Ageing*, 15, 1.

Clayton, P.J., Halikas, J.A., Maurice, W.L., Robins, E. (1973), 'Anticipatory grief and widowhood', *British Journal of Psychiatry*, 122: 47-51.

Coleman, P.G. (1986), *Ageing and Reminiscence Processes: social and clinical implications*, Chichester: Wiley.

Coleman, P.G. (1994), 'Adjustment in later life', in Bond, J. et al (eds) (1994), *op. cit.*

Coleman, P.G. (1996), 'Reminiscence within the study of ageing: the social significance of story', in Bornat, J. (ed) (1996), *op. cit.*

Cumming, E. and Henry, W.E. (1961), *Growing Old: the process of disengagement*, New York: Basic Books.

Daley, C. (1998), 'He would know but I just have a feeling: Gender and Oral History', *Women's History Review*, 7(3): 343-360.

Danish, S.J. and D'Augeli, A.R (1980), 'Promoting competence and enhancing development through life development interventions', in Bond, L.A. and Rosen, J.C. (eds) (1980), *op. cit.*

Dant, T. and Gearing, B. (1990), 'Using biographical research', in Peace, S.M. (ed) (1990), *Researching Social Gerontology*, London: Sage.

Davidson, K. (1999), *Gender, Age and Widowhood: how older widows and widowers differently realign their lives*, unpublished PhD thesis, University of Surrey.

De Beauvoir, S. (1970), *Old Age*, Middlesex: Penguin.

De Beauvoir, S. (1974), *The Second Sex*, New York: Vintage Books.

Delmar, R. (1986), 'What is feminism?', in Mitchell, J. and Oakley, A. (eds) (1986), *What is Feminism?*, Oxford: Blackwell.

Denscombe, M. (1998), *The Good Research Guide*, Buckingham: Open University Press.

Denzin, N.K. and Lincoln, Y. (1994), *Handbook of Qualitative Research*, Newbury Park: Sage.

DiGiulio, R.C. (1989), *Beyond Widowhood*, New York: Free Press.

Di Gregorio, S. (1986), *Growing Old in Twentieth Century Leeds*, unpublished PhD thesis, Leeds University.

Erikson, E.H. (1959), 'Identity and the life cycle', *Psychological Issues*, 1(1), 1-171.

Erikson, E.H. (1965), *Childhood and Society*, Middlesex: Penguin.

Erikson, E.H. (1980), *Identity and The Life Cycle; a re-issue*, New York: WW Norton.

Erikson, E.H. (1982), *The Life Cycle Completed: a review*, New York: WW Norton.

Erikson, E.H., Erikson, J.M. and Kivnick, H.Q. (1986), *Vital Involvement in Old Age: the experience of old age in our time*, New York: WW Norton.

Feinson, M.C. (1986), 'Aging widows and widowers: are there mental health differences?', *International Journal of Aging and Human Development*, 23(4): 241-55.

Fenwick, R. and Barresi, C.M. (1981), 'Health consequences of marital change among the elderly: a comparison of cross sectional and longitudinal analyses', *Journal of Health and Social Behaviour*, 22(2): 106-16.

Ferraro, K. (1984), 'Widowhood and social participation in later life', *Research on Aging*, 6: 451-68.

Ferraro, K. (1989), 'Widowhood and health', in Markides, K.S. and Cooper, C.L. (eds) (1989), *Aging, Stress and Health*, Chichester: John Wiley and Sons.

Ferraro, K.F., Mutran, E., Barresi, C. (1984), 'Widowhood, health and friendship support in later life', *Journal of Health and Social Behaviour*, 25: 245-59.

Finch, J. and Groves, D. (1983), *A Labour of Love: women, work and caring*, London: Routledge and Kegan Paul.

Flick, U. (2000), 'Episodic interviewing', in Bauer, M.W. and Gaskell, G. (eds) (2000), *op. cit.*

Fooken, I. (1985), 'Old and female: psychosocial concomitants of the aging process in a group of older women', in Munnichs, J., Mussen, P., Olbrich, E., Coleman, P. (eds) (1985), *Life Span and Change in a Gerontological Perspective*, Orlando: Academic Press.

Ford, J. and Sinclair, R. (1987), *Sixty Years On*, London: Women's Press.

Forster, M.C. (1996), *Hidden Lives: a family memoir*, London: Penguin.

Frieden, B. (1993), *The Fountain of Age*, London: Jonathan Cape.

Gearing, B. (1998), 'Narratives of identity among former professional footballers in the United Kingdom', *Journal of Aging Studies*, 13(1): 43-58.

Gee, E.M. and Kimball, M.M. (1987), *Women and Aging*, Toronto: Butterworths.

Gibson, D. (1996), 'Broken down by age and gender: the "problem" of old women redefined', *Gender and Society*, 10: 433-448.

Giddens, A. (1991), *Modernity and Self-Identity: Self and Society in the Late Modern Age*, Cambridge: Polity Press.

Giele, J.Z. and Elder, G.H. (1998), *Methods of Life Course Research*, California: Sage.

Giles, J. (1995), *Women, Identity and Private Life in Britain 1900-50*, Basingstoke: Macmillan.

Gilligan, C. (1993), *In a different voice: Psychological theory and women's development*, Cambridge MA: Harvard University Press (first published 1983).

Glick, I.O., Weiss, S. and Parkes, C.M. (1974), *The First Year of Bereavement*, New York: John Wiley and Sons.

Gluck, S.B. and Patai, D. (eds) (1991), *Women's Words: Feminist Practice of Oral History*, New York: Routledge and Chapman Hall.

Goffman, E. (1969), *The Presentation of Self in Everyday Life*, Harmondsworth: Penguin.

Gorer, G. (1965), *Death, Grief and Mourning*, New York: Doubleday.

Gould, R.L. (1980), 'Transformational tasks in adulthood', in Greenspan, S.L. and Pollock, G.H. (eds) (1980), *The Course of Life: Psychoanalytic Contributions Towards Understanding Personality vol.3 Adulthood and the Ageing Process*, Washington DC, National Institute for Mental Health.

Granville, G. (2000), 'Menopause: a time of private change to a mature identity', in Bernard, M. et al (eds) (2000), *op. cit.*

Granville, G. (2001), *Developing a Mature Identity: a feminist exploration of the menopause*, unpublished PhD thesis, Keele University.

Greene, R.W. and Field, S. (1989), 'Social support arrangements and the well being of elderly widows and married women', *Journal of Family Issues*, 10(1): 33-51.

Greer, G. (1991), *The Change: women ageing and the menopause*, London: Hamish Hamilton.

Gubrium, J.F. (1995), 'Voice, context and narrative in aging research', *Canadian Journal on Aging*, 14, supplement 1: 68-81.

Gubrium, J.F. and Sankar, A. (eds) (1994), *Qualitative Methods in Aging Research*, Thousand Oaks, California: Sage.

Gubrium, J.F. and Holstein, J.A. (1994), 'Analysing talk and interaction', in Gubrium, J.F. and Sankar, A. (eds) (1994), *op. cit.*

Gurin, G., Veroff, J. and Field, S. (1960), *Americans View their Mental Health*, New York: Basic Books.

Haas-Hawkings, G., Sangster, S., Ziegler, M. and Reid, D. (1985), 'A study of relatively immediate adjustment to widowhood in later life', *International Journal of Women's Studies*, 8(2): 158-66.

Hall, C.M. (1997), *Women and Identity: value choices in a changing world*, New York: Hemisphere.

Hansson, R.O. and Remondet, J.H. (1988), 'Old age and widowhood', *Journal of Social Issues*, 44(3): 159-74.

Harding, S. (ed) (1987), *Feminism and Methodology*, Brompton and Indianapolis: Indiana University Press.

Harding, S. (1991), *Whose Science? Whose Knowledge? Thinking from women's lives*, Milton Keynes: Open University Press.

Havers, B. (1995), 'Overview of longitudinal research on aging', *Canadian Journal on Aging*, 14, supplement 1: 119-134.

Havighurst, R.J. (1972), *Development Tasks and Education*, New York: David Kay.

Heyman, D.K. and Gianturco, D.T. (1973), 'Long term adaptation by the elderly to bereavement', *Journal of Gerontology*, 28: 359-62.

Hill, C.D., Thompson, L.W., Gallagher, D. (1988), 'Role of anticipatory bereavement in older women's adjustment to widowhood', 28 *Gerontologist* (6): 792-97.

Hilz, S.R. (1978), 'Widowhood: A roleless role', *Marriage and Family Review*, 1: 2-10.

Holloway, I. (1999), *Basic Concepts for Qualitative Research*, London: Blackwell Science.

Holmes, T.H. and Rahe, R.H. (1967), 'The social readjustment rating scale', *Journal of Psychosomatic Research*, 11(2): 213-18.

Houldsworth, A. (1988), *Out of the Doll's House*, London: BBC Publications.

Horowitz, A. (1985), 'Sons and daughters as caregivers to older persons: differences in role performance and consequences', *Gerontologist*, 25 (6): 612-17.

Humphrey, R. (1993), 'Ageing and social life in an ex-mining town', *Sociology*, 27(1): 166-178.

Hunter, S. and Sundel, M. (1989), *Midlife Myths: issues, findings and practice implications*, Newbury Park: Sage.

Hyrkas, K., Kaumonnen, M. and Paunonen, M. (1987), 'Recovering from the death of a spouse', *Journal of Advanced Nursing*, 25: 775-79.

Jacobs, S., Hansen, F., Berkman, L., Kasl, S. and Osterfield, A. (1989) 'Depressions of bereavement', *Comprehensive Psychiatry*, 30(3): 218-224.

Jacobs, D.E. and Ostfield, A. (1977), 'An epidemiological review of the mortality of bereavement', *Psychosomatic Medicine*, 39(5): 345-357.

Jacobson, D.E. (1986), 'Types and timing of social support', *Journal of Health and Social Behaviour*, September: 250-64.

Jaffe, D.J. and Miller, E.M. (1994), 'Problematising meaning', in Gubrium, J.F. and Sankar, A. (eds) (1994), *op. cit.*

Jaggar, A. (1983), *Feminist Politics and Human Nature*, Totowa, New Jersey: Rowman and Allanheld.

Jenkins, R. (1996), *Social Identity*, London: Routledge.

Jerrome, D. (1981), 'The significance of friendship for women in later life', *Ageing and Society*, 1: 175-97.

Jerrome, D. (1990), 'Frailty and friendship', *Journal of Cross Cultural Gerontology*, 5: 51-64.

Jerrome, D. (1991), 'Intimate relationships', in Bond, J. et al (eds) (1991), *op. cit.*

Jerrome, D. (1993), 'Intimacy and sexuality amongst older women', in Bernard, M. and Meade, K. (eds) (1993), *op. cit.*

Johnson, M. (1978), 'That was your life', in Carver, V. and Liddiard, P. (eds) (1978), *op. cit.*

Jones Porter, E. (1995). 'The life world of older widows: the context of the lived experience', *Journal of Women and Aging*, 7(4): 31-46.

Josselson, R. and Lieblich, A. (eds) (1999), *Making Meaning of Narratives*, California: Sage.

Jovchelovitch, S. and Bauer, M.W. (2000) 'Narrative Interviewing', in Bauer, M.W. and Gaskell, G. (eds) (2000), *op. cit.*

Kelly, L. (1988), *Surviving Sexual Violence*, Cambridge: Polity Press.

Kelly, L., Burton, S. and Regan, L. (1994), 'Researching women's lives or studying women's oppression? Reflections on what constitutes feminist research', in Maynard, M. and Purvis, J. (eds) (1994), *Researching Women's Lives From a Feminist Perspective*, London: Routledge.

Kenyon, G.M. (1996), 'Ethical issues in ageing and biography', *Ageing and Society: Special Issue on Ageing, Biography and Practice*, 16: 659-675.

Kirkwood, T. (1999), *Time of Our Lives: the science of human ageing*, London: Weidenfield and Nicholson.

Kubler-Ross, E. (1970), *On Death and Dying*, London: Tavistock.

Lewis, J. and Meredith, B. (1988), *Daughters Who Care: daughters caring for mothers at home*, London: Routledge.

Lieberman, M. (1992), 'Limitations of psychological stress model', in Wykle, M.L., Kahana, E. and Kowel, J. (eds) (1992), *Stress and Health Among the Elderly*, New York: Springer Publishing Co. Ltd.

Lieberman, M. (1996), *Doors Close, Doors Open: widows grieving and growing*, New York: Grosset/Putman.

Lieberman, M. and Tobin, S.S. (1983), *The Experience of Old Age: stress, coping and survival*, New York: Basic Books.

Levinson, D.J., Darrow, D.N., Klein, E.B., Levinson, M.H. and McKee, B. (1978), *The Seasons of a Man's Life*, New York: AA Knopf.

Llewelyn, S. and Osborne, K. (1990) *Women's Lives*, London: Routledge.

Lofland, J. (1982), 'Loss and human connection: an exploration into the nature of the social bond', in Ickes, W., Knowles, E.S. (eds) (1982), *Personality, Roles and Social* Behaviour, New York: Springer-Verlag.

Lofland, J. and Lofland, L. (1995), *Analysing Social Settings: A guide to qualitative observation and analysis*, Belmont CA: Wadsworth (first published 1985).

Lopata, H.Z. (1973), *Widowhood in an American City*, Cambridge, MA: Schenkman.

Lopata, H.Z. (1979), *Women as Widows: Support Systems*, New York: Elsevier.

Lopata, H.Z. (ed.) (1987), *Widows, Volume 2: North America*, Durham, NC: Duke University Press.

Lopata, H.Z. (1988), 'Support Systems of American Urban Widowhood', *Journal of Social Issues*, 44(3): 113-128.

Lopata, H.Z. (1996), *Current Widowhood: Myths and Realities*, Newbury Park, CA: Sage.

Lovell, T. (ed) (1990), *British Feminist Thought: A reader*, London: Blackwell.

Luborsky, M.R. (1994), 'The identification and analysis of themes and patterns', in Gubrium, J.F. and Sankar, A. (eds) (1994), *op. cit.*

Lund, D.A., Dimond, M., Caserta, M., Johnson, R., Poulton, J. and Connelly, R. (1985-6), 'Identifying elderly with coping difficulties after two years of bereavement', *Omega: The Journal of Death and Dying*, 16(3): 210-19.

Macdonald, B. and Rich, C. (1989), *Look Me in the Eye*, London: Women's Press.

Maddisson, D. and Walker, W.L. (1967), 'Factors affecting the outcome of conjugal bereavement', *British Journal of Psychiatry*, 113: 1057-67.

Markides, K.S. and Cooper, C.L. (1989), *Aging, Stress and Health*, Chichester: John Wiley and Sons.

Marris, P. (1958), *Widows and Their Families*, London: Routledge and Kegan Paul.

Martin Matthews, A. (1991), *Widowhood in Later Life*, Toronto: Butterworths.

Martin Matthews, A. (1999), 'Widowhood', in Neysmith, S.M. (ed) (1999), *Critical Issues for Social Work Practice and Aging Persons*, New York: Columbia University Press.

Marshall, P. (2000), 'Older women undergraduates', in Bernard, M. et al (eds) (2000), *op. cit.*

Mason, J. (1996), *Qualitative Researching*, London: Sage.

Matthews, S. (1979), *The Social World of Old Women*, San Diego, CA: Sage.

Matthews, S. (1983), 'Definitions of friendship and their consequences in old age', *Ageing and Society*, 3: 141-5.

Matthews, S. (1986), *Friendship Through the Life Course*, Beverley Hills: Sage.

Maynard, M. (1994), 'Methods, practice and epistemology: the debate about feminism and research', in Maynard, M. and Purvis, J. (eds) (1994), *Researching Women's Lives From a Feminist Perspective*, London: Taylor and Francis.

Maynard, M. and Purvis, J. (eds) (1994), *Researching Women's Lives From a Feminist Perspective*, London: Taylor and Francis.

McCallum, J. (1986), 'Retirement and widowhood transitions', in Kendig, A. (ed) (1986), *Aging and Families: A Social Supports Networks Perspective*, Sydney: Allen and Unwin.

McCrae, R.R. and Costa, P.T. (1988), 'Psychological resistance among widowed men and women', *Journal of Social Issues*, 44(3): 129-42.

McLeod, J. (1999), *Practitioner Research in Counselling*, London: Sage.

McGloshen, T.H. and O'Bryant, S. (1988), 'The psychological wellbeing of older recent widows', *Psychology of Women Quarterly*, 12: 99-116.

Miles, M.B. and Huberman, M. (1994), *Qualitative Data Analysis: 2nd Edition*, Thousand Oaks: Sage.

Miller, N. (1991), *Getting Personal: feminist occasions and other autobiographical acts*, London: Routledge.

Miller, R. (2000), *Researching Life Stories and Family History*, London: Sage.

Minkler, M. and Estes, C.L. (1991), *Critical Perspectives on Aging: the political and moral economy of growing old*, Amityville, New York: Baywood Publishing.

Mitchell, J. (1974), *Psychoanalysis and Feminism*, New York: Vintage Books.

Mitchell, J. and Rose, J. (eds) (1982), *Feminine Sexuality*, London: Macmillan.

Morgan, D.L. (1989), 'Adjusting to widowhood: do social support networks really make it easier?', *Gerontologist*, 29(1): 101-107.

Morgan, D.L., Carder, P. and Neal, M. (1997) 'Are some relationships more useful than others? The value of similar others in the networks of recent widows', *Journal of Social and Personal Relationships*, 14 (6): 745-59.

Morgan, L.A. (1976), 'A re-examination of widowhood and morale', *Journal of Gerontology*, 30(6): 687-95.

Morris, J. (1989), *Able Lives*, London: The Women's Press.

Morris, J. (1996), *Encounters With Strangers: feminism and disability*, London: The Women's Press.

Nagy, M.C. (1982), *Attributional Differences in Health Status and Life Satisfaction of Older Women: a comparison between widows and non-widows*, PhD dissertation: Department of Health Education, University of Oregon.

Neysmith, S. (1995), 'Feminist methodologies: a consideration of principles and practice for research in gerontology', *Canadian Journal on Aging*, 14, supp. 1: 100-18.

Neugarten, B., Moore, J.W. and Lowe, J.C. (1965), 'Age norms, age constraints and adult socialisation', *American Journal of Sociology*, 70: 701-17.

Neugarten, B. and Datan, N. (1973), 'Sociological perspectives on the lifecourse', in Baltes, P.B. and Schaie, D. (eds) (1973), *Life-span Developmental Psychology*, New York: Academic Press.

Neugarten, B. (1977), 'Adaptation and the life cycle', in Schlossberg, N.K. and Entine, A.D. (eds) (1977), *Counseling Adults*, Monterey, California: Brooks/Cole.

Nieboer, A.P., Lindgenby, S.M. and Ormel, J. (1995) *Phase differences in the consequences of bereavement for the well-being of elderly men and women*, paper presented to the European Congress of Gerontology, Amsterdam: 30th Aug.- 2nd Sept.

Oakley, A. (1974), *The Sociology of Housework*, London: Martin Robertson.

Oakley, A. (1981), 'Interviewing women: a contradiction in terms', in Roberts, H. (ed) (1981), *Doing Feminist, Research*, London: Routledge.

O'Brien, P.A. (1985), 'Network analysis of mid-life transitions: a hypothesis on phases of change in micro-structures', in Peterson, W.A. and Quadragno, T. (eds) (1985), *Social Bonds in Later Life*, Beverley Hills: Sage.

O' Bryant, S. (1982), 'The value of home to older persons and its relationship to housing satisfaction', *Research on Aging*, 4: 349-63.

O'Bryant, S. (1987), 'Attachment to home and support systems of older widows, in Columbus, Ohio', in Lopata, H.Z. (ed) (1987), *op. cit.*

O'Bryant, S. (1988), 'Self-differentiated assistance in older widow's support systems', *Sex Roles*, 19: 91-106.

O'Bryant, S. (1991), Older widows and independent lifestyles *International Journal of Aging and Human Development*, 32 (1): 41-51.

O'Bryant, S. and Morgan, L.A. (1989), 'Financial experience and well-being among mature widowed women', *Gerontologist* (29) 2: 245-51.

O'Bryant, S. and Straw, L.B. (1991), 'Relationship of previous divorce and previous widowhood to older women's adjustment to recent widowhood', *The Journal of Divorce and Remarriage*, 15(3/4): 166-90.

O'Connor, P. (1992), *Friendships Between Women*, London: Harvester Wheatsheaf.

Olson, L.K. (1982), *The Political Economy of Aging: the state, private power and social welfare*, New York: Columbia University Press.

Office of National Statistics (1997), '2.4 Marital conditions (de jure) estimated population', in *Annual Abstract of Statistics*, London: HMSO.

Office of National Statistics (2001), *2001 Census*, www.statistics.gov.uk.

Opie, A. (1992), 'Qualitative research: appropriation of the "other" and empowerment', *Feminist Review*, 40 (Spring): 52-69.

Osterweiss, M., Solomon, F. and Green, N. (1984), *Bereavement: Reactions, Consequences and Care*, Washington DC: National Academy Press.

Owen, M. (1996), *A World of Widows*, New Jersey: Zed Books Ltd.

Parkes, C.M. (1972), *Bereavement: studies of grief in adult life*, Harmondsworth: Penguin.

Parkes, C.M. (1986), *Bereavement* (2nd Edition) London: Tavistock Publications.

Parkes, C.M. and Weiss, C. (1983), *Recovery From Bereavement*, New York: Basic Books.

Patai, D. (1987), 'Ethical problems of personal narratives or who should eat the last piece of cake?', *International Journal of Oral History*, 8: 5-27.

Patai, D. (1991), 'US academics and third world women: is ethical research possible?', in Gluck, S.B. and Patai, D. (eds) (1991), *op. cit.*

Peace, S.M. (1986), 'The forgotten female: social policy and older women', in Phillipson, C. and Walker, A. (eds), (1986), *Ageing and Social Policy: A Critical Assessment*, Aldershot: Gower.

Peace, S.M. (ed) (1990), *Researching Social Gerontology*, London: Sage.

Peace, S.M. (1993), 'The living environments of older women', in Bernard, M. and Meade, K. (eds) (1993), *op. cit.*

Pearlin, O. (1980), 'The life cycle and life strains', in Blalock, H.M. (ed) (1980), *Sociological Theory and Research: A Critical* Approach, New York: Free Press.

Personal Narratives Group (1989), *Interpreting Women's Lives: feminist theory and personal narratives*, Brompton and Indianapolis: Indiana University Press.

Petrowsky, M. (1976), 'Marital status, sex and the social network of the elderly', *Journal of Marriage and the* Family, 38: 749-56.

Phillips, J. (2000), 'Working Carers', in Bernard, M. et al (eds) (2000) *op. cit.*

Phillipson, C. (1982), *Capitalism and the Construction of Old Age*, London: Macmillan.

Phillipson, C. (1998) *Reconstructing Old Age*, London: Sage.

Pickard, S. (1994), 'Life after a death: the experience of bereavement in South Wales', *Ageing and Society*, 14: 191-217.

Pihlblad, C.T. and Adams, D.L. (1972), 'Widowhood, social participation and life satisfaction', *Aging and Human Development*, 3: 323-31.

Pihlblad, C.T. and McNamara, R.L. (1965) 'Social adjustment of elderly people in three small towns', in Rose, A.M. and Peterson, W.A. (eds) (1965), *Older people and their social worlds*, Philadelphia: FA David Company.

Plummer, K. (1983), *Documents of Life*, London: George Allen and Unwin.

Plummer, K. (2001), *Documents of Life 2*, London: Sage.

Pollock, G.H. (1977), 'The mourning process and creative organisational change', *Journal of American Psychoanalytic Association*, 25(1): 3-34.

Price, J. (1999), 'In acknowledgement: a review and critique of qualitative research texts', in Jossellson, R. and Lieblich, A. (eds) (1999), *op. cit.*

Rabinow, P. and Sullivan, W.M. (1987), *Interpretive Social Science*, Berkeley: University of California Press.

Ray, R.E. (1998), 'Feminist readings of older women's life stories', *Journal of Aging Studies*, 12(2): 117-28.

Ray, R.E. (2000), *Beyond Nostalgia: Aging and Life-Story Writing*, Charlottesville: University Press of Virginia.

Rees, W.D. and Lutkins, S.G. (1967), 'Mortality and bereavement', *British Medical Journal*, (4): 13-20.

Reinharz, S. (1986) 'Friends or foes: gerontological and feminist theory', *Women's Studies International Forum*, 9: 503-514.

Reinharz, S. (1992), *Feminist Methods in Social Research*, New York: Oxford University Press.

Ribbens, J. and Edwards, R. (1998), *Feminist Dilemmas in Qualitative Research: Public Knowledge and Private Lives*, London: Sage.

Richardson, D. and Robinson, V. (eds) (1993) *Women's Studies*, Basingstoke: Macmillan.

Riessman, C.K. (1993), *Narrative Analysis*, Newbury Park: Sage.

Riley, D. (1988), *Am I that name?: feminism and the category of 'women' in history*, Basingstoke: Macmillan.

Riley, M. (1973), 'Aging and cohort succession: interpretations and misinterpretations', *Public Opinion*, Quarterly, 37: 35-49.

Riley, M., Johnson, M. and Foner, A. (1972), *Ageing and Society Volume 3: a sociology of age stratification*, New York: Russell State Foundation.

Roberto, K.A. and Scott, P. (1986), 'Confronting widowhood', *American Behavioural Scientist*, 29(4): 499-511.

Roberts, E. (1998), *Women and Families 1940-1970*, London: Blackwell.

Rook, K.S. (1989), 'Strains in older adults' friendships', in Adams, R.G. and Blieszner, R. (eds) (1989) *op. cit.*

Rook, K.S. (1987), 'Reciprocity of social exchange and social satisfaction among older women', *Journal of Personality and Social Psychology* (52) 1: 145-54.

Rosik, C.H. (1989), 'Impact of religious orientation in conjugal bereavement among older adults', *International Journal of Aging and Human Development*, 28 (4): 25-60.

Rossi, A. (1986), 'Sex and gender in an ageing society', *Daedulus*, 111: 141-69.

Rowbotham, S. (1999), *A Century of Women*, Harmondsworth: Penguin.

Runyan, W.M. (1982), *Life Histories and Psychobiography: explorations in theory and method*, Oxford: Oxford University Press.

Ruth, J-E., Birren, J.E. and Polkinghorne, D.E. (1996), 'The projects of life reflected in autobiographies of old age', *Ageing and Society*, 16: 677-99.

Ruth, J-E. and Kenyon, G. (1996), 'Introduction', *Ageing and Society*, 16: 633-57.

Ruth, J-E. and Oberg, P. (1996), 'Ways of life: old age in a life history perspective', in Birren, J. et al (eds) (1996), *op. cit.*

Sable, P. (1989), 'Attachment anxiety and the loss of a husband', *American Journal of Orthopsychiatry*, 59: 550-56.

Sapsford, P. and Abbott, R. (1992), *Research Methods for Nurses and the Caring Professions*, Buckingham: Open University Press.

Sangster, J. (1994), 'Telling our stories: feminist debates and the use of oral history', *Women's History* Review, 3(1): 5-28.

Scott, J.P. and Kivett, T. (1985), 'Differences in the morale of older, rural widows and widowers', *International Journal of Aging and Human Development*, 21(2): 121-35.

Sheehy, G. (1997), *New Passages*, London: Harper Collins.

Sheridan, D. (1990), 'Ambivalent Memories: women and the 1939-45 War in Britain', *Oral History*, Spring.

Siddell, M. (1995), *Health in Old Age: myth, mastery and management*, Buckingham: Open University Press.

Silverman, D. (1993), *Interpreting Qualitative Data*, London: Sage.

Silverman, D. (1997), *Qualitative Research: Theory, Method and Practice*, London: Sage.

Silverman, D. (2000), *Doing Qualitative Research: a practical handbook*, London: Sage.

Silverman, P.R. (1986), *Widow-to-Widow*, New York: Springer Publications.

Silverman, P.R. (1987), 'Widowhood as the next stage in the life course', in Lopata, H.Z. (ed.) (1987), *op. cit.*

Skeggs, B. (1995), *Feminist Cultural Theory: Process and Production*, Manchester: Manchester University Press.

Smith, D. (1975) 'Women and psychiatry', in Smith, D. and David, S. (eds) (1975), *Women and Psychiatry: I'm not mad*, Vancouver: Press Gang Publishing.

Sokoloff, S. (1999), 'How are they at home? Community, state and servicemen's wives in England', *Women's History Review*, 8 (1): 27-51.

Sontag, S. (1978), 'The double standard of ageing', in Carver, V. and Liddiard, P. (eds) (1978), *op. cit.*

Stacey, J. (1991), 'Is there a feminist ethnography?', in Gluck. S.B. and Patai, D. (eds) (1991), *op. cit.*

Stacey, J. (1993) 'Untangling feminist theory', in Richardson, D. and Robinson, V. (eds) (1993), *op. cit.*

Standing, K. (1998), 'Writing the voices of the less powerful: research on lone mothers', in Ribbens, J. and Edwards, R. (eds) (1998), *op. cit.*

Stanley, L. (ed) (1990), *Feminist Praxis*, London: Routledge.

Stanley, L. and Wise, S. (1990), 'Method, Methodology and Epistemology', in Stanley L (ed) (1990), *op. cit.*

Stanley, L. and Wise, S. (1993), *Breaking Out Again: Feminist Ontology and Epistemology*, London: Routledge.

Stevens, N. (1995), 'Gender and adaptation to widowhood in later life', *Ageing and Society*, 15: 37-58.

Strain, L.A. and Chappell, N.C. (1982), 'Confidants: Do they make a difference in quality of life?', *Research in Aging*, 4 (4): 479-502.

Stroebe, W. and Stroebe, M. (1987), *Bereavement and Health: the psychological and physical consequences of partner loss*, Cambridge: Cambridge University Press.

Stroebe, M. and Stroebe, W. (1988), 'Current themes in widowhood research', *Journal of Social Issues*, 44 (3): 207-16.

Sugarman, L. (1986), *Life Span Development: concepts, theories and interventions*, London: Methuen.

Summerfield, P. (1989), *Women Workers in the Second World War: production and patriarchy in conflict*, London: Routledge.

Summerfield, P. (1998), *Reconstructing Women's Wartime Lives*, Manchester: Manchester University Press.

Summerfield, P. and Crockett, N. (1992), 'You weren't taught that with the welding: lessons in sexuality in the Second World War', *Women's History Review*, 1(3): 435-454.

Swindells, J. (1995). 'Coming home to heaven: manpower and myth in 1944 Britain', *Women's History Review*, 4(2): 223-234.

Talbot, M.M. (1990), 'The negative side of the relationship between older widows and their adult children: the mothers' perspective', *The Gerontologist*, 30: 5.

Thomas, C. (1999), *Female Forms: experiencing and understanding disability*, Buckingham: Open University Press.

Thompson, P., Itzin, C. and Abendstern, M. (1990), *I Don't Feel Old*, Oxford: Oxford University Press.

Tong, R. (1990), *Feminist Thought*, London: Unwin Hyman.

Torrie, M. (1975), *Begin Again*, London: JM Dent and Sons.

Townsend, P. (1981), 'The structured dependency of the elderly', *Ageing and Society*, 1 (1): 5-28.

Troll, L.E. (1994), 'Family connectedness of old women: attachment in later life', in Turner, B.F. and Troll, L.E. (eds) (1994), *op. cit.*

Troll, L.E., Miller, S. and Atchley, R.C. (1979), *Families in Later Life*, California: Wadsworth Publishing Co.

Turner, B.F. and Troll, L.E. (1994), *Women Growing Older*, California: Sage.

Vachon, M.L.S., Formo, A., Freedman, K., Lyall, A., Rogers, J. and Freeman, S. (1972), 'Stress reactions to bereavement', *Essence: Issues in the Study of Ageing, Dying and Death*, 1: 23-33.

Vachon, M.L.S., Rogers, J., Lyall, W.A., Lancee, W.J., Sheldon, A.R. and Freeman, S.J.J. (1982), 'Predictors and correlates of adaptation to conjugal bereavement', *American Journal of Psychiatry*, 139(8): 998-1002.

Vachon, M.L.S. and Stylianos, S.K. (1988), 'The role of social support in bereavement', *Journal of Social Issues*, 44(3): 175-90.

Van den Hoonaard, D.K. (1994), 'Paradise Lost: widowhood in a Florida retirement community', *Journal of Aging Studies*, 8: 121-32.

Van den Hoonaard, D.K. (1997), 'Identity foreclosure: women's experience of widowhood as expressed in autobiographical accounts', *Ageing and Society*, 17: 533-51.

Van den Hoonaard, D.K. (1999), 'No regrets: widows' stories about the last days of their husbands' lives', *Journal of Aging Studies*, 13 (Spring): 59-72.

Van den Hoonaard, D.K. (2001), *The Widowed Self: The Older Women's Journey Through Widowhood*, Ontario: Laurier University Press.

Verrill, R.L. and Beddoe, D. (1992), *Parachutes and Petticoats*, South Glamorgan: Honno.

Victor, C. (1989), *Health and Health Care in Later Life*, London: Edward Arnold.

Walker, A. (1994), 'Poverty and inequality in old age', in Bond J. et al (eds) (1994), *op. cit.*

Walker, M. (1990), *Women in Therapy and Counselling*, Milton Keynes: Open University Press.

Wenger, C. (1984), *The Supportive Network*: , London: Allen and Unwin.

Williams, F. (1991), *Social Policy: a critical introduction*, Cambridge: Polity Press.

Wolcott, H.F. (1994), *Transforming Qualitative Data*, California: Sage.

Wortman, C. and Silver, R.C. (1990), 'Successful mastery of bereavement and widowhood: a life course perspective', in Baltes, P.B. and Baltes, M.M. (eds) (1990), *op. cit.*

Wright, P.H. (1989), 'Gender differences in adults' same- and cross-gender friendship', in Adams, R.G. and Blieszner, R. (eds) (1989), *op. cit.*

Young, M., Benjamin, B., Wallis, C. (1963), 'The mortality of widows', *Lancet*, 2: 454-56.

Young, M. and Wilmot, P. (1957), *Family and Kinship in East London*, Harmondsworth: Routledge.

Yow, V. (1994), *Recording Oral History*, London: Sage.

# Index

acceptance of the inevitable 202–3
'acquisitive' style of friendship 50, 168
Adams, D.L. 36
Adams, R.G. 45, 47–8
Adlersberg, M. 6, 26
ageing 12, 19–21, 56–62, 210
ageism 18–22, 48, 61, 198, 229, 232
Allan, G. 39, 44–5, 48
Allen, K. 18, 31
Allport, G. 79
aloneness 204–5
analysis of research findings 101–2
Anderson, K. 81–2
Anderson, T.B. 43–5, 75, 77
Andrews, M. 20–21, 70, 74, 97
anticipation of widowhood 19–20, 203
Antonovsky, A. 12
Arling, G. 36–7, 46, 48, 68
assumptions about widowhood 10
Atchley, R.C. 21
Atkinson, D. 77
Atkinson, R. 78–9, 84, 88, 102, 105
autobiographical accounts 11, 28
autonomy, personal 121–2, 127–9, 141,
    236–7

Babchuk, N. 43–4
Bankoff, E. 4, 39–40, 67
Barresi, C.M. 9–10
Beasley, C. 63
Beddoe, D. 13
Bee 116, 131–2, 135, 146, 150, 154,
    160, 167, 169, 178, 186, 202,
    204–6, 208, 210, 235–8, 260
Bernard, M. 46, 59
best friends 216–18, 238

Betty 115, 130–31, 134, 145–6, 154–6,
    158–9, 167, 177–8, 185–6, 195,
    206, 210, 219
Beveridge Report (1942) 16
biographical approach to research 49,
    58–9, 71, 77–86, 90–92, 95, 243,
    263–6, 240–42
    limitations of 265–6
biographical assets 12, 18, 23, 54, 67,
    266
Birren, J.E. 58
Blau, Z. 38, 48–9
Blieszner, R. 47
Bordo, S. 64
Borland, K. 81, 105
Bornat, J. 75, 82
Bowling, A. 5
Browne, C.V. 61
Burgoyne, J. 13
busy lives 209, 238
Butler, R.N. 256

Cain, M. 76
Capper, Dorothy 13–14
'career' orientation for widows 31
Cartwright, A. 5
Chamberlayne, P. 77
change, management of 178–9, 187
Chappell, N.C. 45
Chicago school of sociology 77
child-care 157–8, 182
choices, making of 205–6
coding of data 102–4
Coleman, P.G. 59, 79–80, 261
collaborative approach to research
    265–6

companionship 39, 42–7, 166–7, 183–6, 216–18, 222, 259

confidantes 44–6, 166, 183

confidentiality 86–7, 94, 97, 101–2, 252

connectedness 29–30

continuities and discontinuities in widows' lives 240–42

Crockett, N. 14

Daley, C. 75

Dant, T. 82

daughters, relationships with 36, 42, 53, 185–6, 200, 215, 236, 248, 255, 260

Davidson, K. 4, 11–12, 16–18, 22, 25, 54–7, 67–8

Delmar, R. 63

dependency 25, 37, 40, 136, 185, 192–3, 221; *see also* independence

depression 9, 36, 55

descriptive validity 84

disability issues 70, 81

disengagement theory 57

divorce 3–4, 13

do-it-yourself (DIY) skills 5

Doris 115–16, 132–3, 135, 150, 154, 170, 179, 205, 208, 213, 215, 231–2, 237, 239–40, 256

Dorothy 119–20, 138–9, 154–5, 158, 171, 193–4, 196–7, 199–201, 204, 218, 234–5, 250, 255, 258–9, 261

Edith 109–10, 138, 141, 160, 175–6, 184, 197, 212–14, 220, 223–4, 245–7, 250, 252

education 13–14, 48, 67–8, 87, 154–6, 238

ego-integrity 59

Elder, G.H. 12, 58, 78

Elizabeth 110–11, 125, 128–9, 146–7, 149, 152, 157–8, 176, 179, 183, 205, 207–9, 217, 231, 236–7, 244–5, 252, 257

Ellen 113–14, 134–5, 149–51, 156–7, 159–60, 167–8, 170, 172, 203, 215–16, 218, 220, 224, 252–3

emotional involvement 247

empathy 247

employment, women's 14–16, 139, 158–60, 176

empowerment through research 73, 81–2

epistemology 72

Erikson, E.H. 59–60

ethical issues in research 85–6, 89, 91, 94, 97, 252–4, 260–62

ethnographic research 73

Eunice 118, 123–7, 154–5, 157–60, 166–7, 181, 183–4, 190, 201–2, 205, 211–14, 216, 219–23, 226, 245, 247, 260–61

evacuation, memories of 147–8

Evelyn 102, 110, 124, 126, 128, 152, 154, 158, 160, 176, 184–5, 203–4, 207, 217, 252

expectations of other people 138

experience, mediation of 76

exploitation through research 85–7

family relationships 36–7, 125–6, 139, 172–5, 179–86, 196–7, 240
  as friendship 183–4
  ideology of 179–80
  lack of closeness in 185–6

Farzana 114–15, 124–6, 128, 138, 147, 151–2, 154, 172–3, 181–2, 203, 210, 237, 248–52

Feinson, M.C. 21–2

femaleness, commonality of 63

feminist research practice 57, 60–65, 68–77, 81–97, 103–5, 233, 242–4, 248, 251, 254–5, 261–6

Fenwick, R. 9–10

Ferraro, K. 10, 19, 45, 48, 53

Field, S. 41

field diary notes 96, 100, 244–8, 252–4, 257

fieldwork, stages of 92

financial knowledge 5, 214, 222–3

financial security 205–6

Flooken, I. 20

follow-up interviews 100–101

Ford, J. 5, 34

Forster, M.C. 234

friendships, widows' 38–51, 165–77
closeness of 45–7
importance of 169–72
lack of 172–7, 197, 218–19, 235
maintenance of 171–2
making of 168–71
styles and types 47–51
with couples 43–4, 219–20
with men 43, 165, 222
with other widows 43, 218–19,
236–7
within the family 183–4
*see also* best friends
future, the, attitudes to 200–202, 210,
223–5

Gearing, B. 82
gendered life courses 3, 57, 60, 153–4,
159–60, 164, 187, 215, 233
gendered scripts 75–6, 129, 253–4
generational differences 144–7, 150,
153, 162, 235–6, 242
generativity 59
gerontology 54, 57–62, 65, 68, 233
getting on with life 202–10, 215, 235
Gianturco, D.T. 9
Gibson, D. 62
Giddens, A. 11–12, 58
Giele, J.Z. 12, 58, 78
Gilligan, C. 60
grandchildren, relationships with 186
gratitude to others 140
Green, R.W. 41
Gubrium, J.F. 69–70

Haas-Hawkings, G. 20, 67
Hansson, R.O. 18, 29–30
Harding, S. 72
Mrs Hatch 5
Havighurst, R.J. 29
health, attitudes to 9–10, 192–3, 207–8, 231
Heyman, D.K. 9
historical context 78, 144–5, 153, 162
Holloway, I. 70
Horowitz, A. 36
Houldsworth, A. 13, 16–17
housing 151–2, 182–3

Huberman, M. 89
Hunter, S. 6
husbands, subservience to 156–60,
175–6, 213–15
'hygienic' research 81

identity, personal 11, 23–32, 35, 46–7,
57–8, 121, 141, 172, 178–81,
185–7, 241
incompleteness, feeling of 195–6
independence 127–8, 215–16, 238; *see
also* dependency
informed consent to research 85–9,
93–4, 97, 100–101, 252, 254
interdependence 181–2, 185; *see also*
reciprocity
interpreters, use of 250
interpretivism 69
interview methods 77–103, 245–8,
252–4
inter-war years 144–6, 236
intimate friendships 45–6

Jack, D. 82, 88
Jacobson, D.E. 35
Jaffe, D.J. 69
Jean 107–8, 125, 127–8, 158, 177,
181–2, 204–5, 216–17, 222–4, 238,
255–6
Jennie 111, 123–5, 158, 168–9, 180–82,
212, 216, 221–4, 246
Jerrome, D. 4, 9, 39, 42–50, 98
'jigsaw' metaphor 239
Joan 116–17, 130–31, 135, 148–51,
156–60, 170–71, 178, 183, 203,
220, 242, 255–6, 258
Johnson, M. 56
joining-in 177–9, 238
Jones Porter, E. 23, 52, 56, 70,
239

Katherine 113, 125, 128, 154, 158, 166,
168–9, 203–4, 206–7, 209, 231–2,
249, 252, 261
Kelly, L. 72–3, 88
Kenyon, G. 58
Kivett, T. 68

Lieberman, M. 6, 23–7, 59–60
life course perspective 34, 38, 49,
    52–62, 65, 91, 102, 233, 242,
    264
life span development theory 30–31
life story research 66–70, 75–89, 92–5,
    99–106, 242, 255
    interactive nature of 81–2
    validity and reliability of 83–4
literature on widowhood *see* research
    literature
Lofland, J. 29
loneliness 5, 137–8, 190–97, 200–204,
    215, 231, 235, 239, 241
Lopata, H.Z. 5–7, 24–7, 31, 34–46, 67
loss, widowhood seen as 4–5, 53, 190
Luborsky, M.R. 89

Macdonald, B. 61
McLeod, J. 84–5
Mags 117–18, 133–4, 160, 170, 181,
    184, 190, 208–9, 248
'malestream' views 64, 71
marital relationships 24–5
    exclusiveness of 219
Marris, P. 11
Martin Matthews, A. 4, 11, 20, 24, 26,
    31, 33–43, 53–4, 56, 67–70, 240
Mason, J. 2, 69, 83, 86, 89, 245, 252
Matthews, S. 45, 49–51, 230, 241
Maynard, M. 72, 76
Meade, K. 59
member test of validity 84
memories
    collective 162
    happy and unhappy 204
Miles, M.B. 89
Miller, E.M. 69
Miller, N. 73–4
Miller, R. 77–8, 85–8, 102
Morgan, D.L. 33, 36–40, 43–4, 55–6
Morgan, L.A. 67
mortality rates 10
motherhood 139
multiple narratives 121, 162–5, 190,
    226–34, 239–42, 264–6
mythology of widowhood 5–9, 23, 52

narratives 77–80, 87–9, 103–5; *see also*
    multiple narratives
neighbours, relationships with 46, 170
Neugarten, B. 19, 54
new interests and skills 222–3
Neysmith, S. 74
nieces, relationships with 37, 184–5
nuclear families 17

Oakley, A. 74, 79, 257
Oberg, P. 18, 58, 103
O'Bryant, S. 5, 19–20, 37
O'Connor, P. 45–6
ontological security and ontological
    coherence 12
Opie, A. 73
opportunity sampling 98
Owen, M. 9

Pakistani community 151–2
Parkes, C.M. 10, 26, 29
Pat 112–13, 161, 202, 206–7, 215,
    218–19, 221–2
Patai, D. 85
pathological model of widowhood 6, 52,
    242
patriarchy 64–5
Patricia 111–12, 136–9, 147–8, 173–4,
    179, 181, 185, 192, 195, 197–200,
    204, 231–2, 234–5, 239, 249–50,
    252, 259–61
Pearlin, O. 9
pension provision 159
'personal is political' doctrine 64
Personal Narratives Group 78, 80
personality 18, 27, 31
Phillipson, C. 58
Phyllis 108, 130, 134, 168, 177–8, 201,
    209, 214, 216–17, 222, 261
Pickard, S. 35, 43
Pihlblad, C.T. 36
pilot interviews 93
pleasure gained from life 199
Plummer, K. 78, 84
positivist research 71, 77
post-war period 152, 157, 159
potential for growth 257–60

powerlessness 136
pregnancy 161, 238
pride 134–5
problematisation of widowhood 4–7,
    240, 264
psychiatry 6
psychological well-being 20, 22,
    59–60
purposive sampling 263
qualitative research 68–72, 83, 86–9,
    91–2
  potential of 68–70

Rabinow, P. 265
Ray, R.E. 75–6, 253
rebelliousness 132–4, 237
reciprocity in personal relationships 47,
    55, 69, 166–8, 183–5, 237
reflexivity 73, 80–81, 89, 101–3, 241–4,
    256–8, 262, 266
Reinharz, S. 61, 63, 70, 77
remarriage 221
reminiscence, attitudes to 79–80,
    261
Remondet, J.H. 18, 29–30
research literature on widowhood
    3–11, 18–19, 29–30, 33–6, 45–7,
    50–51, 56, 94–5, 164, 190,
    229–30, 245
  assumption of homogeneity in 67–8
  'support' and 'participant' types 230
research participants, effects of taking
    part on 73, 79–80, 192, 200–201,
    243, 248, 255–62
researchers
  *active* participation by 252–3
  power of 74–5, 81, 85, 89, 91,
    96–100, 248–51, 262
Riley, D. 58, 63
Roberto, K.A. 38
Roberts, E. 16
roles and role theory 16–17, 25, 36, 53,
    57, 64, 222–3, 262
Rossi, A. 62
rule-breaking 160–61
Runyan, W.M. 83–4
Ruth, J.-E. 18, 58, 78, 98, 103

Sable, P. 5
sampling 98, 263
Sangster, J. 74–5, 253
Sankar, A. 69–70
Scott, J.P. 68
Scott, P. 38
Second World War 14–17, 144–50, 158,
    235–8; *see also* post-war period
secrets 99, 254
self, sense of 11, 23–31, 33, 50, 58,
    121–2, 127
self-awareness 211–14, 225, 257–8
self-confidence and self-esteem 121–6,
    129–31, 136–42, 193–5, 232–8
self-help groups 55, 60
semi-structured interviews 77, 81
sexism 18–22, 48, 61, 198, 229, 232
Sheehy, G. 22–3, 54–6
sibling relationships 37, 186, 260
Silver, R.C. 11, 31–2
Silverman, P.R. 30, 55, 60
Sinclair, R. 5, 34
Skeggs, B. 76, 87
Smith, D. 64
Smith, Sidonie 75
'social clock' theory 19, 49, 54
social construction of widowhood 26, 30
social exchange theory 40, 55
social gerontology 57–9
social life (as distinct from friendships)
    175, 237
social participation 41, 51
  barriers to 48
social world of older widows 33–4, 41,
    46–51, 164–7, 171–6, 187, 230–31
socialisation 22, 45, 61
Sokoloff, S. 14
sons, relationships with 36, 42, 139,
    186, 196–7, 218, 248
spouse sanctification 24–5
Stacey, J. 63, 85, 261
Standing, K. 75
Stanley, L. 64, 71
'status passage' concept 22–3, 54–6
stereotypes of widowhood 1, 6–9, 18,
    23, 80–82, 136, 230–34, 240
Stevens, N. 22

stoicism 202–3
Strain, L.A. 45
Straw, L.B. 19–20
Stroebe, M. and W. 21
subjectivity and subjective experience 8,
    18, 23, 51, 57–8, 67, 70–73, 102,
    193, 231–2, 235, 239–44, 254, 266
Sullivan, W.M. 265
Summerfield, P. 14, 263
Sundel, M. 6
support networks 20–22, 29, 33–41,
    167, 171
  functions of 35
Sylvia 118–19, 138, 140–41, 160–61,
    174–5, 203, 213–15, 238, 240,
    255–6
symbolic interactionism 11–12, 53–4, 56

Talbot, M.M. 37
tape-recording 93–4
thematic field analysis 89
Thomas, C. 70, 87
Thompson, P. 83, 94
Thorne, S. 6, 26
Torrie, M. 4
transcription 91–103
transition, widowhood as 211, 237–8
Troll, L.E. 41
turnings' in widows' lives 49, 164,
    178–9, 241

Vachon, M.L.S. 67
validation 208–9, 255, 262
validity, *descriptive* and *personal* 84
values 124–5
Van den Hoonaard, D.K. 16, 28,
    67
Vera 108–9, 136–9, 154, 159–60, 175,
    192–4, 196–200, 205, 209, 232,
    234–5, 239, 251, 257, 261
Verrill-Rhys, R.L. 13

Walker, M. 14
wartime, experiences of *see* Second
    World War
Weiss, C. 29
Wenger, C. 39, 41
'why' questions 88
widowers 21, 221
widowhood
  as a distinct period of life 68
  likelihood of 3–4
  types of (Lopata) 27
Wise, S. 64, 71
womanhood, concept of 63
work ethic 125
Wortman, C. 11, 31–2
Wright, P.H. 45

Young, M. 10
Yow, V. 78–80, 95, 255